WITTGENSTEIN ON PI
OBJECTIVITY, AND

This volume of new essays presents groundbreaking interpretations of some of the most central themes of Wittgenstein's philosophy. A distinguished group of contributors demonstrates how Wittgenstein's thought can fruitfully be applied to contemporary debates in epistemology, metaphilosophy, and philosophy of language. The volume combines historical and systematic approaches to Wittgensteinian methods and perspectives, with essays providing detailed analysis that will be accessible to students as well as specialists. The result is a rich and illuminating picture of a key figure in twentieth-century philosophy and his continuing importance to philosophical study.

JAMES CONANT is Chester D. Tripp Professor of Humanities and Professor of Philosophy at the University of Chicago, as well as Humboldt Professor at the University of Leipzig. He has published widely on topics including philosophy of language, philosophy of mind, aesthetics, German idealism, and history of analytic philosophy.

SEBASTIAN SUNDAY is Lecturer in Philosophy at the University of Oxford. His research covers a range of philosophical areas, with a focus on logic and epistemology.

WITTGENSTEIN ON PHILOSOPHY, OBJECTIVITY, AND MEANING

EDITED BY

JAMES CONANT

University of Chicago

SEBASTIAN SUNDAY

University of Oxford

 CAMBRIDGE
UNIVERSITY PRESS

CAMBRIDGE
UNIVERSITY PRESS

University Printing House, Cambridge CB2 8BS, United Kingdom

One Liberty Plaza, 20th Floor, New York, NY 10006, USA

477 Williamstown Road, Port Melbourne, VIC 3207, Australia

314-321, 3rd Floor, Plot 3, Splendor Forum, Jasola District Centre, New Delhi - 110025, India

79 Anson Road, #06-04/06, Singapore 079906

Cambridge University Press is part of the University of Cambridge.

It furthers the University's mission by disseminating knowledge in the pursuit of education, learning and research at the highest international levels of excellence.

www.cambridge.org
Information on this title: www.cambridge.org/9781316645406
DOI: 10.1017/9781108151764

© Cambridge University Press 2019

First published 2019
First paperback edition 2021

A catalogue record for this publication is available from the British Library

Library of Congress Cataloging in Publication data
NAMES: Conant, James, editor.
TITLE: Wittgenstein on philosophy, objectivity, and meaning / edited by James Conant, University of Chicago, Sebastian Sunday, University of Oxford.
DESCRIPTION: New York : Cambridge University Press, 2019. | Includes bibliographical references and index.
IDENTIFIERS: LCCN 2019008053 | ISBN 9781107194151 (alk. paper)
SUBJECTS: LCSH: Wittgenstein, Ludwig, 1889–1951.
CLASSIFICATION: LCC B3376.W564 W5795 2019 | DDC 192–dc23
LC record available at https://lccn.loc.gov/2019008053

ISBN 978-1-107-19415-1 Hardback
ISBN 978-1-316-64540-6 Paperback

Contents

List of Contributors   *page* vii
Preface   ix
Acknowledgments   xii

1 Anatomy of a Muddle: Wittgenstein and Philosophy 1
  Alexander George

2 Explaining What We Mean 28
  Julia Tanney

3 Objectivity 47
  Alice Crary

4 The Methodological Significance of Intuitions in Philosophy 62
  Oskari Kuusela

5 Wittgenstein on 'Seeing Meanings' 84
  Katherine J. Morris

6 Bringing the Phenomenal World into View 100
  Avner Baz

7 First Steps and Conceptual Creativity 119
  Michael Beaney

8 Wittgenstein and Analytic Revisionism 143
  Martin Gustafsson

9 Demystifying Meaning in Horwich and Wittgenstein 164
  Silver Bronzo

10 What Is Meaning? A Wittgensteinian Answer to an
  Un-Wittgensteinian Question 185
  Hans-Johann Glock

11   Meaning, Use, and Supervenience   211
     William Child

12   Some Socratic Aspects of Wittgenstein's
     Conception of Philosophy   231
     James Conant

References   265
Index   280

Contributors

AVNER BAZ, Tufts University

MICHAEL BEANEY, Humboldt University and King's College London

SILVER BRONZO, National Research University Higher School of Economics

WILLIAM CHILD, University of Oxford

JAMES CONANT, University of Chicago and Leipzig University

ALICE CRARY, University of Oxford

ALEXANDER GEORGE, Amherst College

HANS-JOHANN GLOCK, University of Zurich

MARTIN GUSTAFSSON, Åbo Akademi University

OSKARI KUUSELA, University of East Anglia

KATHERINE J. MORRIS, University of Oxford

SEBASTIAN SUNDAY, University of Oxford

JULIA TANNEY, independent scholar

Preface

Wittgenstein's famous example, in the opening section of the *Investigations*, of the transaction between a shopkeeper and someone who has been sent shopping with a slip of paper marked "five red apples" is followed by this equally well-known dialogue:

> — It is in this and similar ways that one operates with words. – "But how does he [the shopkeeper] know where and how he is to look up the word 'red' and what he is to do with the word 'five'?" – Well, I assume that he *acts* as I have described. Explanations come to an end somewhere. – But what is the meaning of the word "five"? – No such thing was in question here, only how the word "five" is used. (PI §1)

Thus ends the opening section. This dialogue will be as intelligible, or unintelligible, to an otherwise intelligent reader as the shopkeeper example itself and the discussion of a quotation from Augustine which precede it. Most readers are likely to have many questions at this point. Is it true that one operates with words in the same way (or similar ways) as the shopkeeper? Why does Wittgenstein say "explanations come to an end somewhere," before he has even begun to give any explanation at all?

On the other hand, if a reader knows the later philosophy of Wittgenstein well, they might recognize in this brief passage several key elements of it, including Wittgenstein's conceptions of meaning as use; of rule-following as a practice; of a philosophical problem as being of the form "I don't know my way about"; his notion of a language-game as an object of comparison; and his emphasis on description over explanation in philosophy.

It is noteworthy that Wittgenstein's description of the shopkeeper example does indeed give nothing but descriptions as opposed to explanations. In the subsequent dialogue, quoted above, Wittgenstein underlines this feature of the example: first, by adding the qualification that "it is in this *and similar ways* that one operates with words"; and, second, by refusing to give explanations in his responses to the interlocutor's questions ("Well, I assume that he *acts* as I have described"), and even adding—somewhat preposterously—that "explanations come to an end somewhere."

This latter statement ("Explanations come to an end somewhere") is perhaps the clearest indication, in this short dialogue, of the kind of interest that Wittgenstein takes in the interlocutor's two questions ("But how does he know where and how he is to look up the word 'red' and what he is to do with the word 'five'?"; "But what is the meaning of the word 'five'?"). Wittgenstein responds to these questions, which are apparently innocent, as if they embodied some kind of objectionable philosophy. This is a feature that these questions and Wittgenstein's responses to them have in common with the earlier quotation from Augustine and Wittgenstein's response to it. In both cases, Wittgenstein appears to think that there is important philosophical work to be done, although (or, perhaps, because) the relevant type of problem is less well defined than a particular philosophical view or theory; the type of problem that Wittgenstein is interested in appears to lie at a somehow deeper or more general level.

The opening section of the *Investigations* is a nutshell, in many ways. It presents various elements of Wittgenstein's philosophy in a nutshell. And, like Wittgenstein's philosophy as a whole, it too is a hard nut to crack. Given this relative inaccessibility of Wittgenstein's philosophy, it is perhaps not surprising that, nowadays, Wittgenstein scholarship—that is, the historical study of the philosopher and his philosophy—continues to thrive, while Wittgensteinian philosophy—that is, both Wittgenstein's philosophy itself and philosophy practiced in the same manner—is increasingly perceived by many philosophers as being, at best, at the periphery of current concerns and debates. Wittgenstein's influence on the analytic tradition was particularly strong, but analytic philosophers are evidently finding it increasingly difficult to see the relevance of much of Wittgenstein's work for contemporary analytic philosophy. This volume strives to repair this recent disconnection of the analytic tradition from one of its founding figures by analyzing Wittgensteinian methods and points of view both from an exegetical perspective and with a view to the contemporary significance of Wittgenstein's philosophy. For this purpose, we decided that it would be best to give our contributors the freedom to treat their subjects with varying degrees of exegetical detail. Since the volume seeks to both interpret and apply Wittgenstein's philosophy, it seemed to us that more free-spirited variations on it should be permitted, or indeed encouraged.

The thematic focus of the volume is on metaphilosophy, epistemology, and the philosophy of language. Naturally, Wittgenstein's conception of philosophy and various related issues concerning the metaphysics, epistemology, and methodology of philosophy itself figure most prominently as a topic of discussion throughout. The chapters of this volume follow no strict sequence, and may be read in any order. However, those new to Wittgenstein's philosophy would do well to start at the beginning: the first two essays are both in-depth yet accessible discussions of the nature of Wittgensteinian philosophy, with the first one developing its argument largely in the form of exegesis and the second proceeding more freely. The following six essays then bring into focus various more narrowly defined questions. The first of this group tackles one central notion for this volume head-on, namely that of objectivity; the second presents a Wittgensteinian perspective regarding the role of intuitions in philosophy; the third offers a detailed and innovative interpretation of Wittgenstein's famous remarks on what he called "aspects," with a focus on related issues regarding the cognition (or perception) of meaning; the next essay also discusses Wittgenstein's remarks on aspects, and in this way develops a new solution to a problem about the nature of perceptual experience; the fifth applies lessons from Wittgenstein's work on aspect perception to questions of conceptual creativity in philosophical analysis; and the sixth discusses (related) questions concerning Wittgenstein's method and an influential type of revisionism in analytic philosophy. The following three essays each discuss linguistic meaning. The first argues against a prominent Wittgenstein-inspired use-theory of meaning; the second develops an alternative such theory; and the third presents a response to two recent criticisms of the related view that facts about meaning—or, more specifically, semantic facts—supervene on (non-semantic) facts about the use of words and concepts. The final essay in this volume is an exam on Wittgenstein and Socrates.

Acknowledgments

We are very grateful to our fellow philosophers who have contributed to this collection, not only for the brilliance of their work but also for their patience while the volume was in preparation. And we are grateful to our commissioning editor at Cambridge University Press, Hilary Gaskin, for her constant support throughout the editing process. Finally, we wish to thank the Alexander von Humboldt Foundation and the Fritz Thyssen Foundation for funding that made completion of the project possible.

CHAPTER I

Anatomy of a Muddle: Wittgenstein and Philosophy

Alexander George

It is not sufficiently considered, that men more frequently require to
be reminded than informed.

— Samuel Johnson

o   Ludwig Wittgenstein has a problem with philosophy. This claim will
hardly generate dissent. Though perhaps it should: for it might be objected
that Wittgenstein is leery of generalizations, including ones about what
troubles philosophy. He emphasizes that there is not just one way of going
astray in philosophy (PI §133).

Nevertheless, Wittgenstein does have a recognizable approach that he
regularly pursues in his philosophical investigations. There is a problem
that he often presses, a form of criticism that he often develops, against
traditional pursuits of philosophy, though in any given case its true force
only becomes clear in the particularities of its execution.[1] It is surprisingly
difficult to say clearly what this problem is. But it is worthwhile to try, for
not only is this criticism a hallmark of his thought but it is closely
connected to other central features of it, for instance, to his conception
of language and of the nature of philosophical investigation. These features
can be properly understood only in concert with a correct view of his terms
of criticism of traditional philosophy. In what follows, I shall articulate a
problem Wittgenstein sees with philosophy, show how it illuminates
otherwise peculiar features of his investigations, and finally consider an
illuminating way in which his goals might be thwarted.

1.1   It will be helpful to begin by briefly deploying the *calculatus eliminatus* to
explore what Wittgenstein's criticism is *not*. Most obviously, Wittgenstein

---

[1] The general terms of criticism that I describe, and the correlative approaches Wittgenstein develops
to press that criticism, are important *leitmotifs* of his entire later thought; whether this is the only
form of problem he presses does not concern me here.

does not aim to argue for the falsity of a philosophical proposition. If one knows anything about Wittgenstein's thought, one knows this. Of course Wittgenstein is not the only person in the history of philosophy who eschewed judgments of falsity when rejecting a philosophical pronouncement: David Hume, to take but one example, cannot always be read as arguing for the falsity of some opponent's claim. But Wittgenstein, throughout his life, was adamant that the proper critical stance to take toward traditional philosophical claims is *not* that they are false.

Even those with a passing knowledge of Wittgenstein's philosophy will know that his terms of criticism involve the notion of nonsense. But what is nonsense? It is natural to think that Wittgenstein's problem with the philosopher's claim is that it cannot be made sense of because it is couched in a way that somehow violates rules of his language. One might elaborate this thought as follows: claims are made within language, languages employ words that have meanings, and those meanings may occasionally conflict in such a way as to render the entire claim itself unintelligible, that is, in such a way as to render it nonsense. This view may go hand in hand with a view of Wittgenstein as a language policeman, someone who tasks himself with discovering the meanings that guide our use of language and stopping those who do violence to those meanings through illegal combinations of expressions.

This view is not tenable, however, in light of Wittgenstein's regular insistence that he has no objection to the form of words per se used by the philosopher: "It is not our intention to criticize this form of expression," he writes (BB 7). Indeed, Wittgenstein might have no problem with those very same words as spoken by someone else. Whatever Wittgenstein's criticism is, it is not directed just at a "form of expression."

It might be thought that keeping in mind Wittgenstein's focus on the *use* of expressions (as opposed to meanings allegedly attached to them) will be enough to get us back on track. But even with this in view, there are ways of misunderstanding Wittgenstein's critique. For instance, if we recast Wittgenstein's policing as targeting circumstances of use and say that his complaint with the philosopher is just that she uses words in unordinary ways, then we will again not have matters quite right. For Wittgenstein has no problem with familiar locutions being used unfamiliarly. Indeed, a distinctive feature of his method is precisely to conjure up circumstances in which familiar expressions are used differently: his intermediate cases and imagined peoples all involve scenarios in which common expressions are used in alternative ways.

To sum up, we have been considering attribution of the following line of thought to Wittgenstein:

(1) To employ an expression in an unordinary way is to utter nonsense.

(2) Philosophers often employ expressions in unordinary ways.

(3) Hence, philosophers often utter nonsense.

We have just been noting, however, that (1) is at best questionably attributed to Wittgenstein. From the fact that someone employs an expression in an unusual way, Wittgenstein would not conclude that she has lapsed into nonsense. If someone says "I feel the visual image to be two inches behind the bridge of my nose," a form of expression that is alien to us, Wittgenstein will not judge that he "is telling a lie or talking nonsense"; rather, he simply says, "this phrase has sense if we give it sense" (BB 10, 7). Wittgenstein's problem with philosophical claims is not most illuminatingly put by saying that they employ expressions in unusual ways.[2]

1.2 I shall turn now to a positive characterization of Wittgenstein's view. It will be helpful to consider an example of a situation in which Wittgenstein's antennae might begin to quiver. Imagine that someone expects that Bill will attend the party. Now imagine further that she says that she has a certain feeling in her stomach. Should we describe her feeling as that of "expecting that Bill will attend the party"? (Wittgenstein attributes such a view to Bertrand Russell.) It might come as a surprise that Wittgenstein would have no objection to so describing that feeling. Nevertheless, he would immediately caution, it should not be thought that by doing so we have a clear understanding of what "the feeling of expecting that x will attend the party" means for any given value of "x." It is true that a particular feeling has been baptized with a complex name, but the complexity of the name has been given no role in determining to which feeling we are referring. So while there is nothing wrong in itself with dubbing a sensation as "the feeling of expecting that Bill will attend the party," there may be a temptation down the road to assimilate this expression to, say, "the likelihood that Bill will attend the party." And if we do so, then we will be inclined to treat the parameters of the latter expression (for instance, "Bill") as present also in the former.[3] That is, because we can talk about "the likelihood that Bettina will attend the party," we will be

---

[2] There is something else problematic about attributing premise (1)—"to employ an expression in an unordinary way is to utter nonsense"—to Wittgenstein, if it encourages the thought that he takes there to be a determinate totality of uses that constitutes "the ordinary use" of an expression. I return to this issue in Section 1.3 and, again, in Section 2.3.

[3] In the *Blue Book*, Wittgenstein calls these parameters—for instance, "Bill" in the expression "the likelihood that Bill will attend the party"—"arguments" (BB 21).

inclined also to speak of "the feeling of expecting that Bettina will attend the party"; and this is an expression about whose use we are none too clear.

Before exploring the kind of confusion Wittgenstein thinks such assimilations can lead to, it is worth noting that warnings about such a slide—whereby an innocent-looking notation induces a false sense of the intelligibility of some parametric variation—reappear in central texts of analytic philosophy by thinkers who were no doubt influenced by Wittgenstein.

In "Two Dogmas of Empiricism" (1951), Quine considers an objection to his doubts about analyticity. He imagines someone who protests that analyticity is messy to characterize merely because ordinary language is messy. By contrast, we are assured, if we confine our attention to sharply defined artificial languages then the notion of *analytic truth* can be explained as clearly as one pleases. Quine's difficulties in characterizing the analytic truths of ordinary language, according to this objection, stem not from the notion of analyticity but rather from our lack of understanding of the structure of ordinary languages. Following Carnap, for instance, we can articulate a set of "semantical rules" of a given formal language that will settle which of its formulae count as analytic truths. For instance, assume that we are considering a particular formal language, L, and that we have specified what its semantical rules are. Then, by appeal to these, we can specify a certain subset of its formulae, the set of all and only those formulae that are analytic in L. What, Quine's interlocutor continues, could possibly be objectionable about this?

I think Quine would agree that so far there is nothing objectionable at all. A certain subset of the formulae of L has been clearly defined and if one wishes to call the formulae in that subset the analytic truths of L, one should feel free to do so. The problem comes when one thinks that the relation __ *is analytic in* __ has been thereby illuminated in any way. Such illumination would require that we treat "L" in "analytic in L" as a parameter, but nothing has been said so far to give us a handle on, say, the property "analytic in M." Quine puts the point this way:

> We may, indeed, view the so-called rule as a conventional definition of a new simple symbol "analytic-for-L_0," which might better be written untendentiously as "K" so as not to seem to throw light on the interesting word "analytic". .... By saying what statements are analytic for L_0 we explain "analytic-for-L_0" but not "analytic," not "analytic for." We do not begin to explain the idiom "S is analytic for L" with variable "S" and "L," even if we are content to limit the range of "L" to the realm of artificial languages. (Quine 1951, 33–4)

Again, an innocent notational predilection may lead us astray in giving us the impression that we have endowed a range of other locutions with significance.

In 1956, Wilfrid Sellars first presented his paper "The Myth of the Given: Three Lectures on Empiricism and the Philosophy of Mind." One of his targets was contemporary and classical sense-datum theories. At one point he considers the possibility that

> someone might introduce so-called sense-datum sentences as code symbols or "flags," and introduce the vocables and printables they contain to serve the role of reminding us of certain features of the sentences in ordinary perceptual discourse which the flags as wholes represent. In particular, the role of the vocable or printable "sense datum" would be that of indicating the symbolized sentence contains the context ". . . looks . . ., " the vocable or printable "red" that the correlated sentence contains the context ". . . looks red . . . " and so on. (Sellars 1956, 27)

Now Sellars has no objection to so introducing sense-datum talk. Indeed, doing so might be useful for various purposes. The problem is that it is easy to forget how this code was introduced and as a consequence easy to mistake the code elements for the identical strings of symbols in everyday talk. The philosopher, focused on the form of the expression instead of on how it was introduced and is used, easily confuses the two. And from there, it is easy to convince oneself that these code statements have an independent life and indeed involve concepts that help to clarify or explain our everyday discourse about how the world appears to us. Sellars thinks that this is one route down which philosophers have traveled to the idea of an intelligible and explanatory sense-datum language. As Sellars puts it:

> It would take an almost superhuman effort to keep from taking the vocables and printables which occur in the code . . . to be *words* which, if homonyms of words in ordinary usage, have their ordinary sense, and which, if invented, have a meaning specified by their relation to the others. (Sellars 1956, 29)

Absent this superhuman effort, "one may be tempted to try to eat his cake and have it" by both treating "sense-datum talk as *merely another language*" and taking it to "have an explanatory function" (1956, 30).

We can trace back this idea even further if we recall a book that Wittgenstein, Quine, and Sellars all read: the *Tractatus*. For, as Wittgenstein himself notes in the *Blue Book* (BB 21), a version of this idea makes an appearance there. In the context of a discussion of the Tractarian claim that all propositions are truth-functions of elementary propositions, Wittgenstein writes:

> The arguments of functions are readily confused with the affixes of names. For both arguments and affixes enable me to recognize the meaning of the signs containing them.
>
> For example, when Russell writes "$+_c$," the "$_c$" is an affix which indicates that the sign as a whole is the addition-sign for cardinal numbers. But the use of this sign is the result of arbitrary convention and it would be quite possible to choose a simple sign instead of "$+_c$"; in "$\sim p$," however, "p" is not an affix but an argument: the sense of "$\sim p$" *cannot* be understood unless the sense of "p" has been understood already. (TLP 5.02)

Though the details are unimportant here, Wittgenstein goes on to formulate an objection to Frege in terms of this distinction, namely that his "theory about the meaning of propositions and functions is based on the confusion between an argument and an affix."[4] Using this terminology, we can say that in "the feeling of expecting that Bill will attend the party," the name "Bill" functions not as an argument but as an affix.

But in fact, this kind of concern can be traced back yet further and, again, to a source that was certainly read by Wittgenstein, Quine, and Sellars: Frege himself. After arguing that, for instance, *being two in number* is not a property of an object but rather of a concept (in his technical sense of "object" and "concept"), Frege in *The Foundations of Arithmetic* (1884, §55) proceeds to offer a recursive definition of the property *being n in number*. To say that F is 0 in number is simply to say that there exists nothing which is F:

$$(\exists_0 x)Fx =_{df} \neg(\exists x)Fx$$

To say that F is exactly 1 in number (more colloquially, that there is exactly one thing that is F) is to say that at least one object is F and furthermore that the number of things that are F and not identical to that object is 0:

$$(\exists_1 x)Fx =_{df} (\exists x)(Fx \wedge (\exists_0 y)(Fy \wedge x{\neq}y))$$

And likewise, to say that there are exactly 2 Fs is to say that at least one thing is F and furthermore there is exactly one object that is F and not identical to that thing. It can thus be defined as:

---

[4] For a brief discussion of Wittgenstein's objection to Frege's theory of propositions and functions, see Black 1964, 238–40.

$$(\exists_2 \, x)Fx =_{df} (\exists x)(Fx \wedge (\exists_1 \, y)(Fy \wedge x{\neq}y))$$

More generally, we can define what it is for exactly $n{+}1$ things to be F:

$$(\exists_{n+1} \, x)Fx =_{df} (\exists x)(Fx \wedge (\exists_n \, y)(Fy \wedge x{\neq}y))$$

In this way, using just the apparatus of first-order quantification theory and the identity relation, Frege was able to define all the numerically definite quantifiers (see Frege 1884, §55).

Frege was not content with this analysis. But it is important to note that his dissent had nothing to do with the account's correctness: the logical structure of, say, "There are exactly 2 Fs" is exactly as specified by this recursive definition. The problem for Frege was rather that this notation misleads in giving the impression that the definition tells us something about the number 2 or about any particular natural number (which Frege announced as his goal at the outset of *Foundations*). To put the point formally, the notation suggests that the numeral "2" contributes semantically to the meaning of the claim that "There are exactly 2 Fs" just as the name "Hume" contributes semantically to the meaning of "Hume is Scottish." If we were to unpack the truth conditions of the latter statement, we would perforce make reference to Hume. However, if we unwind the truth conditions of "$(\exists_2 \, x)Fx$," we will not find ourselves referring to the number 2. For that reason, Frege thought that the numeral "2" in "$(\exists_2 \, x)Fx$" does not function as it does in, say, the statement "2 is an even prime number." To use the *Tractatus'* terminology, the numeral "2" in "$(\exists_2 \, x)Fx$" does not function as an argument. Given that the *Tractatus* introduces this notion in order to criticize Frege, there is some irony in the fact that Frege himself anticipates that very concern about notation. "It is only an illusion," Frege writes, that "2" in "There are exactly 2 Fs," as defined earlier in this section, functions as it does in "2 is an even prime number," an illusion fostered by our terminology.[5]

Let us now return to Wittgenstein and to a comical example of how our notation can induce such "illusions." At one point, he asks us to imagine someone who, for whatever reason, wishes to call a non-painful form of tooth decay "unconscious toothache." Again, one might think that

---

[5] Frege 1884, §56: "It is only an illusion that we have defined 0 and 1; in truth we have only determined the sense of the phrases

'the number 0 belongs to,'
'the number 1 belongs to';

but this does not allow us to distinguish 0 and 1 here as independent, reidentifiable objects."

in itself this is troubling to Wittgenstein as these words are now being used in an unusual way. But this is not so: "There is nothing wrong about it," he insists (BB 23), "as it is just a new terminology and can at any time be retranslated into ordinary language." We might say that the term "toothache" does not function here as a parameter; it is not an argument but an affix, in the *Tractatus*' terminology. "Unconscious toothache" is not an instance of "unconscious *x*." That is to say, the complex expression has not been explained to us in such a way that we know how to use it in ways analogous to the ways in which we might use the superficially similar "unconscious pregnancy," "unconscious cancer," etc.

How the expression was introduced can easily be forgotten, however, and we may find ourselves transforming "Smith has an unconscious toothache" in ways that we readily transform "Smith has an unconscious pregnancy." For instance, just as we might move from the latter to "Smith is pregnant but does not know it," so we might be tempted to move from the former to "Smith is in pain but does not know it." This, however, is a sentence for which we have no handling.

This kind of slide can be well illustrated by considering how a comparable situation might arise from Frege's account of the numerical quantifiers. Since we readily infer from "2 is an even prime number" that "There is at least one even prime number," the "illusion" of parity with "There are exactly 2 Fs" might encourage us to infer "There is at least one thing such that there are exactly that many objects that are F" or "$(\exists y)(\exists_y x)Fx$." We might, that is, treat "2" as functioning in the same way in both sentences, as occupying an argument position that can be existentially generalized. Now as it turns out, we can assign a meaning to this last claim. But that understanding has to be given to us independently: there is nothing in the recursive definition of the numerical quantifiers that teaches us how to handle this claim. As Frege puts it (1884, §66), our understanding of such new expressions is "no thanks to" his definition. (This independent understanding is precisely what Frege aims to provide in the remainder of his *Foundations*.)

1.3   We are now in a better position to articulate what the difficulty is that surrounds "Smith has an unconscious toothache," according to Wittgenstein. As we have seen, it is not the expression itself or the novel use assigned to it. The full problem is rather our inability to keep this use in focus. For we have a tendency to forget our initial resolve as to its use and instead to imagine that its use is of a piece with that of "Smith is pregnant but not conscious of that fact." To deploy the *Tractatus*' terminology, we had resolved to treat "toothache" as an affix, but we easily drift unawares into treating it as an argument.

As we lose sight of the use on which we had previously settled, we come to see the expression through the lens of syntactically analogous but in fact unrelated locutions. Wittgenstein sketches a number of different ways in which we might then react. We might dub the first that of the bold explorer: he will treat the existence of "unconscious toothache" as a major discovery about the mind and "he will say it like a man who is destroying a common prejudice" (BB 23). Or one might react as a skeptic and "deny the possibility of unconscious toothache" (BB 23). Or one might respond as a theoretician, "perhaps ask such a question as 'How is unconscious toothache possible?'" (BB 23), and then seek to develop a theory to accommodate this strange phenomenon. Or one might find oneself oscillating among all these responses, and yet others.

What these reactions have in common is that they presuppose that the words in question express a claim along the lines of someone's being pregnant without knowing it. But the fact is that we have not yet settled how to use the expression "unconscious toothache" along the lines of "unconscious pregnancy," and the only use we have given it so far—namely that of "painless tooth decay"—is one of which we have now lost sight. The speaker is left with a form of expression that she is convinced is significant but whose significance has yet to be resolved. "The phenomenon," Wittgenstein says, "is that of *irresolution*" (VW 235). Here, the speaker neither has in mind a definite use that has been marked out ("painless tooth decay") nor appreciates that formal analogies ("unconscious pregnancy") will not suffice to settle some use along other lines. This is an unwitting irresolution: the speaker thinks her words have a role in the language when in fact that role is still quite up in the air. Later, Wittgenstein will put this point by saying that the "confusions which occupy us arise when language is like an engine idling, not when it is doing work" (PI §132); idling, he might have added, while we believe the gears to be fully engaged.[6]

Before turning to a different kind of example of such irresolution, it will be worthwhile to make a number of quick observations. First, Wittgenstein speculates throughout his work on the forces that feed such irresolution. One that is of great interest to him is the assumption that

---

[6] While writing this essay, I had occasion to reread Stanley Cavell's "The Availability of Wittgenstein's Later Philosophy." It seems to me there is a congruence between my understanding of Wittgenstein and Cavell's suggestion that for Wittgenstein "the philosopher has no position at all" (Cavell 1962, 83).

words have determinate meanings that accompany them from one circumstance of use to another. We naturally assume that an expression contributes to the significance of a sentence in a manner that is systematically related to the way it contributes to the significance of any other sentence in which it might appear. There are several reasons why this assumption about meaning leads to trouble, according to Wittgenstein, but in this connection it is the fact that it encourages the philosopher to think that in order to endow her words with meaning no further work on her part is required beyond concatenating them in familiar ways. Thus, after Wittgenstein expresses perplexity about the sentence "I feel in my hand that the water is three feet under the ground," he imagines the response: "Surely you know what it means. You know what 'three feet under the ground' means, and you know what 'I feel' means!" To this, Wittgenstein replies: "I know what a word means *in certain contexts*" (BB 9). This sentence, he says, "combines well-known words, but combines them in a way we don't yet understand. The grammar of this phrase has yet to be explained to us" (BB 10).

Secondly, Wittgenstein often suggests that we regularly misinterpret our confusion about how to handle the relevant expression as the product of our grappling with philosophically deep issues. The confusion, which is actually a consequence of our irresolution about how to handle our expressions, is projected by us onto what we think the expressions are about and thereby misconstrued as an indication of the depth of the subject matter (relatedly, see PI §111). A muddle about meaning is mistaken for a problem of philosophy.

Thirdly, it is worth reemphasizing how this criticism differs from that which is often attributed to Wittgenstein. As remarked earlier, Wittgenstein is frequently interpreted to hold that the philosopher goes astray when she uses words in a fashion that conflicts with their ordinary usage. For him, it is said, the way the philosopher insists on applying her words clashes with the ordinary way in which they are used and thus ought to be used. But there are a number of problems with this construal. For one thing, it is misleading to say that Wittgenstein believes there is such a thing as "the ordinary way" in which words are used: his explorations reveal highly varied and perhaps even uncircumscribable ways in which we put our language to use. There is no determinate totality of uses that constitutes "ordinary usage." For another, we have seen that Wittgenstein does not believe that in matters of language use *is implies ought*: even if there were a definite canonical fashion in which we deploy our words, there would be no requirement that we stick to it. And finally, there is the point we have most recently been emphasizing: the philosopher's plight, at least the one here being highlighted, is precisely *not* that of someone who uses her words in a fixed fashion. Quite to the contrary, the problem is that her stance toward her words is irresolute: she has not settled how she wants to use them (and does not realize this).

Appreciation of this last point suggests that premise (2) in Section 1.1— "philosophers often employ expressions in unordinary ways"—is also not happily attributed to Wittgenstein. For this premise seems to saddle him with the view that the philosopher has resolved to use her words in a particular way (albeit one that differs from "ordinary usage"). But Wittgenstein's distinctive criticism is rather that this is precisely what the philosopher has failed to do.

Again, the terms of criticism here are unusual. As he puts it in the *Blue Book*, "the nature of our doubts" about the philosopher's words is not that something false or nonsensical has been said, but rather that "we don't understand the meaning of . . . a phrase" as used by the philosopher (BB 9, 10). This too is slightly misleading in suggesting that the problem is an epistemic one: as if the situation could be remedied simply by the philosopher's conveying the relevant information to us. But the problem is not that we are ignorant of some fact or that the philosopher is holding out on us. We might put the point by saying that the philosopher himself has no relevant information to convey: the philosopher thinks he has settled the work his words are to do when in fact he has not.[7] Wittgenstein's "doubts" are not directed at a form of expression. Rather, they are addressed to a person. They are doubts about whether an individual has lost his way in the use of some parts of his language. The problem he finds is that the speaker has become estranged from a stretch of his language and does not realize it.[8]

Wittgenstein's terms of criticism are very different from those of other philosophers, which partly explains why it can be so difficult to understand him. But the difference is not most helpfully put by saying that he substitutes the term "nonsense" for "false" in his dissent. I find it more instructive to locate the difference in the target of his criticism. It is

---

[7] In such situations when doing philosophy, Cavell writes, "our understanding should lose its grasp. Not only is it true that this can happen without our being aware of it, it is often very difficult to become aware of it—like becoming aware that we have grown pedantic or childish or slow" (1958, 205).

[8] An interesting question raised by Nishi Shah, and deserving more thought, is why estrangement from a stretch of one's language without one's realizing it is a hazard when doing philosophy in particular. It must be relevant that when we philosophize we do not engage with the world as we might in empirical inquiry. Rather, as Wittgenstein puts it, "in philosophizing, we contemplate what we *say* about things" (BB 23). I return to this question in Section 1.4.

directed not at the language a philosopher speaks or at a doctrine that the philosopher believes or at the reasoning the philosopher deploys in defense of his doctrine. It is directed at the philosopher himself. Again, when Wittgenstein writes that "confusions which occupy us arise when language is like an engine idling, not when it is doing work" (PI §132), the metaphor is carefully chosen: for an engine does not idle through any fault of its own, but because its operator has failed to engage it.

1.4   In the examples scouted in the previous sections, an expression was stipulated to have a use with which the philosopher eventually loses contact. Wittgenstein thought that some cases of philosophical confusion arise from such stipulations by philosophers: stipulations which are subsequently lost sight of without there being any real (as opposed to illusory) alternative sources of meaning on the horizon. To take one final example, consider Arthur Eddington's surprising claim that his writing table is not really there. What he actually means by this, at least initially, is that the existential commitments of the best physical theory of his day comprise "aether, electrons, quanta, potentials, Hamiltonian functions, etc." (Eddington 1928, xiii). Such entities are the possible values of variables in a formalization of the theory as opposed to, say, tables, desks, and chairs. His assertion may be an unusual way of putting this fact, but we do understand the gloss, and, so understood, the claim may or may not be of interest to those wishing to know what physicists are up to. But this gloss on "really there" is hard to keep front and center; the expression, after all, already has a rich use in everyday speech which exerts a strong pull. In fact, Eddington himself might quickly lose sight of the fact that he has placed an unusual spin on the expression. Sooner or later, the expression becomes interpreted along the lines of "The sand dunes are really there but the oasis is not." And at that point, Eddington finds himself with philosophical news: his familiar table—of which he says that "it has extension; it is comparatively permanent; it is coloured; above all it is *substantial*"—is not "really there" at all (1928, ix, xii).[9] And now one may find oneself oscillating through the variety of responses described earlier: from denial, to abashment at a presumptuous doubting of physicists, to perplexity which is chalked up to the philosophical depth of the matter at hand.

---

[9] Wittgenstein surely has Eddington in mind in his discussion of solidity in the *Blue Book* (BB 45–6). Wittgenstein says that in the descriptions by "popular scientists ... the word 'solidity' was used wrongly." This may not be the most helpful choice of words here: he has already explicitly stated that there is nothing wrong with putting an expression to a novel use, so long as one clarifies what that is and sticks to it. By "wrongly" here, we do better to understand Wittgenstein to mean: in a way liable to generate philosophical confusion.

A different kind of case is one in which the philosopher fails to see that the expression in question is *already* used in different ways in different contexts. Here, we have not a case in which the philosopher begins (consciously or not) to use an expression in an unusual way, as Eddington did, but rather a situation in which a given expression already has several different uses.[10] Let us return to the *Blue Book* and examine a philosophically potent example of how such a situation might lead to linguistic irresolution.

Sometimes, we experience fear. If we wish to report this experience, we might say "I am afraid." In other circumstances, our fear is directed at some particular object. We might describe such a fear by saying, for instance, "I am afraid of that spider." Now we might be drawn to the parametric variation in this last expression, what Wittgenstein calls its "multiplicity" (BB 29). And we might wish to render explicit the felt ellipticality of the first locution, "I am afraid," by rephrasing it as: "I am afraid of something (but I don't know what)." (A logician might describe this as our treating the transitive variant as the *normal form* of this locution.) We sometimes express our fear in this way. Is there anything inappropriate in doing so? Not according to Wittgenstein: "Both these forms of description can be used," he says (BB 22). If we recall precisely how we use "I am afraid of something (but I don't know what)," then it will be no more troubling to us than the expression it stands in for, "I am afraid."

But our tendency is not to keep these uses front and center, and instead to focus on syntactical parallels. We might, for instance, assimilate the parametrized expression of fear to "I shot something (but I don't know what)." That is, we might come to think that our understanding of "I fear something (but I don't know what)" is of a piece with our understanding of "I shot something (but I don't know what)," that is, to think that the two expressions are, as it were, values of the same function. But this is not so. The trappings that surround the latter are only stumblingly, if at all, extended to the former. For instance, I occupy no special role in settling what I shot. I can, along with anyone else, conjecture about this matter, though I might turn out to be rather poorly placed relative to others to discover what I shot. Have the analogues of such assertions, and countless others, in the case of the unknown object of my fear a clear use? Again,

---

[10] Gregory Carroll has pointed out to me that Eddington's situation could after all be assimilated to the second kind of case, in which a given expression already has several different uses, if we just describe it in such a way that Eddington does not stipulate novel uses for terms but instead uses them in ways they are already used by physicists, and then loses sight of the differences between such uses and the ordinary uses of these terms.

Wittgenstein's point is not that we cannot propose uses for such forms of expression: we can, and in so far as we do and stick to them, we clarify what we mean when we say that the object of our fear is unknown to us. The point is rather that often we do not engage in this work and (mistakenly) trust the grammatical parallelism to have discharged this task for us. Absent this work—and having forgotten the original uses of our expressions—the philosopher unwittingly casts herself into a linguistic limbo.[11]

Another example, of which Wittgenstein was fond, is the word "is": this word, he says, has "led to thousands of confusions" (VW 123).[12] It can be used as part of a predicate, as in "the rose is red," but also as the symbol for identity, as in "the positive square root of 36 is 6." If one were to lose sight of how the first sentence is used and to drift into viewing it through the lens of the second's use, then one might be inclined to wonder in what sense the rose could be identical to a color: we can be led, he says, to "the tormenting question 'To what extent is a rose identical with red?'" (VW 71). That question is tormenting, Wittgenstein says, not because it is ill-formed or nonsensical or incapable of being given a sense. In fact, the problem does not concern the sentence at all. The real problem lies in a user's take on the sentence. The sentence will be confusing to a user who has not yet given it a use but who is under the impression that it has one. "I have nothing against your attaching an idle wheel to the mechanism of our language," Wittgenstein says, "but I do want to know whether it is idling or with what other wheels it is engaged" (VW 73). The philosopher lacks this information: he cannot spell out clearly with which other wheels his expression is engaged and yet he believes it is not idling. The philosopher's perplexity is induced by a form of expression's idling in the context of his ignorance of this fact.

In the case of "is," we want to say that it is an accident that the same word is enlisted in English to do double duty. The final kind of case I shall

---

[11] I have focused on how linguistic similarities can suggest expressions that we do not know how to handle. But there are other sources of such suggestions. For instance, we might tell ourselves stories or imagine pictures about some phenomenon, and these might suggest an ultimately troublesome form of expression. A student describes Wittgenstein as saying:

> It is very pernicious to make a picture (e.g., of thinking as something going on in our head) and then forget the picture and go on using language derived from the picture. We may safely contrive to use this language *only* if we remember the picture e.g., man's spirit was pictured as his breath, then the picture was forgotten but the language derived from it was retained. We must only use language when we *make conscious* the picture, then it becomes harmless (cf. psycho-analysis). ([1930], 5)

[12] The example of "is" is also discussed in the *Tractatus* at 3.323. And it figures of course in Frege's "On Concept and Object" (1892).

mention here is the interesting one in which a word already has distinct uses, but nevertheless we wish to say it is natural or appropriate that we employ a single word. An example that intrigued Wittgenstein is the word "measure" as it occurs in the locutions "to measure time" and "to measure distance" (see, for instance, BB 26–7). Wittgenstein's diagnosis of Augustine's perplexity when he wondered, in *The Confessions*, how time could be measured is that Augustine viewed the former locution through the lens of the latter and its uses. Measurement of length differs enough from measurement of time that we are uncertain how to follow the analogies through—how to understand "the climb took 3 hours" along the lines of "the course was 3 miles"—which can lead, in circumstances of philosophical reflection, to linguistic alienation from our statements about temporal measurement. We forget the family of uses involving such statements and instead get our wires crossed by analogizing them to superficially similar statements with a different, though overlapping, family of uses. Avoiding such crossing, he says, is "particularly difficult when, in philosophizing, we contemplate what we *say* about things," that is, when we contemplate the words we employ, as opposed to how we employ them (BB 23). Nevertheless, the overlap in the uses of the term "to measure" in the different contexts motivates—makes seem utterly natural—our use of just one term.

2.1   If the above understanding of Wittgenstein is on the right track, then we might hope that it illuminates his practice. I shall briefly focus on one distinctive approach of his which can appear quite puzzling but is in fact clarified by the above reflections on his terms of criticism.

Wittgenstein often describes what he calls *language-games*, that is, uses of language that bear some relation to our own but are far simpler: "These are ways of using signs simpler than those in which we use the signs of our highly complicated everyday language" (BB 17). These are not to be thought of as fragments of a more complex practice. To emphasize this, Wittgenstein calls them "primitive forms of language or primitive languages" (BB 17; see also 81). In fact, these are often so simple, relative to our own complex practice, that the question naturally arises why their study should be at all relevant or beneficial. The same applies to the imagined "notations" (BB 59), the "intermediate cases" (PI §122), the fantasized "historical developments" (CV 45e) that fill his work.[13] What point do they serve?

---

[13] CV 45e: "One of my most important methods is to imagine a historical development of our ideas different from what has actually occurred."

The question is made more pressing by the fact that Wittgenstein often stresses that he is engaged merely in description. "We must do away with all *explanation*," he says, "and description alone must take its place" (PI §109). It is quite surprising then to find his writings filled with language-games: imagined uses of words, which precisely do *not* describe how *we* use our words. How are these excursions consistent with his call to stick to description? And again, what is the point of such linguistic fantasies anyway?

Wittgenstein's declaration about description has puzzled his readers even if we put his appeal to language-games to one side. For readers easily imagine that he is therefore concerned to describe and catalog the ways in which we do use our words. And they are then often perplexed as to why someone should think such a bare descriptive task could be of any philosophical interest. Can the above account of Wittgenstein's terms of criticism of philosophy help us understand the import of description in his work as well as the point of his frequent forays into fictional uses of language?

2.2   Let us recall that a major problem Wittgenstein detects is not with language but with a language user. The problem is that of linguistic dissociation: a speaker fails to recall the use a term has in a particular context and imagines that it functions there as it does in other contexts, with the consequence that the speaker arrives at forms of expression she believes to be meaningful but whose role in the language is in fact unsettled. And this in turn can lead to "tormenting" questions, illusions of depth, and fevered philosophical work. Wittgenstein seeks a method that "gives . . . peace" to someone so afflicted (PI §133).[14]

---

[14] In PI §133, Wittgenstein famously compares the philosophical methods he recommends to therapy. This may suggest that, should the therapy prove effective, the philosopher eventually arrives at some truth: he now realizes that something is the case that he had not realized before. A different metaphor is one that Theodore Redpath reports Wittgenstein deploying at the beginning of one of his lectures:

> The first lecture [in 1934] consisted largely of a disclaimer that he proposed to impart to his audience metaphysical "truths," or indeed that he would be concerned to transmit knowledge at all, in the sense in which this could be said of a geographer or a physicist. If that was what any member of the audience was expecting he would be disappointed. What the lectures *would* be offering was, according to Wittgenstein, more like the work of a *masseur*. If anyone happened to be suffering from a particular kind of mental cramp, Wittgenstein might be able to help him. (RAM 18)

How to characterize the upshot—if there is one—of Wittgenstein's "help" is discussed briefly at the end of this essay.

Now Wittgenstein's thought is that one way a speaker can be alerted to confusion is to be presented with a notational variant of his language in which the relevant form of expression is replaced in one of its contexts of use by another form of expression. Recall that, on Wittgenstein's view, a speaker's slide into expressions that exhibit "ineptness or emptiness" (PI §131) is greased by an expression's having different uses in different corners of the language. So by adopting a notation in which an expression no longer performs double duty, the speaker's slide might be arrested. A speaker contemplating such a notation—one that has exactly the same expressive power as her original notation—may come to realize that the troubling bit of language, the one that so perplexed her, was an artifact of her original notation rather than an expression of a deep problem.

In the *Blue Book* (BB 26), Wittgenstein refers approvingly to Hertz's *The Principles of Mechanics* (1894).[15] He does not specify a passage there, but a student at Wittgenstein's lecture in February 1939 reports that he cited the following, which "seemed to him to sum up philosophy":

> With the terms "velocity" and "gold" we connect a large number of relations to other terms; and between all these relations we find no contradictions which offend us. We are therefore satisfied and ask no further questions. But we have accumulated around the terms "force" and "electricity" more relations than can be completely reconciled amongst themselves. We have an obscure feeling of this and want to have things cleared up. Our confused wish finds expression in the confused question as to the nature of force and electricity. But the answer which we want is not really an answer to this question. It is not by finding out more and fresh relations and connections that it can be answered; but by removing the contradictions existing between those already known, and thus perhaps by reducing their number. When these painful contradictions are removed, the question as to the nature of force will not have been answered; but our minds, no longer vexed, will cease to ask illegitimate questions. (Hertz 1894, 7–8; cited in RAM 84)

This passage expresses both the spirit of Wittgenstein's view and also of one of his proposed remedies. Hertz's proposed unraveling of "relations and connections" is just what results in Wittgenstein's new notations.[16]

---

[15] Hertz's *The Principles of Mechanics* is also referred to in the *Tractatus*.

[16] I say that the passage from Hertz expresses "the spirit" of Wittgenstein's view because I do not think the problem is best put in terms of "contradictions" between uses. It is rather that inattention to differences can lead us to expressions which we assume we understand but which we do not really know how to handle.

An example Wittgenstein considers is that of a variant of English in which the word "is" is replaced by two different symbols, say "∈" and "=," to represent predication and identity, respectively (see, for instance, VW 71). Sometimes Wittgenstein will present this variant as a new notation. Sometimes he will ask us to "imagine people who, as it were, thought much more precisely than we, and used different words where we use only one" (PPF §74). Either way, one purpose of the exercise is to break the hold that surface resemblances have on us and to provide us with a clear view of how we use our expressions. This new notation is not intended as an improvement: "ordinary language is all right," after all (BB 28).[17] Again, the problem is not with our language but with a user's stance toward it. The new notation is intended rather to help us appreciate a difference that was not salient to us before. In the new notation, the troublesome questions that we slid into—for example, in what sense a rose can be said to be the same as a color—would no longer result from syntactical analogizing. And yet, everything we wanted to be able to say we still can. We might then acknowledge that the interrogative sentences we had been formulating, which had seemed so bothersome and perhaps indicative of profound metaphysical issues, really expressed no questions at all.

Wittgenstein places great importance on this technique of offering new notations or language-games in which, say, a familiar expression has only some of the uses it has in our language. For these notations provide a "perspicuous representation" of our use of words, which "is of fundamental significance for us. It earmarks the form of account we give, the way we look at things" (PI §122). This importance reflects the facts, first, that Wittgenstein finds this technique helpful in giving us the kind of overview of linguistic use that might arrest our slide into linguistic irresolution and, second, that combating such irresolution is of paramount importance for him.

2.3   Keeping front and center "the form of account" he offers and the reasons for its importance can help deflect a common objection to Wittgenstein and also avert a common misunderstanding. The objection, which we have already broached, is that Wittgenstein is simply in the business of producing descriptions of how we use our words, a business that (a) is at odds with his claim not to be engaged in an empirical inquiry and (b) is of dubious philosophical relevance (at least for those who, like

[17] *Tractatus* 5.5563: "In fact, all the propositions of our everyday language, just as they stand, are in perfect logical order."

Wittgenstein himself, believe that philosophical questions are not to be answered by means of such an inquiry; see PI §109).

It is true, as far as it goes, that Wittgenstein aims to describe language use. However, what the objection misses is that those descriptions are not in the service of comprehensiveness, let alone of an aimless cataloging of linguistic use; nor are they a preliminary exercise to the construction of an empirical theory. Wittgenstein's descriptions are of the facets of use put in relief by his language-games, novel notations, etc. And those language-games, novel notations, etc. are chosen with a view to arresting a particular slide into linguistic irresolution by a particular speaker. Any given slide is the product of specific mis-analogies. The descriptions offered are in the service of making salient those particular crossed linguistic wires.

Again, the goal is not comprehensiveness. And the descriptions are neither presented for description's sake (whatever that might mean exactly) nor as an empirical data-gathering prelude to a theoretical account of use. Rather, they are highly focused presentations whose aim is to help a speaker see that she has drifted into taking an expression to have been given a role to play in her language when in fact it lacks one. As Wittgenstein puts it, a description he might offer "gets its light, that is to say its purpose, from the philosophical problems" (PI §109), where by the latter he means a speaker's muddles induced by linguistic irresolution. If we keep in mind Wittgenstein's conception of philosophical progress—that is, the releasing of someone from a confusion related to language—then we can see how his pointers to facets of use might qualify as (a) descriptive, (b) not in the service of empirical theorizing, and yet (c) philosophically valuable.[18]

Closely related to this common objection is a common misunderstanding: that for Wittgenstein there is such a thing as "the ordinary use" of an expression. The common objection indeed presupposes this misunderstanding in its claim that there is little to no philosophical interest in a bare description of "the ordinary use" of an expression. This promotes the misinterpretation of Wittgenstein according to which he believes that expressions have a canonical use in the language and that the philosopher somehow lapses into nonsense by using her words in ways that conflict with that use.

But it is doubtful that Wittgenstein believes there is such a thing as "the ordinary use" of an expression, if this is intended to designate some

---

[18] An interesting issue, which I cannot take up here, is whether Wittgenstein's descriptions of language use are straightforwardly empirical (even if they are not in the service of empirical theory construction). This question is at the core of Cavell's "Must We Mean What We Say?" (1958).

finite collection of uses. If the uses to which an expression can be put were in practice surveyable, then there would be no bar to articulating necessary and sufficient conditions for correct use (if only in a disjunctive form). But for most common expressions of our language, this is precisely what Wittgenstein believes we cannot do. "There are," he says, "countless different kinds of use" to which we put our words (PI §23).

Still, one might conceive of these uses as forming a determinate totality of techniques that constitutes "the ordinary use." The natural numbers, for instance, cannot in practice be counted and yet most mathematicians believe there is a determinate collection that contains all and only the natural numbers. This conception of "the ordinary use" might be encouraged by the following thought. For the purposes of clearing up confusions in a speaker, which are potentially endless, we find it useful to focus on particular kinds of use. So if we imagine undertaking and completing such an examination for all possible confusions, we would be led to a comprehensive overview of "the infinite variety of the functions of" that expression (BB 83). We would be led, that is, to the determinate infinite totality that constitutes "the ordinary use" of the expression in question. But for Wittgenstein, this thought would be akin to the following "confusion": to think "that a line of a certain length consists of an infinite number of parts because it is indefinitely divisible; i.e., because there is no end to the possibility of dividing it" (BB 15).[19] There may be no end to potential confusions about language, but we should not slide from that to the existence of a determinate infinite collection of all possible confusions and, correlatively, to the existence of a determinate infinite totality of ordinary uses of an expression. For Wittgenstein, it is a confusion to think that there is a determinate totality that is *the ordinary use* of an expression.

3.1   We can arrive at a sharper conception of Wittgenstein's thought here if we consider a particular reaction someone might have to a Wittgensteinian philosophical massage. Let us return to one of Wittgenstein's favored examples: someone who is puzzled about how a rose might be identical to red. As before, Wittgenstein might describe a new notation for her, a variant of English, in which "is" is replaced by two different expressions, "∈" and "=," corresponding respectively to what we might call the "is" of predication and the "is" of identity. In this notation, the sentence "the rose is red" does not appear: it is replaced by "the rose ∈ red." This no longer has the same form as

---

[19] For more on the "confusion" of thinking that a line consists of an infinite number of parts because it is indefinitely divisible, see George and Velleman 2001, chapter 4.

"the rose = the flower in the vase" and so the notation will not encourage moving on from the sentence in ways one might move on from the latter identity, a move that will likely lead to expressions without any clear use. For instance, one will not find oneself asking "Which object is identical to red?" (by analogy with the question "Which object is identical to the flower in the vase?"). How might someone react to such a notation?

One response might be that of relief. A difference in the uses of "is" that had been so salient and yet not hitherto marked by our language has now been recognized. "Such a notation," Wittgenstein writes, "would actually fulfil some of the wishes which are denied us by our ordinary language and which sometimes produce a cramp of philosophical puzzlement" (BB 60–1). The new notation highlights the two distinct uses, we might say, and does justice to our feeling that the double duty to which we put "is" is really accidental. As just noted, such a response to the new notation will be accompanied by a dimming of the tendency to assimilate "the rose is red" to "the square of 5 is 25," with a consequent avoidance of many vexing inquiries, for instance, ones into the kind of thing that a property is.

A different response might be to acknowledge the two different uses of "is" but to insist that this word really should cover both. For instance, Wittgenstein at one point describes different uses of "to understand" but notes that he would reject a notation that, unlike ours, employs two different expressions:

> Then has "understanding" two different meanings here? – I would rather say that these kinds of use of "understanding" make up its meaning, make up my *concept* of understanding.
> For I *want* to apply the word "understanding" to all this. (PI §532)

For whatever reason—or no reason—Wittgenstein is moved to treat "these kinds of use" as of a piece, at least sufficiently so as to want to employ just one word here. Likewise, though less likely, someone might resist Wittgenstein's notational suggestion because he *wants* to use "is" both for predications and identities.

Both of these responses acknowledge the differences in use that Wittgenstein seeks to draw to the philosopher's attention; they diverge in whether they want the given word to cover these acknowledged differences. Since it is acknowledgment of the differences in use that Wittgenstein hopes will arrest slides into irresolution, his massage might provide relief in the face of either of these reactions.

But I would like to focus here on a different kind of response to Wittgenstein's grammatical investigations, that of someone who simply does not recognize the different uses as, well, different. To begin with an outlandish example, say someone appreciates that "is" can be employed to express both equality and predication, but nevertheless finds these employments to be on the order of the application of "to sit" both to sitting on a chair and to sitting on the grass: a difference of application, yes, but not so great as to amount to a difference of use. Is he right to do so? If someone disagrees about how to count uses, how can the dispute be resolved? What kind of dispute is this?

Wittgenstein considers a philosophically more resonant example of such a reaction when he explores our thinking about experience (BB 48–58). One of the voices in this exploration is that of the solipsist, someone who finds enormously salient the differences he sees in his use of "pain" as applied to himself and as applied to others. His reaction to these differences is to embrace a notational change that marks these distinctions, for instance, a notation that allows "Only I feel pain" and "Others, when they behave as I do when I am in pain, are in *shpain*." Such a notation, the solipsist thinks, does better justice to the facts about experience. Most people of course will not have this reaction when these features of use are made plain to them. They will react as Wittgenstein does in the case of "understanding": once made aware of the differences in our use of "pain" they will still feel that they want to apply the word in all these circumstances. The solipsist by contrast "objects to using this word ['pain'] in the particular way in which it is commonly used" (BB 57). Despite this divergence, most of us are in the same boat as the solipsist when it comes to appreciating the distinct ways in which we employ the word "pain"; where we differ is in our response to that appreciation, in particular, in whether we want to apply the word "to all this."

Another voice in this discussion is that of the realist, who, unlike the solipsist, sees no interesting difference in our use of "pain" as applied to ourselves and as applied to others. Even if he grants that one cannot know that another is in pain, the realist will not acknowledge the third-person use of "pain" to be different in kind from its first-person use. The term is really being used in the same way, this realist will insist, only our attributions of pain to another are not confirmable (or knowable or imaginable, etc.) to the same degree as are our self-attributions. (And correlatively, the realist will go on to insist that his uses of "confirm," "know," or "imagine," are univocal as well.)

Wittgenstein says in this case that "the trouble with the realist is that he does not solve but skip the difficulties which his adversaries see, though they too don't succeed in solving them" (BB 48). Solipsists "see," while realists do not, "the difference between different usages of" certain words (BB 49). The realist goes astray by failing to appreciate differences in use. What kind of error has the realist made? Would evidence or argument be pertinent to this dispute? If not, what kind of considerations might Wittgenstein offer the realist to help him "[see] the difference between different usages"?[20]

More generally, what is the status of claims about differences in use? Our ignorance of these differences, Wittgenstein believes, is one root of philosophical perplexity. But what kind of fact is it of which we are ignorant? If someone fails to acknowledge a difference of use, is he in error? If so, what kind of error? That is, what is the status of such claims about use? In resolving such a dispute, which kinds of considerations would be germane?

3.2   As just noted, the solipsist sees a great difference between first-person and third-person uses of "pain": these amount to, he finds, really two different uses. The realist, by contrast, finds there is only one use, though of course applications of the term vary with context. What kind of dispute is this, and does the work of philosophical clarification hinge on its resolution?

Wittgenstein once told his friend Maurice Drury that an apt motto for his *Philosophical Investigations* would be Kent's line in *King Lear*: "I'll teach you differences" (RW 157). For he thought that an appreciation of the differences in our use of expressions might rescue us from irresolution, might help us see that we have unwittingly drifted from one use to another in ways that could result in expressions for which we have no clear handling. Clearly then, the realist's response we are imagining is one that presents a challenge to Wittgenstein. Or at least, so long as someone fails to see the differences in use that Wittgenstein works to bring to light *as significant differences*, she will not feel the benefit of his investigations.

So what is the status of the realist's disagreement with the solipsist? In the first place, for Wittgenstein, the dispute about whether we have here one use of the word "pain" or two is not an empirical one. Our realist and solipsist, we may imagine, are not in disagreement about any facts about

---

[20] Wittgenstein thinks that solipsists also go astray: for they mistake their appreciation of differences of language use for a substantive insight into the nature of experience. Properly understood, the solipsist's error is of a piece with the realist's, just one that occurs further on down the road. For in claiming that his observations about pain signal discoveries of moment, the solipsist himself fails to appreciate the different ways in which certain expressions (like "cannot") get used, for instance, the difference between "You cannot know another person's pain" and "You cannot swim across the Atlantic" (BB 54).

our use of this word. Any feature of our use of "pain" in first-person and third-person contexts that the solipsist might point to will be acknowledged by the realist. Wittgenstein seems to have these matters in mind when he writes:

> There can be two kinds of discussions as to whether a word is used in one way or in two ways: (*a*) Two people may discuss whether the English word "cleave" is only used for chopping up something or also for joining things together. This is a discussion about the facts of a certain actual usage. (*b*) They may discuss whether the word "altus," standing for both "deep" and "high," is *thereby* used in two different ways. This question is analogous to the question whether the word "thought" is used in two ways or in one when we talk of conscious and unconscious thought. (BB 58)

The dispute I am imagining is not of kind (a). I assume that both solipsist and realist know the varied ways in which, say, the word "pain" is used by us. There is no fact about usage to which the solipsist could point that would elicit from the realist the response "Oh, I had not realized we use the word in that way." Theirs is not an empirical disagreement about "actual usage."

Rather, the disagreement is of kind (b): over whether, in using "pain" as they agree we do in first- and third-person contexts, we "*thereby* [use it] in two different ways." In an extended example, Wittgenstein discusses this kind of disagreement but in connection with a physical tool, not a word:

> But is it not right to say that in any case the person who talks both of conscious and unconscious thoughts thereby uses the word "thoughts" in two different ways? – Do we use a hammer in two different ways when we hit a nail with it and, on the other hand, drive a peg into a hole? And do we use it in two different ways or in the same way when we drive this peg into this hole and, on the other hand, another peg into another hole? Or should we only call it different uses when in one case we drive something into something and in the other, say, we smash something? Or is this all using the hammer in one way and is it to be called a different way only when we use the hammer as a paper weight? – In which cases are we to say that a word is used in two different ways and in which that it is used in one way? To say that a word is used in two (or more) different ways does in itself not yet give us any idea about its use. It only specifies a way of looking at this usage by providing a schema for its description with two (or more) subdivisions. It is all right to say: "I do *two* things with this hammer: I drive a nail into this board and one into that board." But I could also have said: "I am doing only one thing with this hammer; I am driving a nail into this board and one into that board." ... The man who says "surely, these are two different usages" has already decided to use a two-way schema, and what he said expressed this decision. (BB 58)

The world does not demand that we individuate uses of a hammer in a particular way. If we have "already decided to use a two-way schema," then we will gravitate toward certain ways of individuating uses; if we have decided on another schema for description, then other individuations may appear natural. And the world itself will not weigh in to rationally constrain our decision about which "schema for its description" to adopt.[21] The realist's judgment that his use of "pain" is unequivocal is an expression of such a decision.[22]

Now Wittgenstein's example of the hammer suggests that there might nevertheless be room for rational assessment of a decision to adopt a schema for description after all (not on account of its accord with the data but rather for its suitability to the describer's interests). Wittgenstein notes in another context that "either tendency [of an individual to use this versus that schema for description] may be justified, say, by his particular practical purposes" (BB 29). To the extent that our imagined realist individuates uses as a result of having certain interests, there is a toehold for rational assessment, at least of a means-end reasoning variety.

But Wittgenstein observes that devices of description are not always adopted because they make sense given our interests. Sometimes it goes more deeply than that. Our descriptive tendencies may reflect how we see the world, our personalities, our ways of positioning ourselves vis-à-vis others. A person's choice, Wittgenstein notes, "often depends on general, deeply rooted, tendencies of his thinking" (BB 30). He offers an example:

> Should we say that there are cases when a man despises another man and doesn't know it; or should we describe such cases by saying that he doesn't despise him but unintentionally behaves towards him in a way – speaks to him in a tone of voice, etc. – which in general would go together with despising him? Either form of expression is correct; but they may betray different tendencies of the mind. (BB 30)

---

[21] For a discussion of similar issues as they arise between Quine and Carnap over analyticity, see George 2000.

[22] Important historical examples of the kind of realists I have discussed are those philosophers deeply attracted to Paul Grice's work and its conceptual machinery of pragmatic versus semantic features of language. (I owe this observation to Nishi Shah.) John Searle, for instance, elaborates a view according to which differences in use of psychological expressions in first-person and third-person contexts are acknowledged but not deemed significant in the way some ordinary language philosophers have suggested (see, for instance, Searle 1969). Wittgenstein might say that Searle's attraction to this apparatus for describing language use manifests his "decision" not to see important differences in our uses of some expressions. Or perhaps he might treat Searle's attraction to this schema of description as of a piece with his not treating certain differences in use as significant. Searle might well reject any such interpretation and claim instead that his embrace of this apparatus of description is a rational response to its explanatory benefits. For a discussion of this fundamental disagreement, see my "'It Will Not Do': What Did Austin Mean?" (unpublished manuscript, co-authored with Nishi Shah).

Such leanings may be untouched by either presentation of facts or means-end reasoning. But as this example suggests, that should not encourage the thought that such "tendencies of the mind" are unimportant, akin, say, to someone's decision to put on his left shoe first. The realist's refusal to agree that we use "pain" in importantly different ways may be inaccessible to forms of reasoning with which philosophers are most comfortable and at the same time revelatory of an important difference in thought or in orientation toward the world and others.

3.3   What kinds of considerations could we possibly lay before such a realist then, if not further facts about the usage of these expressions? John Wisdom observes that there is something blinkered in such an exasperated query:

> When the madness of these questions leaves us for a moment *we can all easily recollect disputes which though they cannot be settled by experiment are yet disputes in which one party may be right and the other wrong* and in which both parties may offer reasons and the one better reasons than the other. (Wisdom 1945, 193; he initially makes the point in the context of disputes about God's existence)

Disputes that resist resolution in the laboratory rarely leave participants with nothing to say to one another. From the fact that there is little disagreement over the empirical data, we should not race to conclude that the practice of offering arguments can get no foothold, that judgments of correctness or reasonableness are out of place. Wisdom reminds us that there is no end to the techniques of reasoning we can, and do, call upon: the presentation of related cases, the drawing of parallels, the highlighting of differences, the tracing of patterns, and on and on. Wisdom calls this vast and varied family of methods "the connecting technique":

> For features of the picture may be brought out by setting beside it other pictures; just as the merits of an argument may be brought out, proved, by setting beside it other arguments, in which striking but irrelevant features of the original are changed and relevant features emphasized; just as the merits and demerits of a line of action may be brought out by setting beside it other actions. (Wisdom 1945, 196, 197)

Though the idea has a long history, the "connecting technique" was much practiced by Wittgenstein, who famously wrote that "the problems are solved, not by giving new information, but by arranging what we have always known" (PI §109). That many disagreements are the product not of factual disputes but instead of different ways of seeing the facts and, consequently, that progress can result from reminders, rather than deductions or measurements, seems uncontroversial once stated and will perhaps surprise only if we are resolutely focused on the methods of mathematics and the sciences.

Wisdom also stresses that such disagreements are all around us and of great variety. They may arise over whether there is an invisible caretaker tending the garden of the world, whether a man's actions legally count as negligent, whether a loved one has behaved with consideration, whether a joke is funny, a work of philosophy insightful, or whether an individual has survived a cognitively devastating illness. I take Wittgenstein's disagreement with the realist who insists he can see only one relevant use of the word "pain" to be of this nature. And so too his disagreement with a philosopher blind to the differences Wittgenstein's grammatical investigations are meant to bring to light. His disagreement with our realist is neither straightforwardly empirical, nor merely definitional. Mustering the data, the bare facts about use of the word "pain," is pointless (since they are not in question). But at the same time, assimilating the disagreement to ones over conventional stipulations on which nothing turns falsifies its character.

At the end of such a discussion, a party to the conversation might say that he learned something, recognized that something was the case, even if no new empirical fact had been discovered. Through his investigations, Wittgenstein might succeed in changing the philosopher's "*way of looking at things*" (PI §144).[23] And this change could express itself in the philosopher's no longer making certain statements or asking certain questions. There is no guarantee that such a change will be forthcoming. (If we kick the debate up one level—to how we use the expression "different use"—we may of course run into the very same situation.) In notes dictated to Francis Skinner, Wittgenstein asks: "How far does the thing I do compel you to remove your doubts?" And he answers himself: "It just can't. Sometimes the thing I do will work, and sometimes it won't work. . . . The puzzle is a sort of misunderstanding and the word which solves it may never be found" ([1934], Feb. 5). It is not an interesting objection to Wittgenstein, or even any objection at all, to point out that his therapy —a most unusual remedy to a most unusual diagnosis of what ails philosophy—will not always bring relief.[24]

---

[23] It is fruitful to explore the connections between Wittgenstein's conception of philosophical progress and his discussion of aspect-seeing.

[24] My thanks to Gregory Carroll and Nishi Shah for helpful discussions and comments.

CHAPTER 2

Explaining What We Mean

Julia Tanney

"The meaning of a word is what is explained by the explanation of the meaning." I.e.: if you want to understand the use of the word "meaning", look for what are called "explanations of meaning".

— Ludwig Wittgenstein

1   Your assertions are claims on my beliefs; your requests and commands are claims on my actions; your expressions—of pain, joy, or opinion—may be claims on my attitudes. But I cannot properly assess, act upon, or react to what you say unless I understand it. If you show me a photograph of a woman you call your mother but at the same time claim that she is not a member of your family, I may not know what to think until I learn what you mean by 'mother' and 'family': how you are using or applying these expressions in the circumstances.

We learn in what Ryle described as the 'hard-school of daily life' (1953, 329) the 'inflections' of meanings or 'elasticities of significance' (1945, 215) for common general terms (such as 'mother' and 'family' in my example above) and the sort of phenomena that count as falling under them. Indeed, most if not all expressions of natural languages have these elasticities and belong to what Wittgenstein called a 'family of structures, more or less related to one another' (PI §108). This network can be revealed when we consider the different logical or implication threads of a sentence as it is employed on various occasions. These logical threads or ties include: what would count as evidence, as justification or warrant, as implied, permitted, or otherwise consistent or compatible; as contrary, contradictory, or otherwise inconsistent or incompatible; as incurred commitments and liabilities, or as a successful or appropriate uptake or reaction, and so on. Mentioning any one of these is among the ways we may spell out what we mean or what we are trying to say. It is for this reason that an answer to the questions 'What is your evidence?', 'What are your grounds?', 'What is your point?', or even 'Show me!' may help us understand what is said. In short, given the elasticities of significance in any given expression, to understand the force of the utterance and its logical ties will often enable us to glean the way its constituent expressions are applied.

As we come to understand English, we learn that in the metaphorical folder labelled 'mother' we tend to include, for example, females who have given birth. We may also include females who have raised their offspring. Often the different considerations that would elaborate, explain, or justify our use of the label 'mother' coincide, but sometimes they do not. On occasion it is important to mark the differences, so if the context does not make it clear, we might use special labels to specify that the subfolder we have in mind is 'birth mother' or 'adoptive mother'. Several decades ago, a separate folder, 'nurse mother' was employed more frequently than it is today. Of course, there are other items collected under the folder 'mother' besides females who have given birth; extending, as a form of address, to very old women, to the head of a female religious community, to institutions or organizations which have 'begotten' other ones; to an extreme example or large specimen of something. It is even used as a synonym for 'starter' (following the French *mère*) used in the production of vinegar and bread. And so on and so forth.[1]

The folder 'family' overlaps in certain places with that of 'mother'; but given the inflections and sub-folders in 'mother' and those in 'family', we may need some time to reflect in order to spell out how. Our cat and dog are members of our family, though some pet owners do not share enough intimacy with their animals to consider them so. This is not just a sentimental claim: it is illuminative to those who might otherwise be bewildered by our lifestyle choices. But although I used to take my sourdough starter on holiday with me (because it needed regular feeding), if there were any sense in regarding it as 'part of the family' this would not be entailed by its being my *mère*.[2]

---

[1] Grammatical variants—adverbs, adjectives, or verbs—such as 'motherly', 'mother-like', or 'to mother' will have overlapping occupations with (that is some affinities with and some differences from) those items collected under 'mother'. Indeed, in many philosophically interesting cases, it will be the applications of verbal, adjectival, or adverbial forms of an expression that will determine how best to understand what is subsumed by the abstract noun. This is exemplified by the present study of the notion of meaning.

[2] Extended uses, we may agree, can be set aside while we concentrate on those that form the central core. In the discussion that follows, we shall quickly set aside several more peripheral applications of 'mother' in order to concentrate on core, more literal uses as opposed to metaphorical or figurative ones. But the contrast between what is literal and what is figurative itself tends to blur as the context changes; and, as we shall see, the number of applications even within an arguably literal use will be innumerable.

On one central, established use of the expressions 'mother' and 'family,' to be a mother is to be a member of a family. Your decision to use 'family' so as to exclude your mother when you showed me her picture, though perhaps not immediately clear, is upon reflection understandable: within the metaphorical folder labelled 'family' are included people who are related to one another and who, because of this, are to be treated with a special loyalty or intimacy. You could well argue that your relation to your mother does not warrant this intimacy; but your relation to your adoptive parents or your pets does, and it is this particular inflection which you are bringing out in your choice not to use the term for your mother.

It was suggested that in the docket labelled 'mother' we may include females who raise their offspring as well as those who have given birth. Because the expression 'raise their offspring' also has elasticities of significance, especially as modern, reconstituted families become prevalent, we find the folder labelled 'mother' may also contain 'stepmother', though this expression itself admits of inflections arising from its use, for example, in fairy tales. It would be understandable if a child were to stick with 'mother' to describe a stepmother to whom she feels close, especially if the birth mother is not around. By contrast, because of the suggestion of age difference or the idea of an extended family unit, I would not dream of calling myself a 'stepmother' to my husband's three adult, middle-aged, male children (and nor would they). 'Given birth' can also be stretched: those who are aptly described as having done so may include, for example, a genetic or non-genetic surrogate, also called 'the gestational mother'. Although presently the egg donor is deemed to be the biological mother, it is not difficult to envisage how this category will undergo further subdivisions as different kinds of procedures for facilitating births or avoiding congenital disorders are invented (for example, when there are two egg donors). At the time of writing, it was announced that artificial wombs are in development for babies born critically premature. Might this one day be extended for the full period of gestation, giving sense to the notion of an artificial mother? Will this category itself divide as robots begin to play a nurturing role? This will depend, of course, on the need we have to make use of such notions.

Often what we mean, if we are to be understood, is settled by factors that override any scope or latitude we might have for drawing boundaries on our part. If you, who do not consider your mother to be family, were asked by your doctor if anyone in your family has a history of heart disease, you would be expected to consider the question in relation to the woman in the photo, whether or not you choose to use the term 'family' in such a way as to exclude her. If the doctor asks of a child born to a surrogate parent whether her mother has such a history, presumably the answer here—how 'mother' is to be understood—would be the egg donor or the biological mother. If the doctor were interested instead in, say, diseases that can be transmitted from the womb to the baby, this would arguably require that 'mother' be applied to the surrogate. These occasions, in other words, would call for a different use or application. When the context is not clear and the relevant applications point in different directions, the question, 'Is this woman your mother?' might invite the response 'Well, she is and she isn't', until it is clear what is to count as your mother in the circumstances.

I have given a rough sketch of a few of the considerations that govern, have governed, and may in the future govern what might be considered core or literal, as opposed to peripheral or figurative, applications of the expression 'mother' and various subdivisions of this general category. Is there any reason to think that I have picked a special case? Or does the discussion of 'mother' instead illustrate a feature of most, if not all, expressions of any given natural language? For the expressions 'knowledge', 'justice', or 'beauty', like those of 'time', 'space', 'random', 'probable', 'about', 'the same as', 'understanding', 'meaning', 'thought', 'belief', 'right', and 'good', for example, have indefinitely many applications and their inference-edges will differ in relation to them. This is especially true for expressions, such as these, which feature in multiple and overlapping areas of discourse. A moment's reflection will show that this is also true of the semi-technical expressions adapted for philosophical purposes, such as 'real', 'idea', 'representation', 'analytic', 'necessary', 'possible', 'entail', 'valid', 'argument', 'property', 'proposition', 'concept', and so on, as these have been and continue to be used and debated in philosophical discussion.

2   Philosophers, it might be responded, are not much interested in expressions, our use of them, or our intuitions concerning them. They are as indifferent to English as they would be to French or any other natural language. To talk about the saying-power of sentences, or the contribution made by their constituent words or phrases, is to talk about something that prescinds from, and indeed determines, the employment of sentences and their word- or phrase-constituents of natural languages such as English. A philosopher's business is with that object or idea for which the words are generally used to stand and which is to be discerned by revealing what is common among its instances. It is these abstract objects, not the natural language expressions, that should absorb our interest. For it is concepts

that we grasp in thought which bestow meaning on words; and the propositions of which they are constituents that are the bearers of truth or falsity.

Further, a philosopher might continue, fully to grasp a concept, or to attach to a word its meaning, is to be equipped with rules for its application. If the linguistician's job is to uncover syntactical rules, the philosopher's job is to uncover semantic ones. The latter, 'meaning rules', fix the relation between a lexical item (such as a general term) and its referent (a constituent of thought or a concept). Indeed, these rules may be revealed by breaking down complex concepts into simpler ones by definitional equivalences. Much like mathematical formulae, these equivalences would in the ideal case lay down context-free, invariant conditions—individually necessary and jointly sufficient—for the application of the word that is thus defined.

Staying with our example, the suggestion might be that our employment of the word 'mother' is governed by the concept MOTHER. Since MOTHER is a complex concept, an analysis might be provided by decomposing MOTHER into its simpler components. Just as the concept BACHELOR is decomposable into those of UNMARRIED and MAN, so might MOTHER be decomposable into FEMALE and . . . and what? Should we opt for a female who has given birth or focus rather on the type of relationship a female has to her offspring? If we suggest that giving birth is a (contextually independent) necessary condition then, since this is manifestly not an adequate description of our practices, we would appear to be stipulating with a wave of our philosophical wands that the relationship the female has with the children she raises is not—even in certain contexts—sufficient for her to be deemed their mother. If, however, we deem this relationship to be necessary, then we rule out the employments that concerned the doctor. With any choice of definition, thus conceived, not only have we ruled out a host of applications, but we have not yet answered the questions of how the newly introduced expressions, 'female', 'given birth', and 'offspring', are to be applied.[3]

---

[3] It is worth noting that even 'bachelor' has inflections of significance that are not captured by the mere combination of 'unmarried' and 'man' (and not merely due to extensions such as 'bachelor of arts' or 'bachelor buttons'). It is the strong suggestion of eligibility (where 'eligibility' comes with its own inflections, of course), mandated in 'bachelor' in a core use, but notably countermanded in 'spinster', which have presumably motivated philosophers to add 'adult' as a qualifier to 'male' in the stipulated decomposition of BACHELOR, and others to mention the Pope as a counterexample even to this qualified definition.

A variant of this classical line of thought—albeit a modest one from our point of view—is that when the notions to be analysed belong to particular domains of interest, it is up to philosophers working closely with their colleagues in the appropriate branches of science to articulate, not the alleged denizens of a Platonic world expressed by these nouns, but the object, property, relation, or event at which the elements of our descriptive apparatus—for instance, predicate expressions—merely gesture. But if this co-operative enterprise is to help reveal the nature—the real nature—of motherhood, this so-called naturalistic line of thought is also controverted by our discussion above for much the same reason. For which of the indefinitely many applications of 'mother' or 'is the mother of' are to be investigated as 'that to which the expression gestures'? Clearly, the question 'Who is the real mother?' makes no sense independently of the kinds of considerations we have examined and innumerable others that we have not. Even if we were to agree to defer to scientists about the nature of motherhood, which scientists are we to consult and for which scientific purposes? Social scientists may well insist that 'mother' is best understood as a functional (or role) concept, and thus the sex of the one who plays this role or his or her biological proximity to the child is irrelevant. Biological science, as we have seen, may be interested in any number of possibilities of applying the notion of 'female', 'birth', and 'offspring'. Mothers themselves, of course, will rightly claim to have a say in the nature of motherhood. But here we have come round full circle. We cannot adjudicate between competing theories and choose which of their proprietary relations, properties, objects, and so forth, should direct us to the nature of motherhood without delineating the boundaries around what we will accept as the relevant sense of 'mother'. In attempting to do so we will find competing claims.

An even less promising alternative would be to suppose that 'mother' expresses an idea or representation in the mind of the individual who 'tokens' it. Whether this token is transported by an image or a sentence of a proto-language in which the word-equivalent 'mother' appears, whether the medium of conveyance is phenomenological space or the neural structure of the brain, the questions remain: what is the method of projection for this image or, if it is embedded in a sentence, how is this word-symbol applied, thus embedded, on this occasion? Most importantly, what grounds or reasons can be produced for a speaker's particular application of the expression on this occasion? How is this latter question even intelligible when it is not the speaker, per se, who applies the term, but rather her brain that 'tokens' it?

3   What, then, of the alleged *rules* that govern the expressions of natural
language? That these expressions are rule-governed, even when their applications are multifarious, is implicit in my frequent references to 'correct',
'incorrect', or 'permissible' applications. Thus, even if natural language
expressions such as 'mother' undergo developments which affect their
logical ties, there must be some, presumably rational, method for obtaining
all and only those which are permissible.

The discussion above should already make us suspicious, if not of
a 'rational method' (of which more, below), then of any reason to suppose
that in speaking and understanding a natural language we employ
a decision-making procedure or a calculus that we operate in accordance
with fixed rules. For as our very first example illustrated, even if the relation
between the notions of mother and family can be fashioned into a lexical
rule for the application of the relevant predicates (for example, the former
a sufficient condition for the latter), then, as Strawson (1952, 230) says, 'we
ought to think of them as rules which everyone has a license to violate if he
can show a point in doing so'. Nonetheless, given the indefinite variability
of expressions of natural languages, we need a tool to circumscribe or draw
boundaries around the implications and other logical ties we wish to allow
or forbid in clarifying the import of what we say. The point and rationale of
such considerations is to avoid misunderstanding and facilitate communication. Like the rules of the road, their *raison d'être* is to minimize
obstructions and to expedite travel.

We say 'and by this I mean . . .', 'that is to say . . .', 'in other words . . .',
'i.e.', and so on, to spell out some of the implication threads or logical ties
of the expression as we have applied it. Doing so is similar to signalling
a turn to indicate the route of travel. It takes the hearer along the particular
inflections of the expression by marking just those differences or affinities
that are to be emphasized. For specific assertions, like specific commands,
questions, and so on, have a function or purpose. Successful communication is a condition of its fulfilment. Thus, here, as in the case of road travel,
there are limits or constraints on how much leeway a speaker or driver has
at her disposal if she is to avoid misunderstanding or bumps along the way.
Both cases depend upon acting in accordance with the common practice,
and this includes the use of signalling devices to indicate deviations.

The doctor could, for example, specify that by 'mother' she meant birth
mother; the state could specify that adoptive and stepmothers will also so
count. Or, what was meant by an utterance can be read off by an observer,
explicating what might have remained implicit. The ability to read this off
from the exchange will require her to ascertain the relevance of what is said,

taking into account, of course, the speaker's purposes and other features of the situation. When we took into account, for example, the purpose of the doctor's enquiry about a history of heart disease in the family, we understood her to be ruling out as irrelevant issues about loyalty and trust in her use of 'family' and to be ruling in issues about genetic inheritance. There is no reason, however, to expect that the actual and possible modifications of the kinds we discussed can be delimited or articulated in advance of our particular needs, discoveries, or aims—let alone in advance of the ways in which these requirements occasion new applications—in order to lay down what is to count as permissible. Further, any specification in a natural language of how the lower-order expression is to be administered will open up additional interpretive possibilities of how the higher-order expression is to be applied. This was illustrated in the specification of 'mother', 'birth mother', 'giving birth', 'gestational mother', and so on. It is a simple consequence of the fact that natural language expressions, including those employed in the higher-order specification, have indefinitely many elasticities of significance.

Eventually, in the normal case, these explanations come to an end. By this I mean that those engaging in the discussion are normally able to go on 'by wont', without needing instructions how to apply the expressions employed in ever higher-order instructions. This is not, however, because the higher-order specifications enjoin how the words are to be understood in abstraction from particular features of the situation. There is nothing in the saying-power of the expressions themselves—at any level of elucidation— that uniquely determines how they are to be applied. In understanding the doctor's purpose, we are able to understand her words, including any instructions about how her words are to be understood. But this in turn demands, to use Wittgenstein's expression, familiarity with a way of life.

Like a pair of pliers, the words or—as Ryle (1953, 324) puts it—the 'block of words congealed into a phrase' do not do anything until they are wielded by a craftsperson or language user who can use them to do any number of things (which, again, is not the same as saying that she can do anything at all). If she wants to say something and be understood, then she will be bound by the customary applications of the expression unless or until she makes manifest the way she is adapting it. Like a pair of pliers that has been modified by a craftsperson for a particular purpose, this new application might catch on. A jeweller will file down the grooves on a pair of pliers that she will use to grasp metal; she will fit them with a smooth, coated material when she uses them to straighten wires. As these uses become established—and efficacious—manufacturers will develop them as specialized pliers for jewellers. The needs of the jewellers, which develop organically, as it were, dictate the rules that manufacturers are to follow when they fabricate and market the specialized tools. Such is the case for natural language expressions. As an application or use becomes prevalent, its description will be 'put into the archives' by a lexicographer, somewhat as the modified pliers will be manufactured from scratch and available for purchase for its particular purposes or specific communities.

If, in our discussion above, the word 'mother' has been put to the service of any unitary function, abstracted from its particular applications, it has figured as a label on a metaphorical file-folder. We have gleaned the kind of person, relationship, attribute (substance, entity, and so on) that may be filed under this label by looking at the contribution it makes, not to sentences considered in abstraction from their particular employments— as, for example, a copy-editor might study them—but to the contribution they make to instances of types of linguistic communication with which we are familiar. That is, by looking at their contribution to actual and possible utterances with a point and rationale, as they figure in particular contexts, circumstances, or situations of the kind we have illustrated. These illustrations, though any number of others might have done just as well, have taken as their starting point extant but fluid practices, those I suppose to be familiar to my reader, in which the expressions 'mother' and 'family' are employed.

Rules for the use of natural language expressions, understood thus, arise within linguistic practices, highly sensitive to purposes, aims, and other contextual matters, and are violable when there is a point in doing so. They do not therefore determine the correct response in the sense of 'determine' understood by analogy with an idealized mechanism that instantiates a mathematical function or algorithm. Far from finding a one-to-one correlation between a word and that for which it stands, our short study of but a fragment of non-technical, everyday discourse belies the idea that we find something in common for which we use the same word for all: instead 'we see a complicated network of similarities overlapping and criss-crossing; sometimes overall similarities, sometimes similarities of detail' (PI §66).

4 Many philosophers consider it to be a platitude that the meaning of a sentence is a function of and determined by the meaning of its constituent terms and its mode of combination; that in grasping a word's meaning, we are equipped with rules that ground its use so as to understand its contribution to any other sentence, including ones we have never seen before. It is

this feature of semantic compositionality that is alleged to be necessary to explain how learning a language is possible.

Another alleged platitude, taking the form of a condition of adequacy for a semantic theory of a given discourse, is that stable propositional or semantic content needs to be available across the particular circumstances of any given expression's employment so that syntactic transformations can be effected for logico-deductive argumentative purposes. Indeed, as one philosopher puts it:

> It is only because propositions have certain stable meanings that we can successfully use them as we do. If it were nothing but use in a context, well, how would we ever learn to communicate? What would ground our rules of use? (Ludlow 1997, 4)

The idea seems to be that without context-invariant propositions or thoughts to bestow sense on one's sentence-utterances, to attach to and detach from other propositions with the help of logical connectives, to embed in attitudinal 'that-clauses', and so on, we would be without the wherewithal to derive the implications of what a speaker says, and how they are imposed on her utterances by transformation rules.

This widely accepted philosophical picture is consistent with and perhaps derives from Frege's (1918, 64) suggestion that what is intimated in speech makes no difference to the thought—the proposition or what is said—and thus to the truth or falsity of the sense of the sentence.

> Somebody using the sentence 'Alfred has still not come' actually says 'Alfred has not come', and at the same time hints – but only hints – that Alfred's arrival is expected. Nobody can say: Since Alfred's arrival is not expected, the sense of the sentence is false. . . . Such conversational suggestions make no difference to the thought.

In the same passage, Frege goes on to suggest that if the various transformations of spoken sentences into ones that can be captured by his concept-notation (or *Begriffsschrift*) are inadmissible because they make a difference to what is intimated in speech, then 'any profound logical investigation would be hindered':

> It is just as important to ignore distinctions that do not touch the heart of the matter, as to make distinctions which concern essentials. But what is essential depends on one's purpose. To a mind concerned with the beauties of language, what is trivial to the logician may seem to be just what is important.

We did not undertake this enquiry, however, with a view to appreciating what is beautiful in language. We began by pointing out that what is said by the employment of a sentence cannot be assessed, including for truth or falsity, until we understand it and, in particular, how its constituent expressions contribute to its sense in the circumstances in which it is employed. Frege's views about what is important in language—leaving aside questions of beauty—are skewed by what is permitted by his concept-notation. For it is not merely hinted that Alfred is expected; it is implied, in the normal sense of 'implied'. We would not—would we?—understand what was said, nor thus be able to assess it as true or false, if someone were to assert that Alfred has still not come but deny that he was expected, hoped for, missing, or otherwise account for the employment of 'still'. To change the sentence so that 'still' is omitted and this implication cancelled is tantamount to admitting that the logical implications—in the reclaimed sense of the expression—that are part and parcel of understanding natural languages are omitted from formal logic.

In any case, the suggestion that context-invariant content is needed for argumentative purposes risks getting things back to front, and in more ways than one. For purposes here, consider Quine's response to Strawson's (1952, 223) suggestion that the symbolic apparatus of modern logic is 'best adapted to the role of systematically exhibiting the relationships between sentences which answer to the ideal of independence of contextual conditions'. Quine (1953, 441) protests that if Strawson were correct, 'formal logic would be a pretty idle luxury'. In quoting, however, from his own *Methods of Logic* (1950, 43) to explain why its scope of applicability is not limited in the way suggested by Strawson's 'dim view', we find something quite telling.

> Insofar as the interpretation of ambiguous expressions depends on circumstances of the argument as a whole—speaker, hearer, scene, data, and underlying problem and purpose—the fallacy of equivocation is not to be feared; for those background circumstances may be expected to influence the interpretation of an ambiguous expression uniformly whenever the expression recurs in the course of the argument . . .
> The fallacy of equivocation arises rather when the interpretation of the ambiguous expression is influenced in varying ways by immediate contexts, . . . so that the expression undergoes changes of meaning within the limits of the argument. In such cases we have to rephrase . . . to the extent of resolving such part of the ambiguity as might, if left standing, end up by being resolved in different ways by different immediate contexts within the proposed logical argument.

If the thread of our discussion is correct, however, whether or not an expression such as a general term undergoes changes of meaning—or changes in the way it is applied—within the limits of an argument is precisely the issue. The sort of ambiguity that threatens is not merely for words with completely different roots (which Ryle terms 'pun' words such as 'bank') but is rather the 'systematic ambiguity' that arises for all natural language expressions that undergo elasticities that affect their logical ties. Only *after* these shifts of meaning have been resolved can one be sure of the univocity required for the proposed interpretation of the formal argument. This, presumably, is why Ryle (1945, 208) suggests that:

> the extraction of the logical skeletons of propositions does not reveal the logical powers of those propositions by some trick which absolves the logician from thinking them out. At best it is merely a summary formulation of what they have discovered.

Although the *écart* between idealized and natural languages tends to be acknowledged by mathematical logicians and others doing formal work, the refusal to acknowledge this schism for the purposes of philosophical investigation has been disastrous. It has long been accepted that there must be a way of specifying the conditions under which a declarative or indicative sentence is true or false by setting aside the purpose or point of what is said, its implications, or other 'pragmatic factors' that might influence what I have been calling its logical ties. But the severe limits on the applicability of quantificational logic to ordinary descriptive speech is shrouded when 'logical implication' is reserved for the formal sense and a new term, 'conversational implicature', is adopted as an easily side-lined proxy for the phenomenon to which I am drawing attention. For understanding logical ties or implication threads (in the reclaimed sense) of any given sentence-utterance in the circumstances of its employment is necessary for understanding how the application of the constituent terms contribute to the sense of the utterance.

5   Earlier (in Section 2) we considered the plausible thought that philosophers are not much interested in our use of expressions and are as indifferent to English as they would be to any other natural language. Yet my focus throughout has been on the employment of a sample set of English expressions which I have suggested constitute a model for others. How is this relatively prosaic task to be reconciled with the more exalted, abstract aims of philosophical investigation? Indeed, what of the glimpse of *realities* that science or metaphysics craves?

Although I have been discussing throughout the saying-power of English expressions, many, perhaps most, of my particular examples would carry over to other natural languages. In other words, my remarks in English about the use of English sentences could be said in French about the use of French sentences, and so on. In this way, my second-order remarks are about the employment of sentences in abstraction from the particular language in which they are mentioned. If this is what is meant in saying that philosophers are concerned with concepts rather than words, or about propositions rather than indicative or declarative sentences, then well and good.[4] To agree, however, that these second-order remarks are about the employment of sentences in abstraction from the particular language in which they are mentioned is importantly different from saying that the remarks are about something abstract, where this 'something' is understood as being logically independent of and explanatorily prior to linguistic practices *tout court*. It may be useful, then, to talk about concepts or propositions when we are describing abstractible or discernible features of any particular natural language. Thus understood, concepts and propositions might be compared to the smile of the Cheshire cat: it is a logical joke to portray a perceptible aspect of the cat as an independently existing part.

So much for the requirement by neo-Fregeans that 'content must be available' for argumentative purposes. The idea that exogenous, context-invariant propositional content must be available for embedding in negations and conditionals (for example) in order to construct arguments and assess them for validity is wrong-footed for another reason as well. It supposes that what belongs to post-inferential levels of discourse—that is, what is best understood as a presumptive warrant for travel—belongs instead to pre-inferential levels which are required for the move from premise to conclusion. In so doing it mistakes the ordinary, but violable, application-dependent inference 'She is my mother; so she is a member of my family' as requiring backing, not from a customary (but modifiable, and therefore discussable) usage of the expressions 'mother' and 'family', but from an exogenous or practice-independent and invariant 'logical' or 'analytic' truth. (For more discussion of this point, see Tanney 2014.)

---

[4] Indeed, to avoid misunderstanding it may be crucial to make a distinction between sentences and propositions. For example, it is true that if English were different, the sentence 'I love my mother' might not have expressed the truth that I now express with it. But this does not mean that English must have been as it is – or even that it must have existed – for me to have told my mother that I love her. (For a criticism of Quine along these lines, see Wisdom 1991, 137–8).

We can speak of propositions, then, as discriminable features of utterances spoken in any language (it does not matter which), but immanent to the context of the conversation in the sense we have been considering throughout. Considered thus, the logical implications of the role of any constituent expression must be discerned in order for it to be paraphrased or translated: choosing, as much as possible, words and phrases that bring out what the speaker wants to say while avoiding inflections that suggest, in the other language, what she does not. (This, after all, is what makes translation so difficult.) Although it may be true that for some particular utterance we can distinguish what is said from what is implied, or what the speaker means or wants to say from what she says, indeed even locutionary from illocutionary acts, these distinctions mark practice-dependent, contextually sensitive, discriminable differences, rather than practice-independent, contextually invariant, separate parts.

I mentioned above that the failure to grasp vast differences between the logic of natural language expressions and that of an ideal one suited to the demands of a calculus has been disastrous for philosophical conceptual investigation. We are now in a position to see why this is so. Consider for example, the question 'What is knowledge?', or 'What is it for a number to be random?' Those attuned to the approach taken for our examination of 'mother' might have expected a cartographical investigation of the reasons or grounds that a competent speaker would adduce for applications of the expression 'knowledge' or 'to know', or their near-equivalents in other languages; or that mathematicians or statisticians, perhaps, would adduce for describing a number or a sequence as random.

For reasons that we have laboured in detail, we should not expect these grounds or criteria to be accommodated within a mould of context-independent conditions that are necessary and sufficient. The trouble in philosophical discussion comes when the failure to accommodate them thus results in their abandonment or, at least, in their demotion as revelatory of that which we are seeking to understand. The incessant focus on what is real, or on what is definitionally or theoretically equivalent to what, manifests a failure to grasp the importance of examining our inclinations to apply or withhold expressions in various actual and possible situations for a better comprehension of the phenomenon in question.

When, for example, mathematicians point out that a desideratum of a truly random number sequence is the unpredictability of any number with respect to that which has occurred before (an epistemic criterion, we might say), they then turn their attention to the way such unpredictability is best achieved (by, say, a throw of a true die). This, we note, evolves into a functional criterion. A still different consideration involves constraints on the pattern or types of numbers that figure in the sequence itself. Call this an intrinsic criterion. Naturally, there will be occasions when these criteria conflict. Sub-categorizations occur: 'pseudorandom' sequences are introduced to accommodate the epistemic criterion, with the suffix 'pseudo' evidently chosen to signal a recognition that the other desiderata may not at the same time be met. What happens when conflicts continue and a 'unifying theory' cannot be met without promoting some of the desiderata but abandoning others? A plausible reaction would be to recognize that we have before us the complex and evolving criss-crossing and overlapping threads that constitute our reasons for deeming a number or number sequence to be random and make a reasoned choice about what would suit the purposes at hand. An unfortunate reaction, evincing a genuine misunderstanding, however, would be to offer excuses or apologies on the grounds that the concept is a slippery one, or to give up too soon on the grounds that we will never know the real nature of randomness.[5]

The whole philosophical sub-discipline known as the theory of knowledge contains some subtle and important reflections on our inclinations to apply or withhold the verb 'to know' in actual and conceivable situations. But these reflections—by which we come to understand the phenomenon of knowledge—are too easily dismissed when epistemologists 'bite the bullet' and reject what they deem to be 'our intuitions'—or worse: the threat of 'pragmatic encroachment'—in their forlorn dream for a unified theory (for more discussion of this point, see Tanney 2019). The fantasy has been all the more calamitous for moral philosophy.

6   Why, then, do we call an individual a 'mother'? How do we determine whether an individual stands in the 'motherhood' relation? Not because 'mother', 'is the mother of', or 'motherhood' stands for a property, relation, or universal from which we can extract inviolable and determinate rules for the application of these expressions or their correlates in other languages. But rather because—to adapt Wittgenstein—the individual has a direct affinity with several things that have hitherto been called 'mother'; and this can be said to give it an indirect affinity with other things that we also call 'mothers'. We extend our concept of mother 'as in spinning

---

[5] For a discussion that roughly follows the trajectory outlined in the text, consult Melvyn Bragg's Radio 4 broadcast for the series *In Our Time*, 'Random and Pseudorandom', first broadcast on 13 January 2011, at www.bbc.co.uk/programmes/b00x9xjb. Discussions between mathematicians about infinity often follow a similar path. Note, in passing, that conflicts in the criteria for the application of types of expression reach their apogee with the difference in grounds for the first- and third-person employment of mental predicates. See Tanney 2013 (chapter 16) for further discussion.

a thread we twist fibre on fibre. And the strength of the thread resides not in the fact that some one fibre runs through its whole length, but in the overlapping of many fibres' (PI §67).

This suggests a method by which we might make reasoned and informed choices as to how we should classify phenomena, whether and in what circumstances to file them under the same label, produce sub-folders with slightly altered labels, or eject them altogether from a particular folder. This involves, as the paraphrase from Wittgenstein suggests, comparing a particular thing with others we call by the same name: a case-by-case procedure. Ryle (1951), observing this method in Wittgenstein's careful examination of various expressions, likens it to that of a tea-taster. Comparing it elsewhere to that of a vintner, Ryle (1966) points to the same technique in Jane Austen's novels as she undertakes her fine-grained studies of moral character.

John Wisdom's 1957 *Virginia Lectures* sets its face against the tendency to think that a dispute is not real unless it is either amenable to investigation (observation and experiment) or to deductive treatment (see Wisdom 1991). Moreover, rather than supposing—as he once did—that such a dispute collapses with the diagnosis that it is *merely* a question of words, Wisdom argues at length that 'there are real questions, and there is at stake a gain in knowledge, even though the procedure for meeting the dispute is that of the comparative, case-by-case sort' (1991, 169). Indeed, he argues, though such a method has often been disparaged in favour of deduction, in fact all deductive reasoning comes in the end to argument by cases. This is an important variation on the theme that a rule does not contain instructions for its own application, which we rehearsed in earlier sections.[6]

'In describing a thing', explains Wisdom, 'we mark its affinities to other conceivable things' (1991, 197).[7] But, as Strawson (1952, 5) notes, we emphasize not only its likenesses:

> When we say what a thing is like, we not only compare it with other things, we also [as an aspect of the same activity] distinguish it from other things.

---

[6] Wisdom 1991, 71: 'Every deductive proof of any conclusion whatever to the effect that something has the predicate P is always no more than the proof which might be offered in what we could call a "one-term" language; that is, a proof in which we use only the predicate P and ask of things, "Isn't this a P?", "Isn't this a P?", and so on. This procedure may lead us to agreement, or it may happen that the other party doesn't use the predicate *at all* in the same way, even when the typical instances are reached.'

[7] Wisdom 1991, 197: 'The proof of the excellence of a description involves comparisons with the conceivable. The proof of the excellence of an explanation involves comparisons with the actual.'

Somewhere, then, a boundary must be drawn, limiting the applicability of a word used in describing things; and it is we who decide where the boundaries are to be drawn.

If we, then, in making a statement, wish not just to be believed but—in the first instance—understood, are we not always *on call*, as it were? Not only are we responsible for providing evidence for our claim, if necessary, to be believed; we are also required to explain what we mean, if necessary, to be understood. For our interlocutor, in applying the same expression, may draw the boundaries differently. How is a dispute to be settled? Consider a disagreement, say, as to whether the length of an object is equal to that of another:

> One has the inclination to say 'You have only to use your eyes and then apply the word' or put the two side by side and see whether the ends coincide. But ... how is this to be settled? Simply by looking and making a noise? No. It involves the comparison of this case with this other case where they're end to end here and not here ... All this process is the process of proof. (Wisdom 1991, 79)

With the realization that even deductive procedures come in the end to the ability to 'go on in the same way' comes a new way of evaluating arguments. For Wisdom, the now discredited position of evaluating arguments as good if and only if their steps are deductively valid should give way to a new outlook in which we take seriously case-by-case arguments (those in which the proffered grounds for the conclusion do not deductively entail it). We neither reject it nor accept it *because* it takes this form. Nor, importantly, do we reject it on the grounds that the usage of words has been stretched; 'whether the conclusion embodies conventional usage is no longer to be a criterion for judging the excellence of the thinking involved' (Wisdom 1991, 71).

In engaging in a case-by-case procedure and not just asking what one would say, for example, about a borderline or paradoxical case, but in examining the grounds for our *inclinations* to apply or refuse a particular predicate, we thus reveal affinities and differences between the new case and others. In so doing 'one is tracing connections that language obscures' (Wisdom 1991, 24).[8] Not surprisingly, this approach will lead to difficulties if the stretched word—a borderline case or paradoxical application—is supposed to set a new standard for all.[9]

---

[8] J. L. Austin writes: 'When we examine what we should say when, what words we should use in what situations, we are looking again not *merely* at words (or "meanings", whatever they may be) but also at the realities we use the words to talk about' (1957, 182).

[9] Wisdom (1991, 70, 83) argues that when Christ (Matthew 5:28) exclaimed 'But I say unto you, that whosoever looketh on a woman to lust after her hath committed adultery with her already in his

With the rejection of the idea that the meaning of a word is the object for which it stands, or that which it represents, we also put into question the traditional dichotomies: *either* matters of fact *or* relations of ideas; *either* further empirical investigation *or* a matter of reflection. This approach opens up a different way of understanding meaning, neither as rules for representation, nor as *Sinn* or 'propositional content' construed as an intermediary between expressions that 'mean the same' and which allegedly accompany our utterances. Instead, it might be construed as a shifting series of commitments that are implicitly undertaken as the target expressions are appropriately employed or redeployed from one circumstance to another. On this view, to learn about meaning is to learn about what is meant: what said, explained, predicted, argued, promised, threatened, and expressed. This involves tracing the logical powers of the sentences, and their constituent expressions, as they take on different inflections of meaning or elasticities of significance within the various situations in which they are employed to perform their multitudinous jobs.

How is it, then, that we can in general understand what is said by a person when she utters a sentence if not in virtue of the fixed meaning of its constituent words and phrases? Perhaps learning to speak and understand a language is like learning to dance: the movements of our feet, the position and trajectory of our bodies, and the ability to move with others are mastered in tandem. This metaphor may help us to remember that it sometimes takes us a long time, and sometimes we fail, to understand what another means by what she says or writes. This is true when she employs a combination of words we have never heard before, and even when she uses those we have. Nonetheless, we should embrace the indefinite capacity of the words to take on different inflections of significance, since it is this that allows us to make connections and see things in a new light. Indeed, it is this capacity of familiar dictions to take on new inflections of logical forces that is, according to Ryle (1945, 216), one of the chief factors making original thought—and, we might add, discovery—possible.

---

heart' he has not only extended the word 'adultery': he has 'altered the geometry of sin'. In wishing to emphasize a certain affinity between the thought and the act, he '*pushed* the word' and enabled us to perceive sin and virtue in a new light. Presumably, however, he would not have been 'taken in' by his own case-by-case reasoning to the point of denying the large differences between those who act out their adultery and those who think about it. Wisdom is less accommodating to Russell's and McTaggart's liberty with 'know' and 'have real reason'. These expressions, Wisdom says,

> have been so considerably modified as they use them that the sceptical statements they make are necessary truisms . . . they bring it out as true without bringing it out as something which couldn't have been false. (1991, 176–7)

To be a participant in a linguistic practice, then, to use one of my own analogies, is like being a dancer with an evolving series of partners: we engage with one another in a common activity, with shared goals, similar natural reactions and complementary training. If we want to take our partners in a certain direction, we will lead and they will follow. Their ability to follow—to understand what we say—will be all the more enhanced by the exercise of our own capacity to explain what we mean.

CHAPTER 3

Objectivity

Alice Crary

One of the core philosophical uses of the term "objectivity" today is to talk about a central and quite helpful metaphysical ideal. The term is employed to pick out aspects of what the world is like in itself or, to put it somewhat more expansively, aspects of the world that are there in the sense that any thinker—without regard to, say, her cultural or historical situation or idiosyncrasies of her temperament—who fails to register them can be said to be missing something. We might speak in this connection of a guiding *concept* of objectivity, and, once this concept has been isolated, it is possible to ask what can be said about the nature of the things that fall under it. We might speak in this further connection of different possible specifications of the concept of objectivity or, alternately, of different possible *conceptions* of objectivity. Throughout the history of analytic philosophy, thought about objectivity—where this is taken to include implicit invocations of the ideal as well as explicit treatments of it—has been dominated by a conception on which objectivity is taken to have as its hallmark the exclusion of everything subjective and on which it is thus construed as "the countering of subjectivity" (Daston and Galison 2007, 36). Starting from a description of the relevant conception of objectivity, this chapter presents and criticizes the kinds of considerations most commonly adduced in the conception's favor. Along the way, the chapter uses passages from the later philosophy of Wittgenstein as its main reference points. A notable virtue of this method is that it sheds light on the transformative significance of Wittgenstein's thought for how we construe the concept of objectivity.

To capture the content of a dominant conception of objectivity on which the exclusion of everything subjective is taken to be objectivity's touchstone, it's necessary to say something about the understanding of "subjectivity" that is at issue. Very generally, the kinds of qualities that here get debarred from objectivity on grounds of their subjective status are qualities that can't adequately be characterized without reference to responses that objects that possess them elicit from subjects. The class of qualities that count as subjective in this sense is internally diverse. It includes, among other things, qualities that an object can be said to possess merely insofar as it in fact elicits certain responses from a subject (for example, the amusing quality that a sudden inadvertent movement of mine can be said to have just because a young child watching me responds to it with amusement). The exclusion from objectivity of such "merely subjective" qualities is not itself of great philosophical moment (for the use of this phrase, see Conant 2006, 16; Crary 2002b; 2007, 17–18; and 2016, 33). But the set of qualities that are subjective in the above sense also includes qualities an object possesses insofar as it is the kind of thing that, in an appropriate setting, would elicit a certain response from a subject. Sensible (or secondary) qualities such as colors are frequently mentioned members of this additional subset of subjective qualities, and it is not hard to see that such qualities are indeed conceptually bound to human sensory capacities. For to be—say—green, just is to be the kind of thing that, in suitable circumstances, would appear green to a requisitely endowed human viewer. This set of more substantial subjective qualities includes, in additional to sensible things, an array of affective qualities such as "humorous" or "annoying." We can take a first stab at specifying the conception of objectivity that prevails in analytic circles by saying that it is distinguished by the expulsion of all qualities that are subjective in the sense specified in this paragraph—and not only the "merely subjective"—from the realm of the objective.

Although many philosophers are content to simply take this conception of objectivity for granted, some of those who favor it draw explicit attention to this fact. For a couple of classic treatments of the pertinent rendering of the concept of objectivity, we can turn to the writings of Thomas Nagel and Bernard Williams. Both thinkers set out to evoke what Nagel calls the "opposition between subjective and objective points of view" (Nagel 1979, 196), and both construe what they take to be objectivity's hostility to subjectivity as extending beyond the merely subjective. Nagel defends an account of the objective world on which none of its properties are "perceptual aspects" (Nagel 1986, 14), explaining that, as he sees it, this is because to have these aspects is just to look a certain way to "normal human observers in the perceptual circumstances that normally obtain in the actual world" (Nagel 1986, 75). Similarly, Williams tells us that he takes sensibles to be excluded from objectivity because they are at bottom "effects on our minds of the objectively existing differences of shape and motion" (Williams 1978, 237; see also Williams 1985, 139).

Additionally, Nagel and Williams make it clear that they take the objective ban on subjective qualities to apply not only to sensibles but also to affective qualities like "humorous" (see, for instance, Nagel 1979, 206, and Williams 1978, 243). Both philosophers in this way offer explicit—and sympathetic—accounts of the prevailing conception of objectivity.

Sympathy for this conception will seem unremarkable as long as there appears to be no alternative, and it may well appear that no alternative is available. What can create this appearance is the in-itself unobjectionable idea that objectivity and subjectivity are conceptual opposites. It would, however, be wrong—a mere bit of terminological sleight of hand—to think that this idea obliges us to construe the objective arena as bereft of all traces of things subject-related. It is certainly possible to use "subjective" to mean "non-objective." But in order to describe the content of the leading philosophical conception of objectivity that is here in question, it is—we saw a moment ago—necessary to take "subjective" to mean not "non-objective" but rather something like "conceivable only in terms of effects on subjects." Granted an understanding of subjective qualities as qualities that are in this sense "subject-dependent" (Conant 2006, 17), and granted a received understanding of objective qualities as qualities that inhere in the world as it is in itself, there is no obstacle to taking seriously the possibility of a conception of objectivity on which some subjective qualities count as wholeheartedly objective.[1] This alternative conception would eliminate the interdiction on subjective qualities distinctive of its philosophically more influential counterpart, and it would thus hold forth the prospect of bringing some subjective elements within the objective domain—and of thereby expanding or "widening" this domain. We might for this reason helpfully refer to the envisioned nonstandard conception of objectivity as "the wider conception of objectivity," and, by the same token, we might well refer to the philosophically more standard conception that it challenges as "the narrower conception of objectivity" (for the use of this monicker elsewhere, see Crary 2007, 18–19, and 2016, 34–5).

The contest between narrower and wider conceptions of objectivity is a philosophically momentous one. Although the narrower conception is often taken to be recommended by reflection on the development of the natural sciences, its influence extends beyond philosophy of science to a comprehensive array of philosophical subdisciplines. Consider, in very

---

[1] For a particularly clear and insightful attempt to show that this possibility, of a conception of objectivity on which some subjective qualities count as wholeheartedly objective, is in principle available, see Wiggins 1987/2002, chapter 5, esp. 201–2.

schematic terms, how a "narrower" approach to construing the concept of objectivity shapes the conceptual space in which—for instance—research in ethics is conducted. Insofar as the narrower conception excludes all subject-dependent qualities from objectivity, it seems to compel us to regard all values as non-objective, so it is fair to speak of the conception's "imprint on ethics" in reference to the clear tendency of moral philosophers to take as a starting point for their investigations an assumption to the effect that ethical values are not among the objective furniture of the universe. Ethics, moreover, is but one case among others. Broadening our conception of objectivity would have transformative implications for inquiry in many areas of philosophy. So, there are good reasons to carefully examine considerations that are traditionally adduced in the narrower conception's favor.

The centerpiece of established arguments for the narrower conception of objectivity is a proposal for distilling reality from appearance. At the most basic level, the idea is that we arrive at an increasingly accurate image of how the world really is by eliminating appearances it presents to us merely in virtue of the fact that we survey it from particular standpoints. This idea has a quite straightforward bearing on the literal—spatial—notion of a point of view or perspective. The literal notion of a perspective is that of a "line of sight on an object . . . when viewed from a particular angle" (Conant 2005, 14), and it belongs to this notion that it is the sort of thing that we must in a way transcend to arrive at an accurate account of the spatial properties of an object. "Transcending" a perspective in the sense that is relevant here involves, in the words of James Conant, placing it in "a *matrix* of alternative perspectives [in a manner that allows] us to *correct* for distortions and achieve a *true estimation* of the spatial properties and relationships of an object (or set of objects)" (Conant 2005, 15, emphasis in the original; for a similar observation, see McDowell 1983, 5–6). Within the proposal for separating reality from appearance that is under consideration, our perceptual and affective resources are effectively treated as resembling literal perspectives in being sources of appearance that must be transcended if we're to see things aright. To be sure, many of the distinctive features of spatial perspectives drop out. There is, for instance, no longer any question of a form of transcendence in which we arrive at a more accurate vision of things by situating a single line of sight in a larger network by appeal to recognized laws. We are dealing with what is aptly seen as a "metaphorical extension" of the literal notion of perspective (for the use of this expression, see Conant 2005, 17, and McDowell 1983, 6), and this extension or leap is asked to bear substantial philosophical weight. For the guiding thought of this strategy for distinguishing reality and appearance is that it is only insofar as we abstract from or transcend our perceptual and affective constitutions that we are justified in crediting ourselves with an accurate image of how things really are. Reasoning along these lines, Nagel, for example, claims that approaching an unobstructed view of the world requires an exercise of "abstraction" away from "the forms of perception and action characteristic of humans" (Nagel 1979, 206); similarly, Williams suggests that, in our effort to bring the real world clearly into focus, we need "to step back from [those] peculiarities of our constitution" relating to color perception, tastes, and interests (Williams 1978, 242–3).

It is a short step from issuing these sorts of calls for abstraction from our subjective endowments to endorsing the narrower conception of objectivity. Insofar as, in trying to get the world in view, we endeavor to step back as far as possible from our subjective makeups, we put ourselves in a position of trying to evacuate from our account of reality all subject-dependent qualities. An initially attractive image of how to distinguish reality and appearance in this way seems to speak for eliminating everything subjective from the fabric of the world or—what amounts to the same—for embracing the narrower conception of objectivity.

The key move in this argument for the narrower conception is the introduction of a requirement to abstract as far as possible from our subjective endowments. But a loose analogy, of the sort described above, between these endowments and literal perspectives provides at best very weak support for such an "abstraction requirement" (for employment of this term elsewhere, see Crary 2007, 21, and 2016, 44). If we are to evaluate the credentials of a "narrower" approach to the concept of objectivity, we need to ask whether we are justified in imposing the requirement.

It might at first blush seem possible to show that we are justified in doing so by identifying discursive resources that are free of any tinge of subjectivity and that thus satisfy the requirement. It might seem as though such resources would supply us with a standpoint that is free of and hence external to everything subjective and that thus positions us to determine not only that our subjective endowments are irredeemably distorting but that we are right to regard our interest in objectivity as compelling us to abstract from them. But this approach to defending the idea of an abstraction requirement, however apparently promising, fails to deliver. The idea that, as Williams dismissively puts it, "not all concepts [are] ours" (1978, 244) may seem like a bit of philosophical fantasy, and there is good reason to think that we are in fact trafficking in mere fantasy here.

A core stretch of Wittgenstein's *Philosophical Investigations* provides support for this conclusion. The passages in question, which are sometimes said to contain Wittgenstein's "rule-following considerations," explore the idea of an ideally abstract conceptual practice where it may seem most plausible, namely, in reference to practices of extending simple mathematical series. Wittgenstein works toward deflating an image of basic mathematical operations as wholly abstract by first encouraging us to do our utmost to breathe life into such an image. He invites us to envision producing the terms of a simple mathematical series in a style that qualifies as suitably abstract in that it is not essentially informed by any of our subjective responses. We are asked to conceive the steps of the series as already—that is, independently of any contribution from our sensibilities—stretched out in front of us, so that we encounter the series' projection in the guise of, to use Wittgenstein's iconic imagery, a rail "laid to infinity" (PI §218). By thus urging us to actively grapple with the idea of abstraction in mathematics that his imagery is designed to capture, Wittgenstein's ambition is to lead us to the recognition that there is nothing we ourselves would accept as realizing this idea and that, by our own lights, the idea is hopelessly confused.

The setting for this exercise within the *Investigations* is a cluster of scenarios in which a child is taught to produce different series. In an initial scenario, the child is taught to come out with the series of natural numbers by first copying its terms (PI §143), and in a subsequent scenario the child is given various "examples and tests" until she can write the series of even natural numbers up to 1,000 (PI §185). After being presented with these episodes of instruction, we are pushed to try to construe the child's accomplishment in a style consistent with an understanding of mathematical thought as satisfying an abstraction requirement. This would mean thinking of her as having, as John McDowell puts it, "a psychological mechanism which, apart from mistakes, churns out the appropriate behavior" (McDowell 2000, 41). Thus conceived, the child's successful performance doesn't essentially reflect her sense of correctness. Generating the series is, for her, like fastening herself to a conveyer belt and letting it pull her ever further along.

An important aim of Wittgenstein's remarks in these portions of his work is to get us to see that, however strongly inclined we are to present ourselves as endorsing this picture of mathematical understanding, we have no clear idea what it would be for it to be satisfied and should hence forfeit it as bankrupt. The trouble is that, in trying to depict mathematical understanding in the wholly abstract manner in question, we deprive ourselves of resources we would need to determine that a pupil has actually understood the rule for—to stick with the last case touched on above—the series of even natural numbers. That is, no expression the student gives of her own sense of how to proceed in accordance with the rule "add 2"—for instance, no account she gives of how she now sees past earlier errors, and no explanation she offers of how to go on from examples she has been given —can be accepted as demonstrating that she has indeed understood; since, under this rubric, her own subjective take on the matter is at best externally related to understanding. So, in attempting to ascertain whether our tutee has understood, we are restricted to appealing to her brute behavior. This is problematic because grasp of the rule for this and other series of numbers manifests itself in an indefinite amount of behavior and because at any moment we have, in McDowell's parlance, "at most a finite fragment of the potentially infinite range of behavior which we want to say the rule dictates" (2000, 42). At no point do we have more than partial and inadequate grounds for excluding the possibility that the recipient of our instruction has failed to understand the command to count by 2s and will subsequently produce the series incorrectly. We cannot rule out the possibility that—to mention the example Wittgenstein adduces in the *Investigations*—having written out the series of even natural numbers rightly up to 1,000, she will go on to write 1,004, 1,008, 1,012 ... (PI §185). The abstract constraints that we impose while seeking to determine whether a novice has grasped the rule for a mathematical series rob us of the resources we would need to make an authoritative determination. That, in compressed form, is Wittgenstein's argument against taking even mathematical discourse to qualify as ideally abstract.

This argument is unlikely to sway thinkers who appeal to an abstraction requirement in their efforts to motivate the narrower conception of objectivity. Champions of the narrower conception generally agree with Williams in holding that our concepts are irrevocably ours, and that the quest for modes of discourse bereft of all subjective traces is therefore, in Nagel's terms, "an unreachable ideal" (Nagel 1979, 208). What may nonetheless seem to speak for allowing a call for abstraction to play a regulative role in our world-directed thought is the conviction that—even if our discursive categories bear the indelible mark of our subjectivity—there are methods for investigating the world that are themselves wholly abstract and that accordingly justify us in believing that movement toward greater objectivity is, as such, movement toward a view of the world "that is as far as possible not the view from anywhere within it" (Nagel 1979, 206). The idea of such ideally abstract or transparent methods is typically associated with scientific inquiry (see, for instance, Williams 1978, 244, and 1985, 136–40), and, with an eye to evaluating this association, it would seem reasonable to at least ask whether research on the history of science supports the idea that transparency is a regulative ideal for scientific thought. Setting this line of inquiry aside for a moment, we may well be struck by the bald implausibility of the idea of scientific methods that don't essentially reflect views about what the world is like that are championed by scientists at a particular time and place.[2] What may seem to make this idea palatable is a view—central to classic empiricism and still very much alive in philosophy of perception today—to the effect that in perceptual experience we make mental contact with the world in a manner that is nonconceptual and ideally abstract. This view, which is sometimes referred to as the mark of *nonconceptualism* about perception, might seem to speak for taking abstraction to be a governing ideal for world-guided thought, and it might thus seem to speak for respecting the constraints of the narrower conception of objectivity.

Although nonconceptualist approaches to perceptual experience enjoy widespread approval, they have outspoken detractors. There are some high-profile thinkers who maintain, in opposition to nonconceptualists, that perceptual thought is conceptual all the way down (for example, Davidson 1974; McDowell 1994/6, 2009a; and Sellars 1956). The critical efforts of these *conceptualists* are by and large driven by the belief that nonconceptualists are obliged to place conflicting requirements on what perceptual experience is like. Conceptualists tend to go about showing this in something like the following manner. They start by observing that perceptual thought has the sort of normative character that permits questions about what justifies it. They also generally suggest—very plausibly but, as will emerge, not uncontroversially—that when it comes to noninferential perceptual thought, perceptual experience is the natural candidate for this justificatory office. So, it appears to them that a reasonable starting point for a critical examination of nonconceptualist projects is a view of such experience as rationally significant. This intuitive view of perceptual experience is, according to conceptualists, a source of trouble for nonconceptualists. The difficulty has to do with the fact that nonconceptualists are committed to construing experiential inputs to perceptual thought as merely causally produced, nonconceptual contents that in themselves lack normative structure. But it is unclear how perceptual

[2] For criticism of Williams' endorsement of this idea (that is, the idea of scientific methods that don't essentially reflect views about what the world is like that are championed by scientists at a particular time and place), see McDowell 1983, 13, and 1986, 380. For influential general criticism of the idea, see Putnam 1981, 1990, and 2002.

experience can play the rational role in perceptual thought it appears to play and be free of the sort of normative organization that would enable it to serve in this role. That is the basic line of thought underlying conceptualists' efforts to show that nonconceptualists impose incompatible conditions on what perceptual experience is like, and—with a view to the fact that this argument targets an outlook on which experiential contributions to perceptual thought are merely causally "given"—conceptualists sometimes gloss the argument as an exposé of "the myth of the Given" (McDowell 1994/6; Sellars 1956).

Wittgenstein's later philosophy is an acknowledged source of inspiration for these critical endeavors. There are prominent portions of Wittgenstein's writings that explicitly explore an approach to our perceptual lives that qualifies as conceptualist (for example, PI §§398–401 and PPF xi). However, the parts of Wittgenstein's work that speak most directly against nonconceptualism are arguably found in sections of the *Investigations* addressing the topic of sensations or inner experience. A sequence of remarks in what get referred to as the book's "privacy sections" (§§243–70) are aptly taken to provide a model for the line of argument against nonconceptualism just sketched.

Especially helpful is a remark, central to the sequence, that presents a vignette in which a man is trying to make mental contact with his sensation in a manner respectful of a construal of it as a merely given, nonconceptual presence in his "inner" life (PI §258). Because the man is committed to understanding his sensation as in itself nonconceptual, he cannot think of himself as relying essentially on a definition to pick it out. For any definition of his sensation to which he appealed—say, a definition of it as a twinge or a pinch or as a smell that he associates with a baby book his mother kept for him—would be conceptually organized and would as such undermine his attempt to realize his image of transparent access. It follows that, in his attempt to isolate his sensation, he is restricted to a sort of bare mental exercise that might be characterized as a form of inward-directed ostension. Having decided to use "S" to refer to his sensation, he accordingly sets out to employ this form of inner ostension to note for himself "the connection between the sign and the sensation." Wittgenstein's aim in recounting this brief narrative is to get us to ask ourselves whether we have an intelligible idea of what it would be for the man to succeed in thereby isolating a definite sensation, that is, of what it would be for him to succeed in thereby putting himself in a position in which it was in principle possible for him to identify it on other occasions. Here we need to keep in mind that there can be no question of the man's justifying a claim to have isolated S by appealing to the sorts of features that might get mentioned in a definition. He is limited, in his attempt to isolate it, to an entirely unmediated mode of awareness, to the kind of thing we might try to capture by speaking of a pure flash of intuition. The trouble is that, as we are envisioning it, such a flash is nonconceptual and hence as such without normative structure, so it lacks the kind of justificatory force that would underwrite "talk about right." This means not only that, by our own lights, the man has no grounds for believing that he has his mind around a definite sensation. Worse, he has no grounds for believing he has his mind around a sensation in contrast to something else or even nothing at all. This is how Wittgenstein attacks the idea that a bare presence might figure in thought in the way that sensations do. He invites us to see that a conception of sensations as mere "givens" falls apart under the weight of our attempts to actualize it.

It is not difficult to see how this Wittgensteinian exercise can inspire critiques of nonconceptualism about ("outer") perception. We need only change the vignette so that now it features a person who, instead of construing her sensations as bare presences, construes perceptual inputs to thought as such presences. Just as we can tell a story about how the person who thinks of sensations in starkly nonconceptual terms fails to account for having her mind around anything at all, we can tell a story about how the person who thinks of perception in these terms winds up in such a vexed position. There is, moreover, a plausible philosophical ratio-nale for approaching a critique of nonconceptualist views of perception via a critique of their counterpart views of sensation. The appeal of noncon-ceptualism is arguably especially strong with regard to "inner" experience (McDowell 1989), and as long as a nonconceptualist stance seems tenable in this case it is likely to seem that it must be possible to defend such a stance also with regard to perception. The sections of the *Investigations* just discussed—sections on "inner" experience—may thus be seen to speak particularly strongly against nonconceptualist doctrines about perception.

There is, admittedly, a large body of philosophical work devoted to countering the sort of conceptualist attack on nonconceptualism that is in question. A fair number of contributions to this body of literature are dedicated to highlighting what are perceived as fatal flaws of any concep-tualist alternative to nonconceptualism. Critics of conceptualist outlooks frequently charge that these outlooks cannot account for the fact that many nonrational or not fully rational creatures—for example, very young children and some nonhuman animals—resemble rational human beings in having perceptual capacities (see, for instance, Dreyfus 2005, 2007;

MacIntyre 1999, esp. 60–1 and 69; Peacocke 2001, esp. 613–14; and Vision 1998). But this charge typically turns for its force on the equation of concept-mongering with full-blown rationality, and this equation is questionable, flying in the face of the fact that the capacities integral to concept-use come in degrees and are possessed by many nonrational and not fully rational beings (Crary 2012). So, it is not clear that this strategy for defending nonconceptualisms holds forth any real hope of success, and, consequently, not clear that it holds forth any lifeline for the narrower conception of objectivity. Nor does it help the prospects of the narrower conception to turn to the work of philosophers who distance themselves from the conceptualist critique of nonconceptualism outlined above by rejecting the—plausible—assumption that experiential input plays a rational role in perceptual thought (see, for example, Brandom 1994, chapter 4, and 2000, chapter 3). Without touching on the tenability of any philosophical enterprises fitting this mold, we can see that the projects don't offer comfort to the narrower conception of objectivity. Although they represent our sensory lives as points of transparent contact with the world, they also deny that sensory input is as such rationally significant (and they thereby distance themselves from an understanding of the relevant transparent contact as in itself thought about the world). In light of these different observations, it would not be unreasonable to conclude that there is no real prospect for the sorts of fully abstract modes of mental contact with the world that would be required to motivate the narrower conception of objectivity.

At this point, we might feel justified in saying that we lack a compelling a priori case for the abstraction requirement needed to motivate the narrower conception of objectivity. Would it be appropriate, therefore, to revisit our "narrower" ideas about what falls under the concept of objectivity? It might appear that, even in the absence of an antecedent philosophical argument for the narrower conception, it is still possible to provide the conception with empirical support, specifically, by showing that respect for its abstract constraints is a guiding element of methods properly deemed scientific. Asking whether this kind of empirical support for "narrowness" is available is certainly worthwhile, but it is important to note that, even if the relevant support were there, it would not amount to a defense of the narrower conception of objectivity. We would still have no reason to impose the abstract restrictions distinctive of the conception on disciplines outside the sciences such as, say, ethics or aesthetics. To issue this caveat is not to deny the sciences their proper due. We don't express a lack of recognition of the cultural importance or distinctive character of the various natural sciences just because we don't assume ahead of time that their methodological precepts have universal applicability. Moreover, if, in the absence of compelling argument, we insist that these precepts apply everywhere—if we insist that "science is the measure of all things" (Sellars 1956, §42)—then we pass beyond proper respect for science to scientism. But these cautions, although important, don't speak against an empirical inquiry into whether the quest for abstraction is an essential feature of scientific thought. They speak only for care in interpreting the results of such an inquiry.

Lorraine Daston and Peter Galison undertake an inquiry of the relevant sort in their 2007 book *Objectivity*. To explain this, it's necessary to say a word about Daston and Galison's terminology. The authors speak of "objectivity" in reference to the epistemic demands of what above is referred to as "the narrower conception of objectivity." To be "objective" is, for Daston and Galison, "to aspire to knowledge that bears no trace of the knower—knowledge unmarked by prejudice or skill, fantasy or judgment, wishing or striving" (2007, 17; see also 124 and 139–40). Moreover, they self-consciously allow for the possibility of modes of thought, in the sciences and elsewhere, that as such do justice to the fabric of the world without qualifying as "objective" in this sense. When, at their book's opening, Daston and Galison announce that they are setting out to determine whether "objectivity," thus conceived, is "a precondition of all science worthy of the name" (2007, 34), they are not asking whether science is always dedicated to revealing the world as it is in itself. They are presupposing that scientific investigations are governed by what earlier in the current chapter is called our "concept of objectivity," and they are asking whether pursuit of the abstractness distinctive of a "narrower" interpretation of this concept is the mark of all scientific endeavor. One of Daston and Galison's larger aims is to defend a negative answer to this question. They argue that "objectivity" in their sense is a historical phenomenon and, further, that, while it plays a significant role in illuminating some scientific advances, it competes with nonabstract ideals that likewise have claims to be shedding light on the progress of science.

A selective overview of Daston and Galison's historical narrative might be given as follows. "Objectivity," understood in their sense as a "form of unprejudiced, unthinking blind sight" (2007, 16), starts to be regarded as pivotal for a range of scientific endeavors around the middle of the nineteenth century. It is initially identified and articulated as a challenge to existing epistemic ideals that encourage the cultivation of researchers' "genius" and treat an original sensibility as contributing substantively to the description of nature. What drives the emergence of "objectivity" is the belief—in tension with the view that the fate of science depends on the original contributions of the "interpretive, intervening" genius (2007, 121)—that we progress toward an undistorted image of nature by eliminating as far as possible researchers' every subjective contribution. But, in early decades of the twentieth century, this sort of "objectivity" becomes an object of partial criticism for scientists who are convinced that it obscures rather than clarifies some aspects of their work. These scientists maintain that the kinds of connections and classifications that interest them only come into view for observers whose modes of sight, far from tending toward abstractness, are shaped by familiarity and experience. Daston and Galison place the resulting epistemic ideal under the heading of "trained judgment" (and, interestingly, they treat the sections of *Philosophical Investigations* in which Wittgenstein speaks of "family resemblance" as providing a philosophical argument for such judgment; see Daston and Galison 2007, 318 and 336). Within their discussion of trained judgment, Daston and Galison stress that the scientists advocating it do so in the name of accuracy and that these advocates are claiming, as one pair of researchers is quoted as saying, that "accuracy should not be sacrificed to objectivity" (2007, 324). In these and other ways—their book also includes an exploratory chapter on the recent emergence of new nonabstract epistemic ideals in relation to nanoscience—Daston and Galison invite us to see that "objectivity," while a significant epistemic ideal for particular sciences at particular times, needs to take its place, in an evaluative landscape that is decidedly "pluralistic," alongside a variety of nonabstract ideals (see 2007, 18). They in this way make a striking case for the thesis that we should reject "an identification of objectivity with science *tout court*" (2007, 28).

This is not the right place for a detailed examination of Daston and Galison's sources and methods. What merits emphasis here is that, although there is certainly room for critical discussion of Daston and Galison's project (see, for example, Kusch 2009), even the critic who somehow succeeds in making a plausible case for thinking, in opposition to their claims, that objectivity *is* an essential feature of science will not thereby have scored a victory for the narrower conception of objectivity. Such a critique will at best show that the sorts of abstract demands internal to this conception are hallmarks of work within that subset of our cognitive practices that we dignify with the label "scientific," and this local conclusion—which Daston and Galison at the very least succeed in making look more questionable than it may once have seemed—would fall far short of establishing the unrestricted authority of the narrower conception as a rendering of our concept of objectivity. There is, we can now fairly say, good reason to doubt that a successful defense of the narrower conception of objectivity is forthcoming (and, as a result, good reason to explore a vision of our cognitive predicament that is no longer structured by this conception's constraints).

At this point, we have before us sketches of a connected series of (largely Wittgenstein-inspired) arguments against the narrower conception of objectivity. These arguments proceed by attacking the coherence of the idea of wholly abstract mental contact with the world, and by thereby presenting us with an image of our modes of thought on which they are invariably *our*—subjectively inflected—modes of thought. The suggestion that we should accept this sort of irredeemably nonabstract picture of our mental lives will seem to have a skeptical ring to it if, in scrutinizing it, we operate with the assumption that abstraction is a regulative ideal for all thought about the world. It is accordingly important to bear in mind that this assumption is itself the main critical target of the above arguments against the narrower conception. It is with an eye to undermining the appeal of an assumption about an "abstraction requirement" that the arguments bring into question the intelligibility of the idea of wholly abstract mental access to the world. If, following up on the arguments, we abandon this idea as unintelligible, we effectively concede that we lack the kind of intelligible grasp of it that would enable us to use it as a resource for assessing the cognitive credentials of our—more or less abstract— modes of thought. Now there is no longer a question of insisting, in the manner dictated by the narrower conception of objectivity, that every departure from abstraction in our thinking is as such a departure from fidelity to how things objectively are. The exercise of washing our hands of the narrower conception, far from threatening us with loss of the concept of objectivity, positions us to refashion our construal of this concept so that abstraction—or antipathy to everything subjective—is no longer its touch- stone. It positions us to exchange the narrower conception of objectivity for a wider alternative capable of encompassing some subjective qualities.

The transition to the wider conception of objectivity has the potential to transform how we conceive legitimate avenues for research within many areas of philosophy. To "widen" our understanding of objectivity is to allow that subject-dependent aspects of the world may qualify as objective. In making this allowance we aren't yet saying anything about which subject-dependent aspects, if any, do in fact qualify. The question of how much, and in what ways, the transition to the wider conception of objectivity promises to change our investigations is thus open and ought to be intensely explored. Encouragingly, in some local settings, this work is already being done. There are projects arguing, in effect, that narrowly objective constraints are artificial and wrongly restrictive in reference to, among other things:

- *aesthetics* (see, for instance, Cavell 1969/2002, chapters 3, 7, and 8; Crary 2016, chapter 6; Diamond 1991, chapters 11 and 12; McDowell 1983; and Mulhall 2009),
- *epistemology* (see, for instance, Alcoff 2010; Anderson 1995; Code 1991; Crary 2002a, 2018; Harding 1991; Hartsock 1983; and Mills 1988),
- *philosophy of mind* (see, for instance, Cavell 1969/2002, chapter 9; and 1979, part four; Crary 2016, chapter 2; Gaita 1998/2000, 2002; and Winch 1981),
- *political philosophy* (see, for instance, Mills 2005 and Zerilli 2016),
- and—perhaps most notably—*ethics* (see, for instance, Crary 2007 and 2016; De Mesel 2017; Diamond 1991, chapters 11–15, and in press; Gaita 1998/2000; McDowell 1979, 1994/6, 2000; and Wiggins 1987/2002).

The kind of rethinking of our domains of philosophical inquiry that is at issue in these projects—and many more could be mentioned—can be urged solely on the sorts of philosophical grounds discussed above. But it would be a serious oversight not to mention that this rethinking can also be recommended on the basis of specifically moral considerations. What unites the thinkers pursuing the specific projects just listed is an interest in defending the cognitive power of world-directed modes of thought that, far from being maximally abstract, are—quite conspicuously—evaluatively loaded. These thinkers are persuaded that the evaluatively non-neutral methods they favor contribute irreplaceably to uncovering genuine moral, political, and aesthetic insights that are not indifferently available, and it is not uncommon for the thinkers in question to claim, sometimes on the basis of alignment with the methodological stances of radical political traditions, that some of these insights are politically transformative and morally liberating. To the extent that the narrower conception of objectivity, with its demand for abstraction, seems to block recognition of the objective authority of such insights, it appears to be not merely philosophically untenable but also morally problematic. Given that this conception has a staying power in analytic philosophy and, indeed, well beyond it, that cannot be accounted for by the—evidently debatable— strength of the arguments that get presented on its behalf, it is fair to say that it has become ideological and that there is moral urgency to the task of addressing it.

CHAPTER 4

The Methodological Significance of Intuitions in Philosophy

Oskari Kuusela

This chapter discusses the methodological and epistemological significance of so-called intuitions in philosophy, that is, whether intuitions can be understood as evidence for or against philosophical claims. A more specific way to pose this question is to ask whether our comprehension of logical, conceptual or metaphysical possibilities and necessities can be explained by reference to intuitions or the capacity of intuition. For, ultimately, to the extent that philosophy is concerned with logical, conceptual, or metaphysical modality, not merely empirical actuality, the possibility of employing intuitions as evidence in philosophy depends on a positive answer to this more specific question. However, if we answer this question in the negative, as I argue we should, then we will also have to answer the following two questions. How should our knowledge of relevant modalities be explained instead? And might intuitions have some other kind of (non-evidential) methodological significance in philosophy?

I begin by discussing the notion of intuition in the work of two leading proponents of the view that intuitions constitute evidence in philosophy, Ernest Sosa and George Bealer. This functions as background for the critical examination of the notions of intuition and intuitions in sections that follow. In response to Sosa and Bealer, I distinguish three ways in which one might talk about intuition or intuitions in philosophy: (1) the capacity or competence of intuition, (2) particular intuitions about simple cases, and (3) particular intuitions about complex cases. I argue that, whilst intuitions in the two first senses cannot do the desired philosophical work, the philosophical significance of intuitions in the third sense is radically different from what Sosa and Bealer suggest. Although I leave it implicit, my argument against Sosa and Bealer is influenced by my reading of Wittgenstein's work, especially his rule-following considerations. I discuss Wittgenstein explicitly only when outlining my alternative to Sosa's and Bealer's accounts of the methodological significance of intuitions in philosophy, at the end of the essay.

1   Sosa and Bealer on Intuitions and Their Philosophical Significance

The key role attributed to intuitions in contemporary analytic philosophy is their serving as a source of knowledge of logical, mathematical, conceptual, or metaphysical necessities and possibilities, or as evidence for relevant knowledge claims. For example, Sosa regards intuition as the source of mathematical and logical knowledge and of other necessary truths, although he emphasises that the scope of intuition need not be restricted to necessary truth (see Sosa 2006, 210 and 215). Its scope is wider, pertaining to whatever is 'directly or immediately' believed to be true by 'considering it with full understanding', whereby the source of knowledge of such truths is not enculturation, perception, introspection, testimony or inferential reasoning (2006, 211). According to Bealer, intuitions concern matters such as 'whether certain situations are possible and whether relevant concepts would apply', whereby questions of concept application arise especially in connection with scenarios that philosophers present as so-called thought-experiments in order to articulate or evaluate philosophical theories (Bealer 1999, 30; see also 1998, 207). According to Bealer, our 'truth-tracking intuitions' can also be used to explain what concept possession is. Moreover, such an intuition-based account of concept possession can then constitute 'the cornerstone of a unified account of a priori knowledge' (1999, 41, 47).

More specially, according to Sosa, an intuition is 'a state distinct from and prior to both belief and knowledge' (2006, 212). A belief can be based on an intuition, and if the intuition is reliable, such a belief may qualify as knowledge. It is in virtue of the distinctness of intuitions from beliefs that an intuition can function as evidence for the truth of a belief. As Sosa says: 'Intuition is . . . a conscious state with propositional content that can serve as a justifying basis for belief while distinct from belief' (2006, 213). Further, Sosa argues, an intuition is a state of conscious attraction to assent to a propositional content, where the attraction derives from certain properties of the content and the subject's relation to it.

> On our account, intuition is a conscious state of felt attraction explained through the content's being (a) either modally strong or self-presenting, (b) understood well enough by the subject, (c) simple enough, and (d) true; and such a conscious state can serve as a justifying rational basis for belief. (Sosa 2006, 216; see also 2007, 101)

By a content's being 'modally strong' Sosa means its being either necessarily true or necessarily false (2006, 217).

Bealer's account is similar to Sosa's. Bealer writes: 'For you to have an intuition that A is just for it to *seem* to you that A' (Bealer 1999, 30). And further: 'When we have a rational intuition, say, that if P then not not P, this presents itself as necessary: it seems that things could not be otherwise; it must be that if P then not not P' (1999, 30). According to Bealer, a seeming of this sort is a 'conscious episode', and it is intellectual, not sensory or introspective. Apparently, part of the point is that intuitions do not just inform us about an individual's psychological states, or whatever she happens to find true, but they can really inform us about matters of, for example, logic. For, unlike experiences which may be merely subjective, the deliverances of reason, at least traditionally, are thought to be the same for all rational beings, unless something goes wrong. Accordingly, 'intuitions are counted as "data of reason" not "data of experience"' (Bealer 1999, 30).[1] Bealer too distinguishes intuitions from beliefs; the latter are not (conscious) seemings. For example, one may believe a mathematical theorem consequent to having seen the proof, but the theorem does not need to *seem* to one true/false, thus lacking the characteristic phenomenology of intuitions. Intuitions are also 'distinct from judgments, guesses, hunches, and common sense' (Bealer 1999, 31; see also 1998, 208). All in all, an intuition as an intellectual seeming is 'like sensory seeming, ... just one more primitive propositional attitude' (1999, 31).

Thus, both Sosa and Bealer argue that there is an intellectual or rational source of knowledge of modalities that explains our comprehension of non-empirical necessities and possibilities, and constitutes the basis of logical, conceptual, and metaphysical knowledge. Sosa's and Bealer's accounts of the nature of intuition can perhaps be summed up as follows (with certain reservations in Bealer's case; see Note 2). An intuition—characterised as either a felt attraction to assent to a content present in one's mind (Sosa) or an intellectual seeming (Bealer)—is an inclination to believe something, to adopt or reject a particular conception or a way of thinking about a matter, for example, a philosophical definition or theory. A relevant kind of intuition is characterised by a phenomenology of things seeming to be in a certain way, which makes one inclined to accept something as true or to reject it as false.[2]

---

[1] This means that Timothy Williamson's argument against reliance on intuitions on the grounds that this constitutes a psychologisation of philosophical evidence does not quite hit Bealer as its target or risks begging questions against Bealer (see Williamson 2004; and 2007, 214 and 235). If intuition can inform us about the logical principles governing thought, for example, it reaches beyond the merely psychological. More philosophical work is required to justify Williamson's critique.

[2] Bealer argues against characterising intuitions as inclinations by pointing out that one may have various inclinations to believe that are not intuitions in the sense of a cognitive episode, while in the case of an intuition 'a sui generis cognitive episode must occur' (1998, 209). However, Bealer's

Finally, regarding philosophical methodology, both Sosa and Bealer maintain that, as Bealer writes, 'it is our standard justificatory procedure to use intuitions as evidence' (Bealer 1999, 30; see also Bealer 1998, 204 and 205, and Sosa 2009, 230). Both Sosa and Bealer defend this procedure, although they seek to justify it in slightly different ways. According to Sosa, a given intuition can be epistemically justified by reference to the reliability of the competence of intuition in general, this competence being something humans share. Whilst the competence of intuition may have some shortcomings which explain our attraction to certain 'deep paradoxes' and, due to circumstances, individuals may make occasional mistakes, the competence is, Sosa maintains, generally reliable (Sosa 2006, 218–20, 222). Thus reliance on intuition can be regarded as a rational way to acquire knowledge. A given intuition, as Sosa puts the point, 'is *rational* if and only if it derives from a *competence*, and the content is explicitly or implicitly modal' (Sosa 2007, 101). Bealer, on the other hand, characterises the reliability of intuitions as a matter of an intuition having 'an appropriate kind of strong modal tie between its deliverances and the truth' (Bealer 1999, 35; see also 34–6). This, he says, is to be understood as an idealisation. An intuition can have such a modal tie in ideal conditions, whilst we may actually only be able to approach such conditions 'by working collectively over historical time' (1998, 202). Assuming that there is such a tie, however, intuition can be regarded as 'a basic source of evidence' in the same way in which perception can be so regarded. Of course, this does not mean that intuition is an infallible source of evidence, only that it holds 'for the most part' (Bealer 1999, 36; see also Bealer 1998, 216ff and Pust 2004).

Naturally, Sosa's and Bealer's accounts of intuition have not gone unchallenged. Some scholars have questioned the reliability of intuitions by reference to empirical findings that suggest their diversity (for example, Weinberg, Nichols, and Stich 2001; but see also Note 6). Others have argued that intuitions cannot serve as evidence, because they are not 'evidential states' (for example, Earlenbaugh and Molyneux 2009). Yet others maintain that intuitions are unnecessary to assume, and that our knowledge of modalities can be explained without any reference to them

requirement can be accommodated by characterising intuitions as a special kind of inclination to believe, namely one that is essentially connected with the occurrence of such a cognitive episode. Bealer further points out that there may be inclinations to believe a posteriori necessities; on Bealer's account, such inclinations are not intuitions either. However, this can be accommodated by treating intuitions as a particular species of inclinations about a priori necessities. For more discussion of the conception of intuitions as inclinations to believe, see Cappelen 2012, 83ff.

(Williamson 2007, chapter 5). More recently, Herman Cappelen (2012) has argued that intuitions do not in fact play a role in philosophy, and that the appearances to the contrary are illusory. Whilst my critique has connections with each one of these criticisms, it is also significantly different, both in detail and regarding its general philosophical outlook. In particular, the scope of my argument includes important normative issues that remain untouched by Cappelen, as I am concerned with the possibility, not merely the supposed actuality, of philosophers' reliance on intuitions.

2   Critical Examination of the Notions of Intuition and Intuitions

I wish to distinguish three ways in which one might talk about an intuition or intuitions. First, one might speak about intuition as a capacity or a competence. As noted, according to Sosa, such a competence underlies people's particular intuitions about specific matters, whereby a relevant kind of question would be, for instance, whether a belief in certain circumstances qualifies as knowledge. Second, one might speak about particular intuitions that someone may have. Hence, we can distinguish between a general competence or capacity and its manifestations, whereby particular intuitions are regarded as manifestations of an underlying capacity or competence. This type of distinction is often not explicitly drawn but assumed implicitly by scholars who, like Sosa, attempt to explain the reliability of particular intuitions on the basis of the general reliability of the competence of intuition. Third, we can subdivide the category of particular intuitions into two classes, namely, intuitions about complex cases and intuitions about simple cases. Intuitions about philosophical matters, as well as certain intuitions about moral matters, are examples of intuitions about complex cases. I shall provide examples and explain the relevant notion of complexity in due course.

In the following two subsections, I shall first discuss the notion of a capacity of intuition and then that of particular intuitions. Regarding particular intuitions, I argue that intuitions about matters such as the applicability of concepts are mostly best not regarded as intuitions at all. The resulting account, according to which concept application does not usually involve intuitions, differs from the majority view in the intuition debate: both supporters and critics of the intuition-based philosophical approach tend to be happy to call the views of language users about the applicability of concepts 'intuitions'. However, ultimately the difference between the proposed view and the majority view is not as great as it might seem. I agree that views about the applicability of concepts may in complex cases be characterised as intuitions. Only, in such cases intuitions cannot serve as evidence.

2.1 The Capacity or Competence of Intuition

A central motive for postulating a capacity or competence of intuition that underlies intuitions about particular matters is that it appears to provide a way to explain and justify particular intuitions. A good understanding of the capacity/competence might also allow one to label areas where our intuitions are not reliable. According to the proponents of intuition, just as the faculty of sight reliably enables one to see, so intuition enables one to comprehend modalities. As the faculty of sight is subject to some illusions, so might intuition be. But we can avoid such illusions through a better understanding of the capacity/competence of intuition (see, for instance, Sosa 2007, 101–2). The problem, however, is, first, that postulating the capacity/competence of intuition, arguably, offers a merely apparent explanation of the capacity to understand modalities. Second, even if the capacity/competence could explain our comprehension of modalities, it cannot justify particular intuitions in just those cases where a justification is needed (as I will explain).

Regarding the first issue, it is noteworthy that a person's comprehension of modalities in one area of the employment of modal notions need not imply competence in other such areas. As Aristotle observes, although young persons may be proficient in mathematics they cannot be that in moral matters, because this requires not only the comprehension of universal principles, but the ability to apply them in particular situations only acquired through experience (Aristotle [2000] / *Nicomachean Ethics* 6.8.1142a1ff). Regardless of whether Aristotle is correct, however, evidently mathematical competence does not imply moral competence or vice versa. Similarly, competence in moral matters or mathematics does not imply competence in philosophy or logic, or vice versa. Consequently, to postulate a competence or capacity of intuition in order to explain the comprehension of modalities either requires postulating several such capacities/ competences in different areas, or if one assumes that there is one general capacity/competence with diverse manifestations, one needs to explain why one can be competent in one area but not another.

On its own, this question of how the manifestations of the capacity/ competence of intuition in different modal realms relate to the underlying capacity/competence does not constitute a serious argument against the postulation of a general intuitive capacity/competence. One might account for the diversity of manifestations by saying that, whilst there indeed is an underlying general capacity/competence of intuition, its development in different modal realms is not uniform. Perhaps the capacity/competence takes longer to mature in the case of morality, and requires specific instruction in the case of mathematics. Or perhaps diversity can be explained by saying that realms of modality differ from one another in that the tasks which the capacity/competence of intuition is required to perform in connection with different sets of modal concepts vary.

However, what such responses presuppose, and what raises more serious questions about the explanatory power of appeal to the capacity/competence of intuition, is the tight correspondence between the presumed intuitive competences, or competences in particular modal realms, and competence in the relevant areas of the use of language, concepts, or relevant symbolic systems. As if by predetermined harmony, one develops a relevant intuitive/modal competence in concert with developing the corresponding competence to use relevant concepts or linguistic locutions. For example, the presumed intuitive competences relating to moral matters or mathematics, and the comprehension of relevant modalities, seem to manifest themselves only when one becomes competent in moral discourse or when one learns mathematics. By competence in moral discourse I mean here the ability to reliably recognise, for example, instances of injustice and to apply the concept of injustice to them but not to other cases (with some margin of error), and *mutatis mutandis* for a sufficient number of moral concepts. Competence in mathematics may be similarly regarded as the ability to employ relevant mathematical notions.

But if there is such a correspondence between modal and linguistic/conceptual competences, why not explain the comprehension of modalities by reference to the relevant linguistic/conceptual capacity/competence? This would be simpler, since in order to explain the linguistic manifestations of our comprehension of modalities we need to postulate a linguistic competence anyway, and if we can say that the comprehension of relevant modalities is part of the linguistic competence, we can avoid unnecessarily postulating multiple explanatory factors (capacities or competences). Indeed, as I argue, the account of our comprehension of modalities by reference to relevant linguistic competences can be developed in such a way as to exclude as unnecessary any appeal to a capacity/competence of intuition. But in order to explain my point, I need, firstly, to clarify what I understand by a linguistic or conceptual competence.

Secondly, I need to discuss questions relating to the attribution of competences in relation to their manifestations.

By a linguistic or conceptual competence I understand in what follows the competence to use relevant concepts, for example, mathematical or moral ones. This is not intended as a general characterisation of linguistic competence or what it is to possess language, but only as a minimal characterisation sufficient for present purposes. (Since linguistic competence involves more than the capacity to apply concepts, a conceptual competence manifested in language use is a narrower notion.) Crucially, a necessary part of the competence to use concepts is their use in accordance with relevant determinations of what is possible and necessary which partly define those concepts. For example, it is part of my comprehension of the concept of a triangle that triangles have three angles, and if I apply the concept to anything with more or fewer angles, this may be a reason to conclude that I do not understand what triangles are and do not possess the concept (for instance, if my mistake were not a mere accident). This is intended to illustrate a general point: if I do not grasp the modal features of my concepts, especially those that are part of the criteria for their application (or part of the criteria of identity of the objects to which they are applied), or if I do not understand the basic modal relations between my concepts (such as $2 < 3$ or that colour cannot be attributed to numbers), then I do not understand or have those concepts. In this sense a comprehension of relevant modalities is a necessary part of the comprehension of concepts.[3]

It is also important that the notion of a linguistic/conceptual competence is normative. Concepts can be employed correctly or incorrectly according to the criteria of their employment, and to attribute to someone a relevant competence is to say that their use of the concept is governed (by and large) by the rules for its correct employment. More specifically, regarding the notions of linguistic signs and concepts, we may say that signs used according to certain rules may give expression to concepts. If so, the ability to use signs according to such rules can count as an expression or

---

[3] The fact that a comprehension of relevant modalities is a necessary part of the comprehension of concepts does not entail that one should necessarily be able to spell out relevant modal properties and relations. The competence to use concepts does not imply a well-developed competence to spell out the criteria of their application or define them, or even reliably judge the correctness of such characterisations. The history of philosophy provides ample evidence for difficulties relating to the task of characterising or defining concepts. Nevertheless, one's comprehension of relevant modalities must be reflected in one's employment of concepts in that one, roughly speaking, only calls triangular objects 'triangles' and does not use language in a way that contradicts the modal relations between the concepts, except as an exception. I return to this issue in Section 3.

manifestation of a relevant conceptual competence or the grasp of relevant concepts. But insofar as a grasp of relevant modal properties and relations is an essential part of the grasp of a concept, then whoever is attributed a competence to use particular linguistic signs as the expression of certain concepts, must also be attributed a grasp of relevant modalities. Insofar as her use of signs gives expression to certain concepts, and manifests her comprehension of those concepts, her use of signs is also an expression or manifestation of her grasp of relevant modalities. In this way a competence to use linguistic signs can be seen as the expression of a comprehension of modalities.[4]

But the grounds or criteria on the basis of which we attribute to someone a capacity/competence to use linguistic signs so as to express concepts are complicated. We exclude, for example, lucky accidents that do not manifest a comprehension of relevant concepts and modalities. It is possible in this and other ways that a person's use of linguistic signs does not manifest a conceptual or modal capacity/competence. For the present argument it is enough, however, that the use of signs *can* manifest or be expressive of a conceptual and modal capacity/competence, not that it must. Granted this, it can then be further argued, as I do shortly, that when we attribute a modal capacity/competence to someone on the basis of how they use particular signs, our doing so does not depend on there being any mental intuitive episodes of the kind that Sosa and Bealer claim to underlie the person's use of concepts. If so, it is not necessary to postulate a capacity/competence of intuition in order to justify the attribution of a comprehension of relevant modalities to a person, and one does not need to explain modal competence as necessarily assuming the capacity/competence of intuition.

Here, a challenge I need to respond to is this: even if a person's competence to use certain signs is sometimes sufficient to show that they possess a relevant conceptual and modal competence, do we not nevertheless need to assume a capacity/competence of intuition that underlies this conceptual competence and upholds it? That is, even if a modal competence always manifested itself through a relevant linguistic/conceptual competence, do we not nevertheless need to presuppose a capacity/

---

[4] A concept understood as something that finds its expression in the use of language or a sign-system, is not a mental entity (*pace* Goldman and Pust 1998). It is something that different language users can grasp and share, to echo Frege on thoughts. For an account of intuitions as based on conceptual competence, see Ludwig 2010. Although not specifically discussed here, my key criticisms are also meant to apply, *mutatis mutandis*, to both the view expressed in Goldman and Pust 1998 and that in Ludwig 2010.

competence of intuition to explain the linguistic/conceptual and modal competence?

With regard to this it is important that in order to attribute someone a comprehension of modalities, we do not need to know anything about how things might seem to the person, or whether she experiences any Bealerian seemings or Sosaian conscious states to assent. For example, marking exam papers in logic requires no knowledge of the inner states of students. Whether or not the students possess the relevant competence is decided on a different basis, not by reference to their inner states, of which markers typically know nothing. Accordingly, anonymous marking is not impossible, unlike marking without reading exam scripts (that is, without recourse to the linguistic manifestations of the students' competence). Thus, in order to justifiably attribute a relevant modal competence to a person, we do not need to assume the occurrence of intuitions in the sense of mental episodes. The attribution of a modal competence is independent of the person's possible intuitive episodes and the justification of the attribution does not depend on the presence of such states. Hence, intuitive episodes are not necessary for the attribution of a modal competence.

Furthermore, the occurrence of such states or episodes is not sufficient for the possession of a modal competence either. Students taking a logic exam might experience relevant seemings and for all that not possess the competence. In such a case they might be under an illusion—for example, a drug-induced one—of possessing the competence. It might seem to them that they know how to construe a certain proof, although they only produce scribbles. To sum up and generalise: however much it may seem to a person that she follows a rule correctly, this does not mean that she actually does so; neither does the correct description of someone, including oneself, as having comprehended a rule require the presence of any seemings. Consequently, states of seeming are neither necessary nor sufficient for a person's possessing a linguistic/conceptual and a modal competence, and it is not necessary to assume intuitions to underlie a person's comprehension of relevant modalities.[5]

---

[5] Cappelen makes a point that is parallel to, though less general than, the point I have made about the relation between intuitions and a person's possessing a linguistic/conceptual and a modal competence. Cappelen points out that the particular phenomenology of intuitive experiences and the presence of such experiences or feelings is not relevant for deciding whether oneself or someone else has correctly understood a philosopher's argument, and in this sense the feeling is not 'argumentatively significant' (see Cappelen 2012, 118ff, 138, 161, and 166).

Let us now turn to how the attribution of a linguistic/conceptual and modal competence is connected with its manifestations, and the sense in which manifesting a competence is a condition for its attribution. What does one commit oneself to, if one accepts that the manifestations of our capacity to comprehend mathematical, moral, and so on modalities are linguistic in the sense that the competence finds its expression in how one employs relevant linguistic or mathematical locutions, and if one accepts that we attribute to someone a relevant modal capacity/competence on the basis of such manifestations? Does this mean that someone must actually manifest a capacity/competence in order for it to be attributed to them?

We can *sometimes* attribute a capacity/competence independently of any manifestations. Nevertheless, this is a limiting case, and not all cases where we attribute the capacity/competence can be of this kind. To maintain the opposite—that we could in general attribute to beings a competence independently of their ever manifesting it—amounts to saying something like that hamsters might have a competence in symbolic logic, even though they never manifest it. But there seems to be no basis for attributing such a competence to hamsters. Arguably, the explanation is that normally the criterion for attributing a capacity/competence to a being is that it manifests it—in some ways, sometimes—and all cases cannot be limiting cases. Therefore, whilst in *each individual* case the attribution of a capacity/competence may be independent of its manifestations, this cannot be true of *every* case. To infer from a possibility pertaining to each individual case to a possibility in all cases constitutes a fallacy. For example, whilst any individual move in chess might contradict the rules of the game, this cannot be true of every move ever made, insofar as the game's identity is determined by its rules, and we do not envisage the game as an abstract object whose existence is completely independent of the existence of chess as a historical phenomenon. The possibility that every move made were incorrect undermines the very possibility of describing anyone as playing the game, because now no standard—such as offered by a practice of playing the game according to specific rules—exists for playing according to rules. The idea that only incorrect moves are ever made is incoherent.

To return to hamsters, the issue is not merely epistemological, concerning the question of whether we know that hamsters do not have a capacity/competence in logic. The point is that in the absence of *any manifestations* the *possibility* of attributing the capacity/competence to them is excluded. Not all cases can be limiting cases. This generalises: whilst the attribution of a capacity/competence is indeed possible in individual cases without it being manifested, this is not possible in every case. This is the connection between the attribution of a capacity/competence and its manifestations that was assumed by the previous argument that rejects the postulation of the competence of intuition as unnecessary.

What do these points regarding the competence–manifestation relation imply for the issue of postulating a capacity/competence of intuition? If there is a necessary correlation between the manifestations of the presumed intuitive competence and the manifestations of the relevant linguistic or conceptual competences such that excludes the possibility of attributing a competence entirely independently of any manifestations, it seems that the way to explain our comprehension of modalities, whenever they have a linguistic expression, is by reference to the corresponding linguistic competence. Whenever the manifestations of the intuitive competence are identical to those of relevant linguistic or conceptual competence, it is unnecessary to postulate a separate capacity/competence of intuition to explain them. This is unnecessary because (1) we already ascribe a linguistic competence to individuals in such cases, (2) a comprehension of relevant modalities is a necessary part of it, and (3) the attribution of a linguistic competence does not require any episodes of seeming, as explained. Thus, the postulate of the intuitive capacity/competence is shaved off by Ockham's razor.

Importantly, here the weak claim suffices for my purpose that whenever the manifestations of the presumed intuitive capacity/competence are linguistic, a person's competence with related modalities is to be explained as part of her linguistic capacity/competence. But there is no need to claim that all manifestations of the grasp of modalities would be linguistic. For example, my comprehension of modalities pertaining to chess might be manifested only in how I play, without ever being given linguistic expression. But in that case, too, my comprehension of relevant modalities can be explained with reference to my competence to play chess. Generally: the media in which intuitive competences manifest themselves may be various, not only linguistic. In all cases, however, a person's comprehension of relevant modalities can be explained in terms of her capacity/competence to operate in the medium in question, for example, to play chess or to use mathematical symbols.

Importantly, we may now regard any intuitions about modal properties or relations as parasitic on the relevant linguistic or other capacity/competence. Although, such episodes of seeming may be typical to those who have the modal competence, arguably it is the linguistic or other capacity/competence that explains the intuitive experiences and their having specific modal content, not the other way around. For example, it seems to me that a triangle cannot have four angles. However, unless we assume that I possess the concept of a triangle—that is, that I have the relevant conceptual competence whose attribution to me assumes that I adhere to certain norms regarding the use of the concept—it is unclear how I can maintain that my mental seemings concern triangles rather than something else. Problematically, if we imagine my comprehension of the modal properties of triangles to be based simply on how things mentally seem to me, there are no grounds for judging me to be wrong when it seems to me triangles could have four angles, as can now be explained.

Norms determined independently of episodes of seeming, such as the norms of a linguistic practice, are required for judging the correctness of the episodes of seeming in particular cases. Such norms provide an independent criterion for the correctness/incorrectness of my seemings without which the identification of mistakes is not possible. In the absence of such an independent criterion, I could simply say that for me triangles can have four angles, if it so seems. But in that case, from the point of view of geometry, there is no reason to accept that my episodes of seeming concern triangles rather than something else I call a 'triangle'. In this sense my possessing the concept of a triangle constitutes a condition for my being able to regard triangles and their modal properties as the content of my mental states. If so, intuitive episodes about conceptual modalities presuppose concept possession, and cannot explain it. Regardless of whether this stronger point is correct, however, the basic weaker point is that our comprehension of relevant modalities is fully explainable by reference to relevant linguistic/conceptual or other capacities/competences, and no intuitive capacity/competence is needed to explain it. (By contrast, see Sosa 2009, 104–5.)

To make a final point about the capacity/competence of intuition, note that one cannot, *pace* Sosa (see Section 1), justify the correctness of any particular intuition by reference to a general competence. Even if the competence is generally reliable, it is possible in particular cases that one's intuitions are mistaken. (As Bealer says, they hold only for the most part.) Hence, to establish the reliability of the competence in general is only to establish that the individual manifestations of the competence (particular intuitions) are generally reliable. Should any questions about the reliability of a particular intuition arise, however, they must be answered independently of appealing to general reliability. The point can be explained by comparing intuition with perception. Assume that we have a generally reliable visual capacity. If doubts arise about the correctness of what we see, it does not help to say that what we see is real because the capacity is generally reliable. This is merely to brush doubts to the side, not to address them. Rather, if we need to double-check the correctness of what we see, we can try to confirm it through independent perceptions. For example, we take another look or refer to another sensory modality. All the while the general reliability of the perceptual capacity is assumed. Appeal to that general reliability, however, cannot do any justificatory work in cases where doubt arises. The case of intuitions is analogous. Even if the competence were generally reliable, this alone cannot ascertain the reliability of its deliverances in particular cases, should concerns arise. The general reliability of the competence cannot help us to decide whether and when particular intuitions can be taken as evidence, because it leaves open the possibility of particular intuitions being wrong.

To sum up the conclusions of the previous arguments, the competence or capacity of intuition is, firstly, not needed to explain our comprehension of modalities, or even more strongly: it cannot explain our comprehension of modalities, but intuitions as seemings about modalities presuppose it and are parasitic on it. Secondly, the competence of intuition cannot be appealed to in order to justify particular intuitions in cases where a separate justification is needed. I conclude that the postulation of the competence of intuition is philosophically unhelpful.

Next, let us discuss particular intuitions and the possibility of their use as evidence in philosophy. Notably, even if one accepts the preceding arguments, this leaves open the possibility that intuitions in the sense of our intuitive judgements about philosophical matters play an evidential role in philosophy. They could play an evidential role, for example, if we assumed that the purpose of philosophical theories is the systematisation of our intuitive judgements about what the theories concern. (To accommodate the results of the preceding arguments with this view, perhaps intuitions/ intuitive judgements are now to be regarded as deliverances of our linguistic competence. In this capacity such intuitions might be a generally reliable and, so, an adequate basis for philosophical theories, even though they may sometimes be questionable.) On this account, intuitions would still play an important, even indispensable, role as evidence in philosophy. As I argue, however, intuitions cannot play such an evidential role.

2.2   Particular Intuitions Including Philosophical Ones

So-called intuitions concerning particular issues—such as whether a certain belief in specific circumstances qualifies as knowledge, or whether a certain action is just—are at the centre of the debate about intuitions and philosophical methodology. One important strand in the debate concerns the issue of whether such intuitions are reliable as evidence in evaluating philosophical theories. Typically, by 'intuitions' one means in this connection philosophers' or peoples' responses, or something that is the basis of their responses, to philosophers' thought-experiments, such as the Gettier examples concerning knowledge. The significance of these examples was, of course, that although Smith's belief in the situations imagined by Gettier may meet the traditional definition of knowledge as true justified belief, most readers would not accept Smith's belief as knowledge. (There would be more to say about whether Gettier's examples meet the definition, but I will leave this to the side.) From the point of view of a Sosa/Bealer-style account of intuitions as evidence, the relevance of such counter-examples can be explained as follows. A counter-example can show the failure of a philosophical theory by presenting us with a case that fits the theory, but which our intuitions tell us not to accept as an instance of whatever the theory concerns. Such an intuition would count as evidence against the theory. In response, however, I wish to question the idea that we generally rely on intuitions in concept application or that concept application generally gives expression to intuitions. I argue that whenever it is right to say that concept application is guided by an intuition or expresses an intuition, such intuitions cannot be taken as evidence for philosophical views.

On grounds discussed earlier, I assume that what is at stake in the Gettier examples is the applicability of the concept of knowledge in relevant situations. To ask whether the concept of knowledge is applicable to Smith's beliefs is to ask whether his beliefs qualify as knowledge. That is, assuming the correctness of the arguments in Section 2.1, philosophers' responses to these examples can now be regarded as manifestations of their capacity/competence to apply the relevant concept in individual cases or as manifestations of their linguistic capacity/competence. If I am granted this, I will be able to reject the view that intuitions can qualify as evidence or constitute the basis for philosophical theories on the following grounds.

If one maintains that a person's application or refusal to apply the concept of knowledge in cases like the Gettier examples is based on an intuition, this will commit one to saying that the application of concepts must everywhere be based on intuition, unless one has some way to distinguish cases in which concept application is not guided by intuitions. (I return to this shortly.) But it is problematic to maintain that when in perfectly ordinary circumstances I call a chair 'a chair' it is because I have an intuition that the relevant object is a chair, or because I have an intuition that the concept of a chair is applicable to the object, or that in such cases intuitions, as episodes of seeming, function as evidence for the applicability of our concepts. This is clearly problematic, insofar as it implies that it can only ever seem to me that a concept applies but I cannot know that it does. Yet, this seems to be the consequence of the intuition-based account of the use of concepts.

I take it that when I am in standard conditions in a room with normal chairs and say to someone 'Here's a chair for you', bringing it for the person to use, the episode of it seeming to me that it is correct to apply the word 'chair' to the object counts as an example of a reliable intuition about concept application, if anything will. Given its reliability, the intuition could then be used as evidence for the claim that the word 'chair' applies to this object, and so intuitions apparently can justify knowledge claims regarding concept application. But the reasoning is too quick. Provided that the general reliability of the capacity of intuition cannot justify the reliability of particular intuitions, as explained, we must ask what other grounds could be given for the reliability of my intuition, if we started doubting it. Is it enough to justify the claim that the concept of a chair applies that the circumstances are standard and the chair normal? No. If all cases of concept application are based on intuition or expressive of intuitions, then it is just another episode of seeming that the circumstances are standard and conditions approximate ideal ones (hence, that those concepts apply). Crucially, in case of doubt, these latter intuitions are just as much in need of justification as the first one regarding the chair. Thus, we are moving in a circle of seemings. Anything I could say to justify my seemings will be just another seeming, and so on ad infinitum. However much anyone is convinced by these seemings, being convinced is merely a psychological state, not the same as knowing.

The intuition-based account therefore seems to imply, absurdly, the impossibility of knowing that a concept applies. But if scepticism or the collapse of the distinction between knowledge and seeming follows from the intuitionist account, other accounts without such consequences are preferable. Of course, there is no similar difficulty with the linguistic account of knowledge of modalities and concept application. Linguistic or conceptual competence does not merely deliver episodes of seeming, but to have the competence is to know how to use concepts, for instance, that the concept applies in the chair example. To conclude this part of my argument, problems with the idea that concept application is based on an intuition, or expresses an intuition, in standard cases like the chair example show that we cannot say that concept application is *in general* based on intuitions or expressive of experiences of seeming. Consequently, intuitions cannot be regarded as evidence for the application of concepts in simple cases like the chair example.

However, if it nevertheless is *sometimes* apt to characterise concept application as guided by intuition or expressive of intuitions, how are we to distinguish such cases from others? I suggest a distinction with reference to the complexity of the case. When the case is complex enough for a language user to have to pause to think whether a concept applies, and when, therefore, two language users might differ without either being obviously wrong, the application of a concept may be described as guided by or as expressing an intuition. If so, however, intuitions cannot be referred to as evidence for philosophical theories or definitions, or for the applicability of concepts. For on this account, it is apt to say we are guided by intuitions only in cases where we might reasonably differ. This means that, although one of two different intuitions might indeed turn out to be correct, neither has any evidential value in the relevant case, because the correctness of both is in dispute. In other words, when the evidential value of particular intuitive judgements is in dispute, they cannot be appealed to as evidence for any particular view or theory. The point is again general: if the evidential status of a suggested piece of scientific or legal evidence is in dispute, that piece cannot be relied on as evidence without establishing its evidential status. This is a sound core in Weinberg, Nichols, and Stich's (2001) objection from diversity. If our intuitions about philosophical cases differ, those intuitions cannot be appealed to as evidence, because it is unclear on whose intuitions we should rely.[6] But let us look more closely at such intuitions regarding complex cases which we might often also describe as philosophical intuitions.

By such a philosophical intuition I mean a philosophical view someone is inclined to accept, or a particular way in which one is inclined to understand a philosophical matter, or to characterise or define a complex concept, or to apply a concept in a complex case. Thus, to have a philosophical intuition is to be inclined to make certain kinds of philosophical statements, to accept or propose certain philosophical characterisations, and so on. Accordingly, for instance, Saul Kripke says that 'we have a direct intuition of the rigidity of names, exhibited in our understanding of the truth-conditions of particular

---

[6] Whether Weinberg, Nichols, and Stich's (2001) empirical studies present us with genuine cases of diversity in concept application or intuitions, or whether this is just a side effect of the design of their studies, is a moot point. We might disagree about concept application for a variety of reasons, including merely verbal disagreements about the interpretation of an example which, Sosa (2007; 2009) suggests, might explain the results about the diversity of intuitions in relevant studies. See also Ludwig 2010.

sentences' (Kripke 1972/80, 14). What Kripke presents us with is a philosophical view about the nature of names, which according to him captures how we use names and sentences, and is supported by 'things we would say' as 'indirect evidence' (1972/80, 14). Similarly, Donald Davidson characterises as intuitions the views that there could not be thought without speech and that thinking is speaking to oneself, and that the mood of a sentence—for example, its being an assertion or a command—is determined by conventions concerning its use (see Davidson 1984/2001, 116 and 155).

Clearly, these intuitions boil down to inclinations to accept particular philosophical views. Similarly, one might have intuitions about the nature of knowledge or justice, thus being inclined to characterise these matters or concepts in particular ways. Not all philosophers share Kripke's and Davidson's intuitions about relevant issues, however, and since philosophical intuitions in this sense may vary, they cannot qualify as evidence for or against philosophical claims. Further, given such differences regarding philosophical views, relevant persons might also differ in their application of relevant concepts, comparably to how subscribing to a Kantian or a utilitarian theory in ethics may give rise to differences in how individuals morally judge a particular case. But if so, we can generally conclude that there are no cases in which intuitions could be used as evidence. As argued, in simple cases, such as the chair, it is not correct to describe concept application as based on intuition, and consequently it is not correct to regard intuitions as evidence. In complex cases it may be correct to describe concept application as based on an intuition, but because intuitions can in such cases be disputed, they cannot be used as evidence.

This negative conclusion, together with the conclusion in Section 2.1 that postulating a competence of intuition is philosophically unhelpful, raises the question of what, if any, is the significance of intuitions for philosophy. Section 3 outlines a conception of the methodological significance of intuitions radically different from Sosa's and Bealer's: the contention is that, insofar as the options discussed above exhaust the possible roles intuitions might play in philosophy, the role outlined, or something along these lines, is the only one left.

3   The Methodological Significance of Intuitions

On the basis of the argument in Section 2.1, I assume that, when discussing issues such as the nature of justice or knowledge, we rely on our competence of using relevant concepts. As explained, our comprehension of relevant modalities is necessarily part of our understanding of the concepts in question. According to this view, we might then say further that when trying to get clear about relevant necessities and possibilities or to define our concepts—for instance, to spell out necessary conditions for knowing —we are reflecting back on our understanding of those concepts. Nevertheless, this does not mean that the task is easy, and need not be taken to imply that everything about relevant modalities is definitely fixed, for instance, that genuinely perplexing cases could not arise or be construed where concepts leave it undetermined (or underdetermined) whether they apply, or that we could not reasonably disagree about their application or how they should be characterised.[7] Moreover, when reflecting back on concepts, part of the difficulty is that the competence to use concepts does not automatically imply a competence to define or to describe them (see Note 3). Rather, the competence to use concepts and to describe their use are two different, albeit connected, competences. The use of language involves largely implicit knowledge of how to use it (which we learn first, as children), whilst describing the functioning of language or concepts is a matter of making explicit what we implicitly know (which we learn only later, if at all). Being able to do the latter, and achieving reflective clarity, may enable one to be more successful in the former 'first order' task, especially when complex issues such as moral matters are at stake. Correspondingly, accepting a bad philosophical theory or definition may also have the opposite effect.

Now, what I have called 'philosophical intuitions' relate to both complex cases of concept application and to cases of reflexive characterisation of concepts. As explained, such intuitions are inclinations to apply (or not to apply) a concept, or to characterise (or not to characterise) it in a particular way, whereby, due to the complexity of matters, it is not obvious what one should say. Regarding the methodological significance of such intuitions, then, I take my cue from Wittgenstein, who remarks about our inclinations in philosophising (that is, our inclinations or temptations to express

---

[7] It is not the case that it would always be determined in advance and for every case whether our concepts apply or not. Sometimes there may be grounds for and against employing a concept. Its criteria of application may be partly met, and the question of its applicability becomes an issue of whether the accord or disaccord is more important. For example, moral questions sometimes leave room for this kind of disagreement. Further, cases may emerge which our concepts are not prepared for, such as the psychological phenomenon of blindsight. Is this seeing or not seeing, blindness or not? Complexities of this kind may make it difficult to decide whether a concept applies in some case, and how it should be characterised or defined. Thus, to determine what, in the light of our concepts, is necessary or possible, may be far from straightforward, even if we assume that we are epistemologically in a good position.

particular philosophical views and to use specific terms and notions for that purpose):

> What we 'are tempted to say' in such a case is, of course, not philosophy; but it is its raw material. Thus, for example, what a mathematician is inclined to say about the objectivity and reality of mathematical facts, is not a philosophy of mathematics, but something for philosophical *treatment*. (PI §254)

Similarly, Wittgenstein writes about relevant kinds of inclination on a different occasion, observing that such temptations may well be widely shared, rather than anything idiosyncratic. Yet, that our inclinations or intuitions are widely shared does not mean, according to him, that what we are tempted to say is therefore correct.

> You say what you are inclined to say. And it has interest only because we too feel the same temptation to say it. However, now it is not yet true nor merely probable, but the object of our investigation. (MS-179, 22v–23r, my translation)

Wittgenstein, therefore, does not accept the view, assumed by many in the intuitions debate, that widely shared intuitions would be more trustworthy.[8] Another distinctive feature of Wittgenstein's view about the significance of intuitions is as follows. According to Wittgenstein, what we are inclined to say when philosophising is important because the statements that express our inclinations may indicate the roots or sources of the philosophical problems we face. Thus, what we are inclined to say requires attention because it can help to reveal the unclarities and confusions that underlie our philosophical difficulties. This is the sense in which our inclinations or intuitions constitute material for philosophical treatment. This feature of Wittgenstein's view requires further explanation of his conception of philosophical problems.

Part of this conception is an emphasis on the importance of paying attention to language as the medium of philosophical thought, and how language, due to its complexity, combined with our inclinations to understand its functioning in particular ways, can mislead us. For notably, not only are philosophers typically interested in highly complex concepts that originate in everyday language (such as knowledge, truth, and justice), they often attempt to characterise their objects of interest—concepts or other

---

[8] Wittgenstein's non-acceptance of this view, that widely shared intuitions would be more trustworthy, is not unique. Similarly, Aristotle—for example—typically starts from views that are commonly held, but gives no special authority to these views; for discussion, see Hintikka 1999.

relevant phenomena—in terms of further, equally complex concepts whose function is not entirely under their control. An example is the definition of knowledge as true, justified belief. Here both 'knowledge' and the defining terms—'true', 'justified', and 'belief'—present us with difficulties. Language should then be a special object of attention for philosophers, because linguistic expressions and our concepts, and how we construe them when philosophising, can guide as well as mislead philosophical thought in various ways. Accordingly, it is part of this conception that our philosophical difficulties may sometimes be self-induced in that, without realising it, they may be rooted in misleading inclinations to think about matters at hand. For example, we try to think about an issue in terms of particular concepts that suggest themselves, but are ultimately unsuited for the purpose, and do not enable us to understand it. Hence, the methodological significance of philosophical intuitions—what we are inclined to say—is that their scrutiny may reveal something important about what makes an issue problematic for us. In this way, examining those intuitions, rather than uncritically following them, may be helpful or even crucial in resolving philosophical problems.

By contrast to Sosa and Bealer, there is no need to assume that we are always fully conscious about such inclinations or intuitions. One's inclinations to think about philosophical matters in particular ways might be inherited from the philosophical tradition or one's home philosophy department through a process that is more akin to enculturation than rational examination. This may make those inclinations seem natural, and yet such inherited inclinations, if unexamined, may constitute a potential source of difficulties. Accordingly, an important part of philosophical work may be to try to become clear about the assumptions and moves one makes almost automatically. Ultimately, the danger is that our reliance on intuitively acceptable views might turn out to manifest lack of rigour in the examination of our views and assumptions. Feeling comfortable with some assumption or idea, we may leave it insufficiently examined, accepting it as an article of faith. A literal example is appealing to God as a guarantor of knowledge of the external world.

It should also be noted that our inclinations to think about matters in particular ways may sometimes be such that we do not really *want* to give them up. For one reason or another one may desire something to be true, and consequently be unable to bring oneself to properly consider alternatives. Thus, when dealing with one's philosophical intuitions, one might also be wrestling with a difficulty of the will, and the problem is not purely intellectual (see, for instance, PO 161). Accordingly, it may be important to try to be aware of extra-philosophical motivations behind one's views, too, so as to be able to subject all potential sources of distortion to scrutiny.

Finally, if one comprehends the significance of philosophical intuitions as I propose, clearly attention to them is not the whole story about what it is to deal with philosophical problems. Clarity about how a certain problem arises may be a crucial step towards solving it, but it is still a different matter to arrive at a positive account of the issue. In this regard our philosophical intuitions may be irrelevant or even a significant hindrance, except perhaps in the lucky case in which they point in the right direction. In such a case, however, the correctness of our intuitions must be established independently of them. Whether an intuition was a good one depends on the justification of the account developed on its basis. Just as in science, intuition can help but is never the way to test a theory.

To conclude, whilst philosophical intuitions—that is, our inclinations to think about philosophical matters in particular ways—are a worthy object of attention, their significance is arguably very different from that envisaged by Sosa and Bealer. Although intuitions cannot provide any evidence for philosophical views, they can provide a starting point for philosophical examination and may reveal something important about the sources of our philosophical difficulties. To postulate a general capacity or competence of intuition, as Sosa and Bealer do, however, is unhelpful. The postulation of such a capacity/competence adds nothing to the explanation of our comprehension of modalities by reference to our linguistic capacity/competence, or, more broadly, our capacity/competence to operate in the medium in which our intuitions manifest themselves.[9]

[9] This work was first presented at a conference on 'Intuitions in Philosophy' held at the University of East Anglia in July 2009. Thanks to participants, and Angela Breitenbach, John Collins, and Marie McGinn for comments.

CHAPTER 5

Wittgenstein on 'Seeing Meanings'

Katherine J. Morris

Wittgenstein came to serious study of Köhler late in his career.[1] His well-known remarks on aspect-seeing are part of this engagement with Köhler, but these remarks are not always read in that context.[2] The argument put forward here arises, in part, from an attempt to do so. And it involves, perforce, seeing Wittgenstein's interests as lying beyond the relatively well-trodden cases of 'aspect-seeing': 'We find certain things about seeing puzzling, because we do not find the whole business of seeing puzzling enough' (PI II 212 / PPF §251).

In the first section of what follows, I examine one main line of criticism which Wittgenstein pursues against Köhler. It is well known that Wittgenstein, in connection with his critique of Köhler, points to two uses of the word 'see' in his remarks on aspect-seeing; most scholarly discussion, however, concentrates on the 'aspect-seeing' use. The first use is more or less unreflectively interpreted in the literature in two apparently contrasting ways. I argue that there is a way of understanding this apparent contrast which makes it, precisely, a contrast between two uses of 'see' which both seem to be distinct from Wittgenstein's aspect-seeing use. (I label it the distinction between 'seeing colours and shapes' and 'seeing things', though both phrases are used in a quasi-technical sense.) Moreover, drawing *this* contrast is precisely one of Köhler's primary polemical aims. (This makes it somewhat strange that neither Wittgenstein nor Wittgenstein commentators have paid it much attention.) In the second section, I explore how the

---

[1] Wittgenstein discussed Köhler's *Gestalt Psychology* (1929/47) extensively in his last lectures in 1947. Students' notes on these lectures are published as *Wittgenstein's Lectures on Philosophical Psychology 1946–47* (LPP). Wittgenstein's written remarks during this period are gathered together as *Remarks on the Philosophy of Psychology* (RPP I, RPP II); some of this material was culled in *Zettel* (Z), and Wittgenstein himself gathered some of it into a short manuscript which was originally published as 'Part II' of *Philosophical Investigations* but is now called *Philosophy of Psychology — A Fragment* in the new translation.

[2] Some authors do contextualise discussions of aspect-seeing within Wittgenstein's Köhler period. See, for instance, Schulte 1987/93, McFee 1999 and Schroeder 2010.

84

'seeing colours and shapes' and 'seeing things' contrast works in two prima facie different situations, namely in looking at the world and in looking at pictures, and suggest on this basis some reasons for apparently fundamental disagreements amongst commentators on aspect-seeing. In the final substantive section, I turn to the remark to which the title of this piece alludes ('It is – contrary to Köhler – precisely a meaning that I see', RPP I 869).

I begin, though, with a few reminders of some of the main concepts of Gestalt psychology by means of which it describes the perceived world.[3] The most basic notion in Gestalt psychology is that of 'organisation'. This term points us in the direction of what the Gestalt psychologists call 'circumscribed units': 'In most visual fields the contents of particular areas "belong together" as circumscribed units from which their surroundings are excluded' (Köhler 1929/47, 80–1), for instance, 'things: a piece of paper, a pencil, an eraser, a cigarette, and so forth' (1929/47, 81). Gestalten essentially possess a figure-ground structure. A 'circumscribed unit' (the figure) is segregated from its surroundings (the ground), the figure having 'the character of solidity or substantiality', the ground being 'loose or empty' and 'unshaped' (1929/47, 120). The Gestalt psychologists did a great deal of work on what they called 'the constancies': the fact that perceived objects maintain their perceived size, shape, colour, etc. through variations in distance, orientation, lighting, and so on (hence they spoke of 'size constancy', 'shape constancy', 'colour constancy', etc.). Their descriptive concepts range far more widely than this, but this is enough to get us started.

i Various Uses of 'See'

I begin by reminding readers of Wittgenstein's two uses of 'see', and point out that the contrast is understood by commentators in different ways. In particular, the non-aspect-seeing use is understood differently, such that there is a case for identifying at least three uses of 'see' which play a role in Wittgenstein's discussions of perception and aspect-perception. The pay-off from making all these seemingly fine distinctions comes in Section ii.

---

[3] I here intentionally speak of Gestalt psychology's 'descriptions' of the perceived world, by contrast with 'explanations'; Wittgenstein also had criticisms of Köhler's explanations (for example, isomorphisms in the brain), but I leave these aside for present purposes, and indeed only touch on a tiny handful of his criticisms of Köhler's descriptions. The phrase 'perceived world' intentionally echoes the phenomenologists and particularly Merleau-Ponty, with whom I bring Wittgenstein into dialogue very gently later in this essay, but more vigorously elsewhere (see, for instance, Morris 2007, 2017).

Wittgenstein's Two Uses of 'See'

Wittgenstein's best-known treatment of the Gestalt psychologists' descriptions occurs in his remarks on aspect-seeing in chapter xi of what was posthumously published first as 'Part II' of the *Investigations* and later, in a revised edition of this work, as *Philosophy of Psychology — A Fragment*.[4] Of particular interest to him, at least initially, are what the Gestalt psychologists call 'reversals' in ambiguous drawings, that is, drawings which spontaneously admit of different organisations. Wittgenstein reproduces a number of such drawings, including most famously the duck–rabbit. He speaks of the different organisations of these drawings as 'aspects' and of reversals as 'changes of aspect'. What appears to strike Wittgenstein about reversals is a kind of paradox, which he expresses thus: 'One would like to say: "Something has altered, and nothing has altered"' (RPP I §966).[5]

One of Wittgenstein's central objections to Köhler (see, for instance, RPP I §1023) is that he supposes that we see organisation *in the same sense* in which we see colours and shapes, hence that what one sees changes in a change of aspect *in the same sense* in which what one sees would change were the colours and shapes to alter. (A change in organisation 'amounts to an actual transformation of given sensory facts into others', writes Köhler; 1929/47, 99.) However, this not only involves a conflation, it leaves Köhler unable either to express or dissolve the 'paradox', because there is no sense, in this case, in which *everything* remains the same. Wittgenstein claims (rightly or wrongly) that to 'put the "organisation" of a visual impression on a level with colours and shapes' is to proceed 'from the idea of the visual impression as an inner object' (PI II 196 / PPF §134). Thus he imagines Köhler saying that the 'outer picture'—for example, the drawing of the duck–rabbit—has remained the same while the 'inner picture' has changed. However, one ought to be able to *represent* the 'inner picture' with a drawing (an 'outer picture'); but if one tried to represent what the duck–rabbit was like before the change of aspect and what it is like now simply by

---

[4] As Graham McFee (1999, 265) rightly points out, unlike other passages where Wittgenstein discusses aspect-seeing, only what was posthumously published as PI II/PPF had been 'prepared with a view to publication'.

[5] The more famous of Wittgenstein's expressions of the apparent paradox of aspect-change, 'I *see* that it has not changed and yet I see it differently' (PI II 193 / PPF §113), may mislead us (and did momentarily mislead Mulhall 2010, 255 and possibly Baz 2010, 232) into thinking that the two uses of 'see' in this sentence are the two uses which begin his discussion. In fact, the italicised 'see' is properly understood as 'I see that *what I see* (in one use of "see") has not changed'.

making an exact *copy* of what one sees in each case, 'no change is shewn' (PI
II 196 / PPF §131; see also PI §196 and RPP I §1041).

Wittgenstein suggests that the phenomena of aspect-seeing and change
of aspect point to 'the difference of category between the two "objects" of
sight' (PI II 193 / PPF §111), corresponding to 'two uses of the word "see"',
which he exemplifies thus: '"I see *this*" (and then a description, a drawing,
a copy)' as opposed to 'I see a likeness between these two faces' (PI II 193 /
PPF §111; see also RPP I §964). How do these exemplars relate to changes
of aspect? We have seen already that any attempt to represent the 'before'
and 'after' in a change of aspect with a drawing or copy would show no
difference; rather, one might (for example) convey the change by first
grouping the drawing with a number of other drawings of ducks, and
then with a number of drawings of rabbits (see PI II 196–7 / PPF §137), and
calling attention to the likenesses in each case. Once we have distinguished
these two uses of the word 'see', the apparent paradox vanishes: what you
see in the first use of the word 'see' does not change, whereas what you see
in the second use changes.

There is no doubt a very great deal more to be said. However, I want to
leave it at this, in order to pursue another point. This is that there seems
to be some lack of clarity—both in Wittgenstein's texts and amongst
commentators—about how exactly to understand the other use of 'see',
that with which 'seeing aspects' is contrasted. Some commentators take
the 'objects' of sight in this use to be ordinary objects such as trees (see,
for example, Schulte 1987/93, 82, and Köhler's 'things: a piece of paper,
a pencil, an eraser, a cigarette, and so forth', 1929/47, 81); this seems like
a fairly natural way to read Wittgenstein's '"I see *this*" (and then a
description, a drawing, a copy)'. Others take the objects of sight here to
be 'shapes and colours' (for example, Mulhall 2010, 263); there is a good
deal of textual evidence for this reading, for instance, 'If I saw the duck–
rabbit as a rabbit, then I saw: these shapes and colours (I give them in
detail), and I saw besides something like this: and here I point to
a number of pictures of rabbits' (PI II 196 / PPF §137). (In fact, the
phrase 'shapes and colours' occurs very frequently in Wittgenstein's
discussions of aspect-seeing.)

How important is this difference? Avner Baz, for example, suggests that
the objects of sight in this use are 'what we ordinarily describe, report,
inform another person of, alert someone to, ask a question about' (Baz
2010, 231). This neutral way of putting it may characterise both everyday
objects like trees and 'shapes and colours'; I can call someone's attention to
that tree, or to the colour of its leaves; I can ask 'What kind of tree is that?'

or 'What do you call that colour?' So maybe there's nothing here worth worrying about.

However, I want to suggest that there is a way of understanding these two interpretations such that they do indeed mark a significant contrast; arguably, they point to two different uses of 'see', both distinguishable from Wittgenstein's aspect-seeing sense. Moreover, the contrast they mark is one that Köhler saw as enormously important. I will label these two uses 'seeing shapes and colours' and 'seeing things', but it must be borne in mind that these labels are quasi-technical, corresponding to a distinction drawn by Köhler between the 'analytic' and the 'normal' attitude of perceiving, brought out in the next subsection.

'Seeing Shapes and Colours' and 'Seeing Things'

A great deal of Köhler's *Gestalt Psychology* is polemical, arguing against the empiricist psychology which then dominated the field. The form of empiricist psychology most important for our purposes is what was known as introspectionism, whose basic premise is 'the all-important distinction between *sensations* and *perceptions*, between the bare sensory material as such and the host of other ingredients with which this material has become imbued by processes of learning' (Köhler 1929/47, 43). On this view, the sensation is 'the genuine sensory fact', by contrast with 'mere products of learning' (1929/47, 44). Central to introspectionism is what Köhler labelled 'the constancy hypothesis', according to which 'the characteristics of true sensory experience depend only upon corresponding characteristics of peripheral stimuli' (1929/47, 55).

The implications of this hypothesis are wide-ranging. It clearly struggles with 'reversals', in which 'with a constant pattern of [retinal] stimuli, we may see . . . two different shapes' (1929/47, 107). But its implications go well beyond this. It implies that we cannot strictly speaking see depth (distance, three-dimensionality), since the image on the retina is two-dimensional. It also implies that none of the 'constancies' (of size, shape, colour, and so on) are strictly speaking seen. The introspectionists claimed that since the projection on the retina of a cow moving away from us gets smaller, what we strictly speaking see is a smaller shape, not a cow of the same size who is getting further away;[6] since the projection on the retina of a tilted circular plate is elliptical, what we strictly speaking see is an

---

[6] Father Ted, to Father Dougal: 'These [toy cows] are *small* . . . but the ones [the real cows] out there are *far away*'. (Thanks, Ian Ground.)

elliptical shape, not a circular plate which is tilted; since different rods and cones are stimulated by the bits of the cushion which are in shadow rather than by those which are well-lit, what we strictly speaking see is a whole variety of colours, not a uniformly coloured cushion.

Moreover, these empiricist psychologists developed an arsenal of laboratory techniques to enable us to get past the learning which interferes with our awareness of what we strictly speaking see. If you look at the retreating cow through a cardboard tube, you will see it shrinking; if you look at the tilted plate through a screen with an elliptical hole cut into it, you will see its elliptical shape; if you squint and shade your eyes when you look at the bit of the cushion that is in shadow, you will see a different colour than you see if you look in this manner at a bit of the cushion that is in the light. All this (strange as it may seem to us today) amounts to techniques for gaining practice in 'introspection'. (Of course, we don't necessarily need to employ such techniques in order to see what the empiricist psychologists say we 'really' see; many of these are techniques which we employ quite spontaneously for various purposes, and painters often use them in their effort to capture 'what they see' on the canvas.)

On this basis, the Gestalt psychologists drew a distinction between the 'analytical' and the 'normal' attitude in perception (see Köhler 1929/47, 47 and 99; see also RPP I §§1110–12).[7] In the analytical attitude, we see what the introspectionists say we strictly speaking see, and their techniques may, through their decontextualisation and laboratory setting, get us into this attitude, but in our ordinary lives, we normally see three-dimensional objects which exhibit constancies of size, shape, and colour and which appear as figures against grounds. The introspectionist unjustifiably reads the experience we have while adopting the analytical attitude into that which we have when taking the normal attitude in perception (Köhler 1929/47, 52; see also 102; and Merleau-Ponty 1945, 9/8 and 38 n.19 / 505 n.26). It is this distinction, between what we see in the analytical and the normal attitude in perception, which I aim to capture by those quasi-technical phrases 'seeing shapes and colours' and 'seeing things' respectively.[8]

---

[7] To be sure, Köhler did not think of the 'analytical' and 'normal' 'attitudes' as corresponding to different uses of the word 'see' (this indeed is one of Wittgenstein's complaints); nonetheless, they arguably do, and Köhler deserves credit for calling attention to the phenomena that inspired the philosophical reflections that show this.

[8] Wittgenstein is as resistant as Köhler to the empiricist temptation to say we don't (strictly speaking) *see* aspects: 'If someone wanted to correct me and say I don't really see [these things, but only shapes and colours], I should hold this to be a piece of stupidity' (RPP I §1101). (In this passage Wittgenstein

Moreover, at times at least, Wittgenstein clearly recognises that there is an important distinction between 'seeing shapes and colours' and 'seeing things'; indeed he accuses Köhler of failing to see how different these two uses are, using arguments which are in some ways parallel to those he uses to argue for the difference between 'seeing shapes and colours' and 'seeing aspects'. Thus he reflects on Köhler's commitment to the idea that 'object' (figure) and 'ground' are 'visual concepts like red and round' (RPP I §1023). (See also: 'Indeed, you may well say: what belongs to the description of what you see, of your visual impression, is not merely what the copy shews but also the claim, e.g., to see this "solid", this other "as intervening space"', RPP I §1118.) Wittgenstein suggests that if one were to ask what, in a drawing, 'corresponded to the words "object-like"', the answer would be 'the sequence, the order, in which we made the drawing', which is not *in* the drawing in the sense that the colours and shapes are (see RPP I §1023). Elsewhere, Wittgenstein considers the question of whether *depth* can 'really be seen' (RPP I §85); he goes on to suggest that the sense in which we see colour and shape and the sense in which we see depth are different senses, the one perhaps to be represented 'using a transparency', the other 'by means of a gesture or profile' (see also RPP I §86).

Are there then three uses of 'see' here? Well, consider one of the reasons which Wittgenstein offers for saying that 'seeing shapes and colours' involves a different use of 'see' than 'seeing aspects': namely, the fact that 'an aspect is subject to the will', that is, that 'it makes no sense to say "See it red"; whereas it does make sense to say "See it as . . ."' (RPP I §899)—at least to ask someone to *try* to see it as . . . —which 'touches the essence' of aspect-seeing (see RPP I §976).[9] We might suggest that the analytical attitude may also be understood as 'subject to the will'; the various techniques which introspectionists ask us to adopt in order to 'see shapes and colours' could, precisely, be understood in this way. (To be sure, we cannot say 'See it red', but we can say 'See it as shapes and colours as opposed to seeing it as a thing [and these techniques may help you to do so]'.) By contrast, we do not normally *try* to see *things*: this *is* the 'normal attitude' in perception. (This is one reason for the peculiarity of saying, at

is actually referring to seeing facial expressions, but it is clear that he would say the same thing about standard cases of 'aspects'.) I take it that it is (and that Wittgenstein would agree that it is) equally 'a piece of stupidity' to hold that we don't really see *things*, but only shapes and colours (although I would also add that both of these are pieces of stupidity which have evidently tempted people very powerfully, and which merit more than mere dismissal as pieces of stupidity for that very reason).
9 Wittgenstein presents as a further criticism of Köhler that he 'does not deal with' (RPP I §971) the fact that aspect-seeing is subject to the will.

the sight of a knife and fork, 'Now I am seeing this as a knife and fork', PI II 195 / PPF §122.) This sounds like *a* reason for taking 'seeing shapes and colours' and 'seeing things' as indicating different uses. No doubt 'the concept of "seeing" makes a tangled impression' (PI II 200 / PPF §160). No doubt, too, there are all kinds of intermediate cases.[10] Still, there seem to be reasons, for certain purposes at least, for distinguishing between *three* uses of 'see' here.

ii   Looking at the World and Looking at Pictures

We might be struck by the fact that whereas much of the discussion around aspect-seeing concerns pictures, much of the discussion around seeing things concerns the world. But it may be suggested that the distinction between the three uses of 'see' applies equally, and in the same way, to looking at the world and looking at pictures. This section makes a few tentative observations in connection with this suggestion.[11]

Looking at the World

We have seen already that the distinction between 'seeing shapes and colours' and 'seeing things' was originally developed (by Köhler) not in connection with pictures but in connection with the world. So one question is: is seeing aspects confined to pictures, or can we also talk of seeing aspects in the world? At the least we can say this: that we frequently encounter perceptual ambiguity in the world. Of course we can talk about an actual three-dimensional wire cube which is ambiguous in the manner of the Necker cube, but there are myriad less artificial cases. For example, Strawson describes a situation in which he is 'looking towards a yellow flowering bush against a stone wall, but I see it as yellow chalk marks scrawled on the wall. Then the aspect changes and I see it normally, that is I see it as a yellow flowering bush against the wall' (1970, 57–8). Strawson's use of the word 'aspect' here goes along with his argument that all seeing is aspect-seeing. And, indeed, can't we imagine saying in these cases 'Something has altered, and nothing has altered'? And doesn't this suggest that Strawson is right to use the word 'aspect' here?

[10] Strawson (1970) makes much of intermediate cases regarding the different uses of 'see' that I have discussed.
[11] Some of the reflections here started life several years ago during conversations with some of the other participants in the second Wittgenstein Colloquium at Porto Alegre, in May 2013, at which I presented an early version of Morris 2017.

Well, first, we might note that it is part of what it is to be-in-the-world (to borrow a phrase from the phenomenologists) that the world contains such ambiguities (as well as indeterminacies, vaguenesses, and so on). 'Being is synonymous with being situated' (Merleau-Ponty 1945, 294/251); and things are given to situated beings perspectivally, so that there are always unseen sides, always more to explore, with our hands or with our gaze. The being of an object is 'a being-for the gaze which meets it at a certain angle, and otherwise fails to recognise it' (1945, 295/253): things looked at from odd angles (see PI II 198 / PPF §151) or out of the corner of our eye lack their normal 'physiognomy'. The 'being of an object' is also a 'being-for the gaze' which meets it at a certain optimal distance: increasing distance means 'that the thing is beginning to slip away from the grip of our gaze' (1945, 304/261). Thus the man who is further away does not look smaller; rather, he 'is a much less distinguishable figure, . . . he presents fewer and less identifiable points on which my eyes can fasten, . . . he is less strictly geared to my powers of exploration' (1945, 304/261). Distance can generate ambiguity: 'If I walk along a shore towards a ship which has run aground, and the funnel or masts merge into the forest bordering on the sand dune, there will be a moment when these details suddenly become part of the ship' (1945, 20/17–18), whereas until that moment they are ambiguous and might equally be part of the forest. It is crucial for this ambiguity that the ship's masts are at a non-optimal distance from me so that I cannot yet fully explore them with my gaze. Strawson plausibly suggests that someone with better eyesight might not have seen the chalk-marks 'aspect', and one might suggest that short-sightedness is (phenomenologically as well as etymologically) connected to distance (to be short-sighted just is for optimal distances to be 'objectively' shorter).[12]

At the same time, such ambiguities are crucially *un*like ambiguities in pictures. In the first place, ambiguities in the world have, in some sense, a 'right' reading (those things are ships' masts, not trees; those other things are roses, not chalk marks, etc.). By contrast, we can't possibly suppose that either the duck or the rabbit is the 'right' way to read the picture. And in the second place, they are in principle resolvable; that is, we can often establish what the right reading is, precisely because we are situated in the world and can move about in it and explore things more closely and from different angles. (Obviously we can get closer to a picture or stand further back, and this can make certain kinds of difference. It can certainly make

---

[12] I don't mean to suggest that only distance creates ambiguity in the world; it just happens that both Merleau-Ponty's and Strawson's cases can both be understood in this way.

the difference between seeing shapes and colours and seeing things in pictures: there is an optimal distance to stand from Monet's water-lily paintings, when suddenly they become depictions of things. Again, *sometimes* standing closer to a picture can enable one to establish that this or that detail is, for example, a tree or a ship's mast. However, were Strawson or Merleau-Ponty to paint 'what they saw' in the cases described, no amount of standing closer to the painting could establish the 'right' reading, any more than standing closer to the duck–rabbit could do so.) It is because Merleau-Ponty is walking towards the ship—that is, the distance between him and it is decreasing—that 'these details suddenly become part of the ship' and not part of the forest. Now, Strawson suggests that his 'aspect-switch' just happened; but didn't he move a little closer, or squint his eyes a bit (which effectively slightly 'lengthens' the sight)?

So, finally, it's not clear that in such cases we could say 'Something has altered, and nothing has altered'. *Everything* has altered: I have moved closer or squinted my eyes or whatever, *and* I now see ships' masts or a rose bush. Thus we have some reason, at least, to say that aspect-seeing is confined to pictures and is not to be found in the world. And by the same token, we have some reason to reject those commentators (like Strawson) who wish to identify 'seeing things' (in the world) with 'continuous aspect-seeing'.[13]

Of course, there are numerous other kinds of cases where we might well say (of things in the world) 'Something has altered, and nothing has altered': an ordinary cottage which we subsequently discover to have been the childhood home of Isaac Newton; the smile of someone whom we used to like and have come to loathe, etc. Here, our reasons for resisting talking of aspect-seeing and a change of aspect may be different: for example, such changes would not *suddenly* strike us; perception of such changes would not naturally be expressed as '*Now* her smile looks false!' (just 'Now her smile looks false'); it is also doubtful that we can switch *between* the 'before' and 'after' 'at will'; and we would anyway be reluctant to talk about ambiguity in such cases. None of this is meant to *demonstrate* that we cannot talk of aspect-seeing when it comes to the world; it is simply meant to call attention to differences.

---

[13] Strawson's view sits uncomfortably with Wittgenstein's observation that it is hard to make sense of saying 'Now I am seeing this as a knife and fork' at the sight of a knife and fork (PI II 195 / PPF §122). He is of course well aware of this, and supposes that 'Wittgenstein was perhaps *over*-impressed by the cases where we are *suddenly* struck by something' (1970, 58, italics in the original).

Looking at Pictures

The distinction Wittgenstein usually makes in connection with pictures is that between seeing shapes and colours and seeing aspects. Yet clearly, at least when it comes to so-called representational pictures, a distinction between seeing shapes and colours and seeing things has some application. We can just about imagine someone who sees pictures *only* in terms of shapes and colours, and never in terms of things (see Mulhall 2010, 263), but even apart from such unusual cases, we are capable (with or without consciously adopting the introspectionists' techniques) of *focusing* just on the 'shapes and colours'. Indeed, as we have noted, some paintings, for example, some of Monet's water lilies, are such that it can be difficult at first to discern anything other than shapes and colours.

However, it may be suggested that we never *simply* see things in paintings, as we may simply see things in the world: such is the burden of Wollheim's (at least more recent) view (see, for instance, Wollheim 2001). (Only of a *trompe l'œil* painting can we say that we *simply* see a thing in a painting. Even then, it is only very briefly and from a very limited standpoint, for reasons linked to the remarks about our insertion in the world: the moment we begin to explore the thing in a *trompe l'œil* painting—stand closer to it, try to move around it, etc.—we stop seeing it *simply* as a thing.)[14] Rather, according to Wollheim, we engage in a kind of 'double-seeing', of both the painted surface and the thing represented; in my terms, in some way or another, we normally *both* see shapes and colours *and* see things (simultaneously and interwovenly, on Wollheim's view) when we look at paintings. To the extent that Wollheim is at least getting at something right, and to the extent that his 'seeing the painted surface' is comparable to my 'seeing shapes and colours', this suggests a further crucial distinction between looking at the world and looking at paintings.

Importantly, there are analogies too: for instance, as Wittgenstein points out, 'in some respects I stand towards it [a picture-face] as I do towards a human face. I can study its expression, can react to it as to the expression of the human face' (PI II 194 / PPF §119). Indeed, 'we *regard* the photograph, the picture on the wall, as the object itself (the man, landscape, and so on) depicted there' (PI II 205 / PPF §197), which is not to say, of course, that we *mistake* the thing in the picture for the thing in the world, as Stephen Mulhall (2010, 263) points out. And as he further points out,

---

[14] Wollheim concludes that *trompe l'œil* isn't a species of representation (see, for example, Wollheim 2001); one can make the point I have made without going this far.

Wittgenstein's explicit cases of what he calls 'continuous aspect-seeing'— in which, for example, I 'have seen the duck–rabbit simply as a picture-rabbit from the first' (PI II 194 / PPF §120)—are cases in which I *regard* the picture-rabbit as a rabbit, in this sense of 'regard as'. At this stage, it may be tempting to say, as indeed Mulhall does, that seeing things in pictures is continuous aspect-seeing.

We might prefer to say that 'aspect-seeing' should be reserved for those pictures where 'we know that it can also be seen differently' (RPP I §1); as Graham McFee points out (citing PI II 195 / PPF §121), Wittgenstein only seems to talk of 'continuous aspect-seeing' from a third-person perspective such that *we* know that a picture can be seen differently but the person who is stuck in one aspect can't see the other (see McFee 1999, 277).[15] Moreover, if aspects are, as Wittgenstein claims, 'subject to the will', then it should be possible to 'try to see a conventional picture of a lion as a lion' (PI II 206 / PPF §203). — Well, *isn't* it possible? Mulhall's person who sees pictures *only* in terms of shapes and colours, and never in terms of things, may try, and fail, in just this kind of case; likewise many of us when faced with a Monet water-lily painting (I take it that this still counts as a 'conventional' painting of water lilies: 'conventional', I think, just means 'unambiguous' here). But this doesn't imply that seeing the lion in a conventional lion painting is seeing an aspect; rather, it implies that in certain circumstances, seeing a *thing* in a *painting* can be 'subject to the will' (compare the earlier suggestion that 'seeing shapes and colours', in the context of seeing the world, is subject to the will, since our normal mode of perception is that of seeing things).

Thus it seems to me that a good deal of the disagreement amongst commentators might be alleviated if we distinguish, first, between seeing shapes and colours, seeing things, and seeing aspects, and distinguish, secondly, between the way that these operate (or not) in connection with looking at the world and in connection with looking at pictures. There are, to be sure, innumerable further distinctions we could make; I have, for example, said nothing whatsoever about seeing human beings, or faces, or expressions; nor have I said anything about seeing meanings in words. But the aim of the distinctions drawn here is simply to introduce some clarity into some of the discussion of these issues, not to sketch out the 'logical geography' of 'see'.

---

[15] Of course, someone who is 'blind' to things-in-a-painting will also be aspect-blind (if one cannot, in the relevant sense, regard a picture-rabbit as a rabbit, then one cannot switch from this to seeing the drawing as a duck and regarding the picture-duck as a duck), but why should someone not be able to regard a picture-rabbit as a rabbit and still be aspect-blind?

iii   Seeing Meanings

'It is – contrary to Köhler – precisely a meaning that I see [when I see an aspect]' (RPP I §869). I will not try to assess this as a criticism of Köhler. I simply want to suggest a way of reading the word 'meaning' in this remark. In using this word here, I submit, Wittgenstein is moving beyond the question of 'what *counts as* seeing shapes and colours, seeing things, seeing aspects' towards the question of 'what seeing shapes and colours, seeing things, seeing aspects *count as*';[16] that is, he is moving towards their significance, the role they play in our lives.[17]

So, finally, I want to make two suggestions: first, that 'to see shapes and colours' in the quasi-technical sense sketched here is, precisely, not 'to see a meaning'; and secondly, that we 'see a meaning' not only when we see aspects but when we see things (and this whether we are looking at pictures or looking at the world).

As for the first suggestion, that 'to see shapes and colours' in the sense sketched here is, precisely, *not* 'to see a meaning': the whole aim of the introspectionists' exercise is to decontextualise what we see, and thereby to *deprive* what we perceive of meaning or significance. Note that in saying this, I do not mean to suggest that 'seeing shapes and colours' in an *everyday* sense—as part of the stream of life, in 'normal' as opposed to 'analytic' perception—is not 'seeing a meaning'. Consider the following observations by Merleau-Ponty (who is far more eloquent than Wittgenstein on, as Merleau-Ponty puts it, 'colour in living [as opposed to analytic] perception', 1945, 355/305). A colour has a physiognomy: my fountain pen 'is black'; this blackness is not so much a 'sensible quality' as 'a sombre power which radiates from the object' even when it is reflecting the sun's rays (1945, 356/305). And corresponding to the perceptual physiognomy of colour is a 'motor physiognomy' whereby a colour is 'enveloped in a living significance' (1945, 243/209), 'a type of behavior which is directed towards it in its essence' (1945, 245/211). Merleau-Ponty invites us to 'rediscover how to live these colours as our body does, that is, as peace or

---

[16]   I owe to Anniken Greve this way of putting the contrast ('what *counts as* seeing shapes and colours, seeing things, seeing aspects' vs. 'what seeing shapes and colours, seeing things, seeing aspects *count as*').

[17]   This use of 'meaning' will be familiar to those in the phenomenological tradition, but Wittgenstein himself, at least sometimes, clearly uses it in something like this way (for instance: 'The characteristic feature of the awakening mind of man is precisely the fact that a phenomenon comes to have meaning for him', PO 129). The context for the remark that I have discussed provides no clue about the meaning of 'meaning', so I make no apologies for the speculativeness of my suggestion in the text.

violence in concrete form' (1945, 245/211).[18] But none of this will reveal itself to analytic perception.

I will expand on the second suggestion at slightly greater length. Wittgenstein often gets at meaning (as I am understanding it here) by asking what would be missing from the life of someone who was 'blind' to such things (PI II 214 / PPF §261; see also RPP I §202 and LPP 181–2). Following the distinction made in the previous section, let us first ask this question in connection with seeing pictures. Here we can be brief, because this is relatively well-worn territory. (I don't mean to suggest that all that can be said here has been said, only that I want to devote more of the space remaining to the under-explored 'meaning' of *things*.) If it is right, as I suggested in the previous section, to confine aspect-seeing to pictures, then Wittgenstein's (hypothetical) individuals who are 'aspect-blind' belong in this part of the discussion. The aspect-blind person is someone who never sees anything *as* anything (see RPP II §478 and PI II 213 / PPF §257), who can 'gather various things about the landscape' from a photograph but cannot exclaim 'What a glorious view!' (RPP I §168); we might 'picture him as making a less lively impression than we do, behaving more "like an automaton"' (RPP I §198), 'as it were sleep-walking' (RPP I §178). (Compare: the impression made by the 'meaning-blind' man might be described as 'prosaic', RPP I §342.) I want to say that the *world* of the aspect-blind person (likewise Mulhall's person who is 'thing-blind' in respect of pictures) is 'less lively', more 'prosaic', than ours.[19] To be blind to such things is to lose that dimension of experience which gives life its magic and enchantment.

What about seeing the world? Can we imagine someone who is 'thing-blind'? It is noteworthy that Wittgenstein does occasionally use the term 'gestalt-blind' (*Gestaltblinde*) (see, for instance, RPP II §478; see also RPP I §170, where it is translated as 'form-blind' although Wittgenstein sometimes equates 'gestalt-blind' with 'aspect-blind', for example at RPP II §478). In this case, Wittgenstein imagines a man with 'the talent to copy objects . . . very exactly, and yet he might keep on making small mistakes against sense; so that one could say "He doesn't grasp an object as an object"' (RPP I §983; see also RPP I §§ 423 and 978). But we might also think of the brain-injured patient Schneider, discussed at length by

---

[18] Merleau-Ponty also speaks of the physiognomy of shapes (although less poetically than he speaks of the physiognomy of colour); see, for instance, Merleau-Ponty 1945, 70/61 and 448/385.

[19] I can't here discuss Severin Schroeder's interpretation of aspect-blindness in detail (2010, 366ff); however, his discussion of 'emotional seeing-as' (even if he wishes to deny that this is 'really seeing') might have some resonances here.

Merleau-Ponty (1945, 151/131). When presented with a fountain pen and simply asked what it is,

> the phases of recognition are as follows. 'It is black, blue and shiny,' says the patient. 'There is a white patch on it, and it is rather long . . . It may be some sort of instrument. It shines and reflects light. It could also be a coloured glass.' The pen is then brought closer and the clip is turned towards the patient. He goes on: 'It must be a pencil or a fountain pen.' (He touches his breast pocket.) 'It is put there, to make notes with'.

Merleau-Ponty comments: 'The patient, like the scientist, verifies mediately and clarifies his hypothesis by cross-checking facts, and makes his way blindly towards the one which coordinates them all', whereas 'in the normal subject the object "speaks" and is significant, the arrangement of colours straight away "means" something' (1945, 151/131). This is surely a real-life case of thing-blindness, of someone who sees *only* 'shapes and colours'; 'the world no longer has any *physiognomy* for him' (1945, 151–2/131–2).[20]

iv   Concluding Remarks

What I have tried to do here is, in a modest way, to contextualise Wittgenstein's remarks on aspect-seeing in connection with his reading of Köhler, and thereby to contextualise them within a wider discussion of seeing. I noted that most commentators devote little attention to the use of 'see' with which aspect-seeing is contrasted, and that it tends to be interpreted in the literature in two contrasting ways. I suggested that these two ways could be lined up with Köhler's distinction between 'analytic' and 'normal' modes of perception, corresponding to the quasi-technical distinction between 'seeing shapes and colours' and 'seeing things'. I argued that Wittgenstein's 'aspect-seeing' use of 'see' contrasts interestingly differently with each of these. I further suggested that the ways in which these three uses of 'see' work is importantly different in the context of looking at pictures and looking at the world, and that such an exploration might help to clarify some of what is at issue between some commentators on these remarks.

Finally, I suggested that Wittgenstein's claim that seeing an aspect is 'seeing a meaning' may be understood as an invitation to contemplate what

---

[20]   Could we imagine someone who was blind to 'shapes and colours' and only saw things (in pictures; in the world)? And why not?

would be missing from the life of the aspect-blind. Moreover, I have suggested that seeing a *thing* is likewise 'seeing a meaning'. In a way, this is the real point of this essay: if we contemplate the world of the thing-blind—a world without physiognomies, a faceless world—we may find ourselves less contemptuous of 'ordinary perception' of 'mere things'.[21]

[21] An earlier version of this essay was presented as the Annual British Wittgenstein Society Lecture at the Welsh Philosophical Society on 29 April 2017. I am extremely grateful for the comments and feedback I had on that occasion.

CHAPTER 6

Bringing the Phenomenal World into View

Avner Baz

Introduction: Travis's "Fundamental Question of Perception" and the Repression of the Phenomenal World

The fundamental question of perception, Charles Travis tells us, is this: "How can perceptual experience make the world bear (rationally) *for the perceiver* on what he is to think and do?" (Travis 2013, 3; see also 242). In taking *that* to be the fundamental question of perception—which means, I take it, the question that philosophers interested in perception should first and foremost attempt to answer—Travis is in very good company. It is the question that virtually all of the contemporary philosophers with whom he critically engages have attempted to answer as well. It is also the question that Western philosophers, at least since Kant (and arguably as early as Descartes), have taken to be fundamental.

It is worth asking why *that* is *the* fundamental question, or the *fundamental* question, that philosophers interested in *perception* should focus on. In asking this, I mean not merely to suggest that there might be other equally important and interesting questions for philosophers to ask about perception. Rather, I mean to suggest that there might be *better* questions—where by "better" I mean "less liable to mislead and more fruitful"—for philosophers interested in perception to ask, including philosophers who wish to become clearer about the relation between the world as it presents itself to us in perception and the world as represented in our thoughts, and in our justifications and rationalizations of our deeds. "Don't think, but look!" (PI §66), says Wittgenstein, whose work is one of Travis's main sources of inspiration. Might it not be better to follow Wittgenstein's general approach here—even if not quite his more specific procedures—and ask what, if anything, can truly be said in general terms about how human perceivers and thinkers *do* (normally, and abnormally) relate to the world *as perceived and responded to* prior to being reflected upon theoretically or becoming the object of true or false judgments or thoughts? Isn't it obvious, and indeed as self-evident and undeniable as our own existence, that we find ourselves always already *situated*, which means perceptually related not just to the world *of* which we think and speak but to a world *in* which we think and speak (a world that elicits words and other behavioral responses from us and against the background of which they acquire whatever sense, or rationality, they have for us)? Even what we attend to and try to capture with our words—and so, if you will, that *of* which we think (judge, speak) truly or falsely—must somehow be present to us perceptually, however indeterminately, prior to becoming the object of a thought; for otherwise, it could not *draw* our attention, nor be something we could *try* to put into words.

Call the world *as perceived and responded to* prior to being *thought*, or thought (or talked) *about*, *"the phenomenal world."* A fundamental problem with Travis's "fundamental" question—at least as Travis and most of his contemporary interlocutors understand it, and as it *needs* to be understood in order to seem *fundamental* —would then be that it is liable to block that world, and our perceptual relation to it, from coming into view.

In recent years, and largely under the influence of John McDowell's appropriation of Kant and Sellars, the philosophical repression of the phenomenal world—which is nothing less than a repression of the world in which we first and foremost find ourselves, including when we philosophize—has often taken the form of opposition to something called "the myth of the (pre-conceptual) given." One of the merits of Travis's work on perception is its powerful affirmation of the pre-conceptualized, perceptually given (to which our judgments may be more or less faithful, or else unfaithful). However, Travis too ends up repressing the phenomenal world and our relation to it in his account. He mostly uses "things," or "things being as they are," whenever he wishes to speak generally of what presents itself to us in perception prior to our making judgments or forming thoughts about it (see, for instance, 2013, 4), without giving any indication of how he thinks we relate perceptually to those "things"—as I've suggested we *must* —when we're not forming true or false thoughts about them. And whenever he needs to say something more specific about the pre-conceptualized, perceptually given, or give a concrete example, he switches to an objective, third-person perspective and talks about "objects in (or features of) the shared environment" (see 2013, 13, 85, 99, and 231), such as a pig or peccary on the path in front of the perceiver, or a chipmunk climbing down a tree (2013, 182, 191, 195, 225–6; see also 134 and 13). Of such objects Travis writes that they "can form images on retinas" (Travis 2013, 100; see also 2013, 19 and 248; and 2016, 5) and are "fully part of a world which is what it is independent of how we stand toward it" (2013, 227; see also 241).

In some moments, Travis seems to find patently absurd the idea that we play *any* role in the constitution, or shaping or unification, of what presents itself to us in perception (see, for instance, 2013, 20 and 257–8). But for the most part his thinking about this issue is framed by his "fundamental" question, and his argument is therefore only directed against the idea that what presents itself to us in perception is "conceptualized" in the sense of having the content (or structure) that an objective, empirical *judgment* might have (see 2013, 193–5 and 226–31). As Travis sees things, the attribution to what presents itself to us in perception of *that* sort of content (or structure), while aiming to secure the rationality of our judgments, actually leaves us with no coherent notion of perceptual *judgment* (understood as a stance, assessable in terms of truth and falsity, that we may take toward what presents itself to us in perception). And with *that* I have no disagreement. I believe Travis has shown conclusively, and I myself have argued elsewhere (see Baz 2003), that it actually makes no sense to think of what presents itself to us perceptually—*as perceptually presented*—as having the content of true or false judgments (Fregean "thoughts," Kantian "cognitions"), even apart from *our judging* (or otherwise *representing*) it to be some particular way or another in a context suitable for endowing our judgment (or representation) with a determinate sense (or content). One of the most important and far-reaching upshots of Travis's argument for the "context-sensitivity" of linguistic sense is that, with respect to the sort of content capturable in sentences of the general indicative form "Such and such is thus and so," what presents itself to us in perception is, as such, *indeterminate* (see especially 2013, 403).

What Travis overlooks is the possibility that we play a role in bringing about, and sustaining, *perceivable unity and sense that are not conceptual.*[1] Recognizing this role (or *power*) which we have, I will later propose, does not commit us to positing metaphysically private intermediaries between us and the perceived world. But in order to recognize *this*, we will need to bring the phenomenal world into view, and distinguish it from the objective world— or, more precisely, from the world as objectively understood—which we, together, construct on the basis, and against the background, of the phenomenal world.

---

[1] I speak of "unity" in order to register the fact that the different elements of the world as perceived *hang together* for us (in a way that I elaborate upon later in the essay). I speak of "sense" in order to register the fact that we (normally) *understand* the world as perceived—an understanding, I propose later, that may not aptly be thought of as conceptual—and respond to it, immediately and apart from any judgment, in ways that may be found more or less *appropriate* (fitting, skillful).

I should say that Travis's repression of the phenomenal world—his shift to the third-person, objectivist perspective whenever he needs to refer more specifically to what presents itself to us in perception—is not unmotivated. For one thing, it follows Wittgenstein's mistrust of phenomenology (for discussion, see Baz 2017; see also Travis 2016, 24). Another source of motivation for the repression is that if you think about language and linguistic expression as in the business, first and foremost, of representing the world truly or falsely—as Travis and most contemporary analytic philosophers do (but Wittgenstein did not)—then you are bound to find paradoxical any attempt to describe, or otherwise elucidate by means of words, the world as it presents itself to us in perception *apart from* being the object of true or false judgments (or thoughts). And even independently from any particular conception of language, there is the inherent difficulty of bringing into view and elucidating, without *thereby* distorting, the world as it presents itself to us in perception *before* we reflect on it (and on our relation to it) from a theoretical perspective. This last is just the inherent difficulty of phenomenology.

For all that, the suppression of the phenomenal world in Travis's work—and not *just* Travis's—is both internally problematic and phenomenologically untenable. To begin to see why it is internally problematic, ask yourself what exactly Travis is (or intends to be) referring to by "world," when he talks about "the world" that perception allows to be brought to bear (rationally) on what we are to think and do, or when he talks about the things we perceive as "fully part of a world which is what it is independent of how we stand toward it." He *might* have been talking about the phenomenal world.[2] As we shall see, however, the phenomenal world is *not* "independent of how we stand toward it."

Travis's talk of a world independent of how we stand toward it brings to mind the Kantian notion of "the world as it is in itself"—that is, the world as it is apart from how *we* perceive and make sense of it. But, as Kant has taught us, thinking of the world in which determinate objects such as pigs and chipmunks relate determinately to each other temporally and spatially (stand on the path in front of us, for example, or climb down trees)—not to mention causally (form images on retinas, for example)—as a world as it is in itself, leads to philosophical nonsense and impasse. In other words, it makes no sense to think of our empirical concepts—of size, location, and

---

[2] Indeed, the phenomenal world is, I will ultimately propose, the world to which our empirical judgments or thoughts may be found more or less faithful, as well as the world against the background of which they acquire whatever sense they have for us.

direction, for example, or of cause and effect—as applying to the world apart from *human judgment* and the shared background against which particular judgments have their particular sense. Travis's work, not only on perception but also on "context-sensitivity" in the philosophy of language, has in fact helped to underscore and deepen this important Kantian lesson (see Baz 2017, chapter 4).

This seems to leave us with the objective, empirical world as the intended referent of Travis's "world." However, by Travis's own lights (2013, 18; 2016, 12), and as Kant has taught us to recognize, *that* world— again, the world in which temporally enduring objects, with their determinate properties, stand in determinate temporal and spatial relations to each other—is constituted by our judgments, against a background of shared practices and standards of measurement, experimentation, calibration, collection of and appeal to evidence, and so on. Though independent of how any particular *individual* might stand toward it (this is just what is intended by calling this world "objective"), the objective world is *not* independent of how *we*—all those who, in practice, accept and respect the abovementioned practices and standards—communally stand, and have stood, toward it. It therefore makes no sense, given the framework of Travis's discussion, to think of *that* world as present to us perceptually *prior* to judgment, and as that to which our judgments are to be true.

I said that the suppression of the phenomenal world was also *phenomenologically* untenable. In Travis's case, the repressed phenomenal world emerges when he tries to accommodate the perception of what Wittgenstein calls "aspects" within the general framework of an answer to his "fundamental" question. I will argue in what follows that the perception of Wittgensteinian aspects cannot be accommodated within Travis's framework; and I will further argue that this reveals the limitations of that framework, precisely by forcing us to recognize and confront philosophically the phenomenal world and our relation to it. But before I argue for all of this, I want us to have before us Travis's answer to his "fundamental" question (partly because this answer seems to me to be correct as far as it goes).

Travis's Answer to His "Fundamental" Question

Travis's answer to his "fundamental" question is actually fairly simple (setting aside complications having to do with his critical engagement with, on the one hand, philosophers such as McDowell who read into the phenomenal world the sort of unity, structure, and sense paradigmatically belonging to empirical statements and, on the other, philosophers such as Tyler Burge who attribute truth- or correctness-evaluable representational content to subconscious states of our perceptual apparatus; see Burge 2005). Travis's answer is also fairly old—as I am going to suggest shortly—since it is essentially Kant's answer to that question. The answer, in a word, is *judgment* (understood as the "subsumption" of a "particular" under a "universal" or, in Travis's terminology, the subsumption of the world as it presents itself to us in perception under "concepts" or "generalities"). Travis's criticism of the two broad positions just mentioned—of the Burgean (see especially Travis 2013, 128) and of the McDowellian (see especially Travis 2013, 247)—could be summed up succinctly by saying that neither of them recognizes, or so much as allows for, the irreducible role judgment plays in moving us from perception to thought (or to true or false *representations* of what perception *presents* to us).

Perception, on Travis's account, presents us with "things" (or "things being as they are"). But it does not *represent* things to us *as being some particular way (or ways).*[3] It is *we*, human perceivers and "thinkers," who may *judge* things to be some particular ways and not others, where the "ways" here are "generalities" in the sense of being variously and indefinitely instantiable: for *any* particular way we may judge things to be, and *however precisely* we individuate that way, things could have been different in indefinitely many respects—though of course not in just *any* respect—and still correctly be judged to be *that* way (see Travis 2013, 187 and 269). A thought, as Travis uses that term, is a linguistically articulable, true or false *representation* of things as being some particular way. Concepts, in turn, are abstractable elements of thoughts, and inherit their generality (see 2013, 223 and 250).

In insisting on the irreducible role of judgment in bringing together two sharply distinct sources of empirical cognition—namely, generalities (or

---

[3] The claim that perception does not *represent* things to us *as being some particular way (or ways)*, is one important respect in which Travis's view *still* differs from McDowell's, even after the adjustments McDowell has made to his view since *Mind and World* (1994/6). For even though McDowell's current official position seems to commit him otherwise, he still talks of perceptual experience as if it presented things to us (competent speakers and reasoners) as being *some particular way (or ways)*—where the ways are capturable in indicative sentences of the general form "this or that is such and such." (For a fairly recent expression of this idea, see McDowell 2013b, 43.) For Travis, such determinate, propositional content is only brought into existence by way of human judgments, which in turn are dependent on suitable contexts for the determination of their content. Apart from human judgment, what presents itself to us in perception is, on Travis's view, *indeterminate* as far as propositional content goes. And this is crucially different from saying, as McDowell (still) does, that what presents itself to us in perception "*includes any* particular way it can be truly said to be" (McDowell 2013a, 346, my emphasis).

concepts) and their perceptually encountered instances—Travis may be seen as following in Kant's footsteps. When Travis says that "conceptual capacities are liable to rely ... on an irreducible *sense* for how the non-conceptual would connect to some given bit of the conceptual" (2013, 191), he is echoing Kant's saying in the third *Critique* that we must presuppose a "common sense ... as the necessary condition of the universal communicability of our cognition" (Kant 1790/3, §21/5:239); according to Kant, the successful communication of cognition requires "a relation between the imagination and the understanding in order to associate intuitions with concepts and concepts in turn with intuitions, which flow together into cognition" (1790/3, §40/5:295). And when Travis argues that "conceptual capacities *cannot* always reduce to recipes" (2013, 191; see also 184), he is in effect reiterating the upshot of Kant's infinite-regress-of-rules-for-the-application-of-rules argument in the first *Critique*, namely, that "judgment is a peculiar talent which can be practiced only, [but] cannot be taught" (Kant 1781/7, A133/B172). (This is arguably also one of the main upshots of Wittgenstein's remarks on rule-following in the *Investigations*.)

In Kant, "intuition" refers to the contribution that, on Travis's account, is made by perception to (an episode of) perceptual judgment: the Kantian intuition "can be given prior to all thought" (1781/7, B132, translation emended), puts us "immediately" into contact with its object (see 1781/7, A68/B93 and A320/B377), and is "single" or "singular" (A320/B377) precisely in the sense that, unlike a concept, it has no "reach" (Travis 2013, 192, 247)—that is, no instances falling under *it*. Concepts, for Kant as well as for Travis, are marked by their generality (see Kant 1781/7, A68/B93 and A106): they have indefinitely many instances that may be different from each other in indefinitely many respects (though, of course, not just in *any* respect). And for both Kant and Travis, what renders thoughts (and hence concepts) *meaningful* rather than "empty" is their possible connection (in judgment) to (what Kant calls) intuition, that is, their being assessable by the light of perceptually given, particular instances (see Kant 1781/7, A51/B75, A62/B87 and A339–40 / B298–9; and Travis 2013, 189 and 249). What Travis calls "thoughts" is what Kant calls "cognitions" (*Erkenntnisse*)—that is, in Kant's terminology, non-empty thoughts (which may be assessed in terms of truth and falsity by the light of the deliverances of intuition).

There is one important respect, however, in which Kant's account goes beyond anything that can be found in Travis's and which brings closer to view the phenomenal world: Kant recognizes—while, as I've noted above, Travis methodically ignores, and sometimes seems

committed to denying—the possibility (indeed, the reality) of perceivable *unity* and *sense* that are nonobjective and nonconceptual—unity
and sense, in other words, that could *not* sensibly be accompanied by
the Kantian "I think"—but which at the same time are not simply
given to us, for we play a role in enacting and sustaining them. So
Kant recognizes, while Travis seems committed to denying, the role *in
perception* of what Kant calls "productive" imagination (see Kant 1790/
3, §22/5:240 and, in contrast, Travis 2013, 257–8).

I am setting aside here the exegetical debate concerning the first
Critique, between those who maintain that, according to Kant, all of our
intuitions are "conceptualized" on pain of being "nothing to us" (see 1781/
7, B132) and those who maintain that, according to Kant, intuitions must
be subsumed under concepts *only* if they are to make a contribution to
cognition (see 1781/7, A111 and B144–5). When it comes to Kant's account of
beauty in the third *Critique*, at any rate, there can no longer be any
question that he recognizes the possibility (indeed, the reality) of nonobjective, nonconceptual unity and sense that are nonetheless genuinely
perceived (or "intuited") and *intersubjectively sharable*. For that is precisely
the possibility (and reality) of what Kant calls "beauty." The beautiful is
described by Kant as manifesting "aesthetic ideas"; and an aesthetic idea, he
says, is a "presentation of the imagination that compels [*veranlasst*] much
thinking, but to which no determinate thought whatsoever, i.e. no concept, can be adequate" (1790/3, §49/5:314, translation emended).
Moreover, while nonobjective and nonconceptual, the unity and sense
exhibited by the beautiful are not merely *given* to us: we play a role in
projecting and sustaining them, not by way of the application of concepts
in true or false judgments, but in the way we perceptually attend to the
object and take hold of it with our "productive and self-active" imagination
(Kant 1790/3, §22/5:240). Kant's anti-empiricist dictum that synthesis
comes before analysis—and that it is not mechanically given but, rather,
actively ("spontaneously") projected and sustained by the subject (see 1781/
7, B130)—therefore still holds true in the case of the perception of beauty as
he understands it; but the synthesis here does *not* take the form of empirical
judgment.

The same is true of the perception of what Wittgenstein calls "aspects"
(see Baz 2016a, 2016b). In the remaining three main sections of the present
essay, I will point out Travis's difficulties in accommodating the perception of Wittgensteinian aspects and propose that those difficulties stem
from Travis's general repression of the phenomenal world in his account of
perception.

The Difficulty Posed by Wittgensteinian Aspects to Travis's Account of Perception

Travis's answer to his "fundamental" question of perception is structured around three interrelated dichotomies that he derives from Frege: the first is that between objects in the environment that can form images on retinas— objects that are wholly independent of their perceivers and, in this sense, are "outside the mind" (see Travis 2013, 226–30)—and (metaphysically private) Fregean *Vorstellungen* (ideas, mental images), each of which has one and only one owner (see Travis 2013, 62ff, 82ff and 387); the second is that between what we are *passively* presented with in perception and our *response* to it, which for Travis is an act of *thought* or *judgment* (see 2013, 399); the third, which I have already discussed, is that between generalities and their perceptually encountered, *singular* instances. The perception of Wittgensteinian aspects gives trouble to each one of these three dichotomies. In this section, I will argue this with respect to the first and second dichotomies. In the next two sections, I will argue it with respect to the third. It should be kept in mind, though, that since Travis's dichotomies are interrelated, the difficulty presented by aspect perception to any one of them may only be fully appreciated by taking into account the difficulties it presents to the other two.

(The following discussion presupposes some familiarity on the part of the reader with Wittgenstein's remarks on aspects. For a more expository treatment of the grammatical and phenomenological features of aspects that I will be appealing to, see Baz 2016a; see also Katherine Morris's "Wittgenstein on 'Seeing Meanings,'" Chapter 5 in this volume.)

I begin with Travis's first Fregean dichotomy: the one between objects in the environment and Fregean *Vorstellungen*. One of Travis's central contentions is that only the former are proper objects of perception, and that failure to acknowledge this would lead us straightaway to positing objects of the second kind as objects of perception and the bases of perceptual judgments (see Travis 2013, 183), which he takes—correctly in my view—to be hopeless (see 2013, 193 and 387). In arguing for this claim, Travis repeatedly reminds us of the grammatical fact that "what someone saw is bounded by what there was, anyway, to be seen" (Travis 2013, 411; see also 2013, 102, and 2015, 47), so that "if Penelope is not sipping [a *mojito*], Sid does not see [her sipping]" (2013, 266). That seems to me exactly right, but only as long as we are talking about the grammar of "see" in what Wittgenstein refers to as its "first use," which Wittgenstein contrasts with the use of the same word in which it refers to the seeing of aspects (see PPF §111).

When Travis turns to consider Wittgensteinian aspects, he remains committed to the dichotomy between environmental objects and Fregean *Vorstellungen*, and suggests that at least many aspects are objective "looks" of things (Travis 2015, 57)—there for *one* to perceive (see 2013, 101 and 107 and 2015, 51) or "register" (2015, 48–9)—while other aspects are perhaps *Vorstellungen* and, if so, not possible objects of true or false judgments (see 2013, 107–9, and 2016, 25–8). For example, objectifying the two aspects of the Necker cube—Travis calls them "the A-cube" and "the B-cube"—Travis suggests at some point that the two aspects are "objects in plain view," which one may nonetheless fail to see (2016, 17); elsewhere he says that "if the A-cube was Napoleon's favourite, then to see it is to see Napoleon's favourite" (2015, 49).

The problem for Travis is that Wittgensteinian aspects are objects of perception that fall on *neither* side of his dichotomy: the presence of an aspect is not objectively establishable (you'd be neither wrong nor literally blind, nor necessarily lacking in attention, if you couldn't see a particular aspect); aspects are not liable to cause *distinct* images on retinas (that is, images different from those caused by the object seen under a different aspect or seen under no particular aspect); they *are* partly dependent on us ("are subject to the will," PPF §256); and they are *not* "to be met with by anyone suitably placed and perceptually equipped" (Travis 2013, 63), at least not if this means that anyone suitably placed and perceptually equipped *will be able* to see *any* aspect that someone else can see. In all of these respects, the Wittgensteinian aspect is *not* part of the objective world and, so, is *unlike* pigs, chipmunks, people sipping mojitos, or any objectively establishable look any of those things might have. For example, if a resemblance between a person's face and her father's has struck me— where this is the perceptual *experience* Wittgenstein uses to introduce the concept of "noticing an aspect" (PPF §114), in which I come to see the father's face in the face I'm looking at, so that the perceived physiognomy of the face I'm looking at changes, as opposed to the perceptual *judgment* that there *is* an objectively establishable similarity between the two faces— then I do not know what it would mean "to learn this was not so" (Travis 2015, 53); similarly, if I'm told that "the A-cube was Napoleon's favourite," the only way I can make sense of that is as meaning to say that Napoleon preferred *seeing* the Necker cube *under the "A" aspect.*[4] And *yet,* for all that,

---

[4] Travis seems to me to fudge the issue by saying that "the Necker [cube], for example, *does depict a cube* in one orientation (call this the A-cube) and a cube in another (call this the B-cube)" (2016, 15–16, emphasis altered), and by suggesting that "the Necker's *depiction* of the A-cube" is an "object of sight" on par with Sid or burnt toast (2016, 18, my emphasis). I can only understand this as

it makes perfect sense to call upon others to share (the seeing of) an aspect with you, whereas—by definition, as it were—it would make no sense to call upon another to share a Fregean *Vorstellung* with you (see 2013, 234).[5]

The second Fregean dichotomy Travis insists on, as I've said, is that between what perception passively presents us with—"things" or "things being as they are," and a little more specifically "objects in the environment"—and *our response* to what it presents us with; for Travis, that response must be an act of *thought* that consists of subsuming what we perceive under a generality, but which cannot affect *what we perceive* or our *perceptual* experience *itself* (see 2013, 257–8 and 410–411, and 2015, 49). The seeing of Wittgensteinian aspects reveals, however, our power to affect—within constraints, to be sure, but *wholly*—what we perceive, rather than (and separably from) what we *think* or *judge*.

At several points in his recent attempts to accommodate aspects, Travis cites with approval Wittgenstein's remark that when it comes to aspect perception "we must be careful not to think in traditional psychological categories . . . such as simply parsing experience into seeing and thinking" (LW I §542; as quoted in Travis 2013, 399 and 410, and 2015, 52). But then, when he attempts to account for the perception of aspects, he continues to hold on to those traditional categories, and proposes that aspect perception should be understood as somehow *combining* seeing and thinking, understood as they have been understood everywhere else in his work on perception (see 2013, 411, and 2015, 55–6 and 62). He suggests, for example, that to see a similarity of one face to another is "to bring [its] look under a certain generality . . . which (within a Fregean perspective, at least) is an exercise of thought" (2015, 57); and then, in order to accommodate the fact that Wittgenstein is talking about a particular sort of *visual experience* (which a judgment, as such, is not), he goes on to say that "one can, so

meaning that the two-dimensional drawing *could serve as*—it is such that, given a suitable context, it would be correct to take it to *be*—a depiction of a cube going this, or that, way (but not both at once). And while it may be that Napoleon liked *the drawing* better when it served to depict a cube going *this* way, rather than a cube going *that* way, or that in general he preferred *cubes* that (relative to him) went this way, we are now no longer talking about the perception of Wittgensteinian aspects (or about the *seeing* of something *as* something).

[5] Travis, as I said, is ready to think of *some* Wittgensteinian aspects—for example, what someone sees when she sees four evenly distributed dots in a straight line as two pairs side by side, or as two dots flanking a pair of others, or when she sees the letter "F" as facing right, or left—as *Vorstellungen*, "things not in view" (2016, 22ff); and he suggests that when it comes to such aspects, the person has "executive authority" over what aspect she sees (2016, 25ff). This seems to ignore, however, the crucial importance of such invitations as "Try to see these as belonging together" or "See this as facing *this* way" in the teaching of mathematics or architecture or in the appreciation of art, and in a whole range of other human activities. It also ignores the potentially far-reaching *consequences* of a person's seeing something one way rather than another (see Diamond 1991, 250).

to speak, drink [the look] in, study it, draw it, fantasize over it, and so on" (2015, 57). This attempt to hold on to the Fregean dichotomy between seeing and thinking—while at the same time doing justice to the phenomenology of aspect dawning—will not do, however. The dichotomy—which has been a useful heuristic in Travis's critical response to positions such as McDowell's that have intellectualized perceptual experience—will need to be rethought from the ground up, if we are to understand the phenomenal world and our relation to it, which begin to come to light in the dawning of Wittgensteinian aspects. Specifically, we will need to recognize and make room for the internal relation between how we stand (or orient ourselves) toward the world and how it presents itself to us *perceptually*. On Travis's account, we are essentially passive with respect to what presents itself to us in perception and how it presents itself. The perception of Wittgensteinian aspects shows we are not.

Aspects and Concepts

The third Fregean dichotomy Travis insists on, as we've seen, is that between concepts (or "generalities") and instances of those concepts (or generalities). The Wittgensteinian aspect, I will argue in this section and the next, is neither: it does not have the generality of a concept (does not transcend any one, or any finite set, of its instances *as a concept does*), and yet there *is* a sense in which it transcends the particular thing perceived under it and connects it with others.[6]

Among interpreters of Wittgenstein's remarks on aspects, the tendency has been to identify aspects with concepts.[7] And this, coupled with the idea that all (normal) human perception is aptly thought of as aspect perception, has been taken to be a way of substantiating the view that what we perceive is always and necessarily "conceptualized."[8] Travis, as we saw, resists this last conclusion; he resists it by denying that all (normal) human perception is the perception of aspects (see Travis 2013, 102 and 411, and 2016, 32). But what of the identification of aspects with concepts, which, at least in the case of *some* aspects, Travis appears to accept (see, for instance,

---

[6] The final two main sections of this essay borrow from my paper "Aspects of Perception" (2016a) but refocus the original line of argument to bear directly on Travis's account of perception.

[7] That aspects may be identified with empirical concepts was first proposed by Strawson (1970). It has since also been proposed in Wollheim 1980, Schroeder 2010, and Agam-Segal 2012.

[8] The earliest version of the idea that all (normal) human perception is aptly thought of as aspect perception is (also) found in Strawson 1970. Later versions may be found in Mulhall 1990 and 2001, Johnston 1993, and Schroeder 2010.

2015, 57)? I believe the identification of aspects with concepts is misguided, for reasons most of which Travis has identified for us.

To be sure, *the same form of words* with which an aspect is described *could*, at least in most cases, *be used to express an empirical judgment* (for example, to the effect that there is an empirically establishable similarity between one face and another, or that *that* is a rabbit, or a picture of a rabbit). But this by itself does not show, or mean, that to perceive an object under an aspect is to perceive it as falling under a concept. Neither the grammar of aspects nor their phenomenology supports the idea that they may aptly be identified with concepts.

Let's take as our stalking horse Wittgenstein's example of being struck by the similarity of one face to another, where the face you are looking at— its physiognomy—appears to change in front of your eyes, and change *wholly* (PPF §114). The candidate empirical concept here is, I suppose, that of *bearing (some) visible similarity to a particular, given face*. Concepts, as Travis correctly insists, are *general*: a concept allows for indefinitely many instantiations that differ from each other in any number of ways. And it transcends any finite set of instantiations: for any particular face, and for any finite set of faces that may all correctly be judged to bear visible similarity to that face, there could always be another face that is visibly distinguishable from all of those faces and yet may correctly be judged to bear visible similarity to the first face. One could go a step further and argue that *any* two faces may, in *some* contexts, correctly be judged to bear *some* visible similarity to each other. This leads us to the further point that—as Travis has taught us to recognize (see 2013, 185)—the concept of *bearing visible similarity to some particular face*, just like any other empirical concept, is "context-sensitive," in the sense that for any given face, and for a wide variety of faces that *in some contexts* would correctly count as bearing visible similarity to it, there could be other contexts in which those same faces would not correctly count as bearing visible similarity to that face. This means that, in judging that one face bears (or does not bear) visible similarity to another, we are beholden not just to the two faces but also to the context—however indeterminate and mostly tacit—in which we make the judgment.

These important Travisian reminders about concepts—which seem to me to speak decisively against the idea that what presents itself to competent speakers whenever they open their senses to the world is (always already) "conceptualized"—should also give pause to anyone who wishes to claim that what dawns on us and affects our perception of, say, a face when its likeness to another face strikes us is a *concept* (not because these reminders show that such a claim might be mistaken, but because they show that it is not even clear what exactly would be claimed).[9]

Let's look closer. Concepts, at least as commonly thought of in contemporary analytic philosophy, are paradigmatically applied in objective (truth-evaluable) *judgments*. On Travis's view, as I've noted, concepts are best thought of as abstracted, or abstractable, elements of such judgments.[10] Seeing something under an aspect, however, is *not* the same as judging it to *be* this or that (way). For example, seeing a face as (similar to) another is not the same as judging it to *be* (similar to) another, so not the same as "bringing what was seen under a given generality" (Travis 2015, 55); and seeing a triangle as having fallen over is not the same as judging it to *have* fallen over. Aspects, according to Wittgenstein, do not "teach us something about the external world" (RPP I §899). This is the flipside of the grammatical and phenomenological dependence of the Wittgensteinian aspect on *being perceived*: unlike a "property of the object" (PPF §247), the aspect "lasts only as long as I am occupied with the object in a particular way" (PPF §237).

Here it might be thought—and Travis sometimes seems to suggest (see, for instance, 2013, 409–12)—that, although seeing something under an aspect is not the same as *thinking* or *judging* that it *is* this or that (way), the aspect may still be identified with a thought about the object that is merely *entertained*, or *imagined* to be true (see Wollheim 1980, 221).[11] This will not do either, however, because to see one face as (similar to) another, for example, is, grammatically, not the same as entertaining the thought that it is (or imagining it to *be*) similar to another. Nor is it the same as "acquiescence in [the] appearance" of their *being* similar (Travis 2013,

---

[9] Strawson talks about aspect perception as a visual experience that is "*irradiated* by, or *infused* with, the concept; or it becomes *soaked* with the concept" (Strawson 1970, 57). Similarly, Wollheim claims that when we see x as *f*, the concept of *f* "does not stand outside the perception," but rather "permeates or mixes into the perception" (Wollheim 1980, 220). Part of my aim here is to raise doubt about the intelligibility of this sort of figurative talk. For a more detailed discussion of Wollheim's account, see Baz 2016a.

[10] McDowell appears to agree with Travis that concepts are best thought of as abstracted, or abstractable, elements of judgments or thoughts (see McDowell 2008, 263). But then he goes on to say that this is compatible with thinking that in discursive activity—and so in judgments which, he says, can be conceived as "inner analogues to assertions" (2008, 262)—"one puts contents together, in a way that can be modelled on stringing meaningful expressions together in discourse literally so called" (2008, 263). For Travis, this idea of McDowell's—of judgments having contents that are put together in the way in which words are put together when we talk—spoils the Fregean-contextualist insight of the primacy of whole thoughts (see Travis 2013, 223 and 250).

[11] Travis suggests that our relation to aspects might usefully be thought of as "Pyrrhonian" (see 2013, 409–12), where a Pyrrhonian attitude "has the content of a belief" but lacks the commitment to (objective) truth that beliefs require (2013, 405).

405). If a concept is something that may contribute to (or is abstractable from) the content of judgments (or Fregean thoughts), however hypothetically or even counterfactually entertained—if, in other words, the application of the concept of C to a case is what may be expressed by asserting, or even just hypothesizing, that the case *is* (a case of) C—then what dawns on us when a Wittgensteinian aspect dawns on us is *not* a concept, nor may it be identified in terms of one. And this is true regardless of whether the application is "committed" (as Travis puts it), or merely entertained or imagined, or acquiesced in.

The same conclusion—that aspects may not aptly be identified with empirical concepts—can also be reached by considering the phenomenological (as well as grammatical) *inseparability* of the aspect from the object perceived under it. An empirical concept does not depend for its identity, as the particular concept it is, on any one of its instantiations. This is just what makes it *general*. Nor can any one of its instantiations serve to fully define it or what Travis calls "its reach" (2013, 237, 269–70). Moreover, the presence of some perceived empirical property—and equally the truth of some perceptual judgment about some object—does not depend upon any (or anyone's) perceptual experience of the object. This is precisely what is meant by calling empirical properties, and empirical judgments, *objective*. Normally, if I want you to know what I see (or otherwise perceive) in Wittgenstein's *first*, "objective" sense of "see" (PPF §111), I only need to tell you what I see; insofar as *that* "object of sight" goes, you may thereby come to know its presence as well as I do and even be entitled to assure others of its presence. By contrast, the aspect is not separable from the object perceived under it; and the presence of the aspect *does* depend on people's experience of it. As already noted, the aspect lasts only as long as one is occupied with the object in a particular way; this, again, is the flipside of the point (reached above) that the aspect is not part of the objective world. If I want you to know what I see (or otherwise perceive) in Wittgenstein's *second* sense of "see," then it will not do just to tell you. I would have to get you to *see* it for yourself. For what I see is not just a rabbit (or a picture of a rabbit, or a similarity between two faces), which would be there even if I wasn't attending to the object perceptually in a particular way. What I see is something (a small rock, perhaps) *as* a rabbit (or an ambiguous figure *as* a picture of a rabbit, or one person's face *in* another person's face). What we have here is perceived, physiognomic sense which, unlike the kind of sense captured in concepts, is inseparable from what has it, and from our perceptual experience of it (see Merleau-Ponty 1945, 170/148).

Aspects as Perceived Internal Relations

I've argued that Wittgensteinian aspects do not have the generality of concepts. Let me say why they are not aptly thought of as just "singular" *instances* of generalities either, and, therefore, do not fit on *either* side of Travis's third Fregean dichotomy. The basic point is that the Wittgensteinian aspect does connect the thing seen under it with other things, albeit not as a concept does.

"What I perceive in the dawning of an aspect," Wittgenstein writes, "is not a property of the object, but an internal relation between it and other objects" (PPF §247). Though the notion of "internal relation" features quite centrally already in the *Tractatus*, where it is used to say something—however ultimately discardable as "nonsensical"—about "[the relation of] depicting that holds between language and the world" (TLP 4.014), I wish to propose that the notion, as Wittgenstein uses it *here*, is drawn from Gestalt psychology and is, importantly, a *perceptual* notion, as opposed to an objective, third-person notion.

Two (or more) perceived things (objects, elements) stand in an *internal relation* to each other when their perceived qualities are not independent of the perceived relation between them. Here is a passage from Kurt Koffka that illustrates the notion: "Two colors adjacent to each other are not perceived as two independent things, but as having an inner connection which is at the same time a factor determining the special qualities A and B themselves" (Koffka 1921/8, 221). According to Gestalt psychology, what we perceive is—at the most basic level—not atomic sensations which we somehow synthesize into significant intelligible wholes but, rather, *unified significant wholes*, where the perceived qualities of the elements of a perceived whole—and, so, the specific contributions those elements make to the overall perceived significance of that whole—are not perceptually independent from that perceived overall significance; so the elements of a perceived whole are internally related.

The well-known duck–rabbit figure provides a simple illustration of the internal relation between elements of the phenomenal world. When you see the drawing as a rabbit, say, you see the two "appendages" as ears; but your seeing them as ears is not independent from your seeing the whole thing as a rabbit. Perceptually, the ears are (seen as) ears only when the whole thing is (seen as) a rabbit. One important implication of this is that your seeing the duck–rabbit as a rabbit cannot be *explained*, or *rationalized*, as the outcome of your seeing this portion of the drawing as ears, that portion as the mouth, another portion as the back of the head, and so on; the rabbit aspect is not synthesized from elements that have their "rabbit-parts" significance independently of being elements of that overall aspect. On the other hand, if you took the basic elements of our perception of the duck–rabbit to only have objectively establishable, geometrical properties—and so to be devoid of any rabbit, or duck, significance—then you would never be able to explain, on *that* basis, why those elements got synthesized into the rabbit aspect, say, rather than the duck aspect. This shows that the perception of significant wholes should be taken as phenomenologically primary.

Now consider Wittgenstein's example of the experience of being struck by the similarity between two faces. A similarity understood as an objective property of the faces is an *external* relation between them: each face has its objective properties, which one may come to know without knowing anything about the other face; and those properties determine whether (and, if so, to what extent) the two may correctly count (context-dependently) as bearing some objective similarity to each other. And so you may look at a face and see (in Wittgenstein's first sense of "see")—or have someone point out, or demonstrate, to you—that there is some visible similarity between it and another; seeing *that* need not involve, or bring about, *any* change in how you visually experience the face you're looking at; its perceived gestalt (physiognomy, expression) need not change at all. "*Seeing that,*" as Travis has noted, refers to a cognitive stance that does not involve any particular *perceptual* experience (see 2013, 238ff). By contrast, in the experience Wittgenstein describes, the perceived gestalt of the face you're looking at changes; and what dawns on you is an *internal* relation between that face and another: the perceived relation (in this case, of similarity) is inseparable from the perceived change in the overall physiognomy or expression of the face you're looking at.

In order to appreciate more fully the way in which an aspect connects the object seen "under it" with other elements of the phenomenal world, it is important to note that internal relations hold not just among the perceived elements of some perceived object or between one perceived object and some other, particular object, but also between the perceived physiognomies of objects and their perceived surroundings. Wittgenstein illustrates the internal relation between a perceived figure and its surroundings when he remarks that "a smiling mouth smiles only in a human face" (PI §583). In the *Brown Book*, Wittgenstein gives a similar example of friendly eyes in a friendly face (BB 145). He notes that, even though the eyes *are* (perceived as) friendly and their friendliness does contribute essentially to the (perceived) friendliness of the face, the same eyes—objectively, geometrically identical ones—could feature in a face that was not (perceived as) friendly and, so, would not be (perceived as) friendly. Indeed, the "context-sensitivity" of perceived significance (or physiognomy), and the internal relation between figure and background, manifest themselves at every level: just as a mouth has its particular expression only in the context of a particular face, so is the perceived expression of a face internally related to a context—however indeterminate—apart from which it would not have been (perceived as) *that* expression.[12] When, to use one of Wittgenstein's examples, one is struck by some particular schematic drawing of a face as having a particular expression which could—"as an approximate description of the expression"—be said to be that of "a complacent business man, stupidly supercilious, who though fat, imagines he's a lady killer" (BB 162), that particular aspect comes with a context (here, an imagined context), however indeterminate: an anticipation of how that character would think, talk, and react, and—as Merleau-Ponty puts it (1945, 225/199)—"a world of meanings" against the background of which this mode of being-in-the-world has the sense it has for us; at this level, too, the perceived physiognomy and its context are internally related (the face's having *that* expression, and therefore invoking *that* context for its perceiver, is not separable from its relation to that context).

Concluding Remarks

Travis has done more than anyone else to bring out the context-dependence—and, hence, the holistic nature—of *linguistically* expressed sense. But in his work on perception he has overlooked the context-dependence and holism of perceived sense *in general*. Travis's account of perception—like so many other accounts of perception given by analytic philosophers in recent years—ignores the fact that, in normal human (and not just human) perception, the perceptual field is *always* organized into figure and background, which relate to each other internally.[13] *Ipso facto*, this kind of account also ignores altogether the role of the perceiver in *effecting* the figure–background structure by *attending* to something in a particular way and "putting its surroundings in abeyance" (Merleau-Ponty 1945, 78/70), both of which we for the most part *find* ourselves doing, rather than *choose* or *decide* to do.

I have argued that perceiving something "under" an aspect, or seeing something *as* something, situates that something in the *phenomenal* world

---

[12] Comic-book illustrators know that it is possible to change dramatically the perceived expression of a drawn face just by changing what the character says or thinks.

[13] I say "normal" human perception, because in some people—for example, some people on the autistic spectrum—the ability to effect the figure–background structure is severely impaired.

(not in the objective world, as the application of a concept would). The phenomenal world is a world of perceivable, physiognomic sense, which, according to Merleau-Ponty (1945, 243–5/217–18), should be understood in terms of *affective* and *motor* value—that is, value, not for our Kantian "understanding," but for our phenomenal *body*. By contrast with Kant—and much of the philosophical tradition Kant inaugurated including Travis's work on perception—in Merleau-Ponty's phenomenology, perception is understood as "in the first place not a matter of 'I think that' but of 'I can'" (1945, 159/139). As I've already noted, perhaps one of the most significant omissions in Travis's account of perception—which becomes conspicuous when he turns to consider the perception of what Wittgenstein calls "aspects"—is his failure to recognize the internal relation between how we stand (or orient ourselves) toward the world and how it presents itself to us *perceptually* (as opposed to how it is *represented* in our Fregean thoughts). The perception of Wittgensteinian aspects reveals our power to project, more or less creatively, perceivable unity and sense that are importantly different from the unity and sense afforded and secured by the application of empirical concepts in objective, true or false, judgments.

And that revelation should actually be welcome to anyone who wishes, as Travis does, to avoid at once the empiricist myth of the mechanically given *and* McDowell's "conceptualization" of perception; and doing all that—in line with Wittgenstein's philosophical approach, and as Travis clearly aspires to do—by bringing out and elucidating what we must *already*, on some level and in some way, be familiar with. There is no better way of putting to rest the spate of philosophizing inaugurated in McDowell's *Mind and World* – with its roots in Kant and the philosophical tradition on which Kant draws—than to bring into view the phenomenal world, and the unity and sense it has for us prior to any objective thought or judgment. For it is the phenomenal world that's perceptually given to us, and in which we first and foremost find ourselves and others. And, although it is of the very essence of this world to be hard to put satisfyingly into words, it is not a myth. It is the perceived background against which our deeds and our words—including our objective thoughts and judgments—have whatever sense they have for us.

CHAPTER 7

First Steps and Conceptual Creativity

Michael Beaney

Introduction

In section 308 of *Philosophical Investigations*, Wittgenstein talks of the first step in philosophizing being 'the one that altogether escapes notice . . . that's just what commits us to a particular way of looking at the matter'. A good example of such a first step is Frege's use of function–argument analysis and the associated conception of concepts as functions, which led to almost all his characteristic doctrines, as well as certain paradoxes, such as the paradox of the concept *horse* and Russell's paradox. And yet there is value in seeing concepts as functions: it made the development of modern logic possible.

Another good example of a first step is Cantor's conception of sameness of number as one–one correspondence, which enabled him to introduce— or 'create'—the concept of a transfinite number. The conceptual creativity involved here is analogous to Frege's reconceiving concepts as functions: in each case a relevant practice needs to be established and 'intuitions' crystallized, as it might be put, for the relevant conception to acquire meaning and objectivity. It is tempting to conceptualize this process as originating in some 'Eureka!' moment and as catching on when others can exclaim 'Now I can go on!'; but all this needs careful description to avoid mythologization.

In this essay I explore some of the connections between conceptual creativity and the kind of first steps of which Wittgenstein spoke. The essay has a straightforward, albeit two-dimensional (4 x 4) structure. I elucidate Wittgenstein's talk of first steps and his interest in the various phenomena of sudden understanding and recognition in Section 1, and clarify some key conceptions and issues concerning conceptual creativity in Section 2. In Section 3 I take Frege's use of function–argument analysis and associated conception of concepts as functions as a fruitful case study of a first step, and in Section 4 I draw out some of the implications of the preceding discussion in considering Wittgenstein's own conceptual creativity. Each section is divided into four subsections, each subsection in each section corresponding to the respective subsections in the other sections. An overview is provided in the table below.

1 First Steps	2 Conceptual Creativity	3 Frege's First Step	4 Wittgenstein's Conceptual Creativity
1 The fly and the fly-bottle	1 Conceptual spaces	1 Wittgenstein and the Fregean fly-bottle	1 Connective creativity
2 The first step	2 Transformational creativity	2 Frege's use of function– argument analysis	2 Therapeutic analysis
3 'Now I understand!'	3 'Eureka!'	3 'Concepts are functions!'	3 'That's exactly how I meant it!'
4 Aspect change	4 Conceptual change	4 Reconceiving concepts	4 Changing our ways of looking at things

1   First Steps

1.1   The Fly and the Fly-Bottle

Wittgenstein's aim in philosophy, he once famously said, was to show the fly the way out of the fly-bottle (PI §309).[1] This is a memorable image, but what did he mean? For someone who urged us to be wary of analogies, metaphors, and pictures embedded in our use of language, as we try to battle against the bewitchment of our intelligence (see, for instance, PI §109), Wittgenstein was not averse to using them in his own thinking. Is this not itself an image that can easily mislead us? The comparison is presumably very simple, however. We are all like flies buzzing around in the open air. But some of us—philosophers, or indeed anyone tempted to make philosophical claims—become attracted by something sweet inside a bottle, fly into it, and then cannot find our way out again. Instead, we just keep banging our heads against the sides of the bottle. The idea here echoes Wittgenstein's concern in the *Tractatus* with the limits of language and thought, which we only recognize by bumping up against them in doing philosophy. But there was no sense in his early work of our being *trapped* by certain uses of language or forms of thinking. This idea is what Wittgenstein adds in his later work. The picture of language that he offered

---

[1] In Subsections 1.1 and 1.2, I am indebted to Peter Hacker's analytical commentary (1990, 1996), which identifies relevant passages from Wittgenstein's other writings and offers much helpful elucidation.

in the *Tractatus* was itself seen as a fly-bottle in which he had become trapped, and his later work was an attempt to find his way out.

The idea of being *trapped* by certain pictures of language, or preconceptions of how particular kinds of expression work, emerged in the first few years after Wittgenstein's return to philosophy in 1929. In the section on 'Philosophy' in the *Big Typescript*, he writes:

> Human beings are deeply imbedded in philosophical, i.e. grammatical, confusions. And freeing them from these presupposes extricating them from the immensely diverse associations they are caught up in. . . . Language has the same traps ready for everyone; the immense network of easily trodden false paths. . . . Therefore wherever false paths branch off I ought to put up signs to help in getting past the dangerous spots. (BT 311e–312e)

This suggests not only that anyone can be trapped, but also that it is *language* that entraps us. Erecting signs to warn people involves a different metaphor than showing them the way out of the fly-bottle, but the idea of entrapment lies at the root of both.

The metaphor of the fly-bottle is first used in notes written in 1936: 'The solipsist flutters and flutters in the flyglass, strikes against the walls, flutters further. How can he be brought to rest?' (LPE 300; see Hacker 1990, 264). That the metaphor should have been first used in discussing solipsism is perhaps unsurprising. For it is natural to regard the solipsist as indeed shut up in their own little world. But here the issue is their being 'brought to rest', rather than anyone philosophically confused more generally being helped out of the fly-bottle.

1.2   The First Step

But how exactly is a philosopher—or anyone suffering from philosophical confusion—to escape from the fly-bottle? The beginning of an answer can be found in the section that immediately precedes Wittgenstein's remark about the fly and the fly-bottle:

> How does the philosophical problem about mental processes and states and about behaviourism arise? — The first step is the one that altogether escapes notice. We talk of processes and states, and leave their nature undecided. Sometime perhaps we'll know more about them – we think. But that's just what commits us to a particular way of looking at the matter. For we have a certain conception of what it means to learn to know a process better. (The decisive movement in the conjuring trick has been made, and it was the very one that seemed to us quite innocent.) – And now the analogy which was to

make us understand our thoughts falls to pieces. So we have to deny the yet
uncomprehended process in the yet unexplored medium. And now it looks
as if we had denied mental processes. And naturally we don't want to deny
them. (PI §308)

This passage occurs in the course of Wittgenstein's sustained critique of
the idea of a private language (see esp. PI §§243ff). A sensation term, he
argues, should not be seen as a name of a private mental state or process.
But it is then tempting to interpret Wittgenstein as denying that there is
any mental state or process involved at all, and as therefore being
a behaviourist in disguise, as indeed he imagines his interlocutor objecting
in section 307. Wittgenstein's response is to criticize the very way in which
the dispute gets going. Philosophical debates typically arise, on
Wittgenstein's view, by making some fundamental assumption that both
sides implicitly accept and that then governs the possible philosophical
positions. In this case, he suggests in section 308, the underlying assumption is that our talk of mental states and processes is straightforward, any
unclarity about them being something that can just be left to future
discovery to remove. With this assumption, the debate then simply
becomes a matter of whether sensation terms refer to such mental states
or processes or not. If they do, then it seems that we have to acknowledge
the existence of language that is necessarily private; and if they do not, or
we reject the claim that they do, then behaviourism seems the only option.

The underlying assumption that governs how this philosophical dispute
gets going is what Wittgenstein calls here 'the first step', the one that
seemed quite innocent and yet where the 'decisive movement in the
conjuring trick has been made'. In the manuscript volume from which
section 308 originated, we find the following additional remark: 'The first
step is the innocent ethereal conception in which one (nevertheless) leaves
open the "kind" of processes or states' (MS-116, 332; as quoted in Hacker
1990, 262). This offers little additional clarification. Indeed, it only raises
the question as to why one would adopt the 'ethereal conception'.

A better clue to what 'the first step' might mean here lies in
Wittgenstein's talk in section 308 of 'the analogy which was to make us
understand our thoughts' and which now 'falls to pieces'. What is this
analogy? In section 571 Wittgenstein writes:

A misleading parallel: psychology treats of processes in the mental sphere, as
does physics in the physical.
   Seeing, hearing, thinking, feeling, willing, are not the subject matter of
psychology *in the same sense* as that in which the movements of bodies, the

phenomena of electricity, and so forth are the subject matter of physics. You can see this from the fact that the physicist sees, hears, thinks about and informs us of these phenomena, and the psychologist observes the utterances (the behaviour) of the subject. (PI §517)

It turns out that section 571 also originates from the manuscript volume from which section 308 was taken, and indeed, the early version of it occurs between two drafts of section 308 (see Hacker 1990, 260). So the analogy to which Wittgenstein alludes in section 308 is presumably the analogy between physical states and processes and mental states and processes.

This suggests that what is really involved in the first step is the assumption that mental states and processes are indeed analogous to physical states and processes, which is why we can leave their precise nature 'open'—to be determined by future discovery. This suggestion is confirmed when we trace the idea back further in Wittgenstein's earlier writings. In *Philosophical Grammar* he writes:

> We say that understanding is a 'psychological process', and this label is misleading, in this as in countless other cases. It compares understanding to a particular *process* like translation from one language into another, and it suggests the same conception of thinking, knowing, wishing, intending, etc. That is to say, in all these cases we see that what we would perhaps naively suggest as the hallmark of such a process is not present in every case or even in the majority of cases. And our next step is to conclude that the essence of the process is something difficult to grasp that still awaits discovery. For we say: since I use the word 'understand' in all these cases, there must be some one thing which happens in every case and which is the essence of understanding (expecting, wishing etc.). Otherwise, why should I call them by all the same name? (PG 74–5)

Wittgenstein goes on to stress the '*primitive*' nature of the underlying conception here, that is, that there must indeed be one kind of thing to which any term such as 'understanding' or 'state' or 'process' refers in all its uses, a conception he comes to reject in talking later of 'family-resemblance' concepts. First steps often do lie in such primitive or naïve conceptions, and once these conceptions are accepted, philosophical confusion easily arises and we end up becoming trapped in the fly-bottle.

1.3   'Now I Understand!'

A theme that runs throughout the *Investigations* is the phenomenon of sudden understanding or recognition, as expressed in such exclamations as 'Now I know!', 'Now I understand!', or 'Now I can go on!' Wittgenstein first mentions these expressions in section 151; and his discussion of meaning and rule-following in sections 143–242, which sets the scene for his private language arguments, examines different accounts of what might be involved in sudden understanding. In repudiating the idea that suddenly understanding the system behind a series of numbers consists in a formula's occurring to me, he asks if it then follows that the understanding must be taken as a process underlying the occurrence of the formula. He answers:

> If something has to stand 'behind the utterance of the formula', it is *particular circumstances*, which warrant my saying that I can go on – if the formula occurs to me.
>   Just for once, don't think of understanding as a 'mental process' at all! – For *that* is the way of talking which confuses you. Instead, ask yourself: in what sort of case, in what kind of circumstances, do we say 'Now I know how to go on'? I mean, if the formula has occurred to me. (PI §154; see also §155)

The most salient circumstance is the experience I have had before of the connection between a formula's occurring to me and my continuing the series (§179). Other circumstances include my knowledge of the appropriate linguistic and algebraic expressions, my ability to do mathematics, my mastery of certain skills and techniques, acquired in learning the relevant language-games, as well as what I go on to do (§§179–80). Of course, this is not to say that I may not subsequently hesitate, go wrong, or realize that I did not, after all, understand. But exactly how we describe what has happened in each individual case is again a matter of the precise circumstances (§181; see also §323).

Here, as elsewhere, the danger lies in getting misled by the kinds of expression we use in characterizing our experiences. In section 191 Wittgenstein writes:

> 'It is as if we could grasp the whole use of the word at a stroke.' Like *what*, for example? – *Can't* the use – in a certain sense – be grasped at a stroke? And in *what* sense can't it? – It is indeed as if we could 'grasp it at a stroke' in a much more direct sense. – But have you a model for this? No. It is just that this mode of expression suggests itself to us. As a result of the crossing of different pictures. (PI §191)

If something happens 'at a stroke', then it happens fully and completely at a single point in time, such as when we speak of swatting four mosquitos at a stroke. But the picture of something happening 'at a stroke' does not really fit grasping the whole use of a word. Wittgenstein goes on to remark:

'You have no model of this inordinate fact, but you are seduced into using a super-expression. (It might be called a philosophical superlative.)' (§192). He does not advocate avoiding such expressions altogether. It is only when they lend themselves to misinterpretation, as in thinking that 'the future development must in some way already be present in the act of grasping the use and yet isn't present' (§197) that we have to take care.

Nor does Wittgenstein deny that we have experiences of sudden understanding (of realizing what a word means, of grasping the rule of a series, or of solving a problem, for example). To deny this would be to fall into the trap that we have already discussed in relation to section 308. The question is not whether we do or do not have the relevant experiences, but how we are to understand the descriptions or expressions of those experiences—and avoid being misled. For example, shortly after section 308, he writes: '"What happens when a man suddenly understands?" – The question is badly framed. If it is a question about the meaning of the expression "sudden understanding", the answer is not to point to a process to which we give this name' (§321). What we must do is look and see how the expression is used (see §340).

1.4   Aspect Change

The theme of sudden changes in experience is discussed at various points, in various guises, in the *Investigations*. It is further developed in *Philosophy of Psychology — A Fragment*, most notably in chapter xi, where Wittgenstein considers aspect perception. One of the main family of cases he explores is noticing a new aspect of something, as in observing a face and noticing its likeness to another (PPF §§112–13), coming to see the duck, having only seen the rabbit, in the duck–rabbit picture (§118), seeing the solution of a puzzle-picture (§131), or suddenly recognizing someone whom you have not seen for years (§143). In all such cases, Wittgenstein remarks, 'I *see* that [what I am looking at] has not changed; and yet I see it differently' (PPF §113), and what intrigues him most is how we try to capture or do justice to both these features. 'The expression of a change of aspect is an expression of a new perception and, at the same time, an expression of an unchanged perception' (PPF §130). We talk of seeing something *as* something, rather than just of seeing something, in such cases, and talk of 'seeing-as' suggests that there is some kind of interpretation or thinking involved as well as 'mere' seeing: 'the lighting up of an aspect seems half visual experience, half thought' (PPF §140; see also §§ 137, 144, 164, 181, 235, 245, and 248).

As in the cases of sudden understanding discussed in the *Investigations*, Wittgenstein urges us to resist the temptation to look 'inwards' for explanation. 'Don't try to analyse the experience within yourself' (PPF §188). To describe the difference between seeing the duck–rabbit as a duck and seeing it as a rabbit in terms of some difference in 'inner picture' makes no sense, since if this is construed as any kind of mental image 'representing' the object seen, then it is presumably the same image in both cases (see PPF §§133–4). Once again, Wittgenstein directs our attention to the *particular circumstances* in which we talk of someone seeing something *as* something. 'Do not ask yourself: 'How does it work with *me*?' – Ask: 'What do I know about someone else?'' (PPF §204).

In discussing how we might see a figure of a triangle in different ways, Wittgenstein writes:

> Only of someone *capable* of making certain applications of the figure with facility would one say that he saw it now *this* way, now *that* way.
>
> The substratum of this experience is the mastery of a technique.
>
> But how odd for this to be the logical condition of someone's having such-and-such an *experience*! After all, you don't say that one 'has toothache' only if one is capable of doing such-and-such. – From this it follows that we cannot be dealing with the same concept of experience here. It is a different concept, even though related.
>
> Only of someone who *can* do, has learnt, is master of, such-and-such, does it make sense to say that he has had *this* experience.
>
> And if this sounds silly, you need to remember that the *concept* of seeing is modified here. (PPF §§222–4)

We here reach the core of Wittgenstein's later philosophy. Our concepts of thinking, understanding, experience, seeing, seeing-as, and so on are complex, inextricably interconnected, and circumstance-dependent, and continually shift as we attempt to express and make sense of our mental lives. This is revealed not only in the philosophical disputes in which we become trapped, but also in such everyday experiences as noticing a new aspect in something we see.

2   Conceptual Creativity

2.1   Conceptual Spaces

'Creativity' and its cognates are not terms that one finds frequently used within analytic philosophy, outside specific fields such as aesthetics. If anything, they are rather dirty words, suggesting fabrication, speculation, and argumentative deficiency. Even in Wittgenstein's *Investigations* the terms are entirely absent.[2] And yet, as we have just seen, the themes of first steps, sudden understanding, discerning the rule of a series, seeing the solution to a problem, noticing new aspects, and so on, are central to his thinking. How could these have nothing to do with creativity? Discourse about creativity is a prime site for exposing first steps and demythologizing the claims that are often made—for example, about the nature of 'genius' and the 'mystery' of the creative process—by clarifying the use of the various expressions that all too readily mislead us. How could Wittgenstein's philosophy not have relevance to such discourse? Should discussions of Wittgenstein's philosophy and of creativity not be brought closer together, enabling us to see different aspects of each?[3]

Over the last fifty years or so, it has been psychologists who have done most to investigate creativity. One of the leading writers is Margaret Boden, who works, in fact, in the intersection between psychology, computer science, and philosophy. Fundamental in her thinking is the distinction she draws between combinational, exploratory, and transformational creativity (see Boden 1990/2004, 1994, and 2010).[4] Combinational creativity is the simplest and most familiar kind, exemplified in combining the idea of a horse and the idea of a horn in forming the idea of a unicorn. The other two kinds require the key notion of a 'conceptual space'—or 'generative system', as Boden also calls it. This is understood as a domain of thinking that is governed by a set of rules and principles that determine what can and cannot be done within it. A conceptual space, she writes, is 'the generative system that underlies that domain and defines a certain range of possibilities: chess moves, or molecular structures, or jazz melodies' (1994, 79). Exploratory creativity is manifested in exploring the possibilities of a conceptual space, and transformational creativity in changing a conceptual space by rejecting one or more of its constitutive rules and principles.

Crucial to the idea of a conceptual space are the *constraints* that it imposes on our thinking. One might see a conceptual space as a kind of fly-bottle which restricts our intellectual movements. Creativity can still be

---

[2] In the English translation of the text of the *Investigations* the verb 'create' is used just once, but only in the phrase 'creates the illusion' (§253). None of the corresponding German words—'schöpfen', 'schaffen', 'erschaffen', 'kreativ', 'Kreativität', or any of their cognates—are used in Wittgenstein's original text.

[3] For a recent collection of papers that does just this in relation to the creativity of language, see Sunday Grève and Mácha 2016.

[4] I have discussed and drawn on Boden's ideas in my own work on creativity; see, for example, Beaney 2005, chapters 6–7; and 2018.

exhibited as we fly around in the bottle, exploring the space inside and its limits. Boden's examples of exploratory creativity include Euclidean geometry and the classical tonal music of Johann Sebastian Bach (as best illustrated in *The Well-Tempered Clavier*). But sooner or later we will get frustrated at banging our heads against the limits and look for a way out. In the case of Euclidean geometry, for example, we may realize that we cannot construct a heptagon using just ruler and compass (PI §517), and seek other methods and hence a way of escaping the system.

2.2   Transformational Creativity

Transformational creativity is exhibited in developing a new conceptual space by dropping or negating one or more of the constituent rules or principles of the old conceptual space. Schoenberg invented atonal music by abandoning the constraint of the home key in classical music, for example, and non-Euclidean geometry arose by rejecting Euclid's fifth axiom, the notorious parallel postulate. Here what is crucial, on Boden's conception at any rate, is that there is indeed an existing conceptual system that is sufficiently well defined for there to be a rule or principle that can be rejected in generating the new system.

Transformational creativity is not exhibited, in other words, by simply smashing the fly-bottle in which we have been trapped. We actually *need* constraints to think at all. Schoenberg is a good case here. He soon realized that having no constraints at all in atonal music was paralysing, and so he invented the twelve-tone system instead. To pursue our metaphor, the aim is not to escape into the open air and fly around wherever we want, but to move to a better fly-bottle. At this point, however, we might do better to treat the metaphor as itself a fly-bottle whose limits require us to leave it.

On Boden's conception of transformational creativity, the first step in developing a new conceptual space is the rejection of a rule or principle of an existing conceptual space. But if our discussion of Wittgenstein is anything to go by, then first steps can also be taken—whether rightly or wrongly—by means of an analogy, metaphor, or picture; and there are plenty of occasions on which this is fruitful. To give just one famous example, Kekulé's dream of a snake devouring its own tail reputedly led him to think of the benzene molecule as having a ring structure. Perhaps we can also see this as abandoning the assumption (in previous chemistry) that the molecule had to have (at least) two ends, but it shows that there might be more to say about how the transformation comes about.

2.3 'Eureka!'

Kekulé's dream of a snake devouring itself is a good example of a 'Eureka!' moment, that moment of inspiration that results in an intellectual breakthrough. According to legend, Archimedes shouted 'Eureka! Eureka!' ('I've found it! I've found it!') when he realized, in stepping into a bath, that the volume of water displaced was equal to the volume of that part of his body that was submerged, and he then proceeded to run naked through the streets of Syracuse in delight. Whatever the true story may be, it has served as the epitome of the defining moment of a creative act.

It also serves as the epitome of the mythologization of creativity to which we all too readily succumb. It is really just one more example of those experiences of sudden understanding which Wittgenstein was so concerned to clarify. And as studies of all such 'Eureka!' moments have shown, the actual facts—or particular circumstances, to use Wittgenstein's phrase—are always far more complex. To return to the apparently simple example of Kekulé's dream, Kekulé would not have been in a position to discover the ring structure of the benzene molecule had he not been working on the valences of atoms in molecules, and the nature of carbon–carbon bonds, in particular, for years. And he still needed to figure out the chemical valences of the atoms making up the benzene molecule and reshape chemical theory accordingly. There is even doubt about whether the dream really did occur to Kekulé at any decisive point in his work, as he only told the story of it much later. Mythologization about one's own discoveries is just as likely to occur as mythologization by others, and both tend only to occur after their significance has become widely recognized.

2.4 Conceptual Change

When we look at examples of conceptual change, we also see that far more goes on than simply rejecting a rule or principle of an existing conceptual space, although they can be interpreted to involve this. A good case study is Cantor's transformation of the conceptual space of arithmetic by introducing the concept of a transfinite number, which arose by comparing the cardinality of infinite sets. Here we need to distinguish two criteria for two sets having the same number of members:

(a)   neither is bigger than the other (in the sense of 'bigger than' for which a set is always bigger than any proper subset of itself);
(b)   their members can be one–one correlated.

In finite cases these two criteria give the same result. Consider the sets $\{1, 2, 3, 4, 5\}$ and $\{1, 4, 9, 16, 25\}$: these have the same number of members on both criteria. In infinite cases, however, the two criteria come apart, and what Cantor did was take the second criterion as primary. On this basis, he showed that the set of natural numbers and the set of rational numbers have the same cardinality, as they can be one–one correlated, while the set of real numbers is bigger than the set of natural numbers, not merely on the first but also on the second criterion. Supposing—*ex hypothesi*—that they can indeed be correlated in two lists, Cantor demonstrated how to construct a real number not on the list, hence contradicting the original supposition: this was his famous diagonal argument. He called the number of the natural numbers '$\aleph_0$' ('aleph-zero') and the number of real numbers '$\aleph_1$,' ('aleph-one'), and showed how to generate a whole series of such numbers—'transfinite numbers', as he called them.

We need not go into further details. (For a fuller account, see Beaney 2017a, chapter 1; 2018; and Beaney and Clark 2018.) The point is that a lot of work had to take place before the new conceptual space was formed. We can see Cantor as dropping one of the two traditional criteria for two sets having the same number of members, and hence as forming a more specific concept of sameness of number, but the concept of a transfinite number itself was only created *through* the development of transfinite arithmetic. Cantor saw himself as 'discovering' transfinite numbers, but here is where Wittgenstein's words in section 401 of the *Investigations* are apt: 'You interpret the new conception as the seeing of a new object. You interpret a grammatical movement that you have made as a quasi-physical phenomenon which you are observing.' This 'grammatical movement' involves the formation of new concepts, and this is what is insufficiently appreciated:

> Here it is *difficult* to see that what is at issue is determination of concepts.
>   What forces itself on one is a *concept*. (You must not forget that.) (PPF §191)

Wittgenstein is talking here of the ways our perceptual concepts get determined, when we describe our experiences of seeing and seeing-as (see also PPF §181), but it applies no less to Cantor's determination of the refined concept of sameness of number and the new concept of a transfinite number.

3 Frege's First Step

3.1 Wittgenstein and the Fregean Fly-Bottle

Frege was the single most important influence on Wittgenstein. Wittgenstein acknowledged his debt to Frege—alongside Russell—in his preface to the *Tractatus*, and he continued to engage with Frege's writings right to the very end of his life.[5] In describing conversations he had with Wittgenstein about Frege in 1949, O. K. Bouwsma reports him as saying: 'Frege is so good. But one must try to figure out what was bothering him, and then see how the problems arise. There are so many of them' (WC 27). Wittgenstein may well have had Frege in mind in section 309 of the *Investigations*: Frege's philosophy was a fly-bottle into which it was tempting to fly, but from which, once in, it was hard to escape, despite the bumps our heads received in banging against its sides.

In his early work, however, Wittgenstein took over some of Frege's ideas, from which he only later managed to extricate himself. The most important of these was the assumption that the logic of our language is essentially the quantificational logic that Frege had first set out in his *Begriffsschrift* of 1879 ('Begriffsschrift'—literally, 'concept-script'—being the term he used for his logical system). Like Frege, Wittgenstein wrote, 'I conceive a proposition as a function of the expressions contained in it' (TLP 3.318; see also 5.47). The first crack in the *Tractatus* appeared when Wittgenstein realized that there were logical inferences that could not be handled within the theory of truth-functions, such as the inference from '*x* is red' to '*x* is not green'. And he soon came to realize that function–argument form was no more a genuine logical form than subject–predicate form, which is just a 'way of expressing countless fundamentally different logical forms' (PR 119).

Wittgenstein criticizes Frege in the *Tractatus* as well, of course, but there is nevertheless an important sense in which Wittgenstein had himself been trapped in the Fregean fly-bottle. His later philosophy was thus, in part, an attempt to find his own way out of the fly-bottle, and in reading his philosophy as offering a diagnosis of certain philosophical confusions, we have to recognize those confusions in his own earlier thinking and not just in the work of others, whether Frege or anyone else.

---

[5] For more on the relationship between Wittgenstein and Frege, see Beaney 2017b, where I make the suggestion about the Fregean fly-bottle and Frege's first step on which I elaborate in the present essay.

3.2   Frege's Use of Function–Argument Analysis

Almost all the characteristic doctrines of Frege's philosophy flow from his thinking through—and attempting to give philosophical support to—his use of function–argument analysis, which he extended from mathematics to logic. The distinction between concept and object, for example, falls straightforwardly out of this, concepts being regarded as what functional expressions with one argument-place represent and objects as what are represented by the names that fill these argument-places. Concepts, he held, are 'unsaturated', reflecting the 'unsaturated' nature of the functional expressions, while objects are 'saturated', and this absolute distinction he took to be grounded in the very nature of things. Concepts, he also maintained, must be defined for all objects, and hence for every concept, there is a set of objects to which it applies—the extension of that concept. Extensions of concepts were also regarded as objects—albeit logical objects—for which even the concepts whose extensions they are must be defined.

Frege's doctrines, however, gave rise to precisely those problems to which Wittgenstein alluded in his remark to Bouwsma. His distinction between concept and object generated the paradox of the concept *horse*, as well as the associated problems in actually stating the distinction, and his assumptions about concepts and extensions of concepts gave rise to Russell's paradox, the paradox that dealt a fatal blow to Frege's logicist project—his attempt to show that arithmetic was reducible to logic. So there is a lot to do in clarifying how Frege went wrong. It would be natural to see his use of function–argument analysis, and the analogy between concepts and functions that this implicitly assumed, as the first step in Frege's philosophizing. If so, then we might offer the following creative paraphrase of section 308 of the *Investigations*, developing the meta-analogy:

> How does the philosophical problem about concepts and objects and about logicism arise? – The first step is the one that altogether escapes notice. We talk of concepts and objects and leave their nature undecided. We assume that in due course we will know more about them, having a definite idea of the use of function–argument analysis in mathematics, and sure enough, we find ourselves committed to regarding concepts as functions. (The decisive movement in the conjuring trick has been made, and it was the very one that seemed to us quite innocent.) – And now the analogy between concepts and functions which was to make us understand our thoughts falls to pieces. We encounter paradoxes, such as the paradox of the concept *horse* and Russell's paradox. So we have to deny that we can state the distinction between concept and object, and that every concept has an extension. And now it

looks as if we have to reject quantificational logic itself, with all its undoubted successes. And naturally we don't want to reject that.

3.3 'Concepts Are Functions!'

It is tempting to say that Frege's fundamental insight was that concepts are functions, and that this is what enabled him to create quantificational logic and develop his philosophy accordingly. But there is no evidence in his writings of a 'Eureka!' moment that enabled him to go on and do all this. On the contrary, his mature doctrine that concepts are functions that map objects onto truth-values was only formulated in 'Function and Concept' (1891), some twelve years after he first presented his logical system in *Begriffsschrift* (1879). In *Begriffsschrift* itself, he seems to have regarded functions as just functional expressions which *represent* concepts (1879, §9), and as far as concepts are concerned, he oscillated between taking them to be what we *understand* by concept-words and what concept-words *refer to*.

What is notable about *Begriffsschrift* is that there is relatively little philosophical discussion. Frege explains his aim to clarify the nature of arithmetic, and the need for a more powerful logic, and offers some justification of his notion of 'conceptual content' (*begrifflicher Inhalt*), but in the main he simply applies function–argument analysis in developing quantificational logic. It does indeed all seem quite innocent. His *Begriffsschrift* received poor reviews, however, and he realized that he needed to explain its logical ideas and provide more justification. Particularly revealing in this respect is a letter he wrote in 1882 (see Frege [1997], 79–83), in which we can find the following theses formulated:

(A) A distinction must be drawn between concept and object.
(B) A distinction must be drawn between subsumption and subordination.
(C) Judgements (judgeable contents) are prior to concepts.
(D) Concepts are unsaturated.
(E) Judgeable contents have no unique analysis.
(F) Concepts must be sharply defined.
(G) The realm of the conceptual is the realm of the enumerable.
(H) Existential judgements are assertions about concepts.

With the exception of (E), all are only formulated *after Begriffsschrift*; and with qualifications to (C) and (E), which are necessary after Frege distinguished between *Sinn* and *Bedeutung*, all are endorsed for the rest of Frege's life and are fundamental to his philosophy. What we do not find, however, is any mention of concepts being functions.

In 1884, Frege published *The Foundations of Arithmetic*, which offers a much fuller informal explanation of his logical ideas and a sketch of his logicist project. Two further theses can be found here:

(I)   Number statements are assertions about concepts.
(J)   Every concept has an extension, which is an object.

(I) is just a generalization of (H), and while not explicitly formulated, (J) is implicit in the footnote to section 68. All the other theses can also be found, with the exception of (C), (D), and (E).[6] (C) might be seen as implicit in the context principle, and (E) as implicit in the argumentation in sections 62–9. But all three would require talk of function–argument analysis if they were to be properly explained, and talk of function–argument analysis is what is completely absent in the *Foundations*, surprising as that might seem. Indeed, beyond a solitary reference in section 1 in noting developments in mathematics, there is no mention of functions at all, let alone any characterization of concepts as functions.

Why? The charitable answer would be to say that Frege's very aim of explaining, informally, his logical ideas precluded such talk, relying as it does on technical notions in mathematics. The less charitable but philosophically more interesting answer is that Frege was somehow aware that what was driving his thinking, his first step, was only an analogy—the analogy between concepts and functions—and that this was too weak a basis on which to justify his logical theory and logicist project. So he quietly covered it up. We certainly find no announcement of a 'Eureka!' moment, no exclamation that 'Concepts are functions!'

3.4   Reconceiving Concepts

As mentioned, it is only when we get to 'Function and Concept', published in 1891, that we finally get an explicit statement that concepts are functions. What has happened by then is that Frege has distinguished, within his earlier notion of 'content', between *Sinn* and *Bedeutung*, and been led to conceive of the *Bedeutung* of a sentence as its truth-value, itself regarded as an object. The story of these developments is a very long one indeed, and

---

[6] For the record, (A) is endorsed as Frege's third fundamental principle (1884, X; see also §§ 27fn, 38, 51, 68fn, and 97); (B) is alluded to in §§ 47 and 53; (F) is stated in §§ 54 (with qualification) and 74; (G) can be found in §§ 14, 24, 40, 48, and 87; and (H) is explained and generalized as (I) in §§ 46, 53, and 57.

I will not even attempt to summarize it here. (I tell at least part of this story in Beaney 1996, chapter 6; and 2007.) I will simply note that it is immediately after his first account of these new ideas in 'Function and Concept' that he writes:

> We thus see how closely that which is called a concept in logic is connected with what we call a function. Indeed, we may say at once: a concept is a function whose value is always a truth-value. (Frege 1891, 139)

This is revealing. Frege begins by talking of how concepts and functions are 'connected', but then immediately *stipulates* an identity: a concept is a type of function.

What can have motivated this? In a piece written shortly afterwards, but only published posthumously, he repeats his claim that a concept is a function whose value is always a truth-value, and then goes on:

> Here I am borrowing the term 'function' from [mathematical] analysis and, whilst retaining what is essential to it, using it in a somewhat extended meaning [*Bedeutung*], a procedure for which the history of [mathematical] analysis itself affords a precedent. (Frege [1997], 173)

In arithmetic, in the simplest case, a function is a mapping from one number to another. The function $y = x^2$, for example, maps a number onto its square. As Frege had explained in 'Function and Concept', he had extended the meaning of 'function' to allow any object whatever, and not just numbers, to be the argument or value of a function. It is this that had raised the question of what the value of a concept is when conceived as a function, for any object taken as argument. Frege's answer was *a truth-value*, which then had to be taken as itself an object. So what we can see happening here is Frege thinking through the analogy between concepts and functions, and coming up with suggestions—or stipulations—to preserve the analogy as it is pushed further. Just as the concept of a function is transformed, by allowing any object to be an argument or value, so correspondingly is the concept of a concept transformed, by being understood as a mapping from any object whatever to one of the two truth-values (conceived as themselves objects).

Are concepts 'really' functions or not? In his early work Frege thought that concepts can be *represented* as functions—for the purposes of making logical relations clearer. But once he had drawn the *Sinn/Bedeutung* distinction, he came to hold that the *Bedeutung* of a concept-word was a concept, just as the *Bedeutung* of a functional expression was a function. Given that concept-words were construed as functional expressions with one argument-place, it followed that concepts were indeed seen as functions. Since concepts had to be defined for all objects, on Frege's view, the only remaining question concerned what their value was for any object as argument, and this is what his conception of the *Bedeutung* of a sentence as a truth-value answered. We thus reach his mature view of concepts as functions whose value is always a truth-value.

Concepts can be *seen as* functions, then, which can be valuable in helping us gain insight into logical relations and validity. But the question as to whether concepts are 'really' functions is badly framed, to use Wittgenstein's phrase. What was said at the end of Subsection 2.4, in discussing Cantor's development of transfinite arithmetic, is no less apt here. What is at issue is the determination of concepts, and what Frege was trying to force on us were *new concepts* of object, truth-value, function, and indeed of concept itself. This may have given rise to a powerful and fruitful conceptual space, in making possible quantificational logic, but any conceptual space can also, at some point down the line, turn into a fly-bottle.

4   Wittgenstein's Conceptual Creativity

4.1   Connective Creativity

To what extent and in what ways was Wittgenstein creative in his own work? In his main remarks on philosophy in the *Investigations* (§§89–133) he makes clear his view that philosophy should merely describe and not explain:

> All *explanation* must disappear, and description alone must take its place. And this description gets its light – that is to say, its purpose – from the philosophical problems. ... The problems are solved, not by coming up with new discoveries, but by assembling what we have long been familiar with. (§109)

> Philosophy must not interfere in any way with the actual use of language, so it can in the end only describe it. ...
> It leaves everything as it is. (§124)

> Philosophy just puts everything before us, and neither explains nor deduces anything. ...
> The name "philosophy" might also be given to what is possible *before* all new discoveries and inventions. (§126)

Faced with these and similar remarks made throughout his later writings, how could one see Wittgenstein in any way as creative? Does he not explicitly deny that there are any discoveries or inventions in philosophy? It was noted above that talk of 'creativity' is entirely absent in the *Investigations*. In the light of these remarks, is it not obvious why?

On the other hand, as we have also seen, Wittgenstein makes use of a wide range of analogies, metaphors, and pictures in his own writings, and he is also responsible for introducing new concepts into philosophy, such as that of a language-game, an *Übersicht*, a philosophical superlative, and aspect blindness, not to mention coming up with numerous phrases and one-liners that are now a staple part of the philosophical lexicon. Indeed, Wittgenstein surely counts as one of the most original thinkers in the entire history of philosophy. So how could he not be regarded as creative?

How are we to resolve this apparent tension? In Section 2 we discussed three different forms of creativity—combinational, exploratory, and transformational—with various examples given, and one only has to reflect on these to realize that there are many ways of being creative. Wittgenstein may not have created a new conceptual space in the way that Frege did, and indeed, may have repudiated such endeavours, but that does not mean that he was not creative in other ways. One important form of creativity is required even for the pure description that Wittgenstein thinks philosophy should provide.

The work of the philosopher, on Wittgenstein's view, 'consists in marshalling recollections (*Erinnerungen*) for a particular purpose' (PI §127). The main purpose, of course, is to resolve a philosophical problem, but to do this we have to find the 'right' recollections. In section 122 of the *Investigations* he writes:

> A main source of our failure to understand is that we don't have *an overview* of the use of our words. – Our grammar is deficient in surveyability (*Übersichtlichkeit*). A surveyable representation produces precisely that kind of understanding which consists in 'seeing connections'. Hence the importance of finding and inventing *intermediate links*.

The right recollections are those that constitute an *Übersicht*, enabling us to 'see connections'. But seeing connections is itself a form of creativity, and in talking of 'finding and inventing intermediate links', Wittgenstein is admitting that creativity is required here. It is analogous to the creativity required for solving problems in Euclidean geometry—finding the right previously proved theorems or introducing auxiliary lines to prove or construct something. (For a worked-out example of this, see Beaney 2005, appendix 1.) One of the most powerful ways in which Wittgenstein was connectively creative in his later work was in inventing simple language-games to shed light on our more complex linguistic practices (see PI §§ 5 and 130).

4.2   Therapeutic Analysis

How can providing an *Übersicht* resolve a philosophical problem? To return to our metaphor, how can it show us the way out of the fly-bottle? As we have seen, one way in which we can become trapped in a fly-bottle is by carrying an analogy too far. Providing an *Übersicht* of all our uses of that analogy can show us its limitations (§§423–6). But more is typically needed than just this. Using an analogy, seemingly innocently and unconsciously, can constitute that first step from which a philosophical dispute then arises. So we must identify this first step. To show someone the way out of the fly-bottle, we have to show them how they got into the fly-bottle in the first place. So some kind of analysis is needed to help them trace their route back to their first step, and this might aptly be called *therapeutic analysis*.

We can see this illustrated in the account I gave in Section 3 of Frege's first step. Convinced by the power of function–argument analysis in representing the logical relations between sentences whose quantificational complexity had resisted clarification up to then, the implicit analogy between concepts and functions slowly worked its way through his philosophical thinking. As in the case of a bug that gradually takes hold of someone's body, however, he soon showed overt symptoms of illness: paradoxes that could not be shaken off by his own conceptual resources. 'The philosopher treats a question', wrote Wittgenstein, 'like an illness' (PI §255; see also §254). But as a mental rather than a bodily illness, there is no medical operation or injection that can cure it overnight. 'In philosophizing we may not *terminate* a disease of thought. It must run its natural course, and *slow* cure is all important' (Z §382). 'This is how philosophers should salute each other: "Take your time!"' (CV 91e; see also 40).

How can creativity be revealed in therapeutic analysis? Isn't it just a matter of diagnosing the first step and then carefully describing how the philosophical disputes and problems arise? In a remark added at the end of section 133 of the *Investigations* Wittgenstein writes: 'There is not a single philosophical method, though there are indeed methods, different therapies, as it were.' So creativity may be required to find the right therapies. These will be the ones that cure the philosophical illness, but as in psychoanalysis, they must be recognized by the patients themselves if their philosophical confusions are to be removed. How can this be done?

4.3 'That's Exactly How I Meant It!'

In the section entitled 'Philosophy Points out the Misleading Analogies in the Use of our Language' in the *Big Typescript*, Wittgenstein writes:

> The philosopher strives to find the liberating word [*das erlösende Wort*], and that is the word that finally permits us to grasp what until then had constantly and intangibly weighed on our consciousness.
>
> (It's like having a hair on one's tongue; one feels it, but can't get hold of it, and therefore can't get rid of it.)
>
> The philosopher provides us with the word with which we can express the matter and render it harmless.
>
> (The choice of our words is so important, because the point is to hit the physiognomy of the matter exactly; because only the thought that is precisely targeted can lead the right way. The railway carriage must be placed on the tracks exactly, so that it can keep on rolling as it is supposed to.)
>
> One of the most important tasks is to express all false thought processes so true to character that the reader says, "Yes, that's exactly the way I meant it". To make a tracing of the physiognomy of every error.
>
> Indeed, we can only prove that someone made a mistake if he (really) acknowledges this expression as the correct expression of his feeling.
>
> For only if he acknowledges it as such, *is* it the correct expression. (Psychoanalysis.)
>
> What the other person acknowledges is the analogy I'm presenting to him as the source of his thought. (BT 302e–303e)

'Yes, that's exactly how I meant it' ('Ja, genau so habe ich es gemeint') is clearly related to those expressions of sudden understanding or recognition that have been a theme of this essay. Indeed, it is precisely an expression of 'Now I understand!' but with the difference that I recognize *where I went wrong* rather than my *correct* grasp of something. It is a 'Eureka!' moment—though not one where I can now go on, but one where I can now go back and find my way out of the fly-bottle. It is as if Wittgenstein had managed to bring Frege (*per impossibile!*) to exclaim 'Yes, I did indeed regard concepts as functions—*and now I see where I was led astray!*'

The 'liberating' or 'redeeming' (*erlösende*) word that the philosopher tries to find, then, is precisely that phrase that someone can be brought to recognize and use as expressing their acknowledgement of where they went wrong: 'Of course, I now see that that was only an analogy', 'You're right, I was indeed misled by that metaphor', and so on. But as in the other cases of sudden understanding, the expressions are not to be construed as representing a mental state or process, but as warranted by the particular circumstances in which their use is embedded, circumstances that involve the 'slow cure' of which Wittgenstein spoke in section 382 of *Zettel*.

The idea of a liberating word is one that we find articulated very soon after Wittgenstein's return to philosophy in 1929.[7] In conversations with Schlick and Waismann in January 1930, Wittgenstein is reported as saying:

> In this matter it is always as follows. Everything we do consists in trying to find the liberating word. In grammar you cannot discover anything. There are no surprises. When formulating a rule we always have the feeling: That is something you have known all along. We can do only one thing—clearly articulate the rule we have been applying unawares. (WVC 77)

This connects the idea of a liberating word with the claim that there are no discoveries or surprises in philosophy. The passage also shows the continuity between Wittgenstein's early and later work. In the *Tractatus* he had stated that there are no surprises in logic (6.1251), and in the *Investigations* he was insistent that there are no discoveries in philosophy. Indeed, the idea of a liberating word is so fundamental to Wittgenstein's philosophy that it would be tempting to see it as his own first step. Right from the beginning, Wittgenstein had seen philosophy—or at any rate, his own philosophizing—as an attempt to gain clarity about our use of language in order to resolve philosophical problems.

Wittgenstein's stress on the liberating word also makes sense of his own way of doing philosophy: writing down remarks, and then continually revising and re-ordering them in trying to find precisely the right formulations—to 'hit the physiognomy of the matter exactly', as he put it in the *Big Typescript*. As a philosopher, he can thus be compared to a poet, as he recognized himself in *Culture and Value*: 'I believe I summed up where I stand in relation to philosophy when I said: really one should write philosophy only as one *writes a poem*' (CV 28e). In the passage cited from the *Big Typescript* alone, he uses two pregnant images—of having a hair on one's tongue and of a railway carriage running on its tracks. 'A good comparison', he noted, 'refreshes the intellect' (CV 3e; translation modified).

---

[7] The term is used much earlier, in remarks he made in his coded notebooks between October 1914 and January 1915. Wittgenstein expresses his concern to find the 'erlösende Wort' that will solve his problems, but the term is not used again, it seems, until 1929, and we never learn if he ever found such a word (see Klagge 2010, 245–6). Its early occurrence, however, lends support to the suggestion I go on to make that what we have here is something of a 'first step'. For later discussion of finding the 'right' (*richtige*) word, see PPF §§295–300.

Culture and Value, in fact, is full of reflections on his philosophical method, style, and originality. Perhaps the most revealing are the following:

> I think there is some truth in my idea that I am really only reproductive in my thinking. I think I have never *invented* a line of thinking but that it was always provided for me by someone else & I have done no more than passionately take it up for my work of clarification. . . . What I invent are new *comparisons*. (CV 16e)

> My originality (if that is the right word) is, I believe, an originality that belongs to the soil, not the seed. (Perhaps I have no seed of my own.) Sow a seed in my soil, & it will grow differently than it would in any other soil. (CV 42e)

Frege is one of those, amongst others, whom Wittgenstein specifically names in the first passage as having influenced him in his work of clarification. In developing the new conceptual space of quantificational logic, Frege did indeed invent a line of thinking, and Wittgenstein saw one of his tasks as finding the liberating words to clarify this.

4.4   Changing Our Ways of Looking at Things

We are now in a position to gain a better appreciation—through the *Übersicht* provided in the previous sections—of the fundamental connection between Wittgenstein's philosophical methodology, his concern with the various expressions of sudden understanding and recognition, including liberating words, and his discussion of aspect perception. In particular, his reflections on aspect perception, written after his work on the *Investigations*, can now be seen as picking up and developing themes whose currents had been running quite deeply throughout his later thinking. (For more on this, see Baker [2004].)

It is not just that there is a profound thematic connection between expressions of sudden understanding and our recognition of a new aspect to something, all of which are embedded in 'particular circumstances', but that lying at the core of our experience of aspect change is that sense, which Wittgenstein formulated in various ways, as we saw in Subsection 1.4, that what we see both stays the same and yet is seen differently (see also CV 45–6). In philosophy what we are looking at, on Wittgenstein's view, does indeed stay the same—our use of words. And yet the aim is to see it differently, by identifying a first step and gaining an *Übersicht*, to enable us to resolve a philosophical problem—to find our way out of the fly-bottle.

Wittgenstein frequently spoke of coming back to the same point over and over again (see, for instance, PI, preface; and CV 9–10). This was not simply a matter of the helpfulness of seeing things from different angles, but of loosening the grip of entrenched ways of seeing things. The theme of seeing different aspects surfaces in various places in the *Investigations* (see, for instance, §§ 122, 387, 401, and 420). But the key section in this regard is the following:

> The aspects of things that are most important for us are hidden because of their simplicity and familiarity. (One is unable to notice something – because it is always before one's eyes.) The real foundations of their inquiry do not strike people at all. Unless *that* fact has at some time struck them. – And this means: we fail to be struck by what, once seen, is most striking and most powerful. (PI §129)

The analogies, metaphors, and pictures that give rise to philosophical puzzlement are so deeply embedded in our use of language that we have to work hard to counteract their effect on us. We have to change our '*way of looking at things*', as Wittgenstein puts it (PI §144; see also CV 70). As in some cases of aspect perception, once we have indeed seen a new aspect, the old one is overridden, so that the problems just drop away (see CV 55). But even if we can switch at will between the aspects, as in the case of the duck–rabbit picture, this will be enough to loosen the grip of the old one.

Seeing new aspects exhibits creativity. To the extent that these aspects are 'ways of looking at things', they are more thoroughly conceptual than the visual examples that Wittgenstein explored in his discussion of aspect perception. Offering us new ways of looking at things, then, exhibits conceptual creativity. This should not be regarded as a lesser form of creativity because what is conceived is somehow 'left the same'; on the contrary, it could be characterized as bringing together combinational, exploratory, and transformational creativity. 'A thinker', Wittgenstein wrote, 'is <u>very</u> similar to a draughtsman. Who wants to represent all the interconnections' (CV 14e). If this is meant as a self-description, then it considerably underplays his own creativity. Seeing and articulating connections is both thinking and creating. That's it![8]

---

[8] See also CV 78. I am grateful to Sebastian Sunday for detailed comments on the first draft of this essay, and to audiences in Berlin, Hamilton (Canada), and Budapest for helpful discussion when I gave talks based on it.

CHAPTER 8

Wittgenstein and Analytic Revisionism

Martin Gustafsson

I Introduction

Wittgenstein's notorious dictum that philosophy "leaves everything as it is" (PI §124) has often been met with incomprehension. It is sometimes read as an expression of a philosophically self-mutilating conservatism, based on nothing more substantive than a sentimental predilection for the inherited vernacular. This line of criticism was central to early attacks on Wittgenstein's philosophy by Ernest Gellner (1959), Herbert Marcuse (1964), and others. In a less hostile but equally incredulous mode of reaction, others have thought that Wittgenstein's dictum is strangely unfruitful and naïve. After all, some reshaping of inherited conceptual apparatuses will be involved in any genuinely groundbreaking search for knowledge; so why should philosophy allow itself to be restricted in the way Wittgenstein suggests? (See, for example, Churchland 2005.)

Set in a broader philosophical context, however, the dictum should not seem so eccentric or unfamiliar. One only has to look at twentieth-century phenomenology: as any reader of Husserl or Heidegger knows, it is a central thought in that tradition that philosophy is an exercise in letting things be what they are, while avoiding any remaking induced by an unwitting or deliberate imposition of preconceived theoretical categories. The fact that many philosophers today do not recognize it as a serious philosophical option is perhaps a sign of a certain narrow-mindedness in contemporary thought, rather than an indication that the dictum itself is obviously mistaken.

In fact, it used to be a seriously debated issue also within analytic philosophy whether philosophy should leave things as they are or not. At that time, those who wanted to reject the sort of conception stated in Wittgenstein's dictum at least felt the need to support the opposite stance with cogent arguments. Thus arose within analytic philosophy a strong and methodologically self-conscious strand of what I am going to call *analytic revisionism*.

According to analytic revisionists, many of our inherited linguistic practices are substantially defective. By the term "substantially defective," I mean to indicate that revisionists conceive the alleged imperfections not just as matters of potentially confusing notation, but as deficiencies that are somehow built into the very functioning of linguistic expressions in their real-life use. Thus, in Carnap's view, much established usage suffers from an inherent inexactness that is philosophically and scientifically unsatisfactory, and he takes it to be an important philosophical task to remedy this deficiency by replacing inexact concepts with more precise ones in a process of *explication* (Carnap 1945, 1950). Quine shares Carnap's dissatisfaction with the imprecision of our inherited linguistic practices, but thinks of the philosophical revision of those practices as having ontological purpose: the revision is supposed to impose a scheme such that ontological commitments are clearly exhibited, and then reduce those commitments to a minimum (Quine 1960). Rorty, on the other hand, does not care so much about formal precision, but is instead keen to identify obsolete ideological or political viewpoints that he thinks are built into much established discourse, arguing that we philosophers should strive to find replacements that are better adjusted to the needs of our own time (Rorty 1979, 1982). So, while there are considerable differences between how individual revisionists conceive of the goal and nature of the needed revision, they share the overall idea that language as we use it is defective, and that it is therefore a central philosophical task to replace those parts of it which are inherently flawed with new and better substitutes.

In recent years, there has been much renewed interest in revisionist methodologies (see, for instance, Gustafsson 2006, 2014a; Carus 2007; Wagner 2012; Novaes and Reck 2017; and Pearson 2017). These discussions have contained few comparisons with the opposite, Wittgensteinian stance (an exception is Reck 2012). My overall aim in this essay is to make such a comparison. I thereby seek to identify what I take to be the fundamentally question-begging character of revisionist methodologies. I will focus on the two perhaps most prominent analytic revisionists, Carnap and Quine. However, the sort of Wittgensteinian worry I shall try to articulate is meant to address revisionist methodologies generally.

II   Early Wittgenstein vs. Analytic Revisionism

The dictum that philosophy leaves everything as it is only appears in Wittgenstein's later work. To fully understand this dictum, however, it is useful first to consider the way in which *early* Wittgenstein is *also* a non-revisionist, and to clarify exactly how his later non-revisionism differs from the earlier version.

In *Tractatus* 5.5563, Wittgenstein writes:

> In fact, all the propositions of our everyday language [*Umgangssprache*], just as they stand, are in perfect logical order.

This expresses a non-revisionist stance, according to which there is nothing logically at fault with the propositions we employ in real-life, meaningful communication.[1] This stance entails that it cannot be a philosophical aim to replace such propositions with others that are somehow in better logical shape. In fact, early Wittgenstein seems to think that the very idea of a proposition which is put to real-life communicative use and which is yet somehow logically defective is confused: "In a certain sense, we cannot make mistakes in logic" (5.473). Arguably, his idea is that to the extent that a proposition is a proposition *at all*—to the extent that it is used to say *anything*—its logical order must be impeccable. Or, better: according to early Wittgenstein, there simply is no such thing as a proposition's being in "defective logical order." Being in less than perfect logical order can only mean having no logical order whatsoever, being mere nonsense.[2] The upshot is that, in early Wittgenstein's view, there is no vantage point from which the philosopher can criticize and try to improve the logical order of propositions that have a meaningful function in actual communication. According to Wittgenstein, there is no more fundamental criterion of logical perfection than being used in such meaningful linguistic exchange.

There are some passages in the *Tractatus* that may appear hard to reconcile with this non-revisionist conception. In such passages, Wittgenstein seems to say that colloquial language is not perfectly adapted to logic, and that it is an important philosophical task to design a replacement, the syntax of which is fully and genuinely logical. Consider the following passage from 4.002:

> Language disguises thought. So much so, that from the outward form of the clothing it is impossible to infer the form of the thought beneath it, because the outward form of the clothing is not designed to reveal the form of the body, but for entirely different purposes.

---

[1] By "*Umgangssprache*," I take it, Wittgenstein means any language we know and actually make use of. Contrary to what Pears and McGuinness's translation suggests, there is little evidence that his discussion depends on any contrast between "everyday" language and, say, the more specialized languages used in less "everyday" contexts such as legal, medical, or scientific ones.

[2] See also James Conant's illuminating treatment of early Wittgenstein's non-revisionism (Conant 2002b, esp. 416–18). My discussion in Section II is indebted to Conant's at several points.

And then there are these excerpts from 3.323–3.325:

> In everyday language it very frequently happens that the same word has
> different modes of signification ... or that two words that have different
> modes of signification are employed in propositions in what is superficially
> the same way.
>
> In this way the most fundamental confusions are easily produced (the
> whole of philosophy is full of them).
>
> In order to avoid such errors we must make use of a sign-language that ...
> is governed by *logical* grammar – by logical syntax.

However, it is crucial to early Wittgenstein's conception of logic, language, and
philosophy that such apparently revisionist passages are meant to be compatible
with the Tractarian notion that all colloquial propositions are in perfect logical
order just as they stand. Admittedly, Wittgenstein later came to realize that
things are not quite as simple, and that there *is* a conflict between a consistently
non-revisionist stance and the Tractarian conception of what sort of clarity
a notation governed by logical syntax can be used to achieve. Importantly,
however, this conflict is not visible from within the Tractarian framework, but
can be recognized only if one radically questions the early Wittgenstein's very
idea of what logical order must amount to (see Section III below).

So, why—from the viewpoint of the author of the *Tractatus*—is there no
conflict here? How can early Wittgenstein hold that all the propositions of
colloquial language are in perfect logical order just as they stand, while at the
same time say that colloquial language disguises thought and is not governed by
logical syntax?

In short, his view is that the only philosophically relevant sort of "defect"
present in colloquial language is a matter of surface appearance—more specifically, notational features—that are potentially confusing since they do not
perspicuously mirror the logic of the thoughts that are being expressed. His
point is that the notation of colloquial language does not allow us to read off
the logical structure directly from the notational structure itself—whereas
a notation governed by logical syntax allows us to do precisely that.
Importantly, Wittgenstein thinks those confusing notational features are
only *potentially* confusing. His view is not that they *normally* confuse us
when we use language in real life. Nor does he think that such potentially
confusing surface features prevent users of colloquial language from using
propositions to express thoughts that are in perfect logical order.[3] Indeed,

---

[3] Throughout Section II, I use "proposition" to refer to a logical unit, a sentence *in meaningful use*.
Such a unit is identified not in terms of its phonetic or orthographic characteristics, but in terms of its
location within a network of fixed and perfectly determinate inferential relations to other

from the viewpoint of early Wittgenstein, it is doubtful to describe the potentially confusing surface appearance of colloquial language as a defect, since colloquial notation was "designed for entirely different purposes" than to perspicuously mirror logical structure. Such talk of defectiveness is a bit like saying that clothes are bad to the extent that they hide the form of the body— as if all clothes should ideally be made of latex.

So, even if Wittgenstein says "the most fundamental confusions are easily produced" by the lack of logical perspicuity characteristic of our inherited colloquial notation, he never suggests that lack of such perspicuity constitutes a general obstacle to the successful communication of logically well-ordered content. All he does is to register the following fact: "Man possesses the ability to construct languages capable of expressing every sense, without having any idea how each word has meaning or what its meaning is" (TLP 4.002). He *starts from* the observation that we can express and communicate determinate, logically well-ordered thoughts even by means of a notation that disguises the logic of those thoughts. This communicative capacity is not something he aspires to explain, and he is not committed to any determinate view of how it is possible. Presumably he would regard the search for such an explanation as an empirical rather than a philosophical undertaking.

So, according to the author of the *Tractatus*, even if the notation of colloquial language lacks logical perspicuity, sentences couched in such notation are for the most part successfully used to communicate determinately true-or-false thoughts. Indeed, his view is that being a competent speaker is precisely a matter of being able to use colloquial sentences to such an effect. For example, as a competent speaker, I may use the sentence "Short is short" under circumstances in which it is clear to my listeners what is being said, for instance circumstances in which it is clear that a certain individual (my boss, Mr. Short, say) is being referred to and that it is said of him that he is short in terms of bodily length (relative to a contextually determined comparison class, say). Certainly, a logically perspicuous notation would not employ the sign "short" (or any other sign) in two different modes of signification, or in such a way that its meaning shifts between different contexts of utterance. But again, Wittgenstein does not think that the sort of perspicuity such a logically perspicuous notation offers is needed for the communication of

propositions. Crucially, this is how Wittgenstein talks of propositions (*Sätze*) in 5.5563; and thus conceived, he claims that a proposition and a thought are the same thing (see TLP 3.5 and 4). For more discussion of this point, see the beginning of Section III.

determinate thoughts. Indeed, given Wittgenstein's view of how extensive the fully analyzed versions of even the most humdrum colloquial sentences are, he would certainly say that a thorough employment of a notation governed by logical syntax would severely impede rather than facilitate the real-life use of language.

Now, even if Wittgenstein holds that colloquial sentences are for the most part successfully used to communicate determinately true-or-false thoughts, it is of course true that his whole approach to philosophy is based on the observation that lack of logical perspicuity in colloquial notation *can* lead to confusion, both in philosophy and in ordinary communication. Such confusions can often be resolved by simple maneuvers of disambiguation and other straightforward moves—there is usually no need to introduce a special notation. However, when it comes to confusions which are severe enough to cause persistent philosophical trouble, the entanglements are often more difficult to sort out, and thus more far-reaching clarification may be needed in order to get a sufficiently clear overview of the logical situation. Early Wittgenstein's view is that in response to such deep-going confusions, a notation specifically designed to exhibit logical structure may be of genuine use.

We can now identify four central and interrelated elements of early Wittgenstein's non-revisionism, each marking a difference between him and most analytic revisionists:

(i)   Early Wittgenstein agrees with revisionists such as Carnap and Quine that it can be philosophically useful to replace sentences in colloquial language with sentences couched in a logically perspicuous notation. However, he thinks the gain is not that we thereby manage to express more precise thoughts than in colloquial language. Rather, the point is to offer an absolutely clear way of expressing *already* precise thoughts. By contrast, most revisionists conceive of such replacement as involving a more substantive achievement. According to them, logically perspicuous *ersätze* do not just make transparent what was already expressed by the colloquial sentences, but make the use of language itself logically more satisfactory. Roughly, their idea is that it is only once the logically perspicuous replacement has been found that we manage to say something fully precise, with perfectly determinate entailment relations to other things we might say, with perfectly determinate ontological commitments, and so on.[4]

---

[4] *Tractatus* 4.112 may seem to go against my non-revisionist reading. As Conant convincingly argues, however, Wittgenstein's correspondence with C. K. Ogden strongly suggests that he did not intend this paragraph to have revisionist implications (Conant 2002b, 416–17).

(ii) Most revisionists agree with early Wittgenstein that it would be a futile aim to make ordinary people *abandon* established modes of expression in favor of a philosophically more satisfactory notation (an exception is Rorty; see Gustafsson 2011). Carnap and Quine both emphasize that colloquial language has been adapted to handle the practicalities of human life, and that it would hamper the purposes of daily communication if people were to actually make use of a logically satisfactory *Begriffsschrift*. However, according to the revisionists there is a *trade-off* to be made between the practical aims of real-life communication and the logical orderliness or determinacy of what thus gets communicated. They think the practical aims of everyday linguistic exchange can be fulfilled only *at the expense* of the logical orderliness of the messages conveyed. Whereas for early Wittgenstein, perfect logical order is necessary for meaningful communication to occur in the first place, and thus there can be no conflict between logical orderliness and the practicalities of everyday communication. The only trade-off Wittgenstein recognizes takes place at the level of notational perspicuity, in the sense that the aims and circumstances of everyday linguistic exchange make the use of a logically perspicuous notation hopelessly impractical.

(iii) The upshot of early Wittgenstein's conception is, therefore, that replacing a colloquial sentence with one couched in logically perspicuous notation has little rationale except as a *response* to an actual confusion. As long as language use proceeds without such confusion, replacement is pointless. Or, to be more precise: there might be special contexts in which the danger of conceptual confusion is imminent enough to motivate a preventive introduction of a logically perspicuous notation. But in the vast majority of cases such a replacement is out of place. In particular, replacing a colloquial sentence with one couched in logically perspicuous notation does not mean that the message conveyed by the sentence gets in any better logical shape. By contrast, a revisionist thinks of the revision proposed not just as a remedy to confusions *about* what is being said, but as an improvement of *what* is being said. Certainly, the revisionist grants that the gain of such an improvement will have to be weighed against the practical inconvenience of using a logically satisfactory language, and that the practical inconvenience may in the end carry greater weight. But what Wittgenstein questions is the very idea that there is such a weighing to be made in the first place.

(iv)   It follows from early Wittgenstein's conception that it is *we*, the
confused ones, who are the real and fundamental objects of philosophical treatment. Language itself is philosophically problematic
only to the extent that we get confused by its notational peculiarities.
This is not to say that early Wittgenstein thinks of philosophical
confusions as individual whims, gratuitously varying from one person to another and arbitrarily induced in unpredictable ways by
random linguistic quirks. At the beginning of the thirties, he
would write about how language involves "misleading analogies"
against which philosophy has to fight a "constant battle" (BT
302e); and he would notice that "language has the same traps ready
for everyone; the immense network of easily trodden false paths"
(312e). As I understand his early non-revisionism, it is to be viewed as
entirely compatible with such a view of the misleading potentials of
colloquial language. This is why there are occasions with regard to
which early Wittgenstein might acknowledge that a preventive introduction of a logically perspicuous notation is in place, namely,
occasions at which the threat of philosophical confusion is predictable and imminent, and where the introduction of such a notation
would not be in conflict with other and more important purposes of
communication.

III   Later Wittgenstein vs. Analytic Revisionism

When early Wittgenstein says that all the propositions of our everyday
language are in perfect logical order just as they stand, he means by
"propositions" not units that are individuated in terms of their phonetic or
orthographic characteristics, but *logical* units, that is, units that are identified
in terms of their location within a network of other propositions that stand
in fixed and perfectly determinate inferential relations to each other (see also
Note 3). This is why he can consistently say that colloquial sentences are
couched in a notation the structure of which does not reflect the logical
structure of the propositions that those sentences constitute qua sentences-in
-use. In the one case, Wittgenstein talks of sentences qua units in logical
employment, whereas in the other he talks about what is logically arbitrary
about such sentences—their phonetic or orthographic appearance.

One thing the early Wittgenstein resists here is the mentalist notion that
thoughts or propositions are non- or prelinguistic entities hidden in the
minds of speakers, and that language consists of phonetic and orthographic

units that those speakers can use to somehow codify and transmit such hidden thoughts despite the fact that the phonetics and orthography disguise logical structure. Instead, early Wittgenstein conceives thinking in terms of linguistic activity: a thought or proposition *is* a propositional sign in its logico-syntactical employment (TLP 3.5; 4).

Still, it is arguable that early Wittgenstein's notion of language use is too much of an a priori artifice to completely uproot the prejudices and confusions of mentalism. For the early Wittgenstein's conception of "use" does not proceed from any detailed recollection of the actual linguistic habits of real-life language users, but from an already settled view of what description and inference must essentially be like. His idea is this. From a strictly logical point of view, language must consist of a totality of possible propositions that stand in fixed and perfectly determinate inferential relations to each other—relations that show exactly how the complex propositions of the language are constructed from elementary propositions. Each elementary proposition pictures a determinate state of affairs, and the way in which a complex proposition is constructed shows what combinations of such states of affairs would make the proposition true and what combinations would make it false. The logical pattern that constitutes the structure of this totality of propositions *is* the pattern of use that early Wittgenstein has in mind when he talks of "the use" of language. According to him, to the extent that we describe the world and make inferences, what we do simply has to conform to this pattern; for the presence of this pattern is a condition for the very possibility of picturing reality and drawing conclusions from premises. Certainly, if we stare ourselves blind at the surface of colloquial notation, the linguistic activities do not seem to exhibit such clear-cut precision and determinacy. However, Wittgenstein holds, this apparent mismatch can only be apparent. If we translate colloquial sentences into a notation governed by logical syntax, the underlying pattern is brought to the immediately visible surface of the notation itself; but as a pattern of our *activities* of describing and inferring, the pattern must have been present all along.

The worry about this Tractarian way of thinking is as follows. Even if it distances itself from a mentalism according to which thinking is separable from (and perhaps prior to) language use, it still seems to conceive of the thoughts that get communicated in linguistic exchange as in a radical sense *hidden beneath the surface* of colloquial language. If early Wittgenstein had thought that familiar maneuvers of disambiguation, exemplification, and so on, would suffice to clearly spell out these thoughts or contents, this might not have been a huge problem. However, his view is that exhibiting the full logical structure requires a much more far-reaching analysis—so much so that he himself is not able to give one single example of what an elementary constituent of a fully analyzed proposition would be! The closer one looks at the discrepancies between the simple and clear-cut logical structure that the early Wittgenstein thinks characterizes the descriptive and inferential roles of propositions, and the variability of colloquial language as it actually functions in the multifarious circumstances of human life, the Tractarian vision seems more like an imposed a priori requirement than a genuine insight into the essence of description and inference.

And this, of course, is precisely the criticism that later Wittgenstein delivers against his earlier self:

> The more closely we examine actual language, the greater becomes the conflict between it and our requirement. (For the crystalline purity of logic was, of course, not something I had *discovered*: it was a requirement.) The conflict becomes intolerable; the requirement is now in danger of becoming vacuous. (PI §107)

Interestingly, this is a criticism with which revisionists such as Carnap and Quine would feel sympathetic. To understand why, notice that early Wittgenstein's non-revisionism can be seen as an instance of a traditional philosophical attitude that both Carnap and Quine want to combat.[5] A philosopher who has such a traditional attitude thinks that logical law and order is a prerequisite for the very aspiration to infer and make true-or-false statements about the world. When such a traditional philosopher looks at colloquial usage, what he conceives as such law and order is not present at the visible surface. Rather, there seems to him to be a huge gap between the visible mess and the requirements of logic. However, the traditional philosopher's conclusion at this point is not that the users of colloquial language must therefore be deluded in their belief that they are describing the world, drawing inferences, and justifying beliefs. Nor does the traditional philosopher conclude that there is something at fault with his own conception of what logic, truth, inference, and justification require. Rather, his conclusion tends to be that a properly ordered logical activity must still be taking place, even if it cannot be directly read off from the visible surface. Perhaps he calls this activity *thinking*, and holds that the elements and structure of thought must be perfectly determinate as far as

---

[5] In the five paragraphs following the quotation of PI §107, I have drawn on my 'Quine's Conception of Explication – and Why It Isn't Carnap's' (2014a, esp. 511–12).

their logical properties are concerned. Thus he arrives at a picture according to which colloquial language might be said to express logically determinate thoughts, albeit blurrily as it were. This sort of picture opens up the prospect for constructing a more adequately designed symbolism, which lets the logical structure shine through in a perfectly undistorted manner.

A view along these lines may seem persuasive as long as one is convinced that there is just one compulsory logical framework within which description and inference can take place. Given this conviction, even if there is a huge gap between the surface of colloquial language and the logical order of such cognitive activities, claiming that these cognitive activities have precisely this logical order may seem virtually unavoidable. After all, the presumption is that this order is the only order such activities *can* have, qua cognitive.

At the beginning of the 1930s, Carnap finds himself in a situation where it has become increasingly difficult to retain the conviction that there is just one logical framework to which one must adhere as long as one aspires to engage in genuinely cognitive activity. For there are now an increasing number of different but formally well-behaved logical systems available, some of which seem to be as good as standard logic at capturing practices like ordinary arithmetic. In this situation, any claim to the effect that the speakers of a language in actual use—be it the language of ordinary arithmetic, of ordinary physics, or of some more everyday practice— must *really* adhere to the logical framework F1 (rather than F2, or F3, . . . and so on, all of which are such that visible colloquial practice can be made to fit them) seems hard to justify. Indeed, it is unclear what it would *mean* to justify such a claim, especially if one wants to avoid mentalist speculations about contents hidden in speakers' minds.

In this situation, a possible reaction is to abandon the very idea of "logical law and order" which makes colloquial language seem so disastrously messy to begin with, and argue instead that it is the traditional philosopher's abstractedly conceived conception of what such order must amount to that creates the problem. Later Wittgenstein's reaction is along these lines. Carnap, however, does *not* react in this sort of way. Instead, he retains the traditional idea that the presence of the sort of law and order which characterizes a formal system of logical symbolism is a prerequisite for an adequately precise application of terms such as "truth," "valid inference," "evidence," and "justification." So, while he rejects the notion that there is just *one* calculus or one semantic system which gives us *the* order necessary for such talk, he does not reject the idea that *some* such system needs to be in place if such talk is going to be applied in a properly strict fashion.

For the traditional philosopher, the messiness of colloquial practice is a mere surface phenomenon. At the deeper level of logic, law and order reigns; and this is the order that a properly constructed symbolism is designed to articulate. For Carnap, by contrast, there is no such deeper level of stable and well-determined thoughts. He thinks the messy surface is all there is to colloquial language use. In offering a re-articulation in logical symbolism, what we do, according to Carnap, is to impose rigor from without—we engage in conceptual engineering. And this is something we can do in various ways: the "correspondence" between colloquial language and the imposed system is always loose enough to allow for a multitude of different alternatives (see Stein 1992, 281–2, and Ricketts 2003, 261ff). As philosophers we should tolerate all these possibilities, as long as they are formally precise. Which of these different explications eventually turns out to be the most fruitful one cannot be decided a priori, but will have to show itself in future scientific practice. As philosophers, we must therefore leave it to the working scientist to determine which framework is fittest for survival.

Quine's view is different. He does not share Carnap's tolerance toward alternative logical frameworks, but insists that colloquial language should be revised to fit a "canonical notation" that employs only the austere extensional resources of first-order predicate logic. This is not because Quine is any closer than Carnap to the sort of traditional attitude sketched above. His view is not that his canonical notation captures a structure that somehow already underlies established linguistic practices. Rather, his aim is to tweak colloquial language into a framework that allows us to raise ontological questions in a precise manner for the first time. According to Quine, it is only once we have regimented our descriptions of the world according to the strictures of first-order predicate logic that we can be said to have committed ourselves clearly to a determinate ontology; and it is only once this first step has been taken that we can fruitfully look at possible ways of reducing our ontological commitments to a minimum (see also Hylton 2007, 237). So, like Carnap, Quine thinks of logical rigor as something we invoke as philosophers, rather than something that is to be found somehow already present in, albeit hidden underneath the surface of, colloquial language use. Unlike Carnap, Quine does not think of this as a matter of imposing logical rigor "from without"; rather, he sees regimentation as a matter of ordinary language's "disposition to keep on evolving" (Quine 1960, 3). I have discussed the differences between Carnap's and Quine's revisionisms at length elsewhere (Gustafsson 2014a). In what follows, I focus instead on what they have in common, and compare this shared revisionist position with Wittgenstein's later approach.

Both Carnap and Quine agree with later Wittgenstein that the crystalline logical purity envisaged in the *Tractatus* is a requirement rather than something that must already be present (albeit hidden) in colloquial usage. However, such purity is something both Carnap and Quine self-consciously *want* to impose on what they see as our logically messy practices. By contrast, later Wittgenstein's attitude toward such imposed regimentation is different and more hesitant. Why, exactly?

One place to start in order to understand how Wittgenstein's viewpoint differs from Carnap's and Quine's is to note his warning at the very end of the passage from the *Investigations* quoted above (§107), that the requirement of crystalline purity is in danger of becoming *vacuous*. When precision and systematization are legitimately pursued for some specific purpose in scientific, legal, or other contexts, there is no such threat of vacuity. The purpose gives the pursuit a meaningful point, and makes contrasts such as those between the "less precise" and the "more precise," or between the "imprecise" and the "completely precise," intelligible and clear. Wittgenstein's worry about the *Tractatus* is that its requirement of crystalline purity has no such specific point. Rather, the author of the *Tractatus* takes himself to have identified an order that has to be there as soon as there is meaningful language at all, and which is therefore not conditioned *by* any specific aim but a condition *for* the intelligibility and pursuit of *any* aim, so to speak. What later Wittgenstein points out is that when the alleged identification of such an order is aprioristically detached from any specific purpose as well as from any real examination of actual language use, what remains is not simply a requirement but a *vacuous* requirement, motivated by no legitimate scientific or practical need but only by a philosophical fantasy of what absolute, unconditioned logical orderliness must be like.

Again, the immediate target of section 107 of the *Investigations* is the Tractarian idea that a crystalline logical order must already be there, innocently present, in any meaningful use of language. As we have seen, this idea is crucial to early Wittgenstein's version of non-revisionism. In consequence, however, it may seem as if revisionists such as Carnap and Quine are not within the target range here. Again, both Carnap and Quine self-consciously impose logical order on colloquial language, and they seem to think of such regimentation as having quite specific goals. For Carnap, explication of colloquial concepts often happens within science: it is then carried out in order to develop a precise, systematic, and scientifically fruitful conceptual scheme. Carnap also thinks that full-fledged regimentation helps us get rid of philosophical worries, as it allows us to introduce sharp distinctions between logico-linguistic frameworks and assertions made within such frameworks, between analytic and synthetic sentences, between formal science and factual science, and so forth. Carnap's idea is that once these distinctions are sharply drawn, many apparently deep philosophical problems disappear: mathematics falls readily into place as analytic, the principles constitutive of logico-linguistic frameworks wear their identity as constitutive principles (rather than metaphysical theses) on their sleeves, and any need to think of the truth of synthetic statements as knowable otherwise than a posteriori evaporates. Thus he thinks explication allows us to abandon the metaphysical aspiration to limn the true and ultimate structure of reality, as it transforms philosophy into a technical investigation of various syntactical calculi or (after his acceptance of Tarski's treatment of truth) semantic systems (Carnap 1939, 28–9; see also Richardson 2004 and Friedman 2007). Quine instead thinks of the envisaged revisions as allowing us to pursue ontological questions with full clarity and scientific rigor: his aim is indeed to limn the true and ultimate structure of reality, but to clarify this task as one which is wholly continuous with the work of natural scientists. Given that Carnap and Quine are so aware of what they are doing and why they are doing it, mustn't we conclude that Wittgenstein's criticism (in PI §107) has no bite against them?

My sense is that such a conclusion would be premature. Despite their methodological self-consciousness, it is arguable that the goals that Carnap and Quine associate with regimentation and explication are not always as specific and well motivated as they make them seem. If this is correct, Carnap and Quine may be more similar to early Wittgenstein than they themselves recognize, in that they presume a certain formalistic and ultimately vacuous conception of what clarity and rigor must always amount to. Carnap is in fact notoriously wobbly when it comes to the purpose-relative character of explication. On the one hand, he often uses instrumentalist analogies to describe the significance of explication: "A natural language is like a crude, primitive pocketknife, very useful for a hundred different purposes. But for certain specific purposes, special tools are more efficient, e.g., chisels, cutting-machines, and finally the microtome" (Carnap 1963, 938–9). Here, it is clear that he wants to tie explications very closely to specific and well-defined purposes. On the other hand, in his discussions he frequently seems to take it for granted that there is a context-independent measure of logical order and precision, such that the ultimate height of such order and precision—what he does not hesitate to speak of as "complete clarity"—is reached by "the use of symbolic logic and a constructed language system with explicit syntactical and semantical rules" (1963, 936). Certainly, Carnap is tolerant to the extent that he allows different such systems of symbolic logic, systems with different rules. However, he is *not* tolerant enough to acknowledge that the sort of precision reached by the use of symbolic logic is *itself* an ideal that can give substantive content to a notion of "complete clarity" only in relation to the point of particular pursuits of clarification. Certainly, he acknowledges that there are many contexts in which striving for such formal precision is impractical or unnecessary. However, this only amounts to acknowledging that the practicalities of human life are such that we cannot always expect full logical order and precision; it is *not* to reject the notion that the use of symbolic logic provides a universal measure of such order and precision, in principle applicable in all circumstances. Carnap notes that the demands of life make it practically impossible to live up to the ideal of crystalline purity, but this is a fairly trivial observation and cuts little ice against later Wittgenstein's criticism. The real lesson of section 107 of the *Investigations* is more radical, namely, that this ideal makes no sense at all as a universally applicable measure as it decontextualizes the very notions of "clarity" and "precision" to the point where they become empty. Despite his willingness to admit that the striving for formal order and precision is often out of place, it is arguable that Carnap has not taken fully to heart the sort of purpose-specific engineering attitude that would indeed protect him against the criticism Wittgenstein delivers.

Of course, to actually show that Carnap is vulnerable to this criticism would require a much more detailed discussion of his work than I have room for here. (For an excellent criticism of Carnap along similar lines, see Reck 2012.)

When it comes to Quine, a similar criticism may seem even harder to vindicate. In his case, it is even less clear in what sense and to what extent—if any—the sort of order and precision characteristic of formal logical symbolism gets inflated into a supposedly universally applicable ideal. Of course, Quine would deny that he engages in such inflation, and insist that he has a quite specific goal in mind: he wants to do ontology, to "limn the true and ultimate structure of reality," in a rigorous and scientific manner. So, one would have to look closely at his pursuit of and motivation for this project in order to decide whether his notions of "reality," "rigor," and "science" really do genuine work, or whether they are in effect transformed into decontextualized ghosts—empty caricatures of their real-life counterparts.

In the remainder of this essay, I want to emphasize another aspect of the difference between later Wittgenstein and the revisionisms of Carnap and Quine. I shall bring out how later Wittgenstein retains certain non-revisionist elements of his early conception, while reshaping those elements in light of the criticism in the *Investigations*. More specifically, I shall bring out what later Wittgenstein thought was *right* about the Tractarian claim that the propositions of colloquial language are in perfect logical order just as they stand. I thereby aim to lay bare a fundamental continuity between early and later Wittgenstein, a continuity having to do with similarities in their conceptions of what a philosophical problem is and how it may be solved. Thus I will show how deeply foreign the revisionist approaches of Carnap and Quine are to Wittgenstein, early *and* late.

Later Wittgenstein's view of how formal logical symbolism can be of use in philosophy is complex. On the one hand, he rejects as philosophically disastrous the notion that tweaking colloquial discourse into formal symbolism constitutes a universally suitable mode of clarification. On the other hand, he never claims that formal symbolisms must always distort the complex realities of real-life language use. According to later Wittgenstein, formal symbolisms *can* be useful in philosophy, as long as we know what we are doing when we employ them for purposes of clarification:

> In philosophy we often *compare* the use of words with games, calculi with fixed rules, but cannot say that someone who is using language *must* be playing such a game. (PI §81)

Wittgenstein thinks constructed formal calculi can be helpful if we self-consciously employ them as simplified models that highlight certain features of our use. To be sure, this means that other features of our use will be downplayed as they are not represented in these models. However, an undistorted view of certain features at the expense of others may sometimes be precisely what we need in order to resolve a given confusion. This is a central theme in Oskari Kuusela's work on Wittgenstein's method (Kuusela 2008, 2014, 2019; see also Sunday Grève 2018). As Kuusela notes, the language-games Wittgenstein invents are meant to function in a similar fashion. Here is Wittgenstein:

> Our clear and simple language-games are not preliminary studies for a future regimentation of language – as it were, first approximations, ignoring friction and air resistance. Rather, the language-games stand there as objects of comparison which, through similarities and dissimilarities, are meant to throw light on features of our language. (PI §130)

In section 81, Wittgenstein distances himself from the Tractarian view that anyone who uses a language *must*—at some deep level—be following the fixed rules of a logical calculus. In section 130, he further takes a clear stand against the idea that in philosophy we introduce simplified language-games or systems of logical symbolism in preparation for "a future regimentation of language." Rather than blueprints for revision, these models function in philosophy only as objects of comparison, used with the specific purpose of throwing light on features of our language the overlooking or misunderstanding of which has led us into philosophical puzzlement.

Here we find an important point of continuity with the *Tractatus*: such objects of comparison are constructed and employed *in response to actual philosophical confusions*. According to later Wittgenstein, what such objects of comparison can show is not that colloquial language is somehow logically flawed. Rather, they serve to highlight certain features of colloquial usage in order to remind us about them, or in order to make us see clearly what those features amount to. It is our misconstruing or forgetting about those features that such comparisons address and are meant to remedy. Once again, there is continuity with the *Tractatus*: it is not language itself, but *we*, the confused ones, who are the real and fundamental objects of philosophical treatment. Certainly, our confusions may have been prompted by certain notational peculiarities of the colloquial language we happen to have inherited; the vernacular may have "traps" ready for us, traps into which many of us are inclined to fall. However, for later Wittgenstein, falling into those traps is still a matter of misunderstanding those vernacular practices, rather than being victim of misunderstandings that are somehow inherent in those practices themselves. The traps are traps set at the level of notation, and are not reflections of a somehow logically defective *usage*. Just like his early self, later Wittgenstein thinks the idea of logically defective usage makes little sense.

However, later Wittgenstein never puts this point by saying that the propositions of colloquial language are in perfect logical order just as they stand. From his later viewpoint, the notion of "perfect logical order" makes no more sense than the notion of "flawed logical order." Language works in *various* ways; as philosophers, we often do well to remind ourselves of features of these various usages; but there is no single or fixed pattern that constitutes "perfect logical order." The idea of such a single order, such a fixed ideal of perfection, is precisely what leads to the sort of vacuity he warns against in section 107 of the *Investigations*.

It deserves to be emphasized that later Wittgenstein is no more committed than his early self to the idea that philosophical problems are individual whims, unpredictably induced by random linguistic quirks. As I just noted, he would acknowledge that colloquial language contains traps into which we often fall collectively. Consequently, he may well be open to the idea that a preventive introduction of a new and less misleading notation may be in place in special contexts where the threat of confusion is imminent and predictable. However, this would still amount only to a notational change, and not a change in the logic of established usage. Indeed, the change would be made precisely in order to make that logic easier to read off from the notational structure itself.

Importantly, later Wittgenstein's non-revisionism is limited to the treatment of *philosophical* problems. He would not deny that there might be good reasons to revise certain inherited linguistic habits—scientific reasons, ideological reasons, reasons of administration and legislation, and so on. And he would presumably simply agree with the point ventured at the beginning of this essay, that some reshaping of inherited conceptual apparatuses is involved in much groundbreaking search for knowledge. So, Wittgenstein's non-revisionism is tied to the identification of a special class of problems—*philosophical* problems—that he thinks differs from problems in science in that they can be thoroughly resolved only if we refrain from revising established usage and instead remind ourselves of features of that usage which we have misunderstood or forgotten about. Analytic revisionists do not recognize any such special class of problems; or, at least, they believe that most problems in philosophy worth taking seriously are not of this sort.

Not that analytic revisionists think all problems standardly classified as "philosophical" are good problems that deserve positive answers in the form of a substantive thesis or theory: in fact, analytic revisionists usually argue that the revisions they propose help us get rid of (rather than answer) certain bad philosophical questions (as opposed to those good philosophical problems to which the revisions help us give positive answers). Indeed, such revisionists sometimes claim that they thereby fulfill Wittgenstein's intentions more proficiently than his self-proclaimed followers. I have already mentioned that Carnap thinks explication allows us to stop worry about mathematical knowledge, the status of metaphysics, and the synthetic a priori. And here is Quine:

> It is ironical that those philosophers most influenced by Wittgenstein are largely the ones who most deplore . . . explications . . . In steadfast layman-ship they deplore them as departures from ordinary usage, failing to appreciate that it is precisely by showing how to circumvent the problematic parts of ordinary usage that we show the problems to be purely verbal. (Quine 1960, 261)

The term "circumvent" is indeed an appropriate term for the sort of procedure Quine has in mind. His idea is that there are inherently problematic parts of ordinary language that we should find ways to abandon, and once we have abandoned them the problems that they involve will have disappeared together with those defective linguistic habits. However, it is difficult to see how this sort of procedure can avoid begging the very questions it claims to dissipate. For it is crucial to Quine's strategy that he is able to draw a line between uses of language worth keeping and uses of language better abandoned. Thus, he must invoke criteria according to which such a line can be drawn. The problem is that there is no reason to believe that anyone who is genuinely troubled by the problems associated with those habits will accept the criteria in question. If your sense is that the problems address substantive issues of fundamental importance, and if you are then presented with the proposal that the very vocabulary in which those problems are formulated is to be replaced by a vocabulary in which they cannot be formulated, why not conclude that this replacement is inadequate precisely *because* the new vocabulary fails to address those fundamentally important issues? Why not conclude that the significance of the philosophical issues itself shows that those criteria are *mistaken*? Truly deep and difficult philosophical worries are deep and difficult largely because they resist treatment by reference to any such external measure of adequate usage.

To illustrate, consider Quine's attempt to get rid of the philosophical problems associated with talk of mental states and events. His strategy is to offer a physicalist explication of such talk:

> any subjective talk of mental events proceeds necessarily in terms that are acquired and understood through their associations, direct or indirect, with the socially observable behavior of physical objects. If there is a case for mental events and mental states, it must be just that the positing of them, like the positing of molecules, has some indirect systematic efficacy in the development of theory. But if a certain organization of theory is achieved by thus positing mental states and events behind physical behavior, surely as much organization could be achieved by positing merely certain correlative physiological states and events instead. (Quine 1960, 264)

It seems fair to say that anyone who is willing to accept an explication along these lines must already be happily unbothered by the central philosophical problems associated with the notion of the mental. For these problems depend for their apparent inevitability, urgency, and depth on a conception according to which mental states and events are *not* just theoretical posits made in order to achieve some indirect systematic efficacy in the prediction of the observable behavior of physical bodies. If such theoretical positing were all that talk of mental states and events was meant to achieve, then *of course* Quine would be right: there would be no reason to think of such states as distinct from physiological states of the physical body. But in fact, those who are philosophically troubled by the mental are troubled largely because mental states seem so radically *different* from theoretical posits like molecules. To them, Quine's explication will just seem question-begging.

Similar worries can be raised with regard to Carnapian explication. Consider a defender of the synthetic a priori. As I have already mentioned, Carnap thinks explication allows us to introduce sharp distinctions such as that between logico-linguistic frameworks and assertions made within such frameworks; and he thinks one of the major gains of making such sharp distinctions is that no room is left for synthetic a priori truths (since the Carnapian scheme itself is designed to guarantee that any synthetic proposition will be classified as empirical and a posteriori, and any a priori truth will be classified as analytic). Again, Carnap is tolerant in the sense that he allows different frameworks—but his very notion of "framework" precludes the possibility of synthetic a priori truths. Indeed, from the viewpoint of someone who thinks the synthetic a priori is of fundamental significance, Carnap's notion of logical framework (and his associated pluralism) seems to intolerantly foist upon us precisely the sort of empiri-cist-conventionalist confusions that stand in the way of genuine philoso-phical clarity. And since Carnap's conception of explication is inseparable from his notion of logical framework and his pluralism, his method will beg the question against anyone who seriously believes that the notion of the synthetic a priori should *not* be abandoned.

At the beginning of this essay, I mentioned the common worry that Wittgenstein's non-revisionism imposes unnecessary restrictions on how philosophy should be done and on what it can achieve. Instead of such intellectual self-mutilation, why not opt for a revisionist conception according to which it is the philosopher's task to provide us with new and better ways of describing and investigating the world? However, my discussion has now taken us to a point at which we can see Wittgenstein's resistance toward philosophical revisionism in a different and more favor-able light. His resistance can now be seen as motivated by the worry that it is in fact the *revisionist* stance that imposes unfruitful restrictions on what can be seen as good or genuine philosophical problems. For such revision-ism will invoke criteria by reference to which it distinguishes between ways of using language worth preserving and ways of using language better discarded. The revisionist will reject problems that are tied to the allegedly dispensable modes of language use, and he will reject those problems as not worth taking seriously at all. However, some of those problems will be deep enough to involve a questioning of precisely those criteria that the revisionist invokes to distinguish between good and bad uses of language in the first place. Thus, with regard to those problems, the revisionist procedure of circumvention will be question-begging, and therefore not even start to engage with those who are genuinely troubled by the problems. If Wittgenstein is right, problems that are deep in this sense are problems we identify as characteristically philosophical problems. And they can be adequately dealt with only if we do *not* proceed along revisionist lines, but are instead patient enough to leave everything as it is.

CHAPTER 9

Demystifying Meaning in Horwich and Wittgenstein

Silver Bronzo

For more than two decades, Paul Horwich has been refining and defending a use-theory of meaning that seeks to demystify meaning by reducing it to pure regularities of use. He has presented this theory as a development of ideas from later Wittgenstein. Even though he acknowledges that his proposal goes beyond what Wittgenstein explicitly says, he doesn't take it to go against Wittgenstein's central commitments. Horwich's views have changed in some respects over time, and he has occasionally distanced himself from Wittgenstein, but these differences do not affect the reductionist ambitions, the main structure, and the alleged Wittgensteinian roots of his proposal. This chapter argues, contra Horwich, that Wittgenstein's demystification of meaning involves no reduction.

1 Horwich's Reductionist Reading

Consider this passage from Horwich:

> [Wittgenstein] was aiming to demystify the concept of meaning (and derivative intentional concepts such as *belief* and *desire*) by specifying in comparatively unproblematic terms, what meaning *is* ... He wanted to explain how "life" is injected into signs that are otherwise "dead." And his answer, to put it bluntly, is that meaning facts *reduce* to underlying non-intentional facts of word use ... (including physical, behavioral, and certain psychological aspects). (Horwich 2010b, 19)

According to this reading, Wittgenstein takes the notion of meaning to be problematic. More specifically, he takes it to be mysterious, and thus in need of demystification. In order to demystify it, one must give a reductive account of what it is for a sign to be meaningful. A "sign" is here an item "individuated non-semantically," for example in terms of its shape or acoustic properties (Horwich 2005, 28 n.4; see also 1998, 1, and 2005, 6). The "comparatively unproblematic terms" to which meaning is to be reduced are dispositions to internally assent to sentences in conformity with certain regularities, plus feelings of satisfaction and dissatisfaction issuing in acts of self-corrections (see Horwich 2010b; and 2012, chapters 4 and 5). It is crucial that all the elements that figure in the base of reduction should be construed in a manner that does not presuppose the notion of linguistic or mental content; otherwise the account would not be truly reductive, and thus not truly demystifying. This applies, remarkably, to the notions of "sentence," "assent," and "self-correction." Moreover, the base of reduction must not include normative notions. Horwich states explicitly that meaning, according to Wittgenstein, is ultimately constituted by "regularities of word-use" that are "wholly non-normative" and "non-regulative" (2010b, 24 n.10, 21).

Horwich emphasizes that the use-theory of meaning he attributes to Wittgenstein is not *behavioristic*. This is because the base of reduction includes psychological phenomena—such as the internal assent to sentences—that need not be expressed in outward behavior (see 2010b, 23 n.1). The theory is also not committed to *physicalism*: it demands that the psychological items figuring in the base of reduction be free of intentionality and normativity, but leaves open the question of whether they should in turn be reduced to physical phenomena. Horwich, for example, cashes out the notion of "internal assent to sentences" in terms of "cognitive role": "The sentences to which S internally assents are those deployed as premises in his reasoning (i.e. computations), and are the ground for his dispositions to *overtly* assert their vocal correlates" (Horwich 2012, 113 n.5; see also 1998, 94–6; 2005, 30; and 2010a, 139). This characterization, which exploits the apparatus of cognitive science, is meant to be non-intentional and non-normative; but Horwich does not suggest that the success of his theory is conditional on the reducibility of cognitive science to physics. On the other hand, the theory does not *rule out* the prospect of a physicalist reduction of all the notions that figure in its own base of reduction—which perhaps explains why Horwich refers to such notions as "comparatively" unproblematic.

Horwich often characterizes his use-theory of meaning as "naturalistic" (see, for instance, 1998, 114; and 2005, 44, 64, 105, and 116). This makes good sense, since many forms of contemporary naturalism share the ambition of reducing meaning to a non-intentional and non-normative base. It can be puzzling, at first, to find out that Horwich firmly rejects "naturalism" and denies that Wittgenstein was committed to it (Horwich 1993, 156; 2013, 124–7; 2014, 37–40). But the puzzle is simply due to equivocation. The sort of naturalism that Horwich opposes and does not ascribe to Wittgenstein is the view that "everything that exists is located within [the] spatiotemporal, causal domain" (2014, 38; see also 1993, 155 and 2013, 112). Against this view, Horwich holds that we should recognize "phenomena that fall *outside* the spatiotemporal causal order," such as "numbers, values, universals, possibilities, and so on" (2014, 38, 40; see also 2013, 26–7); and he maintains that Wittgenstein was perfectly open to this recognition (1993, 156–7). This position is consistent with the view that all the phenomena belonging to the "spatiotemporal causal order"—which for Horwich include meaning—are reducible to non-intentional and non-normative notions. This is the form of naturalism that Horwich accepts and attributes to Wittgenstein.

There are two features of the context in which Horwich began to present his use-theory of meaning that are worth mentioning. First, it had already become widely accepted that any theory of meaning must account for its "normative" character. The idea is that the meaning of a word places *constraints* on how it should be used: it is a standard against which the use of the word is to be measured. Some applications of a word *accords* with its meaning and others *fail to accord* with it. To use a meaningful word is precisely to subject oneself to the constraints dictated by its meaning, and thus to expose oneself to the possibility of violating them, which amounts to committing a *mistake*. For example, if I want to use the word "green" in its most common English sense and I want to use it to make a serious assertion, then it will be correct for me to predicate it, say, of the grass, but not of the sky. I shall refer to this idea as the "normativity constraint."[1]

Secondly, many had already become convinced that the normativity constraint poses a serious challenge to dispositional accounts of meaning. This was largely due to Kripke's influential critique of those accounts (see Kripke 1982, 22–37). An important part of this critique is that dispositional accounts, in order to be even prima facie plausible, must appeal to dispositions that operate under "ideal conditions"—which, however, cannot be specified without circularity. One way to see this is to notice that we are disposed to make *mistakes* in the application of our words under certain circumstances. For instance, I might be disposed to misapply the word "green" when I take certain drugs. So what I mean by "green" can be identified, at most, with how I am disposed to use the word under circumstances that exclude my taking those drugs. But—so the challenge goes—the idea that we can specify all the relevant "distorting factors," and

---

[1] For some early formulations of the normativity constraint on theories of meaning, see Wright 1980, 19; Kripke 1982, 37; and McDowell 1998, 221 and 235.

thus the correlative ideal conditions, without appealing to the very notion that we are trying to analyze is hopeless: the ideal conditions that we need are simply those in which I apply the word "green" in a manner that accords with the relevant meaning of the word (see Kripke 1982, 28–32).

Kripke argues, however, that this sort of difficulty is only a symptom of a deeper problem with dispositional theories. The fact that they cannot specify non-circularly the ideal conditions in which our dispositions are supposed to operate shows that they cannot give an account of the meaning of a word that tracks our competent judgments about which applications of the word accord or fail to accord with its meaning. But the deeper problem with dispositional theories is that they leave no room for the idea that an application of a word can accord or fail to accord with its meaning. This is because they construe the relation between the meaning of a word and its application in "descriptive" rather than "normative" terms (1982, 37). What they tell us is that, given what one "means" by a word, one *will* apply it in certain ways and not in others. But what they should account for, in order to satisfy the normativity constraint, is that given what one means by a certain word, one *should* apply it in some ways and not in others. Dispositional theories do not so much as fail to satisfy the normativity constraint, but simply choose to *ignore* it. And by doing so—the challenge continues—they relinquish any ambition to provide an account of *meaning*.[2]

Horwich is well aware of these challenges and has devoted great efforts to showing that the normativity constraint, when appropriately construed, can in fact be satisfied by his theory. Here we need to have in view at least the main structure of his theory. There are actually two versions of the theory: a more complex one, which Horwich ascribes to Wittgenstein, and a simpler one, which Horwich takes to be "neater and cleaner" (2005, 77 n.14; see also 2010a, 133–5; 2010b, 24 n.7; and 2012, 121 n.15). The simpler version involves three main steps. Starting "from above," we have:[3]

1) An account of the "normative implications" of the truth-theoretic import of words in terms of various sorts of pragmatic and moral values. For example, given the extension of the word "green," we *ought*

---

[2] In connection with the failure of dispositional theories to satisfy the normativity constraint, Kripke speaks of these theories as being "misdirected," "off-target," and as having an "air of irrelevance" (1982, 23, 37).

[3] My reconstruction of the three main steps that Horwich's simpler version of his theory involves is based on Horwich 2005, chapters 1–3 and 5; 2010a, chapters 6 and 7; 2010b; and 2012, chapters 4 and 5.

to apply it only to objects that fall under that extension, *because truth is valuable.*

2) A "deflationist" account of the truth-theoretic import of words in terms of a prior and independent notion of meaning and a number of schemas *defining* the truth-theoretic notions of *truth*, *reference*, and *being true of.* For example, the fact that "green" is true of the green things and nothing else follows by definition, and thus trivially, from the fact that "green" means the concept *green*. This is because the notion of *being true of something* is defined by a schema that has among its instances the following conditional: If "green" means the concept *green*, then "green" is true of x if and only if x is green.

3) An account of meaning in terms of law-like regularities of word use. The account is modeled on constitution theses advanced by the empirical sciences, such as the thesis that water consists of H_2O. The criterion of adequacy of these reductions, for Horwich, is their capacity to explain in terms of the base of reduction all the "symptoms" of the target phenomenon—for instance, the fact that water boils at a certain temperature, freezes at another temperature, and so on. But the symptoms of meaning, for Horwich, are the patterns of actual deployment of words (characterized in non-intentional and non-normative terms). On these grounds, Horwich maintains that for a word to have a certain meaning consists in its being governed by an ideal law of word use (more specifically, by an ideal law concerning the acceptance of a basic set of sentences containing the word). The use of the word, here, is "governed" by the law in the same sense in which the movements of the planets are governed by Kepler's laws; and the law is "ideal" in the same sense in which Kepler's laws are ideal (for example, in treating the planets as point masses). The process of sorting out "ideal laws" and "distorting factors" in the explanation of the overall use of a word is subject to the same epistemic norms that apply elsewhere in the empirical sciences (such as considerations of explanatory power, simplicity, and coherence with other accepted theories). Finally, the identification of the *specific* ideal laws of word use is an empirical task for linguistics, and it is to be expected that these laws will be different for different classes of words. For example, my meaning the concept *green* by "green" might consist in the fact that what I do with the word is governed by the ideal law "Silver accepts any sentence of the form 'x is green' when he has a visual experience normally produced in humans by observed green things." (This is the

same as saying that my meaning *green* by "green" might consist in my being disposed to assent to those sentences under those circumstances.) By contrast, my meaning the concept *truth* by "true" might consist in the fact that what I do with the word is governed by the ideal law "Silver accepts any instance of the schema '<p> is true iff p.'"

It is worth noting that, in spite of verbal appearances, the part of the account that is meant to address the normativity constraint, as specified above, is *not* the first step, but the conjunction of the other two. There are of course many different kinds of reasons for using words one way or the other. The point of the normativity constraint is that the meanings of words impose *characteristic* demands on how to use them. So the question is not, say, why I should use "green" to make true predications as opposed to false ones; rather, it is why, *assuming that I want to use "green" to make a true predication and that I want to use it in its common English sense,* I should apply it to the grass but not to the sky.

Another feature of the account that is worth emphasizing is the crucial role of the second step, which severs the concept of meaning that Horwich purports to reduce from any truth-theoretic notion. This constitutes the core of Horwich's response to Kripke's circularity objection to dispositional theories. Horwich concedes that it is indeed hopeless to give a *direct* reduction of truth-theoretic content to use-regularities, but holds that the demand for such a direct reduction rests on an illegitimate, "inflationist" theory of truth. Truth-theoretic content can indeed be reduced to use-regularities, according to Horwich, but only in an indirect way *via* the definitional schemas mentioned in the second step of the reduction.

This was the simpler version of Horwich's proposal. In the more complex version, the last step splits into two. So we have:

3a) An account of meaning in terms of implicit rule-following; that is, rule-following that does not involve the explicit articulation of the rule. For example, my meaning the concept *green* by "green" consists in my implicitly following certain rules for its use (for instance, possibly the rule "Accept any sentence of the form 'x is green' when you have a visual experience normally produced in humans by observed green things").

3b) An account of implicit rule-following in terms of ideal natural laws (which operate in the absence of "distorting factors," like Kepler's laws) and acts of self-correction caused by feelings of satisfaction and dissatisfaction with one's performances. For example, my implicitly following the rule mentioned in (3a) would consist in the fact that my use of the word "green" is governed by the ideal law "Silver accepts any sentence of the form 'x is green' when he has a visual experience normally produced in humans by observed green things," in conjunction with the fact that I am occasionally dissatisfied with how I am inclined to use the word and correct myself accordingly, which shows that I have a *desire to conform* to the ideal natural law governing my use of the word.

As one can see, Horwich's reductionist account in either of its versions is a mechanism with many moving parts. Evaluating whether it succeeds in meeting, or debunking, the normativity constraint is not an easy task, and goes beyond the scope of this chapter. As I anticipated, I am only going to take issue with Horwich's grounds for attributing that sort of account to Wittgenstein and for thinking that a demystification of meaning must take the form of a reduction. I will begin, in Section 2, by looking at several well-known passages from the *Investigations* that deal with meaning, understanding, and rule-following. In those passages, I will argue, we can see what Wittgenstein's demystification of meaning actually looks like, and how it differs from Horwich's reconstruction. Then, in the subsequent three sections, I am going to examine the main textual evidence that Horwich takes to support his reductionist reading of Wittgenstein.

2   Demystification in *Philosophical Investigations* §§185–242

A pervasive theme of the *Investigations* is how, when we do philosophy, some of the most familiar things in the world—such as naming something, understanding the meaning of a word, or obeying an order—can come to strike us as being mysterious: for instance, as involving "a strange connection," an "occult" or "odd process" (§§ 38, 196), "a strange medium," "an odd kind of being" (§196), "a pure intermediary" (§94), or "a shadow" of actual events (§194).

As we have seen, it is natural to think, in accordance with the normativity constraint, that the meaning of an expression determines which applications of the expression accord and fail to accord with it—and thus how one *ought* to use it, if one wants to use it in accordance with its meaning. To take one of Wittgenstein's examples: if you understand what the order "Add 2" means, it seems to be already determined that if you were asked to add 2 to 1000, and you wanted to satisfy the order, you ought to answer 1002 (and not, say, 1004). Moreover, it seems that this is the answer you ought to give even if you never explicitly thought about that particular application of the order. But now it can seem that understanding the meaning of an expression, as well as meaning it in some particular way, must be an *extraordinary* mental accomplishment. Here is how Wittgenstein describes the aura of extraordinariness that may be thought to surround the act of meaning the order "Add 2" in the usual way:

> Your idea was that this *meaning the order* had in its own way already taken all those steps: that in meaning it, your mind, as it were, flew ahead and took all the steps before you physically arrived at this or that one.
>
> So you were inclined to use such expressions as "The steps are *really* already taken, even before I take them in writing or in speech or in thought." And it seemed as if they were in some *unique* way predetermined, anticipated – in the way that only meaning something could anticipate reality. (PI §188)

To use an image that Wittgenstein introduces later on in the course of the same discussion, we are led to think of the meaning of a linguistic expression as a pair of "rails invisibly laid to infinity" (§218), that is, rails that go through the space of all the possible applications of the expression and determine in each case what counts as a correct and what as an incorrect application. Understanding the meaning of the expression (or meaning it in a particular way) is then pictured as a mental act that consists in instantaneously going through these infinitely long rails. The actual applications that we are going to make of the expression (in writing, speech, or even merely in thought) are going to be correct or incorrect precisely because they have been anticipated by the initial act of understanding. But how can our finite mind go through—and in an instant!—all the countless possible applications of an expression? And how can it do so without even actually *thinking* of them? Understanding the meaning of an expression, we are inclined to conclude, is an impenetrable mystery.

But according to Wittgenstein there is no real mystery here. We come to think that there is one, he believes, because we misunderstand the forms of expressions that we use when we talk about meaning and understanding:

> We do pay attention to the way we talk about these matters, we don't understand it, but misinterpret it. When we do philosophy, we are like savages, primitive people, who hear the way in which civilized people talk, put a false interpretation on it, and then draw the oddest conclusions from this. (PI §194)

Similar remarks occur earlier in the *Investigations*, in the context of a discussion of the impression that a proposition is something "remarkable," "extraordinary," and "unique" (§93)—for instance, "a pure intermediary between the propositional *sign* and the facts" (§94). This impression, Wittgenstein writes, is due to a "misunderstanding of the logic of language" (§93): "For our forms of expressions, which send us in the pursuit of chimeras, prevent us in all sorts of ways from seeing that nothing extraordinary is involved" (§94).

Now, what are the forms of expression that we savagely misunderstand when we think about meaning and understanding? A prominent example is discussed right after the passage that compares us to savages:

> "But I don't mean that what I do now (in grasping the whole use of a word) determines the future use *causally* and as a matter of experience, but that, in a *strange* way, the use itself is in some sense present." – But of course it is, 'in *some* sense'! Really, the only thing wrong with what you say is the expression "in an odd way." The rest is right; and the sentence seems odd only when one imagines it to belong to a different language-game from the one in which we actually use it. (PI §195)

We can rephrase the form of expression that causes trouble here this way: *Understanding the meaning of an expression does not determine its future use in a causal way, but in some sense already contains it.* Wittgenstein emphasizes that the form of expression is, in itself, all right: there is nothing strange and mysterious about it when it is used in its original language-game. It *becomes* strange and mysterious only when we fail to get into view its original language-game and think of it on the model of expressions that belong to quite different language-games, thereby casting on it a strange interpretation.

So far we have identified a representative example of the forms of expression that mislead us into thinking that meaning and understanding are mysterious phenomena. Now we need to distinguish the correct and incorrect interpretations of this form of expression. How should it be understood in order to be "all right"? And how exactly should we characterize its misinterpretation? The most direct answer to these questions, I suggest, comes in sections 219–21:

> 219 "All the steps are really already taken" means: I no longer have any choice. The rule, once stamped with a particular meaning, traces the lines along which it is to be followed through the whole of space. — But if something of this sort really were the case, how would it help me?
>
> No; my description made sense only if it was to be understood symbolically. – I should say: *This is how it strikes me.*
>
> When I follow the rule, I do not choose.
>
> I follow the rule *blindly*.

220 But what is the purpose of that symbolical proposition? It was supposed to bring into prominence a difference between being causally determined and being logically determined.

221 My symbolical expression was really a mythological description of the use of a rule.

Wittgenstein speaks here of obeying a rule, but the discussion is closely connected to—and indeed a special case of—the overarching discussion of meaning and understanding. For a rule is said to be "stamped with a particular meaning"; thus a "rule," here, is equivalent to what Wittgenstein calls else-where the "expression of a rule" (§198). It can be, for instance, a signpost that tells us to go in some particular direction. The passages I quoted, then, are about the idea that the meaning of a rule determines what counts as obeying and violating the rule. The troublesome forms of expressions that Wittgenstein discusses in this connection are variants of the one we encoun-tered before: "*[When I understand a rule,] all the steps are really already taken*"; "*The rule, once stamped with a particular meaning, traces the lines along which it is to be followed through the whole of space.*" The first thing to notice is that, for Wittgenstein, there *is* a way of interpreting these propositions so that they *make sense*. They make sense, he says, *only if* they are understood *symbolically*. I take it that symbolical understanding contrasts here with *literal* understand-ing (see also Baker and Hacker 1980/2009, 197). In order to make perspicuous the symbolical character of such propositions, Wittgenstein points out, it would be helpful to frame them with a phrase such as "This is how it strikes me." A prefix of that sort would help to make clear that what follows should not be taken at face value.

But what do the troublesome propositions mean, when they are under-stood symbolically? Their meaning, Wittgenstein suggests, can be para-phrased by means of more straightforward propositions such as the following: "*When I follow the rule, I do not choose*"; "*I follow the rule blindly*"; "*[When I follow a rule,] I no longer have any choice*" (see also §230). These are good examples of what Wittgenstein calls "grammatical remarks" (§232). Grammatical remarks are meant to remind us of the way we use our words (so, of their grammar, or logic); they are not meant to be controversial, but to capture what everybody would agree on (see §§ 89–90 and 127–8). The grammatical remarks in question concern our use of the expressions "rule" and "following a rule." It is part of our concepts of rule and following a rule that we don't have to arbitrarily choose at each step what counts as following the rule: to follow a rule is precisely to subject our will to *constraints*. I suggest that, in spite of its technical language, the following is also presented as a grammatical remark: "*[There is] a difference between being causally determined and being logically determined.*" The meaning of a rule *determines* what course of action accords or fails to accord with the rule; but this form of determination is different from causal determination.

The symbolical propositions, when properly understood, are ways of expressing these grammatical points. They are, Wittgenstein says, "mythological description[s] of the use of a rule." They point out aspects of the grammar of "rule," and they do achieve their purpose, in so far as the mythology is understood symbolically (rather than *mis*understood literally). The problem arises when we forget, so to speak, the symbolical operator in which the mythological descriptions are embedded, and take them literally. Only at that point the propositions appear to express something astonishing and mysterious.

To summarize, I have argued that in the cluster of sections I have focused on, Wittgenstein distinguishes three kinds of proposition. We have *grammatical remarks*, which are meant to remind us—in a straightforward and uncontroversial manner—of features of our concepts of meaning, rule, and understanding:

G1) "When I follow the rule, I do not choose." (§219)
G2) "I follow the rule *blindly*." (§219)
G3) "[When I follow a rule,] I no longer have any choice." (§219)
G4) "[There is] a difference between being causally determined and being logically determined." (§220)

Then we have *symbolical propositions*, which serve the same purpose but seek to achieve it through a symbolical employment of images and "mythologies":

S1) Understanding the meaning of an expression does not determine its future use in a causal way, but in some sense already contains it.
S2) "[When I understand a rule,] all the steps are really already taken." (§219)
S3) "The rule, once stamped with a particular meaning, traces the lines along which it is to be followed through the whole of space." (§219)

And finally, we have propositions that express a misunderstanding of symbolical propositions. They give a literal construal of symbolical propositions, and thus take them to describe mysterious phenomena. We may call them *mysterian propositions*:

M1)   "I don't mean that what I do now (in grasping the whole use of a word) determines the future use *causally* and as a matter of experience, but that, in a *strange* way, the use itself is in some sense present." (§195)

M2)   "[When I understand a rule,] all the steps are [*in some mysterious way*] really already taken." (§219)

According to Wittgenstein, these are propositions to which we are drawn "when we do philosophy" (§194), and which are part of what philosophy (as he seeks to practice it) aims to criticize.

The first moral I want to draw from this discussion is that there is an obvious sense in which Wittgenstein *is* concerned to demystify meaning. When doing philosophy, he argues, we are inclined to construe meaning and understanding as mysterious phenomena. But these are misconceptions, mainly due to the fact that we misunderstand the forms of expressions that we use to talk about those phenomena. They are mystifications in the sense that they *render* mysterious something that, in itself, is *not* mysterious. Wittgenstein seeks to undo these mystifications by clarifying the way we talk about meaning and understanding. In the passages I have examined, mysterian propositions are unmasked as misunderstandings of symbolical propositions, which can in turn be paraphrased by means of grammatical remarks about our concepts of meaning and understanding. This process of demystification—and this is the second moral I want to draw—does not involve any attempt to reduce meaning and understanding to something else. What we are left with, when the process is over, are remarks such as G1–G4. These remarks aim to spell out features of our concepts of meaning and understanding by connecting them with a number of other concepts—such as an appropriate notion of choicelessness, or of determination. But there is no intention to show that what meaning and understanding (really) are can be specified in a different and supposedly more fundamental conceptual apparatus. (See also Hans-Johann Glock's "What Is Meaning?," Chapter 10 in this volume.)

3   The Shopkeeper and the Builders

Horwich claims that his interpretation is supported by the discussion of various simple language-games in the opening sections of the *Investigations*. He refers, in particular, to the shopkeeper's language-game described in section 1, and to the builders' language-game as described in sections 2 and 8. For Horwich, the presentation of these and other similar language-games is meant to illustrate the "meaning-constituting uses" of words, which are "never couched in semantic or intentional terms" (2012, 112; see also 2010b, 19). But this reading can be questioned.

Consider, to begin with, the shopkeeper's language-game. The section where it is described begins with a quotation from Augustine's *Confessions* that conveys, Wittgenstein says, a certain idea about the essence of language: the idea that the meaning of a word is the object it stands for. He goes on to suggest that we come to that idea only if we think primarily of words such as "table" and "chair," and not about words such as "five" or "if." At that point, he tells the shopkeeper story:

> Now think of the following use of language: I send someone shopping. I give him a slip of paper marked "five red apples." He takes the slip to the shopkeeper, who opens the drawer marked "apples"; then he looks up the word "red" in a chart and finds a colour sample next to it; then he says the series of elementary number-words – I assume that he knows them by heart – up to the word "five", and for each number-word he takes an apple of the same colour as the sample out of the drawer. — It is in this and similar ways that one operates with words. (PI §1)

The main point of the story is to show how different are the uses of words such as "apple," "red," and "five." In particular, it is meant to show, as Wittgenstein goes on to point out, that the question of what the word "five" stands for does not come up: all that matters is how the word is used. Now, I agree with Horwich that the story illustrates the general idea that the meaning of a word is constituted by its use—by what we *do* with it. But I reject Horwich's claim that the story is meant to show that this use can be specified in non-semantic and non-intentional terms. The meaning of the words used by the shopper and the shopkeeper are indeed constituted, at least in part, by what they do with them. But their doing is (already) *informed* by meaning and understanding. The shopper is *fulfilling the request* to go shopping. The slip marked "five red apples" is something like a *shopping list*: by giving it to the shopkeeper, the shopper is requesting the shopkeeper to sell her what is written on the list. And the shopkeeper goes on to fulfill *that request*. Making requests, fulfilling them, and reading shopping lists are activities that presuppose semantic or intentional notions. The whole episode, moreover, takes place within the framework of a practice of economic transactions; and it is far from obvious that such a practice can be intelligibly specified in non-semantic and non-intentional terms, as Horwich's reading requires. Furthermore, the claim that a reduction in such terms is possible is completely unnecessary for the kind of claim that Wittgenstein actually appears to be making, namely, that words have very different functions and do not have to stand for anything in order to have meaning. Horwich's reductionist reading of the shopkeeper example is only a projection of his own theoretical agenda.

Next, here is how Wittgenstein describes the builders' language-game:

> Let us imagine a language for which the description given by Augustine is right: the language is meant to serve for communication between a builder A and an assistant B. A is building with building stones: there are blocks, pillars, slabs and beams. B has to pass him the stones and to do so in the order in which A needs them. For this purpose they make use of a language consisting of the words "block," "pillar," "slab," "beam." A calls them out; B brings the stone which he has learnt to bring at such-and-such a call. — Conceive of this as a complete primitive language. (PI §2)

As before, we need to look at the role that the description of this language-game is intended to play in Wittgenstein's argument. He says he introduces it in order to show that Augustine's description of language can be regarded, on the one hand, as expressing a conception of meaning that is "at home in a primitive idea of the way language functions"—and thus as an inadequate description of our language—but also, on the other hand, as an adequate description "of a language more primitive than ours" (§2). The builders' language-game is meant to be such a language. Wittgenstein asks us to conceive it "as a complete primitive language." But as several commentators have pointed out, this request is not easy to interpret (see, for example, Goldfarb 1983 and Cavell 1996). We need to pause and ask *what* exactly we are supposed to imagine here. There are various options.

One option is to suppose that the life of A and B is by and large like ours. But then it is mysterious why they choose to speak only when they are working on the building site, and why they choose to use only those four words. Maybe because of some kind of prohibition or vow? In that case, it is not clear why their language should be called "primitive." Moreover, while what they do with their words may be regarded as meaning-constituting, it won't be describable in purely non-semantic terms: as in the shopkeeper's case, their actions will be permeated by semantic and intentional notions. A, for example, won't be merely producing noises, but will be uttering words to *make requests*, which B *understands* and goes on to *satisfy*, and all this on the background of a *collaborative activity of building* that presupposes the capacity for intentional action, practical reasoning, and social coordination.

Alternatively, we might suppose that A and B are in fact like marionettes, or rather simple automata. At the end of the day, when the building activity is over, they simply shut down. In that case, it is not clear that they can be said to have a "primitive language." What they do may indeed be describable in purely non-semantic and non-intentional terms, but it won't be meaning-constituting. A and B communicate with one another, and have a language, only in the derivative sense in which, say, my cellphone and laptop may be said to communicate with one another and use a language.

Yet another option is to suppose that A and B resemble those monkeys that, apparently, use a system of communication consisting exclusively of a small number of signals in order to alert the group about the presence of different kinds of predators. In that case, it makes good sense to say that they master a "primitive language." There are enormous similarities, as well as striking differences, between the life of the monkeys and our own, and between the roles that the respective forms of communication play in these lives. In virtue of these similarities and differences, we are able to recognize some primitive form of meaning in their signals. Nevertheless, there appears to remain a qualitative difference between the scream of one of these monkeys and what we do when we shout "Snake!" in order to warn another about the presence of a snake, even though the monkeys' scream is unquestionably more similar to our warning than, say, the sounds emitted by a smoke-detector. We may hold, with Horwich, that the form of meaning sensibly ascribable to the monkeys' signals is constituted by *how they use* those signals. But it is plausible to maintain that the extent to which we may regard that use as meaning-constituting is *directly proportional* to the extent to which it is *not* describable in non-intentional and non-semantic terms. The proto-semantics that we can sensibly ascribe to the signals of the monkeys—or to the "calls" of Wittgenstein's builders—goes hand in hand with the proto-semantic and proto-intentional character of the activities in which those signals are embedded.

I have distinguished three ways of understanding the builders' language-game, arguing that none of them supports the view that the meaning-constituting use of words is describable in non-intentional and non-semantic terms. What is crucial for our present purposes is that, as we have noted about the shopkeeper example, here too there is no need of saddling Wittgenstein with that reductionist claim; good sense can be made of what Wittgenstein wants to do with the builders' language-game without ascribing to him any such reductionist intentions. His aim, we have seen, is simply to give an example of a "primitive language." Indeed, as I have shown in my discussion of the third way of understanding the builders' language-game, one can achieve this aim, while insisting that use is meaning-constituting only to the extent that it is already infused with meaning and intentionality.

4 Meaning, Truth, and Deflationism

Another piece of textual evidence that Horwich mentions in support of his interpretation is Wittgenstein's supposed endorsement of a "deflationary view of the truth-theoretic notions" in section 136 of the *Investigations* (Horwich 2012, 110). After arguing that Wittgenstein wants to explain meaning in terms of use, Horwich appeals to that section in order to show that the sort of use that Wittgenstein invokes is specifiable in non-semantic terms, and hence without any reliance on truth-theoretic notions such as truth conditions, reference conditions, and satisfaction conditions. In the relevant section, Horwich maintains, Wittgenstein accepts the schema "p is true = p (where 'p' stands for the proposition that p)" (2012, 110). This shows, he argues, that Wittgenstein wants to explain the notion of truth in terms of a prior and independent notion of sentence meaning:

> The notion of truth ... is explained in terms of that of [proposition] (i.e. sentence meaning), which will on pain of circularity have to be explained *independently* of truth. Therefore, he cannot be supposing that the notion of proposition be analyzed in terms of the notion of *truth* condition. (Horwich 2012, 110)

If truth is to be analyzed non-circularly in terms of sentence meaning, then the analysis of sentence meaning in terms of use cannot take for granted the notion of truth. Analogous considerations, Horwich argues, apply to the other truth-theoretic notions and to Wittgenstein's use-theoretic account of non-sentential meaning.

Wittgenstein does indeed mention, in section 136, the schema "'p' is true = p," and I agree with Horwich that Wittgenstein mentions it in an approving manner. I can also grant Horwich's rephrasing of the schema as "The proposition that p is true = p." But I question whether there is any evidence that Wittgenstein takes the schema to express the sort of deflationism that Horwich wishes to ascribe to him (namely, a reductive analysis of truth in terms of sentence meaning). No direction of reductive analysis can be inferred from the schema itself; it only states an equivalence. Moreover, anyone who cares to look at the relevant context in the *Investigations* will find that there is nothing that would support Horwich's reading.

Wittgenstein mentions the schema in the course of a discussion of his earlier specification of the general form of the proposition. In the *Tractatus*, he said that the general form of the proposition is "This is how things are" (TLP 4.5). And now he says:

> At bottom, giving "This is how things are" as the general form of propositions is the same as giving the explanation: a proposition is whatever can be true or false. For instead of "This is how things are," I could just as well have said "Such-and-such is true." (PI §136)

If anything, this passage suggests that the notion of a proposition is defined in terms of truth and falsity, rather than the other way around. However, Wittgenstein actually goes on, from the passage just quoted, to introduce the equivalence schema with the adversative phrase "*Nun ist aber*," translated simply as "but": "But 'p' is true = p." I suggest that the role of the schema, in this context, is to block the impression that the notion of a proposition can be defined in terms of a prior and independent notion of truth. However, its role is *not* to make the reverse claim, as Horwich would have it, that truth can be defined in terms of a prior and independent notion of proposition. Rather, Wittgenstein wants to convey the idea that the notions of truth and proposition *come together* (so that neither can be non-circularly defined in terms of the other).

Support for this reading comes from the way section 136 continues— Wittgenstein writes that the use of the words "true" and "false" is correctly treated "as *belonging* to our concept 'proposition'"—as well as from the following later sections of the book:

> 224 The word "accord" and the word "rule" are *related* to one another; they are cousins. If I teach anyone the use of the one word, he learns the use of the other with it.

> 225 The use of the word "rule" and the use of the word "same" are interwoven. (As are the use of "proposition" and the use of "true.")

The notions of *proposition* and *truth* are interwoven, just as the notions of *agreement* and *rule,* and *rule* and *same*. There is no way of learning or understanding the one without learning and understanding the other. In other words, there is no definitional or conceptual priority among them.

Thus, Horwich's reading of section 136 of the *Investigations* is incorrect. Wittgenstein's discussion of the relation between propositions and truth in this section provides no reason to believe that he aims to specify the meaning-constituting use of words in non-semantic terms.

5   Meaning and Dispositions

Horwich purports to find direct textual evidence for his reading in this passage:

> "But I already knew, at the time when I gave the order [to continue the series +2], that he should write 1002 after 1000." – Certainly; and you may even say you *meant* it then; only you shouldn't let yourself be misled by the grammar of the words "know" and "mean." For you don't mean that you thought of the step from 1000 to 1002 at that time – and even if you did think of this step, still, you didn't think of other ones. Your "I already knew at the time . . . " amounts to something like: "If I had then been asked what number he should write after 1000, I would have replied '1002.'" And that I don't doubt. This is an assumption of much the same sort as "If he had fallen into the water then, I would have jumped in after him." (PI §187)

Horwich comments: "Thus Wittgenstein's view, quite clearly, is that the meaning consists in the disposition" (2012, 141). For Horwich, of course, the disposition must be specifiable in non-semantic and non-intentional terms. According to Horwich, then, what Wittgenstein is saying is that meaning the order "Continue the series +2" in the usual way is partially constituted by one's being causally disposed to write down certain marks after hearing certain noises (for instance, to write down "1002" after hearing "What should be written after 1000, if you want to continue the series +2?"), where "writing" and "hearing" must be construed without presupposing semantic or intentional notions. As we saw in Section 1 above, to have such a disposition is equivalent to being governed by a *ceteris paribus* causal law, where the *ceteris paribus* conditions of the law (which correspond to the activation conditions of the disposition) must be specifiable without any appeal to the meaning of the order under discussion, and indeed (assuming that we are dealing with the meaning-constituting uses of primitive expressions) without appealing to *any* linguistic or mental content.

Once again, Horwich's reading is far from obvious. Here is an alternative interpretation of Wittgenstein's point. Meaning the order "Continue the series +2" in the usual manner entails having the *capacity* to determine that the only answer that satisfies the order, when one reaches 1000, is "1002." More generally, meaning something by an expression—and, conversely, understanding the meaning of an expression—requires the capacity to determine which uses of the expression accord or fail to accord with its meaning. This capacity differs from Horwich's dispositions in three interrelated respects.

First, it is the capacity to carry on with the use of the expression *in accordance with its meaning*: the meaning of the expression enters into the specification of the capacity, which cannot therefore be used to provide a reductive account of the meaning.

Second, the capacity in question is specified in *normative* terms: it can be successfully or unsuccessfully exercised, where the standards of success are fixed by the requirements of the meaning of the expression that one is using. By contrast, the purely causal dispositions which Horwich invokes do not admit of such normative distinctions. There is no such thing as *failing* to act in accordance with a causal disposition. If something does not behave in accordance with a causal disposition (say, if a planet does not move in accordance with Kepler's laws), it simply means that the *ceteris paribus* conditions under which the disposition becomes operative are not satisfied—or, alternatively, that the thing in question does not actually have that disposition.

Third, the capacity to carry on with the use of an expression in accordance with its meaning will be successfully exercised in some conditions and not in others, but there is no reason to expect that these conditions can be specified *without circularity*: the conditions for the successful exercise of the capacity are simply the conditions under which one manages to live up to the demands of the meaning of the expression.

Taken in isolation, the passage from Wittgenstein that Horwich considers (PI §187) does not rule out his reductionist reading. But when we look at the immediate context of the passage, there are some good reasons for preferring the kind of reading that I have suggested over Horwich's reading. As we saw in Section 2, in section 220 of the *Investigations* Wittgenstein contrasts causal and logical determination. From the perspective of Horwich's reading, Wittgenstein's drawing of this contrast makes little sense, because the whole point of Horwich's reading is that Wittgenstein wants to *reduce* logical determination to causal determination. Wittgenstein discusses an analogous contrast in sections 193–4. (These sections have been plausibly interpreted by some commentators as an explicit criticism of dispositional theories of meaning; see, for example, Kripke 1982, 25 n.24.) In those sections, Wittgenstein distinguishes two concepts of machine. When we talk about a "machine," he argues, we can be talking about a "machine *qua* symbol," or about an "actual machine." In the former case, we look at the machine from a functional perspective (that is, from the perspective of how the machine is *supposed* to work), and so we may derive from it the movements that *accord* with its function. In the latter case, we look at the machine from a merely causal perspective, and so we may derive from it the movements that it *will in fact make* in different circumstances. Wittgenstein observes that "the movement of the machine *qua* symbol is predetermined in a different way from how the movement of any given actual machine is" (§193). The whole point of this discussion of machines is to clarify through an analogy the sense in which the meaning of an expression predetermines or "already contains" all its possible applications. Thus, Wittgenstein is here anticipating the contrast drawn in section 220 between causal and logical determination. Again, it is not clear why Wittgenstein should emphasize such a distinction in the way he does, if he really wanted to claim, as Horwich maintains he did, that logical determination is *reducible* to causal determination.[4]

6   Concluding Remarks

I have argued that for Wittgenstein meaning becomes mysterious when we misunderstand its grammar or logic—that is, when we misconstrue the language-games in which we talk about meaning and related phenomena, mainly because we model them on quite different language-games. His attempt to demystify meaning takes therefore the form of an attempt to clarify the concept of meaning. In order to achieve this purpose, Wittgenstein investigates the connections between meaning and a host of other notions, including appropriate notions of choicelessness, determination, truth, and capacity. All these notions are interdependent. In particular, the notions that Wittgenstein takes to be part of the conditions of intelligibility of meaning have meaning as part of *their own* conditions of intelligibility. We are here dealing, we might say, with a distinctive metaphysical layer of reality, which is thoroughly colored with meaning and intentionality. Meaning becomes visible, in all its ordinariness and unmysteriousness, when we attend to the place that it occupies within that layer of reality.

Horwich is well aware of extant anti-reductionist conceptions of the demystification of meaning. For example, he gives the following apt description of John McDowell's approach to intentionality: "Since our puzzlement about meaning is merely an artifact of self-inflicted

---

[4] I have not discussed *all* of the passages that Horwich marshals in support of his reductionist reading. I believe that in each of the remaining cases, the text can be shown to be at least compatible with an anti-reductionist conception of meaning. Some of the relevant passages have already received interpretations that are explicitly at odds with Horwich's reading. See, for example, Gustafsson 2014b, 1200 and Bronzo 2017, 1351–4.

mystification, the illumination we need will have to come from a rooting out of confusions rather than from the development of a reductive theory" (Horwich 2005, 7). Indeed, this statement would also serve as an accurate description of the approach ascribed to Wittgenstein in the present chapter. Horwich finds it unviable: he rejects as "perverse" an account of meaning that does not seek to avoid circularity (2012, 113 n.5). However, he assures us that his reason for demanding a reductionist account of meaning is not "some gut metaphysical conviction that *all* facts *must* be grounded in physical (or 'naturalistic') phenomena" (2005, 36). Horwich's substantial objection to anti-reductionist accounts of meaning is that they render mysterious how meaning and understanding can cause physical events, such as actions and speech acts. The main difficulty, he thinks, is to vindicate this causal efficacy without denying the causal closure of the physical world and without positing causal overdetermination (Horwich 2010a, 103 n.4; see also 2005, 6 and 36; 2008, 472 n.4; and 2012, 160).

Horwich is right that this is a serious challenge. However, reductionist theories of meaning also face a serious challenge. In order to be successful, they must refrain from presupposing in any way the notion of meaning, while also managing to provide an account that is recognizable as an account of *meaning* (rather than simply changing the topic and describing a scenario in which meaning is completely absent). If the argument of the present chapter is correct, Wittgenstein is open to the prospect of meeting the challenge raised by Horwich about the causal efficacy of meaning and understanding, but regards a reductionist theory of meaning à la Horwich as a hopeless undertaking.

CHAPTER 10

What Is Meaning? A Wittgensteinian Answer to an Un-Wittgensteinian Question

Hans-Johann Glock

Although the *Tractatus* was intimately concerned with linguistic meaning, it had put semantics on the index. The things which cannot be 'said' include the meaning of signs and that two signs have the same meaning (see TLP 3.33, 3.332, and 6.23), what a given symbol signifies (4.126), and the sense of a proposition (2.221, 4.022). But these things can be 'shown': they reveal themselves in bipolar propositions with a sense, provided that the latter are properly analysed. On his return to philosophy from 1929 onwards, Wittgenstein abandoned the saying/showing distinction, though gradually and hesitantly. As a result, matters of meaning assumed a central role not just implicitly, but officially. Wittgenstein even declared the 'transition from the question of truth to the question of meaning' (MS-106, 46, my translation) to be central to his philosophical method. This clear and succinct statement of the linguistic turn makes the meaning of expressions central to philosophy. The later Wittgenstein also revolutionized analytic philosophy by following through another incipient idea of the *Tractatus*, namely by completing the latter's partial move away from a referential conception of meaning. According to this conception every meaningful expression stands for an object, the latter being its meaning. Wittgenstein's main objections match the simplicity, if not the simplemindedness, of the target.

Not all meaningful words refer to objects. The referential conception is modelled mainly on proper names, mass nouns, and sortal nouns. It ignores verbs, adjectives, adverbs, connectives, prepositions, indexicals, and exclamations (PI §§1–64). Moreover, even the meaning of a referring expression is not the object it stands for. If it were, referential failure would have to render a proposition like 'Mr. N.N. died' senseless (PI §40).

One should add Ryle's criticism (1971b, chapter 27): identifying the meaning of a word with its referent is a 'category mistake', namely of confusing what a word stands for with its meaning. I can be twenty kilometres away from the referent of the definite description 'the highest peak on earth', but not from its meaning. One should further add an argument inspired by Austin (1946, 96–7; see Rundle 1979, 380). Consider

(1)   *A* knows what the expression *e* means.

In (1), 'what the expression *e* means' is *not* a *relative pronoun* ('that which', Latin *quod*) as in

(2)   She repaired what he had broken.

It is rather an *interrogative pronoun* (Latin *quid*). (1) does not amount to

(1′)   There is an *x* such that (A knows *x* and *e* means *x*)

but to

(1″)   *A* knows the answer to the question 'What does *e* mean?'

It introduces a question, albeit indirectly. The same holds for 'the meaning of *e*', which is equivalent to 'what *e* means'. It obliquely introduces a question rather than referring to an entity. That is why the premises

(3)   *A* knows the meaning of 'superfluous'

and

(4)   The meaning of 'superfluous' is identical with the meaning of 'redundant'

do not entail

(5)   *A* knows the meaning of 'redundant'.

That is to say, 'knows the meaning of *e*' is *intensional*; it creates a context in which co-referential terms cannot necessarily be substituted *salva veritate*. By contrast, when 'knows *x*' does signify acquaintance with an entity, it is *not* intensional. That is why

(6)   Rosa Luxemburg knows Lenin

and

(7)   Uljanow is identical with Lenin

do entail

(8)   Rosa Luxemburg knows Uljanow.

In addition to criticizing the referential conception, Wittgenstein presented an alternative. He famously writes in *Philosophical Investigations*: 'For a large class of cases — though not for all — in which we employ the word "meaning" it can be defined thus: the meaning of a word is its use in the language' (PI §43). It is unclear what kinds of meaning or what types of words the restriction excludes. For better or worse, Wittgenstein had no qualms about ascribing meaning to, for instance, proper names (see §§ 40–2 and 79). If it excludes certain senses of 'meaning', then Wittgenstein might have had in mind natural significance as in 'These clouds mean rain', teleological significance as in 'the meaning of life', and speaker's meaning. The reference to 'use in a language' shows that section 43 is concerned with the *lexical* meaning of type-expressions in a language. At any rate, I shall restrict myself to that topic.

Wittgenstein's dicta on meaning and use are often taken to evince a 'use-theory of meaning'. But he explicitly denied that philosophy should be in the business of constructing theories. Moreover, he was notoriously sceptical about 'What-is . . . ?'-questions in general. Finally, his slogan 'Don't ask for the meaning, ask for the use!' can be read as an attempt to circumvent the question 'What is meaning?' in particular. Sections 1 to 3 resolve this tension as regards its substantive though not as regards its exegetical dimension. Wittgenstein's ambivalence and the proclivities of many of his followers notwithstanding, there is no merit in avoiding our title question. Fortunately, while Wittgenstein's reflections may be incompatible with a formal theory of meaning, they lay the foundations of a viable account of the concept of linguistic meaning, namely by elucidating its connections with other concepts like those of rule, explanation, and understanding. My aim is to make a case for a use-theory of meaning thus understood. I consider whether meaning has a normative dimension, how semantic rules of language use can be distinguished from pragmatic ones, and whether a Wittgensteinian approach can do justice to semantic compositionality. An explanation of meaning along these lines threatens to be circular (see also Silver Bronzo's 'Demystifying Meaning in Horwich and Wittgenstein', Chapter 9 in this volume); the final sections avert this threat by invoking the legitimacy of connective rather than reductionist analysis.

1   A Theory of Meaning?

The basic idea of a use-theory is roughly this: the meaning of an expression *e* is not a *bona fide* object—whether physical, mental, or abstract—for which it stands; it is rather the use competent speakers make of *e*. The idea that meaning is use not only informs—often implicitly—the philosophy of

Wittgenstein and postwar conceptual analysis, it is also accepted by some of their opponents, notably Quine (1981, chapter 5) and Dummett (1993b, chapter 4). It has often been taken for granted by field-linguists (for instance Crystal 1987, 102) and is currently defended by eminent philosophers of language like Paul Horwich (2005). Indeed, it is one of the few Wittgensteinian dicta which are immediately plausible. Nevertheless, the claim that meaning is use has attracted vigorous criticism from different angles (see Hallett 1977, 129–48, and Lycan 1999, chapter 6). Sometimes Wittgenstein's followers try to bypass the latter *ab initio* by pointing out that he did not proffer a *theory* of meaning (for instance Hanfling 2000, 42–8). This is correct, but does not immunize his remarks on meaning against criticism. Wittgenstein and other conceptual analysts profess to investigate the meaning of words. This presupposes a *conception* of meaning. Furthermore, that conception must at least allow of being spelled out in a coherent fashion, and hence of sustaining an *account* of meaning. This holds all the more so if philosophical investigations of meaning are contrasted with systematic theories (see also Dummett 1993a, chapter 14). Whether meaning is the sort of thing one ought to have a theory about depends on the concept of meaning. It also depends on what is meant by a 'theory' in this context.

Traditionally, a theory of meaning was supposed to provide an analysis—in a suitably loose sense—of the concept of meaning and related notions. Theories of meaning in this *analytic* sense include the referential theory, behaviourist and causal theories (like that of Quine), verificationist theories, speech act theories influenced by Austin, and Grice's theory of communication intentions, as well as Wittgensteinian accounts of meaning as use. These analytic theories are theoretical only in a minimal sense. They provide more or less sustained and orderly accounts of the concept of meaning, as well as arguments in their support.

By contrast, formal semantics envisages a *constructive* theory, notably for natural languages. Such a theory does not directly explain what meaning is. Instead, it generates for each actual or potential sentence s of a particular language a theorem 'that, in some way yet to be made clear, "gives the meaning" of s', and shows in particular how this meaning depends on that of its components (Davidson 1984/2001, 23).

Analytic theories of meaning should be compatible with the way the meaning of particular sentences is specified or explained (see Section 10). Yet unlike constructive theories they do not prescribe an algorithm for generating such specifications (see Glock 2003, 141 and 152–3).

Wittgenstein's conception of language is inimical to the very project of a constructive theory of meaning (see Baker and Hacker 1984). He also denied that theories had a role to play in philosophy, for example in the following well-known passage from the *Investigations*: 'We may not advance any kind of theory. There must not be anything hypothetical in our considerations. All *explanation* must disappear' (§109). Arguably, however, that denial is based on an unduly narrow conception, which confines theories to those conforming to the hypothetico-deductive model supposed to characterize theories in the natural sciences (see Glock 2017, 245–6). One might defend section 109 on the grounds that any theory worthy of the name must provide *explanations* of its topic. But although Wittgenstein wishes to ban causal explanations from philosophy, he would be the first to accept that explanations of *meaning* have a role to play (see Glock 1996a, 111–14). Furthermore, the substantive issue is whether linguistic meaning allows for or demands a theory in either a minimal or a more demanding sense. Answering that question requires an account of the concept of meaning that is philosophically serviceable.

2 'What Is . . . ?'-Questions

Ever since Socrates, philosophers have been concerned with 'What is *X*?'-questions, for example, 'What is justice?', 'What is knowledge?', 'What is truth?' In response to these questions, they have traditionally sought *analytic definitions* (of *X*). Such definitions specify conditions or features which are individually necessary and jointly sufficient for something's being *X*. Furthermore, these features should not just *in fact* be possessed by all and only things that are *X*; rather, only things possessing all of the defining features *can be X*, and anything possessing them all is *ipso facto X*.

Wittgenstein was adverse to 'What is … ?'-questions as posed in philosophy. He suspected them—our title question explicitly included—of inducing a 'mental cramp' (BB 1). Several important lessons emerge from his reservations; yet none of them disqualifies 'What is … ?'-questions per se.

First, we ought to shed the essentialist prejudice that one can clarify a concept only by providing an analytic definition (PG 119–20; PI §§64–88). Many philosophically important notions defy analytic definition. Fortunately, however, there are other respectable ways of *explaining* concepts, notably contextual, recursive, and ostensive definitions, surveys of family resemblances and explanations by exemplification (see also Section 11).

Secondly, we must avoid the ('Socratic') mistake of thinking that a cast-iron definition of 'X' is needed in advance of further investigations (PG 121–2; TS-302, 14), whether they be empirical theory-formation about the phenomenon X or philosophical reflection on the concept of X. Nevertheless, we *do* need a grasp of what topic we are addressing. This requires at least a preliminary understanding of the meaning of 'X', an understanding subject to critical elucidation in philosophical reflection and modification in scientific theory-building. Small wonder, then, that Wittgenstein willy-nilly gave or suggested numerous answers to Socratic questions! By no means all of them are hedged with qualifications; and 'What is meaning?', along with related queries like 'What is understanding?', is no exception. Indeed, such a procedure is a prerequisite for dissolving or avoiding questions of the metaphysical kind Wittgenstein regarded as misleading or confused.

Thirdly, some 'What is ... ?'-questions are best addressed through pondering related questions, rather than head on. As we shall see, such an indirect approach is crucial to a tenable use-theory of meaning.

For all that, setting out deliberately to answer 'What is ... ?'-questions with their complications remains alien to a strand in Wittgenstein's later thinking:

> If one describes simple language-games to illustrate, let's say, what we call the 'motive' of an action, one will repeatedly be confronted with more complex (*verwickelten*) cases, in order to show that our theory does not yet conform to (*entspricht*) the facts. Whereas more complex cases simply are more complicated cases. To wit, if a theory were at issue, one could indeed say: there is no use in regarding these special cases, they do not provide an explanation exactly of the most important cases. By contrast, the simple language-games play an entirely different role. They are poles of a description, not the basis (*Grundstock*) of a theory. (RPP I §633, my translation)

Wittgenstein puts his finger on the crux of the matter. Yet his reaction is unwarranted. More complex cases need not occasion throwing up one's arms in despair. Nor do they license shrugging one's shoulders in the vain hope that exclusive contemplation of simple cases by itself will somehow resolve philosophical problems notorious for their complexity through (say) a mysterious kind of cathartic 'aspect change' or intellectual vision. Instead, more complex cases do indeed provide reasons for adjusting our 'theory' (analysis). We are called upon to fit the pieces of the conceptual jigsaw puzzle together. In this respect, conceptual analysts like Ryle, Austin, and Strawson have the edge over Wittgenstein and many of his disciples. Note, however, that Wittgenstein himself counselled 'the quiet weighing of linguistic facts', precisely as an antidote to 'turbulent specula-tion' of a metaphysical kind (Z §447).

There is no philosophical premium on being squeamish about 'What is . . . ?'-questions. After all, Wittgenstein purports to resolve philosophical problems by elucidating the concepts in terms of which they are phrased. Next, although concepts cannot simply be equated with 'meanings', to specify what general terms like 'mind', 'thinks', or 'is conscious' mean is to specify *what concepts they express*, and vice versa (see Glock 2010, 312–15). Thus, Wittgenstein is committed to a stance on 'What is *X*?'-questions, provided that these are understood as inquiries into the concept of *X* rather than scientific inquiries into *X*. Throwing in the towel and revelling in the diversity and alleged chaos of our linguistic practices can only be a last resort.

3 Eliminativism about 'Meaning'

Even if one leaves aside blanket qualms about 'What is . . . ?'-questions in general, one might avoid this question as regards *meaning* in particular. One can take the shortcomings of referential conceptions as an argument not in favour of a use-theory, but of the view that the notion of meaning is misleading and obsolete.

Once again, one might invoke Wittgenstein's authority in support of this eliminativist stance. He was fond of dispensing the advice: 'Don't ask for the meaning, ask for the use!' This slogan appears to manifest a downright refusal to engage with the nature of meaning. According to this interpretation, Wittgenstein does not provide even an account of meaning; in linking meaning and use, he was simply giving a piece of methodological advice. When investigating philosophically contentious terms, the very notion '*the* meaning' misleads us, since its nominal form suggests an object beyond the sign; this is even more true of the German '*Bedeutung*', which derives from the verb '*deuten*' (to point). The concept of meaning is obsolete save for expressions such as 'means the same' or 'has no meaning' (AWL 30, PG 56, M 51–2, PI §120).

Quine took a similar line. He rejected the idea of mental or abstract meanings as 'the myth of a museum in which the exhibits are meanings and the labels are words' (1969, 27). That an expression is meaningful is not due to it being associated with an object which is its meaning. Rather, the 'useful ways in which people ordinarily talk or seem to talk about meanings boil down to two: the *having* of meanings, which is significance, and *sameness* of meaning, or synonymy. . . . But the explanatory value of special and irreducible intermediary entities called meanings is surely illusory' (1953/61, II–12).

Warnings that the concept of meaning carries risks of reification are well taken. Semantic eliminativism is doomed, nonetheless. We need at least *a notion* of linguistic meaning. This holds for everyday life, where the notion of meaning serves to enable, facilitate, and explain crucial aspects of linguistic communication, both within and across linguistic communities. It also holds for successful, semantically clear, and epistemically controlled disciplines like formal logic, linguistics, (parts of) cognitive science, (intellectual) history, jurisprudence, and (certain branches of) philosophy.

Not coincidentally, Wittgenstein continued to operate with the notion of meaning. In line with the *Tractatus* he continued to write of the *Bedeutung* of words and the *Sinn* of sentences. Quine for his part availed himself of a behaviourist ersatz, 'stimulus meaning'. But this marks a point at which agreement between the two ends. For neither outright eliminativism nor replacement by a more or less remote substitute is compatible with Wittgenstein's methodology.

Replacing or modifying philosophically troublesome expressions like 'meaning' by a 'logical explication' à la Carnap will merely sweep the problems under the carpet, *unless* the *explicatum* is properly understood. Once we have elucidated the established concepts, we no longer require an artificial one (PI §130; Strawson 1963), *unless* the established concepts were semantically inadequate (obscure, incoherent). But if so, how could we introduce better ones? For these perforce need to be explained in terms that are already understood, and ultimately in ordinary terms of a mother tongue (PI §120; Strawson 1992, 10–16). Even if intensional notions like meaning could be replaced by extensional terms, or terms less liable to suggest meaning entities, elucidating the established notion would remain a *propaedeutic precondition* for logical explication. (See also Martin Gustafsson's 'Wittgenstein and Analytic Revisionism', Chapter 8 in this volume.)

Still, the numerous paradoxes and antinomies blighting philosophy show that *some* notions may be incoherent. Yet even if these would have to be eliminated, that drastic step must be preceded by prior clarification. We need to know at least what the expressions earmarked for elimination purport to mean and what role they were supposed to fulfil. Because of the notorious troubles in defining the concept of knowledge, for instance, it has been suggested that the latter should be replaced by the concept of true belief. If that counsel were sound, we could appreciate this by comprehending 'knowledge' and its cognates sufficiently in order to assess what surplus value over true belief it purports to signify. The same holds, *mutatis mutandis,* for methodological maxims like 'Don't ask for the meaning, ask for the use!' They had better be based on a clear understanding of the concepts involved. For methods are cognitive instruments accountable to the topics to which they are applied—in our case the philosophically contested notions of meaning and of use.

4   Meaning, Use, and Rules

Wittgensteinian strategies for evading an investigation of the concept of meaning lead astray. There is no licence for shirking the question of how the meaning of an expression is related to its use, if conceptual-*cum*-semantic questions are tackled by investigating the use of the pertinent expressions. At the same time, many critics of the idea that meaning is use go wrong in ignoring the fact that the pertinent concept of meaning is the one used in everyday parlance and in studies of language such as dictionaries and non-formal branches of linguistics, rather than the newfangled concepts they may have introduced for diverse and more or less sound reasons. My use-theory is to be measured against the same standard, namely whether its analysis of 'meaning' and of related terms conforms to the way in which they are used, explained, and understood by competent speakers.

There are undeniable connections between the established concept of meaning and linguistic use. For example:

- whether an expression like 'sesquipedalian' means something in a given language depends on whether it has an established use in the linguistic community;

- what an expression means depends on how it can be used within that community; and

- we learn what an expression means by learning how to use it, just as we learn how to play chess not by associating the pieces with objects, but (initially) by learning how they can be moved.

Nevertheless, the *identification* of meaning with use is untenable (see Rundle 1990, chapters 1, 9, and 10; but compare Schroeder 2006, 168–81). However, while some passages appear to identify meaning and use (see, for example, LFM 192, PG 60, and PI §§ 30 and 138), others stop short of doing so (see, for example, PI §§ 43 and 139). Advisedly! For although the notions of meaning and of use overlap, they diverge in important respects. Some of these differences are accommodated by keeping in mind the contrast between use in the sense of 'employment of a sign-token' and use in the sense of 'way of using' or 'manner of use' (OC §61), as well as Ryle's distinction of 'use' and 'usage' (1971b, chapter 31). The semantically relevant notion of use is that of a way of using a type-expression, its method of employment. By contrast, usage is constituted by the prevalence or non-prevalence of this method of employment in a certain linguistic community. While certain social pressures shape usage, it lacks at least one normative dimension of use: there is the misuse of expressions, but there is no such thing as the 'misusage' of an expression.

Another step towards aligning use with meaning also revolves around normativity. We must avoid reducing linguistic use to a causal process between speakers and hearers after the fashion of causal and behaviourist theories. The meaning of a type-expression does not depend on the actual causes or the actual effects of uttering a token of it, either on a particular occasion or in general (*pace* causal and behaviourist theories). Nor does it depend on the effects intended by the speaker, however complex and high-order they may be (Grice notwithstanding).

If I say 'Milk me sugar!' this may well have the result that my hearers stare at me and gape. Yet it obviously does not follow that this combination of words means 'Stare at me and gape!' It does not even follow if this amusing effect can be repeated. Indeed, it does not follow even if I utter these words with the intention of bringing about this reaction (PI §§493–8). Meaning is a matter *not* of how an expression is actually used and understood, but of how it is (or ought to be) used and understood by members of a linguistic community. What is semantically relevant is the *correct* use of expressions. This also puts paid to the popular yet short-sighted objection that meaning cannot depend on use because speakers frequently misuse expressions. Summarizing this normativist conception of use, the later Wittgenstein maintained that the linguistic meaning of an expression is 'constituted', 'determined', or 'given by' rules which lay down how it is to be used correctly (AWL 3, M 51, OC §§61–3, PG 62–4, PI §108). The idea also underlies his comparison of language to a game like chess. On the one hand, like a chess piece, a token-word is a physical phenomenon. On the other hand, one cannot explain either the significance of a chess piece or the meaning of a word in purely physical terms. Yet the difference between a chess piece and a simple piece of wood or a meaningful word and a meaningless sound is not that the former are associated with an abstract entity or mental process. Rather, it is that they have a role in a rule-guided practice.

At this point anti-normativists have a riposte: if the meaning of an expression *e* in a language *L* is determined or constituted by the use speakers make of *e*, the meaning of *e* cannot at the same time prescribe a certain use to the speakers of *L* (Davidson 1990, 310). But one must distinguish between the use an individual speaker makes of *e*, and the use that the linguistic community makes of it. *Communal* use may *constitute* meaning, while *individual* use is *responsible* to it. The existence of lexical norms and their independence from the utterances and intentions of individual speakers is no more mysterious than the existence of legal norms and their independence from the acts and motives of individual agents (see Glock 2015).

Unfortunately, a normative restriction of the pertinent type of use fails to resolve another difficulty. 'Use (of a linguistic expression)' is a wider term than '(linguistic) meaning'. In pursuance of a correct account of meaning, this observation needs to be sharpened. There are at least three pertinent divergences (see Glock 1996b, 207–10). First, the notion of use has a wider extension, in that it applies to expressions like proper names and certain exclamations ('tally-ho', 'abracadabra') to which the notion of linguistic meaning arguably does not apply. Second, 'use' is acceptable in a wider range of sentence-frames: even the correct way of using a word can involve gestures or be fashionable, but this cannot be said of its meaning. Third, not all aspects of the use of a term are relevant to its meaning.

This last difference applies equally to use conceived in normative terms. Synonymous expressions can have distinct (rule-guided) uses. 'Cop' and 'law enforcement agent' are synonymous ('cop' does not mean *tough law enforcement agent*). But while the former should not be used in a legal document, for example, there is no such convention concerning the latter. Consequently, meaning does not determine use. At the same time, use determines meaning not causally, but logically—just as for Frege sense (*Sinn*) determines reference (*Bedeutung*) (PI §§ 139, 197; PPF §§ 250, 303). While sameness of meaning co-exists with difference of use, every difference in meaning entails a difference in use. Meaning *supervenes* on use. Given the use of a word, we can infer its meaning without additional data, yet not vice versa. One cannot tell from a dictionary explanation of 'cop' whether the term is frequently employed in British courtrooms or whether in that surrounding it is subject to censure. By contrast, one can write the dictionary entry on the basis of a full description of the term's employment. (See also William Child's 'Meaning, Use, and Supervenience', Chapter 11 in this volume.)

In sum, there are incontestable differences between the way we use 'meaning of a word' and the way in which we use 'correct way of using a word'. As a result, the identification of meaning and overall linguistic use faces a *fatal dilemma*. On the one hand, if all aspects of overall use are semantically relevant, it follows that the two expressions do not mean the same. On the other hand, if not all aspects of overall use are semantically relevant, the identification of meaning with overall use is equally mistaken, since the latter exceeds the former.

At the same time, we can learn from the use of a word everything there is to its meaning; use remains the guide to meaning, and conceptual analysis, even of a revisionist kind, must start out from investigating linguistic use. Unfortunately, this consolation does not remove the aforementioned problem, namely that the term 'use' *in vacuo* is too wide. But it brings the difficulty into sharper focus. We have settled for the idea that rule-guided use determines meaning, rather than being identical with it. A difference in meaning entails a difference in use, not vice versa. The paramount semantic question therefore is: *what aspects* of our rule-guided linguistic practices are relevant to meaning; are there aspects differences in which entail differences in meaning?

I shall briefly consider five answers to this question.

5   Verificationism

Verificationism attempts to restrict the semantic rules for the use of *e* to those that are relevant to verifying or falsifying sentences in which *e* occurs. Now, strictly speaking, what is true or false are not sentences, but propositions expressed by their use on a particular occasion of utterance. Adjusting for this, a verificationist account takes the following form: the meaning of a declarative sentence is determined by the methods for verifying or falsifying the propositions expressed by its use. By the same token, the meaning of the components of simple sentences of subject–predicate structure—singular terms and predicates—is determined by the method for establishing whether something belongs to their extension (that is, whether or not a singular term refers to a particular object and whether or not a general term applies to an object).

Having toyed with verificationism around 1930, Wittgenstein came to realize that not even all declarative sentences express propositions allowing of verification; this holds in particular of first-person present-tense psychological utterances. Moreover, non-declarative sentences do not allow of verification. One might try to avoid this problem in line with

Wittgenstein's distinction between the meaning of words and the sense of sentences. Meaning is in the first instance a feature of sentence components, roughly items in the lexicon of a language. The sense of sentences in turn depends on the meaning of their constituent words and their mode of composition, though, as Wittgenstein recognized, not exclusively. The meaning of words is determined by the contribution they make to sentences in which they can occur. Even the sense of non-declarative sentences could then be explained by reference to the meaning of their components as determined by the contribution they make to the sense of declarative sentences, that is to the latter's method of verification.

However, as we shall see, not all meaningful expressions can be used in declarative sentences. Furthermore, *under what conditions* a term is applicable to something is part of its meaning—but not automatically *how* the application of a term is to be verified or falsified. For that may hinge on *factual* considerations. Even if there is a link between meaning and verification, not all aspects of the method for establishing the truth-value of a sentence matter to its meaning, but only those which must be known by someone in order to qualify as a competent speaker. In 1932 Wittgenstein suggested that the fact that we can learn who won the boat race by reading a newspaper goes some way towards explaining the meaning of 'boat race' (see M 59–60). But this is obviously wrong; 'boat race' will not have altered its meaning when all newspapers have been driven to extinction by the internet. Later on, Wittgenstein recognized that only some aspects of 'methodology' are 'conceptual', while others are 'physical' (PPF §338). For instance, that the length of playing fields is measured through the use of tripods is a matter of physics; by contrast, that measuring involves the possibility of comparing the lengths of different objects is partly constitutive of the meaning of 'length'.

6 Conceptual Role Semantics and Inferentialism

Conceptual (or inferential) role semantics is an attempt to improve on previous use-theories by making the notion of use more specific (Whiting 2018). It identifies the meaning of *e* with its *role* or *function* within a language (in the case of lexical meaning) and with a person's idiolect (in the case of speaker's meaning). A particular brand of conceptual role semantics is inferentialism (see Peregrin 2014). It diverges from other versions in following Wittgenstein by recognizing the normative dimension of meaning: the pertinent role of *e* is the one it has in communication, and that role is in turn conferred by rules. As a further step, inferentialism identifies the semantically relevant rules. It is all and only those that govern the inferential relations of the expression.

Though neat, this solution to our challenge is unsatisfactory. On the one hand, without something like an analytic/synthetic or conceptual/factual distinction of the kind envisaged by Wittgenstein under the heading 'grammatical' vs. 'empirical', the appeal to inferences is overly permissive. For it makes all inferential relations (deductive, conceptual, inductive) part of the meaning of an expression. This implies, implausibly, that any difference or alteration in general beliefs amounts to a difference or change of concepts, with the consequence that two scientific theories featuring apparently incompatible empirical claims cannot be talking about the same phenomenon (see Fodor and Lepore 1992, chapter 1).

On the other hand, with an analytic/synthetic or conceptual/factual distinction in place, inferentialism runs the risk of being overly restrictive. There are semantic rules for expressions that do not feature in inferences, not to mention conceptual inferences, except when they are quoted in assertions. Think of greetings like 'hello' or exclamations like 'ouch'. Of course, the overwhelming majority of expressions do have a role in declarative sentences and hence in inferences. Their meaning is at least partly determined by rules pertaining to conceptual inferences. With the exception of logical operators, it is nonetheless problematic to confine the semantic dimension of words to rules of inference, if only because the conditions under which a general term is satisfied by something given in experience is also part of the term's meaning. Sellars (1974), the official founder of inferentialism, was alive to this point. In addition to norms governing 'intra-linguistic moves' which qualify as inferences *sensu stricto*, he also brooked norms for 'language entrance' and 'language exit transitions'.

This concession does not go far enough, however. In the spirit of Wittgenstein, we need to recognize that the notion of a semantic rule is itself a *functional* one. Whether a sentence expresses a rule does not depend on its linguistic form, but on whether it has a normative function, either in general or on a given occasion of utterance. Rule formulations need not contain a deontic verb. And formulations of linguistic rules need not be metalinguistic statements that mention the expressions for which they provide a rule.

By these lights, semantic rules encompass anything which, in natural languages, functions as a standard of semantic correctness and hence of linguistic competence and understanding, including explanations of meaning of various kinds (see Glock 1996a, 150–55). Ostensive definitions, for instance, can function as transformation rules. But they can also be invoked to explain, criticize, and justify uses that are *not inferential,* unless that label is stretched out of proportion.

Imagine the following sequence. I call a grey wall 'sepia'; you correct me by uttering the sentence 'The wall is not sepia, *that* is sepia' while pointing to an antique photographic print; I fall in line simply by starting to call things of the same colour as the wall *grey,* and things of the same colour as the print *sepia,* yet without any statements like 'If the wall is grey all over, it is not sepia all over.' In that case, no inference is in play. Furthermore, while no linguistic community can make do without inferences of *some* kind, it is a hoary question whether all linguistic communities draw logical and conceptual inferences. Finally, even if, as I suspect, there are no exceptions on this score, fictional language-games—significantly more complex than that of Wittgenstein's builders—can be devised that satisfy two conditions: (i) they dispense with logical and conceptual inferences; and (ii) the sounds and inscriptions employed qualify as meaningful.

7   Function, Role, and Combinatorial Possibilities

Having considered two overly restrictive conceptions of semantic rules, we need to take a step back. The immediately appealing option is to retreat to the more general idea that the meaning of an expression is linked to its role (or function) as determined by rules. But where to go from there? Remember, semantic rules should treat, for instance, 'cop' as equivalent to 'policeman', while pragmatic rules permit use of the latter yet not of the former in court or in a legal document. Appeal to role (or function) will not by itself overcome the difficulty, since an expression can have *different kinds of roles* (for example, syntactic, psychological, social, institutional, legal, and aesthetic). Along a different parameter, expressions can have a role in an idiolect or a role in a lexicon, and these roles can coincide or come apart.

Conceptual role semantics of a non-inferentialist kind allows for a wider conception of role than either verificationism or inferentialism. It also recognizes that the meaning of sentence components is connected to their combinatorial possibilities in sentences. However, its prevalent naturalistic manifestations are uncongenial to a theory of lexical meaning. For one thing, they assimilate the notion of sentence-meaning or sense to that of propositional content; for another, they start out from the mental states of individuals rather than inter-subjective linguistic practices; for a third, they conceive of both mental operations and linguistic activities in a way tinged by (computational) functionalism, as mechanical processes rather than intentional and rule-guided activities.

One way of pursuing the idea of role or function that avoids these pitfalls is Wittgenstein's. He was aware of the need to single out the conceptually/ semantically relevant aspects of our linguistic practices; we need to separate the 'essential' from the 'inessential' ones (RPP I §666). Commenting on a fictional language in which one and the same type of tool is called by a different name on different days of the week, Wittgenstein claims that 'not every *use* ... is a meaning' (LW I §289). And he suggests that what guarantees a difference in meaning is a difference in the 'function' (§290) of the word, but admits that this idea is itself imprecise ('a blurred concept', §290). He takes a first step in putting flesh on it by recognizing that what matters is not the function an expression has in a particular situation of utterance or within the idiolect of an individual speaker, but function as conferred by rules governing a whole language. Thus he explains both the sense of sentences and the meaning of words by reference to their 'place,' 'role', 'purpose', or 'function' within an overall linguistic system or 'grammar' (see, for example, BB 5, PG 59–63, and OC §64).

But expressions have distinct types of roles even within a linguistic system, to wit: syntactic, morphological, semantic, and pragmatic roles. Now, the syntactic dimension is intimately connected to the semantic one. As the *Tractatus* recognized, the 'rules of logical syntax' determine the combinatorial possibilities of terms. They specify for any given lexical element (or 'name') with what other elements it can be combined into elementary propositions with a sense. Yet they do so without talking about the relation between an element and the 'object' it stands for. Inferentialism goes in a similar direction, since it ties the meaning of a word to its role in inferences, which in turn presupposes a role within sentences.

Rules of logical syntax specify with what other expressions a given one can combine to yield a sequence of signs that is not just grammatically well formed (like Chomsky's 'semantic anomalies') but has a sense. Such rules are crucial to any workable use-theory. According to an influential line of criticism, such theories are incapable of explaining complex sentences, since ways of using and conceptual roles are not 'compositional' (Fodor and Lepore 1991). For instance, the respective ways of using the expressions 'the', 'cow', 'is', and 'radioactive' do not determine the way of using 'The cow is radioactive'. Fortunately, a use-theory is not committed to the erroneous claim that there are semantically relevant rules not just for the use of words but for the use of whole sentences as well. Semantic rules of use concern *lexical items*, such as words and entrenched figures of speech. At the same time, these rules specify how the item can be used within sentences and what contribution it makes to the latter's senses. Someone who has mastered the use of 'cow' knows, among other things: (a) that it is the name of a kind of animal; (b) that such a name can be combined with the definite article to form a singular term referring to a particular specimen; and (c) that this singular term can in turn combine with the copula and an adjective to characterize the specimen it refers to. And someone who has mastered the adjective 'radioactive' knows, among other things, that it can be meaningfully combined with singular terms referring to spatio-temporal objects, yet not with singular terms referring to, say, numbers, events, or character traits. This is one of several respects in which the link between meaning and understanding provides succour to a use-theory (more on which in Section 10).

8   Form-of-Life Holism

The *Tractatus* notwithstanding, however, confining semantic rules to those of logical syntax for the meaningful combination of words is, once again, too restrictive. The mere ability to manipulate symbols does not suffice for understanding, as Searle's Chinese Room argument shows. Furthermore, there could be rules for combining words without either these words or the resulting combinations being meaningful, for instance in a play of words. At this juncture Wittgenstein's analogy between language and a game breaks down. Still, the difference between a meaningful use of *e* and a mere game involving *e* does not lie in the former being based on a connection between *e* and mental processes or abstract entities. Rather, it lies in meaningful uses of *e* being embedded in a practice. In a language-game, linguistic and non-linguistic actions are interwoven. Both are also embedded in the environment, notably through perception. As a result, unlike mere word-plays, *bona fide* linguistic acts have a role within a 'form of life' (PI §273; PLP 158–9).

Alas, in developing this insight, the later Wittgenstein often goes astray. Taking Frege's context-principle to extremes, he maintains that 'to imagine a language is to imagine a form of life' and that the meaning of a word is determined by its 'role in the whole life of a tribe' (EPB 149, my translation). Admittedly, it may well be necessary to consider the overall role of a concept in a form of life for (certain) philosophical purposes. Nevertheless, a word's social role does not determine its lexical meaning. 'Indigestion' has the role of referring to the default complaint of English hypochondriacs. In German that role is fulfilled by '*Kreislaufbeschwerden*' (circulatory disturbance). To this extent, the two expressions have the same social function. Yet this indicates divergence in form of life—repression here, *Angst* there—rather than sameness of meaning. The point becomes even plainer when one recognizes that sexual swear-words have the same role in some linguistic communities as sacrilegious or faecal ones in others, but I shall refrain from labouring this case. More generally, the conditions something must fulfil to fall under a general term—the features it must possess—are crucial to its meaning. But the things possessing these features can obviously change their social role, without the application conditions and hence the meaning of the term being affected. And in some cases the new role of those instances of the term draws in its wake a new role for the term itself. Consider the contrast between two developments in the overall usage of a single expression. 'Gay' acquired a new meaning when it came to be used as a synonym for 'homosexual'. Yet that meaning has not changed since then simply because, mercifully, most of us now have learnt to use the term without negative connotations.

9   Speech Act Potential

We still face the task of distinguishing semantic from pragmatic rules. Formal semanticists in the philosophy of language and representationalists in the philosophy of mind tend to demean the latter as 'merely pragmatic', relying on Grice's theory of conversational implicatures in their endeavours to keep the notions of meaning and intentional content 'minimal' (that is, logically pure and amenable to formalization). Even for pragmatists who are sceptical about the motives and prospects of this project, however, the challenge remains.

Given our concern with lexical meaning, the kind of role we are looking for is one that expressions have in whole languages. A promising way of pursuing this hint derives from speech act theory. It appeals to the idea of a 'speech act' (or 'illocutionary act') potential (Alston 1964; 2000; von Savigny 1983). The sense of a type-sentence is determined by the type of speech act that speakers perform by uttering it, insofar as that type is determined by general linguistic conventions. For its part, the meaning of a type-expression is its contribution to the speech act potential of sentences in which it occurs.

Taking a cue from Austin ([1962/75], chapter 10), the relevant conventions concern the illocutionary rather than the perlocutionary role of expressions. Austin distinguished between the 'illocutionary' force of an utterance (what is done *in* making it, as a matter of general linguistic conventions) and its 'perlocutionary' force (what is done *by* making it, the effect it has on others in a particular situation). For example, the illocutionary force of 'I'm going to strangle you' is that of a threat or warning, while its perlocutionary force may be anything from intimidating, offending, or even encouraging, depending on the circumstances in which it is uttered. Only illocutionary force is semantically relevant, because it alone is a function of the conventions which govern the use of words in a language. At the same time, the illocutionary force potential of, for example, 'racist' is not exhausted by the speech act performed by asserting (say) that Trump is a racist. It includes among other things the appropriate responses to this speech act by hearers. They might deny that Trump harbours prejudices about humans of different racial origins, challenge the speaker to provide evidence for this claim, invite her to explain her understanding of 'racist', or accept the assertion either with or without drawing damning conclusions about Trump.

The idea of illocutionary act potential embodies valuable insights into the nature of linguistic communication and the role meaning plays in it. Nevertheless, as a definition of the meaning of type-expressions it faces a formidable stumbling block. Though more specific than form-of-life holism, its conception of meaning is still too wide. For the speech act potential of specific words or sentences is tied to rules or conventions which cannot be counted as part of the lexical meaning of expressions. Some of these pertain to communication and communicative competence in general rather than to an individual expression *e* and the knowledge of *e*'s meaning. These include the 'conversational maxims' highlighted by Grice, which concern 'general features of discourse'. Rules like Grice's 'cooperative principle' may contribute to 'the total signification of an utterance'. Yet they contribute neither to 'what the speaker has said' nor to 'what is conventionally implicated' by the utterance, that is, 'implicated by virtue of some word or phrase which [the speaker] has used'. Instead they determine 'what is nonconventionally implicated', in particular by way of 'conversational implicatures'. Such implications fall 'outside the specification of the conventional meaning of the words used' (Grice 1989, 26, 39, 41, 118). The rules which engender them are pragmatic rather than semantic.

It might be feasible to disregard these rules by demonstrating that they have an impact exclusively on the perlocutionary acts that can be performed with *e*, whereas only illocutionary acts count towards speech act potential. But another problem remains. There is a second class of rules which contribute essentially to the speech act potential of an expression *e*, without being part of *e*'s lexical meaning. These are the very rules around which speech act theory revolves, namely those conventional rules which govern specific types of illocutionary acts. The best-known example is the rules for the speech act of promising which Searle (1969, section 3.1) tried to capture. From a pragmatist-*cum*-normativist perspective, at any rate, these are partly constitutive of the meaning of 'promise' and its cognates. But they are not partly constitutive of other expressions, all of which have a potential to be used in promises. The same holds, *mutatis mutandis*, for semantic competence. Knowledge of these rules is a prerequisite for understanding 'promise' and its cognates, yet not for understanding 'chair', 'bachelor', 'drake', 'run', or 'quickly' (for example), not to mention logical operators.

10 Meaning, Explanation, and Understanding

We have reached an impasse and need to pursue an alternative route. This alternative route exploits an unduly neglected aspect of Wittgenstein's reflections on meaning. The general idea is to elucidate the notion of meaning *indirectly*, through its conceptual connections to other pertinent notions (see Baker and Hacker 1980/2009, chapter 2, and Glock 2010, 315–19). More specifically, Wittgenstein focuses on the connections between meaning, on the one hand, and the explanations and understanding of specific expressions on the other. (See also Julia Tanney's 'Explaining What We Mean', Chapter 2 in this volume.)

> 'The meaning of a word is what an explanation of its meaning explains.' That is, if you want to understand the use of the word 'meaning', look for what one calls 'an explanation of meaning'. (PI §560)

At first sight, this looks singularly uninformative. If someone were to clarify what etymology is by saying that it is the history of an expression and then proceeding with 'The history of an expression is what an explanation of its history explains', wouldn't we regard that as a rather feeble joke? The same would seem true of 'The American Constitution is what an explanation of the American Constitution explains.' But compare this last case with 'The British Constitution is what an explanation of the British Constitution explains.' This contrast indicates that a triviality can refer to more or less important and even essential aspects. Simplifying somewhat: unlike the US constitution, the British constitution is *nothing other than*— nothing over and above—what is explained by British courts. The same holds, *mutatis mutandis*, for the meaning of an expression: it does not have an existence independently of the expression being explained, used, and understood. In the spirit of the Austinian argument mentioned at the beginning, one might try to capture this by saying that 'meaning' is just an internal accusative noun for what we explain and understand when we explain and understand words or sentences. The off-shot: section 560, though literally trivial, captures an essential feature of meaning.

To home in on this feature, one needs to recognize that the type of explanation conceptually connected to meaning is not a causal explanation (of *why* an expression *e* means what it does). Instead it is an explanation of what *e* means which proceeds by way of explaining how *e* is to be used. Note the following three meta-semantic lessons. First, the meaning of 'meaning' is connected to that of 'explanation'. Second, the truism reinforces the normative dimension of meaning, since semantic explanations have a normative status; they function as standards of semantic correctness and competence. Third, as regards the proper way for determining the meaning of specific expressions: if you want to know which rules for *e* are semantic, look at which rules are invoked to explain the meaning of *e*.

Does that solve the problem of distinguishing semantic from other rules? It does, but only up to a certain point. Acceptable (notably lexical) explanations of 'cop' distinguish conditions of correct application from, among other things, characterizations of legal legitimacy and social propriety. This is evident from, among other things, the entries in standard lexica. The *explanans* of such an entry explains or specifies the meaning of the *explanandum* at the start of the entry. That *explanans* will specify conditions of application, but not other rules concerning the *explanandum*. To be sure, after the *explanandum* there may be additional information about its use in parentheses. Some of these will be syntactic or morphological, for example, '(adj.)'. But others will specify pragmatic features of use, for instance, '(colloq.)', '(pej.)', and '(anc.)'. Even a parenthesis of that kind, however, falls way short of specifying specific rules concerning the impropriety of 'cop' in a legal context. This is another respect in which following up our apparently stale truism is illuminating: lexica provide a well-established, clear, and generally reliable (though by no means infallible) way of distinguishing the semantically pertinent from other features of use.

Wittgenstein's strategy for clarifying meaning also appeals to how competent speakers understand an expression. The meaning of *e* cannot transcend the understanding of competent speakers. It cannot be at odds with explanations of that meaning which competent speakers are capable of proffering on reflection, or at least capable of accepting when they are formulated by experts. Meaning is immanent rather than 'hidden' (PI §§126–8). The meaning of *e* is determined by how competent speakers understand *e*. The connection of meaning to semantic competence and knowledge of meaning furnishes a second way of demarcating semantic rules. To single out the semantic rules for *e* consider whether a speaker needs to be familiar with them to count as a competent user of *e*. Like the connection to explanation, it also highlights a normative aspect: competent users and uses are those satisfying certain standards.

II Connective Analysis

We have worked our way towards two conceptual claims, which I will call 'meaning–explanation' (*ME*) and 'meaning–understanding' (*MU*).

> (*ME*): The linguistic meaning of an expression *e* is what the explanation of *e* (as opposed to an explanation of the phenomena *e* refers to or applies to) explains.

> (*MU*): The linguistic meaning of an expression *e* is what a competent speaker or user of *e* (as opposed to someone who knows everything about the phenomena *e* refers to or applies to) understands by *e*.

The claims *ME* and *MU* provide criteria for identifying rules as semantic in a particular language. Alas, appeal to these criteria does not provide a non-circular explanation of what 'meaning' means. For in the sense pertinent to *ME*, 'explanation' must be understood as explanation of meaning, whether directly ('what the explanation of meaning explains') or indirectly ('as opposed to causal explanations …'). The same holds, *mutatis mutandis*, for *MU* and 'understanding'. The attempt to single out semantic rules appeals to conventions that can only be separated from other rules governing language by *presupposing* the notion of meaning. It would appear that the desideratum of demarcating semantic from other rules and the desideratum of analysing the concept of meaning are mutually exclusive. Thus Davidson complains: 'It is empty to say that meaning is use unless we specify what use we have in mind, and when we do specify, in a way that helps with meaning, we find ourselves going in a circle' (2005, 13).

At this juncture we should appeal to a distinct conception of conceptual analysis. Strawson (1992, chapter 2) distinguishes between 'atomistic', 'reductive', and 'connective' analysis. Atomistic analysis seeks to break down concepts and propositions into components that are absolutely simple. Strawson repudiates it as 'distinctly implausible'. Reductive analysis tries to explain complex concepts in terms that are regarded as more perspicuous or less problematic from an empiricist or naturalistic perspective. Strawson resists this ambition on the grounds that the fundamental concepts with which descriptive metaphysics deals 'remain obstinately irreducible, in the sense that they cannot be defined away, without remainder or circularity, in terms of other concepts' (1995, 16). He is right on both counts. Developments in the wake of Wittgenstein and Quine undermine the quest to find simpler, let alone ultimate, semantic components for all our expressions.

Accordingly, we should abandon the idea that philosophical analysis decomposes or dismantles a complex phenomenon, and thereby the analogy between philosophical and chemical analysis. Strawson's alternative—connective analysis—is the description of the rule-governed use of expressions, and of their connections with other expressions by way of implication, presupposition, and exclusion. It need not result in definitions, but can instead rest content with elucidating features that are constitutive of the concepts under consideration, and with establishing how they bear on philosophical problems, doctrines, and arguments.

We were faced with a circularity: we explained meaning by reference to semantic rules; yet the latter were to be demarcated from other linguistic rules by appeal to semantic explanation and understanding. However, all explanations of meaning eventually move in a circle. It is not circles *as such* that vitiate an explanation of meaning, but only those that are too narrow or unilluminating. The circles—in turn interconnected—summarized by *ME* and *MU*, respectively, do not suffer from such defects. They shed light on the problematic notion of meaning by reference to notions that do not tempt us into reifying 'meanings', and which are less confusing in philosophical contexts. Both *ME* and *MU* also highlight normative dimensions of the concept of meaning that Wittgenstein was rightly keen on.

12 Correctness, Truth, and Meaning

At the same time, defending that normative dimension against recent sceptics threatens to revive the spectre of circularity. Most of these anti-normativists grant that an expression has a specific meaning only if there are conditions for its correct use. They accept a principle that I have called 'bare normativity of meaning' (Glock 2015).

(*BNM*): e means $F \Rightarrow \forall x$ (it is correct to apply e to $x \leftrightarrow x$ is f)

Here 'e' is a general term, 'F' gives its meaning, and 'f' is the feature in virtue of which e applies to an object x. The consequent of *BNM* provides the scheme for a 'semantic principle' of the kind employed in formal semantics.

(*SP*): $\forall x$ (it is correct to apply e to $x \leftrightarrow x$ is f)

For 'drake', such a principle might read as follows.

(*SP$_D$*): $\forall x$ (it is correct to apply 'drake' to $x \leftrightarrow x$ is a male duck)

Principles of this format play a marginal role at best in our practices, as compared with the diverse types of explanations of meaning highlighted by Wittgenstein. But if one waives that worry, an anti-normativist objection arises. For then it might be objected that 'correct' in *BNM*, *SP*, and *SP$_D$* is not genuinely normative, but is simply a place-holder for 'true': 'it is correct to apply e to x' boils down to e holds true of x (Hattiangadi 2007, 51–61).

This objection can be met (even if we disregard the question of whether 'true' is really as normatively sterile as the objection assumes). For it presupposes that semantic norms would have to be norms of truth, norms to the effect that one ought to think and state what is true. But the contrast between *correct* and *incorrect* applies to language in a variety of ways, and their connection to the notion of meaning differs. In particular, one can use a word meaningfully, in a sentence with a sense that expresses a thought, without that thought being either true or justified.

There is a fundamental contrast between saying something *false or unjustified*, for instance 'Drakes cannot contract avian influenza', and saying something *meaningless* (something unintelligible when understood literally) as in 'Most prime numbers suffer from avian influenza.'

Some uses of words are mistaken solely because of what these words mean, irrespective of any other facts, syntactic rules, or social expectations. Conversely, one can apply a word in a way which is semantically correct— based on a proper understanding of its meaning—without applying it correctly in the sense of saying something true, namely if one errs about pertinent facts.

Even if semantic rules are understood as principles that specify conditions for making a true statement—application/truth-conditions—their violation does not consist simply in saying something false. The proper distinction between semantically correct and incorrect does not amount to that between true and false but is closer to that between meaningful, on the one hand, and meaningless or nonsensical on the other. In the spirit of *MU*: there is a difference between using an expression with understanding and using it to say something true and with the knowledge that what is said is true.

Semantic principles lay down not what *e* actually applies to, but the *conditions* under which it applies to an object *x*. Whether *e* actually applies in a given case then depends on whether *x* satisfies these conditions; it is a matter of fact rather than meaning. One commits a factual error, for instance, if one applies 'drake' to *x* on the mistaken assumption that *x* is a male duck. One commits a semantic mistake if one applies 'drake' to *x* on grounds other than *x* being a male duck. In both cases, one does something which is assessable as incorrect against a standard, but only in the latter case is the standard (the mistake) semantic.

But now, in the context of explaining what meaning is, this normativist riposte appears to come at a steep price. To avoid reducing the incorrectness involved in violating semantic principles to *falsehood*, we have explained it in explicitly semantic terms—'meaningless', 'nonsensical', 'senseless', 'without understanding', and so on. The desideratum of identifying the semantically relevant features of use and the desideratum of pinpointing the normative dimension of meaning seem to stand in a potentially fatal tension.

Fortunately, we can once again take comfort from connective analysis, and appeal to non-trivial and important conceptual connections between meaning, explanation, and understanding. Explanations of meaning play normative roles in teaching, justifying, and criticizing linguistic use; yet they specify conditions under which *e* applies to or is true of (anything), not whether it applies to or is true of a given case. By the same token, understanding a sentence requires knowing the conditions under which it is true, rather than knowing its truth-value. Using words in a way that fall foul of recognized explanations and betrays misunderstanding is a ground for *correction*. While there is more to the normativity of meaning, this suffices to justify the normativist perspective on meaning and use that unites Wittgenstein with inferentialism and the speech act potential approach.

The lexical meaning of an expression *e* in a language *L* is determined by rules specifying conditions that must be fulfilled for *e* to be applied by a speaker. They also lay down appropriate ways of responding to the use of *e* for hearers. Such rules are invoked in acceptable explanations of the meaning of *e* in *L*. Knowledge and mastery of these rules is a precondition of being a competent user of *e* in *L*. In the case of general terms, these rules specify features that an object must possess to fall under *e*. Using *e* in accordance with these rules is sufficient for saying something intelligible, and satisfying the criteria for understanding *e*, but not for saying something true. That is my Wittgensteinian, albeit relatively straightforward, answer to my straightforwardly un-Wittgensteinian question.

CHAPTER 11

Meaning, Use, and Supervenience
William Child

1 Wittgenstein's Anti-Reductionism

What is the relation between meaning and use? Wittgenstein says that 'the meaning of a word is its use in the language' (PI §43).[1] He makes a parallel claim about the sense of a proposition: 'The use of a proposition – that is its sense' (BT 80e). But what sort of illumination are we supposed to derive from those ideas?

Consider a particular expression: the word 'red', for instance. Part of Wittgenstein's point is that the word 'red' means what it does because we use it in the way we do. But the significance of that point depends on how we understand the notion of use. We can distinguish between a reductionist and an anti-reductionist view. The anti-reductionist thinks of the use of a word in a wholly quietist or pleonastic way. On this view, all we can say about how use determines meaning is this: the word 'red' means *red* because we use it to mean *red*; the words 'add 2 each time' mean *add two each time* because they 'are used by us to mean that two is to be added each time' (Stroud 2012, 27); and so on. As Barry Stroud puts it, a description of the use of an expression that 'suffices to fix its meaning' must itself 'employ the idea of meaning' (2012, 27). That is the view that Stroud both endorses and attributes to Wittgenstein.[2]

For the reductionist, by contrast, the point of the idea that meaning is use is to explain linguistic meaning in more basic terms. She agrees that we use the word 'red' to mean *red*. But she thinks we can spell out what is involved in using the word 'red' to mean *red* in a way that does not employ semantic concepts: in terms, for instance, of people's dispositions to

---

[1] Wittgenstein restricts the 'explanation' of the word 'meaning' that he offers at PI §43 to 'a *large* class of cases of the employment of the word "meaning"'. For present purposes we can focus on that class of cases, leaving aside those to which Wittgenstein's explanation is not intended to apply.

[2] For other statements of Stroud's anti-reductionism about meaning, see Stroud 2000, ix, 91–2 and 130. For similarly anti-reductionist readings of Wittgenstein's view of meaning and use, see McDowell 1984; McGinn 1984; and Child 2011, 95–104. Boghossian 1989 advocates an anti-reductionist view of meaning as the best response to Kripke's Wittgenstein; he does not take a stand on Wittgenstein's own position.

produce and respond to sounds or symbols containing 'red' in specified observable circumstances. That is a view that many readers have ascribed to Wittgenstein. According to Michael Dummett, for instance, when Wittgenstein describes the use of language, 'what is described is the complex of activities with which the utterances of sentences are interwoven; and ... the description does not invoke psychological or semantic concepts, but is couched entirely in terms of what is open to outward view' (Dummett 1978, 446). Paul Horwich agrees: Wittgenstein's 'examples of the meaning-constituting uses of words', he writes, 'are never couched in semantic or intentional terms' (Horwich 2012, 112).

My own view is that Wittgenstein is an anti-reductionist about meaning and intentional content. And I think Wittgenstein is right; facts about meaning and content cannot be constructed from or reduced to facts about use characterized in wholly non-semantic, non-intentional terms. But Wittgenstein does not adopt the most flat-footed, uncompromisingly anti-reductionist position on these matters. For, though he insists that meaning cannot be explained or accounted for in other terms, he does think that there are interesting and non-pleonastic things to say about what it takes for an expression to be used with a particular meaning, including things about the relation between a word's meaning what it does and facts about its use, characterized in non-semantic terms. That strand in his thinking emerges in many passages. I will give two examples.

Wittgenstein writes:

> Let us consider very simple rules. Let the expression be a figure, say this one:
> |– –|
> and one follows the rule by drawing a straight sequence of such figures (perhaps as an ornament).
> |– –||– –||– –||– –||– –|
> Under what circumstances should we say: someone gives a rule by writing down such a figure? Under what circumstances: someone is following this rule when he draws that sequence? It is difficult to describe this.
>
> If one of a pair of chimpanzees once scratched the figure |– –| in the earth and thereupon the other the series |– –||– –| etc., the first would not have given a rule nor would the other be following it, whatever else went on at the same time in the minds of the two of them.
>
> If however there were observed, e.g., the phenomenon of a kind of instruction, of showing how and of imitation, of lucky and misfiring attempts, of reward and punishment and the like; if at length the one who had been so trained put figures which he had never seen before one after another in sequence as in the first example, then we should probably say that the one chimpanzee was writing rules down, and the other was following them. (RFM VI §42)

That passage illustrates a point that Wittgenstein makes a few remarks earlier: 'What, in a complicated surrounding, we call "following a rule" we should certainly not call that if it stood in isolation' (RFM VI §33). What each chimpanzee does can be described in terms that do not presuppose that a rule is being given and followed; the first chimpanzee scratches the figure |– –| in the earth and the second scratches the series |– –||– –| etc. If that is just a one-off occurrence, no rule has been given or followed. When it happens in the right kind of context, we do have a case of giving and following a rule. But what is the right kind of context? What exactly are the circumstances under which we should say that a rule is being given and followed? The most uncompromisingly anti-reductionist response to that question would be simply to say this: that the circumstances under which we should say that a rule is being given and followed are those in which people (or chimpanzees) are participating in a practice of giving and following rules or, more simply, in which a rule is indeed being given and followed. But in the passage I have quoted, and others like it, Wittgenstein does not give that unhelpful answer. Instead, he tries to say something genuinely informative and non-pleonastic about what it takes for there to be a custom of giving and following such rules, and what it takes for two people (or chimpanzees) to be participants in such a practice.[3] We can highlight two points.

First, Wittgenstein thinks that the existence of a custom or practice of following rules requires there to be a whole pattern of rule-involving activity. Some of the activities he mentions in the passage I have quoted are specific to the situation of learning: instruction, showing how, imitation, etc. Others are more general: reward and punishment, for instance. But the most basic feature of rule-following, which is implicit in all the activities Wittgenstein mentions, is that giving or following rules involves *acknowledging* or *understanding* actions as being correct or incorrect. The idea of acknowledging an action as correct or incorrect is no more basic than the idea of following a rule itself: to the extent that it is unclear whether two chimpanzees are really giving and following rules (as opposed to merely acting in a regular way), it will be equally unclear whether they are really acknowledging their actions as being correct or incorrect; and

---

[3] Wittgenstein writes, in a context related to the one I have discussed: 'Here there is nothing more difficult than to avoid pleonasms and only to say what really describes something' (RFM VI §21). He thinks it is difficult to say something substantial and non-pleonastic; he does not think it is impossible.

vice versa.[4] As before, there is no prospect of a reductive account of rule-following. Nonetheless, it is philosophically illuminating to set out the kind of structure of holistically related activities that provides the necessary background for something to count as an instance of rule-following.

Second, it is a characteristic feature of Wittgenstein's work to approach the task of saying something substantial about the circumstances in which an interaction counts as a case of a rule being given and followed by focusing on the procedure of someone's *learning* to follow a rule. (As Wittgenstein puts it elsewhere: 'What the correct following of a rule consists in cannot be described *more closely* than by describing the *learning* of "proceeding according to the rule"', RFM VII §26.) In describing the process of learning, we describe a process in which there is a transition from the learner's doing things that do not yet involve following a rule—making marks, copying the teacher, etc.—to her engaging in rule-following activity. In giving such a description we are not explaining what rule-following consists in in non-rule-involving terms. Nonetheless, we are charting one kind of link between non-rule-involving facts and facts about following rules. And that, Wittgenstein suggests, is as close as we can get to giving an informative account in non-rule-involving terms of what rule-following consists in; 'we can go no further' (RFM VII §26).

Now consider a second passage, in which Wittgenstein insists that the existence of a practice of multiplying requires the existence of lower-level regularities in linguistic behaviour.

> What if we said that mathematical propositions were prophecies in *this* sense: they predict what result members of a society who have learnt this technique will get in agreement with other members of the society? '25 x 25 = 625' would thus mean that men, if we judge them to obey the rules of multiplication, will reach the result 625 when they multiply 25 x 25. – That this is a correct prediction is beyond doubt; and also that calculating is in essence founded on such predictions. That is to say, we should not call something 'calculating' if we could not make such a prophecy with certainty. This really means: calculating is a technique. And what we had said pertains to the essence of a technique. (RFM III §66; for related comments, see for instance RFM VI §23)

---

[4] I disagree with Hannah Ginsborg, who argues in recent work that there is a primitive way of taking a performance to be appropriate in its context which is independent of any prior grasp of meaning or rules (see Ginsborg 2011). She appeals to this 'consciousness of . . . primitive appropriateness' (248) to offer a 'partly reductionist' explanation of facts about meaning and rule-following in terms of 'facts that are in a sense more primitive', though not purely naturalistic (2011, 230). I plan to discuss this interesting proposal elsewhere.

We could put the lesson of that passage like this. Mathematical propositions are not prophecies, in any sense. Nonetheless, take a group of people whom we judge to have learnt to multiply and to obey the rules of multiplication. Now say to them, 'What is 25 x 25?' We can predict that they will, by and large, respond by saying '625'. That is an empirical prediction about their behaviour, non-semantically characterized. And it is a correct prediction; people who have been through a certain training and whom we judge to have mastered the rules of multiplication do generally respond in that way in these circumstances. Wittgenstein's point is that the existence of a practice of multiplication in a community depends upon the obtaining of patterns of non-semantic facts in virtue of which such prophecies, if someone chose to make them, would be true.[5] If we could not make such prophecies 'with certainty', the people in question would not be calculating. In this particular case, Wittgenstein is talking about the rules of multiplication and the technique of calculating. But he would make the same points about rules and meaning in general.

2 Supervenience

It is natural to characterize the picture that emerges from passages like those discussed in Section 1 in terms of supervenience. Facts about meaning cannot be reduced to, or explained in terms of, non-semantic facts about use. But facts about meaning do supervene on non-semantic facts about use. That is to say, two worlds cannot differ in a semantic respect without differing in some non-semantic respect. Equivalently, if two worlds are alike in all non-semantic respects, they must be alike in all semantic respects. In the rest of this essay I shall defend this supervenience thesis against some significant criticisms. My primary goal is to defend the supervenience thesis itself. But I shall also argue that the position I defend is consistent with Wittgenstein's views.

---

[5] In several passages, Wittgenstein stresses a distinction between genuine predictions (for instance 'if you follow the rules of multiplication as best you can, you will get 625') and propositions that look like predictions but are actually 'pleonasms' because they are really just ways of stating what the rule in question requires (for instance 'if you follow the rules of multiplication, you will get 625'). 'It is not a prediction', he writes, 'if the concept of *following* the rule is so determined, that the result is the criterion for whether the rule was followed' (RFM VI §15). Someone might object that the 'predictions' Wittgenstein describes in the passage I have discussed are not supposed to be genuine predictions at all: that they fall on the 'pleonasm' side of his distinction. In the context of the quoted passage, however, it is clear that Wittgenstein does mean to be describing genuine predictions: 'In a technique of *calculating*, prophecies must be possible' (RFM III §67).

The thesis that semantic facts supervene on non-semantic facts about use can be understood in many different ways. I shall follow Stephen Kearns and Ofra Magidor in spelling out the target thesis in the following way (see Kearns and Magidor 2012, 323–4). First, the *semantic facts* that are claimed to supervene on non-semantic use facts are to be understood as inclusively as possible, as encompassing both facts about the meanings of words ('The English word "plus" refers to the *plus* function'; 'Jane said that the rose was red') and facts about the contents of thoughts and attitudes ('Jane thought that Brexit was a terrible idea'; 'Jim intended to buy his son a present'). Second, the *non-semantic facts about use* that make up the supervenience base are also to be understood as widely as possible. In particular, the facts about an expression's use are to include the following: (1) facts about the community's use of the expression, and not simply about any particular individual's use; (2) facts about the physical environment in which the expression is used (this accommodates semantic externalism's insight that the meanings of many expressions are determined in part by which natural kinds and which individual things are present in speakers' environments; see Kripke 1972/80 and Putnam 1975); (3) facts, if there are such facts, about the relative naturalness of the properties and individuals to which expressions refer. As Kearns and Magidor note, a common picture in contemporary philosophy is this. Speakers' linguistic dispositions, taken by themselves, are compatible with numerous different assignments of meaning. Nonetheless, the English word 'plus' refers to the *plus* function rather than to any quus-like alternative, the word 'green' refers to the property of being green rather than to any grue-like alternative, and so on. And what makes 'plus' mean what it does is in part that the *plus* function is objectively more natural than any such alternative, and hence more eligible to be picked out by our word (similarly for the word 'green' and the property of being green, and so on). (For this picture, see especially Lewis 1983 and 1984.)

There is room for debate as to how far this conception of the non-semantic facts on which semantic facts supervene is consistent with Wittgenstein's views. I cannot resolve that question here. But I will make two observations. First (concerning point 2 above), some readers of Wittgenstein think that semantic externalism in the style of Kripke and Putnam is incompatible with Wittgenstein's views, because it severs the essential connection between the meanings of people's words and their own use of those words (see, for example, Glock and Preston 1995). I have argued elsewhere that that is a mistake; there is nothing in Wittgenstein that conflicts with the idea that we may use terms to refer to natural kinds in the way described by Kripke and Putnam (see Child 2010, 65–9). Second (concerning point 3), the idea that objective naturalness plays any role in determining meaning will seem to many readers to be directly opposed to Wittgenstein's views. In my view, however, the issue is not clear-cut. I have argued elsewhere that Wittgenstein gives an important role in the determination of meaning to a notion of naturalness that is not constrained by the limits of our actual classificatory capacities, and thus that there is less distance between Wittgenstein's position and the 'natural-properties' view than is generally assumed (see Child 2017). But whether or not I am right about that, the important point for present purposes is a conditional one; if facts about the naturalness of properties and individuals *do* play a part in fixing the meanings of expressions, then the defender of semantic supervenience should count those facts as part of the non-semantic supervenience base.

The thesis I want to defend, then, is this. Semantic facts, taken to include facts about both linguistic meaning and intentional content, supervene on non-semantic facts, taken to include facts about the community's use of words and concepts, facts about the physical environment, and facts (if such there be) about the naturalness of properties and individuals.

3 Supervenience and Dispositional Properties

In 'Wittgenstein on Following a Rule', John McDowell presents an anti-reductionist view of meaning and rule-following in terms of a distinction between two levels at which we can describe linguistic behaviour. On the one hand there are descriptions at (or above) 'bedrock': descriptions in which language-use is characterized in semantic terms ('She said that the post-box was red', 'He said that 1000 plus 2 equals 1002'). That, says McDowell, is the 'deepest level at which we can sensibly contemplate the place of language in the world' (1984, 341). On the other hand, there are 'sub-bedrock' descriptions, in which speakers' behaviour is characterized without reference to meaning or rules ('She made the sound "The post-box is red,"' 'He put "1002" after "1000"'). There is, McDowell says, 'an intimate relation' between facts about rule-following and patterns of sub-bedrock facts such that 'a certain disorderliness below "bedrock" would undermine the applicability of the notion of rule-following' (1984, 349). But 'recognizing the intimate relation must not be allowed to obscure the difference of levels' (1984, 349); no account of language in sub-bedrock terms can capture facts about meaning and rules. That is the kernel of McDowell's anti-reductionism.

McDowell briefly considers the idea that 'statements about rule-following *supervene,* in Wittgenstein's view, on sub-"bedrock" statements'. He comments: 'There may be an acceptable interpretation of this; but on the most natural interpretation, it would make statements about rule-following vulnerable to future loss of mutual intelligibility' (1984, 362 n.43), in a way that would falsify the epistemology of meaning and fail to accommodate common-sense truths. So, he suggests, the 'intimate relation' between bedrock and sub-bedrock facts is not to be captured in terms of supervenience. I agree with McDowell that the particular version of semantic supervenience he has in mind is unacceptable. But working through his objections will point us to a better version of the supervenience thesis, as well as preparing the ground for a response to further objections that we will meet below, in Section 4.

McDowell associates the supervenience thesis with the following picture of the epistemology of meaning. What we detect when some-one speaks are in the first instance non-semantic facts about the sounds he makes and the circumstances in which he makes them. Knowledge of what he means by an expression depends on an infer-ence from such non-semantic facts about his use of the expression and involves hypotheses about his future use, non-semantically character-ized. So, when I claim to understand someone, 'I bind myself to a prediction of the uses of language he will make in various possible future circumstances, with these uses characterized in sub-"bedrock" terms' (1984, 349). The consequence of that picture, McDowell (1984, 348) objects, is that any claim to know what someone else means by an expression is

> indefinitely vulnerable to the possibility of an unfavourable future. Below
> 'bedrock' there is nothing but contingency; so at any time in the future my
> interlocutor's use of the expression in question may simply stop conforming
> to the pattern I expect. And that would retrospectively undermine my
> present claim to be able to vouch for the character of his understanding.

But that, McDowell thinks, is a mistake. It is true that mutual under-standing rests on a 'tissue of contingencies' (1984, 349). And it is true that those contingencies might break down; an interlocutor who currently uses a word in a way I seem to understand might go on to use it in a bizarre and unexpected way that I did not understand. If that were to happen, how-ever, the fact that I did not then understand her would not entail that I do not currently know what she means. Common sense distinguishes two different possibilities.

(a) I know what she currently means by the word. Then her use of the word changes. I do not know what if anything she means by the word after the change.

(b) I do not know what she currently means by the word, though I initially appear to understand her. Her use of the word is consistent over time. What emerges from my failure to understand her later uses of the word is that I did not understand what she meant by it earlier.

The thesis that semantic facts supervene on sub-bedrock facts, McDowell suggests, represents every case in which my interlocutor's use of an expression stops 'conforming to the pattern I expect' as a case of type (b); it implies that a current claim to know what someone means will always be undermined if her subsequent use of the expression diverges from the pattern I expected. But that overlooks the possibility of cases of type (a).

McDowell is right that we must allow for the existence of both kinds of case: (a) and (b). But the defender of supervenience can do that perfectly well. In criticizing supervenience, what McDowell has in mind is the thesis that what a person means by an expression at a given time supervenes on non-semantic facts about her actual applications of the expression at that and subsequent times. But it is natural to offer this different formulation: what a person means by an expression at a given time supervenes on non-semantic facts about her use of the expression *at that time*, including facts about how she is then disposed to use it. We can explore this latter formulation in connection with a different example of Wittgenstein's.

Wittgenstein writes:

> Let us imagine the following example: A writes down series of numbers; B watches him and tries to find a rule for the number series. If he succeeds, he exclaims: 'Now I can go on!' (PI §151)

He considers a particular case:

> A has written down the numbers 1, 5, 11, 19, 29; at this point B says he knows how to go on. (PI §151)

The discussion continues:

> Suppose B says he knows how to go on – but when he wants to go on, he hesitates and can't do it. Are we then to say that it was wrong of him to say he could go on; or rather, that he was able to go on then, only now is not? – Clearly, we shall say different things in different cases. (PI §181; for further discussion, see PI §323 and BB 115–16)

It seems clear that the truth or falsity of the claim 'Now I can go on!' does not supervene on facts about what actually happens when the speaker does in fact try to go on. If it did, we would lose the common-sense distinction between someone (call her Able) who was able to go on when she said she could but cannot now and the person (call her Unable) who was never able to go on but only thought she could. But that does not mean we should abandon the idea that semantic facts supervene on non-semantic facts. It just means that we need to specify the right non-semantic supervenience base. And the obvious thought is that the non-semantic facts on which the truth or falsity of the claim 'Now I can go on!' supervene include dispositional facts. At the time when she spoke, Able was disposed, *ceteris paribus*, to put '41, 55, 71, 89, 109, . . .' after '1, 5, 11, 19, 29 . . .'. Unable was not.

There are well-known difficulties in any attempt to spell out dispositional conditions for the truth or assertability of individual claims about meaning and rule-following, taken one by one (see Kripke 1982, 22–37). For one thing, what someone who can develop a particular series would do if she were to attempt to develop it depends not just on her knowledge of the series but also on her desire to develop it correctly, the strength of any competing desires, her belief about what stage of the series she has reached, and so on. For another thing, even if she tries to develop the series correctly, she may make a mistake. And so on. So there is no question of pairing individual semantic facts about a person with facts about individual dispositions, characterized non-semantically. If it is to be plausible, the supervenience thesis must be that the semantic facts about a person, as a whole, supervene on non-semantic facts about her, including dispositional facts, as a whole.

It is tempting to think that differences in non-semantic dispositions must in turn supervene on something more basic: on differences in underlying physical states. After all, if two people differ in some dispositional respect, there will be possible circumstances in which one person would do something that the other would not do. We naturally think that there must be some causal explanation of any such difference in behaviour and that the explanation must ultimately come down to some difference in underlying brain states. (We can, for present purposes, safely leave aside differences in behaviour that depend entirely on differences in the external environment, such as the difference between the behaviour I exhibit in drinking a glass of water and the behaviour my Twin Earth doppelgänger exhibits in drinking a glass of XYZ.) So, it is tempting to argue, semantic facts ultimately supervene on occurrent physical facts. But the defender of semantic supervenience need not accept this argument. And if dispositional properties can be fundamental features of things, she should certainly not accept it.

Wittgenstein, for one, explicitly accepts that a person's dispositional properties need not supervene on her occurrent brain states; dispositional properties may be fundamental.

> It is . . . perfectly possible that certain psychological phenomena *cannot* be investigated physiologically, because physiologically nothing corresponds to them.
>
> I saw this man years ago: now I have seen him again, I recognize him, I remember his name. And why does there have to be a cause of this remembering in my nervous system? Why must something or other, whatever it may be, be stored up there *in any form*? Why *must* a trace have been left behind? Why should there not be a psychological regularity to which *no* physiological regularity corresponds? If this upsets our concepts of causality then it is high time that they were upset.
>
> . . .
>
> Why should there not be a natural law connecting a starting and a finishing state of a system, but not covering the intermediary state? (Only one must not think of *causal efficacy*.) (Z §§ 609–10, 613)

Applied to our case, the possibility that Wittgenstein is envisaging is this. Able and Unable both say 'Now I can go on' but cannot continue the series when they try to do so. What Able said was true; she really could go on when she said she could. What Unable said was false; she thought she could go on but she couldn't. There is a dispositional difference between them: at the time when they spoke, Able was disposed *ceteris paribus* to continue the series correctly; Unable was not. But there is no further physical difference underlying and explaining this dispositional difference. It is just a brute fact that Able's exposure to the initial steps in the series left her with the disposition to develop the series in that way, while Unable's exposure to the same thing left her with no such disposition.

The point I want to stress here is that the possibility we have just described is entirely consistent with the idea that semantic properties supervene on non-semantic properties. There is (in our extended sense) a semantic difference between Able and Unable: Able understands the series and knows how to continue it; Unable does not. That semantic difference is underpinned by a non-semantic difference; there is a difference between what Able is disposed to do and say, characterized non-semantically, and what Unable is disposed to do and say, similarly characterized. The dispositional difference is fundamental; it does not supervene on any further, more basic, physical difference between Able and Unable. But to make that point is not to reject the thesis that semantic facts supervene on non-semantic facts. It is just to acknowledge that the non-semantic facts on which semantic facts supervene may be, or include, irreducibly dispositional facts.

With that in mind, we can return to the distinction McDowell draws between two cases in which someone's future use of an expression confounds our expectations: case (a) where we now understand our interlocutor but no longer understand her in future; and case (b) where we never understand what she means by the expression, though we initially seemed to understand. As I said above, I agree that an adequate account of meaning must make room for that distinction. And I agree that the specific version of supervenience that McDowell has in mind does not make room for it. But a different version can accommodate the distinction perfectly well, treating it as we treated the distinction between Able and Unable. There is a semantic difference between the two cases; the speaker is using the expression with one meaning in case (a) and a different meaning in case (b). That semantic difference does not supervene on any difference in the non-semantic facts about her actual past or future applications of the expression; those are the same in both cases. But there is a non-semantic difference between the two cases: a difference at the level of the two speakers' non-semantic dispositions. In case (a) she is currently disposed, *ceteris paribus*, to use the expression in one way, non-semantically characterized. In case (b) she is currently disposed to use it in a different way. As before, we naturally expect the dispositional difference between the two cases to supervene on a difference at the level of underlying physical states. As before, however, there is no reason why things must work like that; the difference in non-semantic dispositions could be a brute difference. But even if the dispositional difference is a brute difference, that does not threaten the thesis of semantic supervenience. For there will still be a non-semantic difference between the two cases, (a) and (b); it will simply be an ineliminably dispositional difference. And, as we saw in the case of Able and Unable, that is consistent with the thesis that semantic facts supervene on non-semantic facts. (We will return to the lessons of these cases in the next section.)

McDowell is certainly right to reject the inferential picture of knowledge of another person's meaning that he associates with the claim that semantic facts supervene on non-semantic, 'sub-bedrock', facts about use. But that is consistent with accepting the supervenience thesis itself, which is a claim about the metaphysics of meaning and rule-following, not a claim about our knowledge of meaning and rule-following. Of course, an acceptable account of the metaphysics of meaning has to be consistent with a plausible account of the epistemology of meaning. But nothing in the thesis of semantic supervenience, as I have presented it, conflicts with that requirement.

4   Intentional Ghosts and Semantic Magic

In a recent paper, Kearns and Magidor offer a series of arguments against the thesis of semantic supervenience and in favour of 'semantic sovereignty: the thesis that semantic facts do not supervene on use facts' (Kearns and Magidor 2012, 322). Their arguments fall into two general kinds. First, they offer a range of counter-examples which, they argue, show that the thesis of semantic supervenience is false. Second, they consider a family of familiar arguments, due to Quine, Putnam, and Kripke's Wittgenstein, that 'purport to show that use facts are insufficient to determine semantic facts' (2012, 335; see Quine 1960; Putnam 1977; and Kripke 1982). Kearns and Magidor argue for the plausibility of a 'neglected response' to such arguments: that semantic facts are a fundamental and irreducible feature of reality and thus that the fact (if it is a fact) that use facts under-determine semantic facts is no threat to the reality of semantic facts.[6] Though these more general considerations certainly deserve attention, I shall focus here on Kearns and Magidor's argument from counter-examples.[7]

Kearns and Magidor start with a series of counter-examples that are targeted at the claim that semantic facts supervene on *physical* facts—which, they say, is the 'commonly accepted picture' (324)—rather than at the more general claim that semantic facts supervene on non-semantic facts about *use*. These initial counter-examples involve pairs of worlds, w_1 and w_2, such that w_2 is a physical duplicate of w_1 but also contains non-physical subjects ('ghosts'), or non-physical properties, that are absent from w_1. Kearns and Magidor argue that these non-physical differences between w_1 and w_2 make room for words in w_2 to have different semantic properties from their counterparts in w_1. For instance, a word that has one meaning in w_1 may have a different meaning in w_2 because of the way that ghosts use the word in w_2, even though all the physical facts about its use by physical language-users are the same in both worlds (see 327 and 328–9); or a word that refers to a physical thing or property in w_1 may refer to a non-physical thing or property in w_2 (see 329–30). So physically duplicate worlds can differ in their semantic properties; semantic facts do not supervene on physical facts.

---

[6] Kearns and Magidor cite Boghossian's proposal (mentioned in Note 2 above) that 'the so-called "Kripkenstein puzzle" ought to be solved by accepting a non-reductive view of semantic facts' as a 'rare exception' to the general neglect of anti-reductionism as a plausible option in this debate (2012, 336 n.30). As noted above, anti-reductionist responses to Kripke's Wittgenstein are also offered by McDowell, McGinn, and Stroud, amongst others.

[7] For reasons of space, I set aside one class of Kearns and Magidor's counter-examples: those involving worlds that are non-semantic duplicates but which allegedly differ in haecceitistic semantic properties (2012, 331–5, 342–4). I hope to consider that class of counter-examples elsewhere.

Examples of this kind may challenge the thesis that semantic facts supervene on physical facts. But, as Kearns and Magidor acknowledge, they do not by themselves threaten the thesis that semantic facts supervene on use facts (see 339–40). For in these cases the differences between the semantic facts in w_1 and in w_2 are explained by differences in the use of words between w_1 and w_2; it is just that, in the presence of non-physical language-users and non-physical properties, there can be differences in use between two worlds without those worlds differing in any physical respect. For present purposes, then, we must concentrate on those of Kearns and Magidor's counter-examples that specifically target the thesis that semantic facts supervene on use facts.

The first of these more specific counter-examples appeals to the possible existence of 'purely semantic (and in particular, purely intentional) entities': 'purely intentional ghosts', in their terminology. Purely intentional ghosts, they say, 'have various mental states (beliefs, desires, etc.) but lack any (interesting) non-semantic properties. Such ghosts seem readily conceivable. Indeed, they seem to be what are normally called Cartesian minds' (2012, 340). Suppose that purely intentional ghosts are indeed possible. And suppose that w_2 is a non-semantic duplicate of w_1 but contains in addition a number of purely intentional ghosts, which are absent from w_1. That creates an immediate challenge to the thesis of semantic supervenience. For, though w_2 does not differ from w_1 in any non-semantic respect, it will differ semantically from w_1: most obviously, by containing the thoughts and attitudes possessed by these purely intentional ghosts; but also, because the existence of the ghosts and their thoughts will affect the reference and truth-value of some of the thoughts and utterances of ordinary subjects.[8] How should a defender of semantic supervenience respond to this kind of example?

In the first place, when Kearns and Magidor offer counter-examples that appeal to the possible existence of purely intentional ghosts, they are not really offering an *argument* for the falsity of semantic supervenience; they are in effect simply asserting that the supervenience claim is false. For the supposition that there can be subjects that have intentional (and thus, semantic) properties without having any non-semantic properties *just is* the supposition that semantic properties do not supervene on non-semantic

---

[8] Kearns and Magidor also offer a counter-example that appeals to the possibility of ordinary human thinkers having purely intentional properties: intentional properties whose possession by a person is completely independent of her possession of any non-intentional properties (2012, 340). The issues raised by that case are not fundamentally different from those raised by the alleged possibility of purely intentional ghosts, which I discuss in the text below.

properties. If there is an argument here, it is one that proceeds from the conceivability of purely intentional ghosts to their possibility.[9] Such an argument invites one of the standard responses to arguments of this kind; either purely intentional ghosts are not really conceivable or else they are conceivable, but their conceivability does not entail their possible existence.

However, even if Kearns and Magidor have given us no positive reason to think that purely intentional ghosts are possible, they might say that the defender of supervenience, for her part, has given us no reason to think that purely intentional ghosts are not possible. The onus, they might argue, is on the defender of supervenience to give us some positive reason to think, first, that every possessor of semantic properties must have some non-semantic properties and, second, that its semantic properties must supervene on its non-semantic properties. That is a legitimate challenge. What positive reason is there to think that the thesis of semantic supervenience is true?

There is a rich history of philosophical argument against the intelligibility of Cartesian subjects, or purely intentional ghosts. There are arguments, originating with Kant and Strawson, that contend that we can only make sense of the existence of individual subjects if they are substantial entities that possess non-intentional as well as intentional properties (see Kant 1781/7, A341–405 / B399–432, and Strawson 1966, 162–9). And there are arguments, originating with Wittgenstein, that contend that we cannot make sense of the existence of mental phenomena in the purely first-person way that is all that remains if we try to think away the embodiment and behavioural expression of the mental (see PI §§ 243–315 and 350–1; for related considerations, see Strawson 1959, chapter 3, and Williams 1978, 100–1). I think those arguments make a compelling case against the conceivability of Cartesian subjects. But not every philosopher finds them convincing. Can we appeal to arguments of a different kind to support the thesis of semantic supervenience?

One obvious suggestion is that we could argue for semantic supervenience on causal grounds, in a way that mirrors a standard argument for the

---

[9] There are some indications that Kearns and Magidor are indeed thinking of their considerations about purely intentional ghosts as involving an argument from conceivability to possibility. When they introduce the idea of purely intentional ghosts they point out that such beings 'seem readily conceivable' (2012, 340). And they stress in a different but related case that 'there is nothing clearly incoherent about the scenario we have presented' and argue that 'our case presents a challenge to the proponent of [supervenience] precisely because the scenario we describe seems perfectly possible' (2012, 342).

supervenience of mental properties on physical properties. In outline, the argument would go like this: (i) semantic phenomena play a causal role in producing and explaining other phenomena (for instance, my turning right is causally explained by your saying 'Turn right'; and the fact that 'Turn right' means what it does plays a role in that explanation; if 'Turn right' had meant *turn left*, your saying what you did would not have caused the effect it did cause); (ii) every phenomenon has a complete non-semantic cause; (iii) the effects of semantic causes are not over-determined by their semantic and non-semantic causes; so, (iv) semantic phenomena must supervene on non-semantic phenomena. Despite the popularity of this form of argument, however, it seems dialectically inef-fective to appeal to that line of thought in the current debate with Kearns and Magidor.

In the first place, if Kearns and Magidor are right that there could be purely intentional ghosts, that will immediately undercut the causal argu-ment for supervenience. For, in a world containing purely intentional ghosts, premise (ii) would be false; it would not be true that every phenomenon had a complete non-semantic cause (in particular, the actions of purely intentional ghosts would not have complete non-semantic causes). In the second place, even without appealing to the alleged possibility of purely intentional ghosts, the opponent of super-venience may simply deny that every phenomenon must have a complete non-semantic cause. It is perfectly possible, she may argue, for two things to have different effects, in virtue of having different semantic properties, without differing in any non-semantic respect. So, she will say, we should reject premise (ii) of the causal argument; it is not true that every phenom-enon must have a complete non-semantic cause. And that undermines the causal argument for supervenience. It is no coincidence that Kearns and Magidor's second series of counter-examples to semantic supervenience takes precisely this form (2012, 341–2).

Consider two worlds, w_1 and w_2, that are exactly alike in every non-semantic respect. They are also alike in every semantic respect, with one exception. In both worlds, the word 'cat' refers to cats. In both worlds, the word 'cat' has never in fact been uttered by anyone to refer to cats.[10] But w_1 and w_2 differ in the following respect. In w_1, if someone were to utter the word 'cat', thereby referring to cats, their doing so would have no special

---

[10] How can the word 'cat' refer to cats without ever having been uttered by anyone? Well: it may have been written down, described, gestured at, and so on. Compare the case of a society with a deity whose name, for religious reasons, is never uttered by anyone. It seems unproblematic that the name really is a name of the deity.

effect. But in w_2, if someone uttered 'cat' to refer to cats, their doing so would have the effect of magically turning their interlocutor into a unicorn. Since w_1 and w_2 are alike in all non-semantic respects, there would be no natural, non-semantic causal explanation of that effect; that is the point of describing the effect as magical. And, Kearns and Magidor stress, the magical effect really would be causally explained by the semantic properties of the action of uttering the word 'cat' to refer to cats; merely making the sound 'cat', rather than uttering the word 'cat' to refer to cats, would have no such effect. (I will return to this point shortly.) Kearns and Magidor then argue as follows. The difference between w_1 and w_2 is a semantic difference. But w_1 and w_2 are non-semantic duplicates. So worlds can differ semantically without differing non-semantically; semantic facts do not supervene on non-semantic facts.[11]

Is this argument convincing? I agree with Kearns and Magidor that there is a semantic difference between w_1 and w_2 in their example. The semantic action of uttering the word 'cat' to refer to cats would have different causal consequences in w_1 and w_2; and that is itself a semantic difference between the two worlds. But, I shall argue, when we reflect on the causal differences between w_1 and w_2, it is clear that, *pace* Kearns and Magidor, there is also a non-semantic difference between the two worlds; so the case is not an effective counter-example to the thesis of semantic supervenience.

The basic structure of Kearns and Magidor's case is this. The semantic difference between w_1 and w_2 is a difference in dispositional properties: a difference in what would happen if someone were to utter 'cat' to refer to cats. And the difference in dispositional properties, or causal powers, is fundamental: it does not supervene on any underlying difference in occurrent non-semantic properties; w_1 and w_2 are alike with respect to all such non-semantic properties. Now that, of course, is exactly the structure that we saw in the previous section in the case of Able and Unable. There is a semantic difference between Able and Unable. The semantic difference involves a difference in dispositional properties: at the point when they both said 'Now I can go on', Able understood the series and would *ceteris paribus* have continued it correctly had she tried to do so; Unable did not understand the series and would not have continued it correctly. And, we supposed, the dispositional difference does not supervene on any underlying difference in occurrent non-semantic properties; Able and Unable are alike with respect to all such properties. Nonetheless, we said, the case does

---

[11] I have slightly adapted the cat case, for ease of presentation. But its essentials are taken from Kearns and Magidor.

not threaten the supervenience thesis. For there is a non-semantic difference between Able and Unable; they have different non-semantic dispositional properties. In particular, Able is disposed, *ceteris paribus*, to put '41, 55, 71, 89, 109, . . .' after '1, 5, 11, 19, 29 . . .'; Unable is not.[12]

We can treat the case of words whose utterance would have magic effects in w_2 but not w_1 in essentially the same way. In particular, even though w_1 and w_2 are alike with respect to all occurrent non-semantic properties, they differ with respect to their non-semantic dispositional properties.

In order for me to utter the word 'cat' to refer to cats, two conditions must be satisfied: (i) I must make the sound 'cat'; and (ii) I must do so in a context in which making the sound 'cat' counts as uttering the word 'cat' to refer to cats. With that in mind, consider the two worlds, w_1 and w_2, in the 'cat' example. In both worlds, the context is such that, if I were to make the sound 'cat', I would count as uttering the word 'cat' to refer to cats. Given the context, therefore, my making the sound 'cat' would have different effects in w_1 and in w_2. But then there is, after all, a non-semantic difference between w_1 and w_2: holding context fixed, my making the sound 'cat' in w_2 would turn someone into a unicorn; doing the same thing in w_1 would have no such effect. That is a difference at the level of dispositional properties, non-semantically characterized. There is, *ex hypothesi*, no further non-semantic difference between w_1 and w_2 that *explains why* making the sound 'cat', in this context, would have such different effects in the two worlds. It is just a brute fact that it would. It remains the case, however, that there is a non-semantic difference between the two worlds: w_1 and w_2 are not non-semantic duplicates. So the case of words with magical properties is not an effective counter-example to the thesis of semantic supervenience.

It might be objected that this argument overlooks Kearns and Magidor's specification that what causes my interlocutor to turn into a unicorn in w_2 is not my making the sound 'cat' but my uttering the word 'cat' to refer to cats. I have argued that there is a non-semantic difference between w_1 and w_2 at the level of dispositional properties, on the grounds that making the sound 'cat' in w_2 would cause someone to turn into a unicorn but doing the same thing in w_1 would have no such effect. But, the objector will protest, that is not true. Making the sound 'cat' would have no special effect in

---

[12] Someone might object that to characterize something as a case of '*putting* "41, 55 . . ." after ". . . 19, 29 . . ."' is already to characterize it in semantic terms (in our extended sense), on the grounds that it involves characterizing it as an intentional action. Even if that is true, however, it remains the case that there will be *some* way of characterizing non-semantically what would have happened had Able tried to develop the series. That is all that the defender of supervenience requires.

either world; what does the causal work in w_2 is uttering the word 'cat' to refer to cats. So, contrary to what I have claimed, w_1 and w_2 really are alike with respect to all non-semantic properties, both occurrent and dispositional.

But the idea that what turns my interlocutor into a unicorn in w_2 is not my making the sound 'cat' but my uttering the word 'cat' to refer to cats needs to be handled with care. The context we are considering is one in which, in both w_1 and w_2, my making the sound 'cat' counts as uttering the word 'cat' to refer to cats. In that context, my action of making the sound 'cat' *just is* an action of uttering the word 'cat' to refer to cats. So it cannot be true that what causes the magical effect in w_2 is my uttering the word 'cat' to refer to cats *rather than* my making the sound 'cat'. The point the objector is reaching for can be put in terms of counterfactuals: if I were in a different context, in which my making the sound 'cat' did not count as my uttering the word 'cat' to refer to cats, then making the sound 'cat' would have no magical effect. That is true. But it is irrelevant to the current argument. The crucial question is whether there is a relevant non-semantic difference between w_1 and w_2 in the case in which making the sound 'cat' *would* count as uttering the word 'cat' to refer to cats, and *would* therefore produce different effects in w_1 and w_2. And, as I have argued, there clearly is such a difference: given the context, there is a difference in what would happen in w_1 and w_2 if I were to make the sound 'cat'. So the semantic difference between w_1 and w_2 is underpinned by a non-semantic difference between them. The case does not challenge the thesis of semantic supervenience.

5 Conclusion

We have rejected two arguments against the thesis that semantic facts supervene on non-semantic facts about use. McDowell, I argued, was right to reject the particular version of the supervenience thesis that he had in mind. But a better version, which includes non-semantic dispositions in the supervenience base, is not vulnerable to McDowell's criticism. Kearns and Magidor offered two kinds of counter-example to semantic supervenience. The first depended on the possible existence of purely intentional subjects. But to suppose that purely intentional ghosts are possible, I said, is in effect simply to suppose that semantic supervenience is false; it does not constitute an argument against the supervenience thesis. And, I suggested, there are good reasons for thinking that purely intentional ghosts are not possible, though I have not defended the arguments here. Kearns and Magidor's second kind of counter-example involved the possibility of semantic phenomena having magical effects. I agreed that that kind of case is possible. But, I argued, that possibility is consistent with semantic supervenience, once we acknowledge, as we should, that the non-semantic facts on which semantic facts supervene can include brutely dispositional facts.[13]

---

[13] Earlier versions of this material were presented at the University of Helsinki, the Higher School of Economics in Moscow, and York University Toronto. I am grateful to the audiences on those occasions for very helpful discussion.

CHAPTER 12

Some Socratic Aspects of Wittgenstein's Conception of Philosophy

James Conant

This text will come in three parts: (1) an examination testing your knowledge of Socrates and Wittgenstein, (2) a reflection on why the claim that a philosopher's conception of philosophy bears a Socratic aspect was once a *tautology*, and (3) a meditation on how Wittgenstein's philosophy does bear *some* Socratic aspects and why a claim to that effect is *no longer* a tautology.

There is no point in reading this text, if you are not willing to take the exam yourself. The assumption is that you will find it difficult to answer the exam questions correctly—that even if you know both these philosophers well it will still prove difficult. If it does, then it can open up the question that the second third of the text seeks to prepare and the latter third seeks to explore: why are these questions hard to answer correctly and what does this show about Wittgenstein?

I The Exam: Socrates or Wittgenstein?

The exam itself will have three parts: (i) a practice test, so that you can get the hang of the exercise and warm yourself up; (ii) the exam proper; and (iii) a concluding extra credit portion. (If you would wish to administer any or all three of these parts of the exam to someone—perhaps in order to challenge one of your students or humiliate one of your friends—all three are provided, detached from this text, in the form of three appendices; a fourth appendix contains answers to exam questions including references.)

The preliminary exam starts now! It is to be taken, here and now, by *you*. It will consist largely of quotations. The first quotation on this preliminary portion of the test is, in fact, about tests:

> "Everyone has a simple test to tell whether a cobbler makes good shoes. There is no test of this sort to discover whether a philosopher does his job or not."

Is that Socrates speaking or Wittgenstein? [Please keep track of your answer.]

Next quotation:

> "I give you permission to define each word the way you like just so long as you make clear the application of whatever word you use."

Socrates or Wittgenstein? [If you have to guess, just guess.]

A third quotation:

> "Call me a truth-seeker and I will be satisfied."

Is that Socrates speaking or Wittgenstein? [Don't rush ahead until you have selected your answer.]

The appearance of three asterisks on the page will indicate that the answers to the exam questions are about to be given. Don't look further down, below the asterisks, until you have earned the right to do so!

***

Now let us see how you did. The answer to the first question is "Wittgenstein," to the second "Socrates."[1] The answer to the third question will come in for further discussion near the end of this text.

Here are two more sample questions. The philosopher in question notes, halfway through one of his dialectical excursions, that, at the point thus reached in the proceedings,

> "... we have helped [our interlocutor] to some extent toward finding the right answer; for now not only is he aware that he is ignorant of the answer, but he will be quite eager to look for it."

The philosopher in question remarks:

> "Anything [your interlocutor] can do for himself, leave it to [your interlocutor]."

Which is of those two Socrates and which Wittgenstein? [Again, slow down and do not look ahead until you commit yourself to an answer!]

***

The first is Socrates; the second Wittgenstein.

Here are a few more warm-up questions. Now we will hear from four commentators, scholars, or comrades, speaking in each case *about* one of our philosophers.

---

[1] Compare the following remark from *Philosophical Investigations*, section 79: "Should it be said that I am using a word whose meaning I don't know, and so am talking nonsense? – Say what you choose, so long as it does not prevent you from seeing the facts. (And when you see them there is a good deal that you will not say.)"

"He shows his interlocutors a projection of their own selves. . . . [He] splits himself into two, so that there are two [of him]: the [one] who knows in advance how the discussion is going to end, and the [one] who travels the entire dialectical path along with his interlocutor."

Is this said here about Socrates or Wittgenstein?

"He was constantly fighting with the deepest philosophical problems. The solution of one problem led to another problem. [He] was uncompromising; he had to have *complete* understanding."

Said of Socrates or Wittgenstein?

"It is a telling fact that everyone got carried away when they talked about [him], whether it was [someone] singing his praises or his enemies ranting against him."

Said of Socrates or Wittgenstein?

"[He] had an extraordinary gift for divining the thoughts of the person with whom he was engaged in discussion. While the other struggled to put his thought into words [he] would perceive what it was and state it for him. This power of his . . . sometimes seemed uncanny."

Said of Socrates or Wittgenstein?

***

Here, in order, are the answers to the last four questions: Socrates, Wittgenstein, Socrates, and Wittgenstein.

Here are four more instances of commentators, scholars, or comrades, speaking in each case about one of our philosophers.

"One of [his] beliefs was that philosophy . . . cannot accurately be captured in a lecture or a treatise."

Said of Socrates or of Wittgenstein?

"When [he] invented an example . . . in order to illustrate a point, he himself would grin at the absurdity of what he had imagined. But if any member of the [audience] were to chuckle, his expression would change to severity."

Said about Socrates or Wittgenstein?

"Most of the paradoxical views that can be attributed to [him] are based on things which he said . . . for a distinctive purpose and in a distinctive context."

Said about Socrates or Wittgenstein?

"[He] was not an easy guru to follow, not least because a guru was the one thing that he resolutely refused to be. Still, it is hardly surprising that after his death several of his friends wanted to carry on the good work somehow. Since it was, and is, no simple matter to say exactly what the good work amounted to, it should be equally unsurprising that these would-be successors of [his] ended up championing very different causes."

Said about Socrates and his would-be successors or about Wittgenstein and his?

***

Here, in order, are the answers to those four questions: Socrates, Wittgenstein, Socrates, and Socrates.

That concludes your practice exam. That handful of practice-test examples will have to suffice to prepare you for the real thing. Now we turn to the exam proper. Please keep track of your own score.

The exam proper falls into two halves. The first half, in turn, falls into seven parts, while the second simply contains an additional five questions.

Each of the seven parts of the first half begins with a numbered question. The numbered questions each have at least two answers. If you cannot get the two most obvious answers to each of the numbered questions immediately, then you immediately fail the exam. The numbered questions will be followed by comparatively challenging questions. Here is the first of our numbered questions. Remember: this question is meant to have two equally obvious answers.

1 Which great philosopher lived an ascetic existence, spurning wealth and fame, but did not hold up his own way of life as a model to his friends and students, often encouraging them instead to take up ordinary professional trades and to immerse themselves in the world from which the philosopher himself had withdrawn?

Now comes the first series of follow-up questions.

Looking back upon his life, one of our philosophers finds he is able to claim this about himself:

"I did not care for the things that most people care about – making money, having a prosperous household, high military or civil rank."

Socrates or Wittgenstein?

Looking back upon the life of one of our philosophers, a comrade is able to remark the following:

"A great simplicity, at times even an extreme frugality, became characteristic of his life."

Said of Socrates or Wittgenstein?

***

The first is Socrates speaking to the court; the second is a famous Finnish philosopher speaking of Wittgenstein. (You get extra credit if you are able to guess who the famous Finnish philosopher is.)

Starting now, in between our exam questions, I will occasionally pause to comment on the questions—reflecting on what the difficulty of answering these questions might be taken to show—thereby finally beginning to engage in stretches of behavior approximating that of an author of an essay about Socrates and Wittgenstein. Here comes the first bit of commentary. The point of our opening numbered question is that in neither case—neither in the case of Socrates nor in that of Wittgenstein—did our philosopher take the ethos of frugality in accordance with which he himself lived to be binding upon those who wished to learn philosophy from him.

Socrates in no way considered making money, having a prosperous household, achieving distinguished military or civil rank, or for that matter many another aspect of a conventionally successful Athenian life, to be the sort of thing which was bad in itself. [2] His asceticism did not reflect a central precept of his philosophy, as it did for many a subsequent Greek philosopher. Socrates never preached abstinence. Indeed, he was able to drink others under the table if it befitted the occasion. He often encouraged interlocutors to excel in the trade they had already chosen as their way of life and often wanted only to help clarify for his interlocutor what it would be for them to thus excel. The philosophical life for Socrates did not compete with some other sort of life; rather he viewed it as forming a dimension of any well-lived life.

Though Wittgenstein would have agreed with this last thought, his own relation to the philosophical life remained far more tortured than that relation ever was for Socrates. Unlike Socrates, he did not regard himself as simply constitutionally so inclined as inevitably to become fully occupied with the life of the mind, and thus free of any inclination to bother with such things as clothing, food, and money. Rather he viewed such external goods as positive temptations and distractions from the life he wanted to lead. He also sometimes experienced human society as a threat to his ability to do rigorous philosophical work. He would withdraw for months at a time to remote locations in Norway or Ireland to ensure that he could not be distracted from

---

[2] The translation of the *Apology* cited here (by Hugh Tredennick, from the Hamilton and Cairns edition *The Collected Dialogues of Plato*) translates "οἰκονομία" with "comfortable home." I have amended it to "prosperous household."

the philosophical problems with which he wished to struggle. He gave away his inherited family fortune with a ferocity that suggests he feared what it might do to him if it remained in his possession. One has the sense that he forced the rigors of the simple life upon himself rather than that he naturally fell into such a way of living. He is famous for always wearing the same clothes, especially the same gray tweed jacket. He once explained his personal philosophy of food as follows: it does not matter what you eat as long as you always eat the same thing.[3] Yet, as with Socrates, Wittgenstein never adduces any of these features of his own way of life as prescriptions for what ought to be generally regarded by his friends or pupils as a well-lived life.

Quite the contrary (and with an edge of urgent concern about how philosophy might damage someone who devotes himself to it—a concern that one never encounters in Socrates), Wittgenstein encouraged some of his pupils (though certainly not all of them) to abandon the full-time study of philosophy and consider becoming doctors, carpenters, or practitioners of some other honorable conventional trade. Wittgenstein was genuinely concerned about what the effect on his students' souls might be of their entering into philosophy as a full-time profession. But the significance of this particular dimension of contrast between the two philosophers is easily overestimated.

After all, in Socrates' time, "philosopher" had not yet become the putative title of an established trade. Socrates never needed to worry about what might become of the souls of his students if they were to spend their entire lives inhaling nothing but academic air.[4] In ancient Athens being a philosopher was not yet an imaginable way of living the life of what in contemporary Japanese is known as a サラリーマン [sararīman]—"a salaried man." The closest thing in ancient Athens to a career option both resembling that of a philosopher and allowing of financial

---

[3] WAM 69: "Wittgenstein declared that it did not much matter to him *what* he ate, so long as it was always the *same*."

[4] The situation had already changed substantially only twelve years after Socrates' death, when Plato, at the age of forty, in the year 389 BC, saw fit to found the Academy. After a handful of years laboring away within the confines of this new form of life, which he himself helped to bring about, Plato arguably became the first post-Socratic philosopher to suffer from nagging doubts about the academic way of life. In the *Seventh Letter*, we find this: "I feared to see myself at last altogether nothing but words, so to speak—a man who would never willingly lay hand to any concrete task" (*Seventh Letter* 328c). Socrates and Wittgenstein are sometimes subjected to a facile contrast along the following lines: Socrates thought the philosophical life was good for everyone, whereas Wittgenstein thought it was anything but good for most. There is a genuine contrast to be drawn between these two thinkers somewhere in this vicinity, but it requires delicate handling. The first step toward elaborating a less facile version of the contrast is to notice that one needs to distinguish Wittgenstein's estimate of the value of the philosophical life from that of the academic life and to further notice that it is not clear that Wittgenstein and Socrates would have necessarily disagreed markedly about the latter, had the value of the latter been something that could have been a possible topic of reflection for Socrates.

remuneration was to go into business for oneself as a sophist. Then you could charge money for your services, but you were also then, by Socrates' lights, at most nothing more than a mere simulacrum of a philosopher.

2 Which great philosopher was especially renowned for the intensity of his intellectual concentration, liable to fall into a state of complete absorption in a philosophical problem—a state in which he became utterly oblivious to the world around him?

It is said of our philosopher:

> "When he was trying to draw a thought out of himself, he would prohibit, with a peremptory motion of the hand, any questions or remarks. There were frequent and prolonged periods of silence, with only an occasional mutter from [him], and the stillest attention from the others. During these silences, [he] was extremely tense and active. His gaze was concentrated; his face was alive; his hands made arresting movements; his expression was stern. One knew that one was in the presence of extreme seriousness, absorption, and force of intellect."

Socrates or Wittgenstein?

> "He started wrestling with some problem or other about sunrise one morning, and stood there lost in thought, and when the answer wouldn't come he still stood there thinking and refused to give it up."

Is the first Socrates or Wittgenstein? The second?

***

The second passage continues as follows, making it absolutely clear who is at issue:

> "Time went on, and by about midday the troops . . . began telling each other how [he] had been standing there thinking ever since daybreak. And at last, toward nightfall, some of the Ionians brought out their bedding after supper . . . partly to see whether he was going to stay there all night. Well, there he stood till morning, and then at sunrise he said his prayers to the sun and went away."

The first passage continues in this way, making it equally clear who is at issue:

> "[His] personality dominated these meetings. I doubt that anyone in the class failed to be influenced by him in some way. Few of us could keep from acquiring

imitations of his mannerisms, gestures, intonations, exclamations. These imitations could easily appear ridiculous when compared with their original."

The latter is Norman Malcolm speaking. When Wittgenstein went to the United States to visit Malcolm at Cornell in 1950, Malcolm invited all of his students over to his house to meet the great philosopher. One of Malcolm's students had been out of town, arriving only that evening. He was told that he should go to Prof. Malcolm's house immediately but not told why. He rushed over there. Mrs. Malcolm let him in. As he was taking off his galoshes by the front door, he asked her: "Who is that man with the German accent in the next room imitating Prof. Malcolm?"[5]

3 Which great philosopher's mode of discussion with others was no less intense than his aforementioned capacity for isolated absorption in thought?

It is said of our philosopher:

> "Each conversation with [him] was like living through the day of judgment. It was terrible. Everything had constantly to be dug up anew, questioned and subjected to the tests of truthfulness."

Socrates or Wittgenstein?

> "Anyone who is close to [him] and enters into conversation with him is liable to be drawn into an argument, and whatever subject he may start, he will be continually carried round and round by him, until at last he finds that he has to give an account both of his present and his past life, and when [his interlocutor] is once entangled, [he] will not let him go until he has completely and thoroughly sifted him."

Socrates or Wittgenstein?

∗∗∗

The first remark is again from that Finnish philosopher talking about Wittgenstein; the second remark is about Socrates.

4 Which great philosopher received a military decoration for bravery in battle?

Consider the following four quotations:

---

[5] The anecdote about Wittgenstein, Malcolm, and Malcolm's student was recounted by Malcolm to Peter Winch, who shared it with me.

"You are mistaken . . . if you think that a man who is worth anything ought to spend his time weighing up the prospects of life and death."

Which of our two philosophers said or wrote that?
    And consider the following:

"Now I . . . have an opportunity to be a decent human being, because I am face to face with death."

Socrates or Wittgenstein?
    And the following:

"I may die in an hour, I may die in two hours, I may die in a month, or not for a few years. I cannot know about it and I cannot do anything for or against it: *such is this life.* How then ought I to live in order to hold my own at that moment, to live amid the good and the beautiful until life stops of itself?"

Which of the two?
    Finally:

"Those who pursue philosophy rightly, study to die."

Socrates? Or Wittgenstein?

***

The first is from the *Apology*; each of the middle pair of remarks was penned under duress by Wittgenstein while serving as a soldier in the Austrian army on the eastern front of World War I; the fourth is from the *Phaedo*.

All four quotations serve to make the following clear. The relevant parallel between our thinkers is underestimated if taken simply to consist in the fact that each of them happens to fall under both of the following two descriptions: *great philosopher, decorated soldier.* Each viewed his conduct on the battlefield as a forging and testing ground of his philosophical mettle. Each of them viewed learning *how to die well* as part of what it means to live well.

5 Which great philosopher's decoration in battle was regarded by those who knew him as merely one conspicuous outward sign of a much broader capacity for self-mastery?

Which of the following two quotations is about Socrates and which about Wittgenstein?

"He was by all accounts supremely disciplined and a master of rational self-control. Maybe that was the problem. Perhaps it explains why he had such impossibly high expectations for others ... It has been said of [him] that 'in the strength of his character lay the weakness of his philosophy.'"

"There was practically nothing he was not, or could not have been, able to do unusually well if it belonged at all to the sort of thing that can be brought under voluntary control, where training and practice are essential in the learning process."

Is the first remark about Socrates? Or about Wittgenstein? And the second: about Socrates, or about Wittgenstein?

***

The first is said of Socrates; the second of Wittgenstein.

6 Which great philosopher often seemed to cast a spell on others, either powerfully attracting or repelling those around him?

For example, in which of the following two remarks do we hear the voice of Alcibiades speaking of Socrates?

"It seems he cannot avoid casting a spell, and some are repelled by it as strongly as others are attracted. Those that are drawn to him, are bound by an affection which has in it something that can perhaps be called love. It happens to fishermen and farmers as well as to philosophers."

"I've been bitten in the heart, or the mind, or whatever you like to call it, by [his] philosophy, which clings like an adder to any young and gifted mind it can get a hold of."

Now in which of the two do we hear the voice of Alcibiades speaking of Socrates?

***

Alcibiades speaks second here; Wittgenstein's Norwegian friend Knut Erik Tranøy speaks first.

7 Which great philosopher is often credited with the capacity of being able to see a philosophical problem as if for the first time?

And which of the two is this?

"He would talk about almost anything and always with the same intensity. He impressed me, time and time again, by lifting familiar problems into the light as if he were the first to see the problem, unhampered by conventional and received views."

Said of Socrates or Wittgenstein?

***

Answer: Wittgenstein.

Here now are the final five exam questions of the official portion of the exam.

Our first quotation touches two sides of a single question that was equally live for both Socrates and Wittgenstein:

> "Is it just *I* who cannot found a school, or can a philosopher never do so?"

Is this Socrates speaking or Wittgenstein?

A further recurrent topic for Socrates and for Wittgenstein concerns what it takes to fully acquire capacity to speak the truth in philosophy and in life:

> "One *cannot* speak the truth if one has not yet conquered oneself. One *cannot* speak it—but not, because one is still not clever enough. The truth can be spoken only by someone who is already *at home* in it; not by someone who still lives in untruthfulness, and does no more than reach out towards it from within untruthfulness."

Is that Socrates? Or is that Wittgenstein?

A related topic, of no less abiding concern to both, is the tortuous character of the path one must take in philosophy to arrive at the truth. Being told the truth will not do the philosopher any good if he is not ready for it. Hence one of our two philosophers remarks:

> "One must start out with error and convert it into truth. That is, one must reveal the source of error, otherwise hearing the truth won't do any good. The truth cannot force its way in when something else is occupying its place. To convince someone of the truth, it is not enough to state it, but rather one must find the *path* from error to truth."

Which of them speaks here? Socrates or Wittgenstein?

Our last pair of quotations pose a pair of philosophical questions:

> "If someone thinks, mustn't he think *something*? ... And if he thinks something, mustn't it be something *real*?"

> "And mustn't someone who is painting be painting something – and someone who is painting something be painting something real?"

Are these both questions asked by Socrates? Or both asked by Wittgenstein? Is one of them asked by Socrates and the other by Wittgenstein? If the latter, which is which?

***

Here now are your final five answers: Wittgenstein, Wittgenstein, Wittgenstein, Socrates, Wittgenstein.

That concludes the official portion of your exam. Please remember your test score.

In posing and answering the above questions, I have often needed, in order to elaborate the extent of the parallels between Socrates and Wittgenstein, to resort to quoting memoirs and biographical works recounting *anecdotes* told about each. This mode of displaying what is essential in a given philosopher's conception of philosophy lies at the heart of an *ancient* understanding of the way in which philosophy as such is to be accessed. This way of thinking about what it is *to get a philosophy into view*, however, no longer lies anywhere near the heart of our contemporary understanding of what philosophy is. Yet Wittgenstein seems an exception to this rule about the nature of contemporary philosophy. He is a figure whose conception of philosophy has seemed to many a commentator precisely to require that access to it be opened up, at least in part, via the deployment of anecdotes and related instruments of biographical depiction. This is itself a datum of philosophical interest. We will return to it in a moment.

Before we do, we will conclude this first part of the text with the extra credit portion of the exam. As is customary in such a concluding of a test, these final questions will be trick questions. But you yourself have to work out what the trick is. Here are four quotations by four different commentators:

> "[He] used a very simple language and [was] sure that [he] would be understood only by a few. [He] sought for friendship through philosophy and [was] certain that [he] would be rejected by many."

Said of Socrates or Wittgenstein?

> "An encounter with [this philosopher] ... can be radically unsettling precisely insofar as it does not merely reveal that reality is not what it appeared to you to be, but that you no longer know how it appeared to you. It is not that your belief was mistaken or that nothing in the world answers to your desire; instead you lose your grasp, or rather realize that you never had a grasp, on *what* you 'desired' or 'believed' in the first place, on what should be most intimately your own."

Does this describe an encounter with Socrates or one with Wittgenstein?

> "It is no wonder that no new knowledge needs to be added to the philosophical work. The only thing needed is to work with what one already knows;

for the problems are not problems external to ourselves, but rather precisely
a part of our selves."

Said about Socrates or Wittgenstein?
   And this one:

> "If there are no doctrines to be learnt, are there only things to be unlearnt? –
> And, importantly, here the answer should be: No. But . . . there is no one
> single determinate point to take home either."

Is this said about Socrates or Wittgenstein?

***

It is easy to get partial credit on these four questions, but more difficult to
get full credit. In all four cases, the correct answer is: *both*. All four
commentators are here seeking to bring out parallels in the philosophies
of Socrates and Wittgenstein.

II   A Time When Every Philosophy Had a Socratic Aspect

Socrates was the model in the ancient world of the sage. Precisely because
he did not *write* anything, in the case of Socrates it is impossible to draw the
sharp distinction—a distinction that it makes perfect sense to apply to
most contemporary philosophers—between the life of the philosopher and
his work.[6] Socrates's life is his work and his work is his life. He strived to
live—and to provide an example of what it means to live—a certain kind of
life: the life of one who loves wisdom, which is quite literally what the
conjunction of the two ancient Greek words *philo* and *sophia* means. There
is no understanding of Socrates' philosophy apart from this—that is, apart
from an understanding of the sort of life he sought to live.
   What the example of Socrates makes immediately evident is something that
is equally true, but less perspicuously so, in the case of Wittgenstein: in order to
understand the philosopher, we need a way of understanding the relation
between his philosophy and his life that allows us to see that life as something
internally related to his philosophy—the life as an *expression* of his philosophy
and his way of philosophizing as an expression of his conception of how to live.
   When and how Socrates challenges the charge (of corrupting the youth
of Athens) brought against him, when and how he accepts the verdict of
the court against him, when and how he refuses the opportunity to flee

---

[6] The second part of this text borrows heavily from my "Philosophy and Biography" (2001).

from prison, when and how he behaves in his final moment when he drinks the hemlock and lies down to die: these are all expressions of Socrates' philosophy, and his modes of reflection on each are part and parcel of his conception of how to live. No understanding of what Socrates thought philosophy was is possible apart from an appreciation of how philosophy is meant to find expression in a life such as *this* — that is, in a life such as the one that Socrates himself sought to live.

When Aristotle asks his rhetorical question "What more accurate standard or measure of good things do we have than the Sage?" ([1955], 33 / fragment 5), he is the first of a long line of philosophers to bear implicit witness to the way in which the figure of Socrates leaves its mark on the whole of ancient philosophy. If one turns to the great schools of Hellenistic philosophy (the Skeptics, the Stoics, the Epicureans, the Neo-Platonists), they all sought to practice (what we might call) a broadly Socratic conception of philosophy. Each such school encourages the pursuit of a kind of life: the life of the Sage. The schools have very different conceptions of what exactly such a life comes to. Yet for all their differences, they all took Socrates to offer a (more or less adequate) model of *that* life. So each philosophical school is not only competing with each of the others for the title of the true representatives of philosophy, but also for the title of the true heirs and practitioners of the Socratic life. Philosophy, so understood, was not something you simply learned, say, by reading certain books and taking an examination on them—it was something you practiced. And Socrates' life was exemplary of such a praxis. Yes, of course, there figured in the course of such a life, among other things, the activity of grappling with arguments; but those arguments were an integral part of a set of (what Pierre Hadot has called) *spiritual exercises* through the employment of which one sought to transform oneself—through the practice of what Wittgenstein calls *work on oneself.*

The spiritual disciplines internal to each of the Hellenistic schools of philosophy seek to promote a certain kind of *telos*: for the Skeptics, the *telos* is *ataraxia*; for the Neo-Platonists, ecstatic union with the cosmos; etc. And the *telos* in question is neither merely a theoretical achievement as opposed to a practical one, nor the opposite: it is a matter of successfully giving a certain sort of shape to one's self, where this is achieved in part by giving a certain sort of shape to one's life, where both in turn are achieved through the achievement of a certain form of understanding. With respect to a great many controversial philosophical points, if the Epicureans were inclined to champion it, then the Stoics were apt to proclaim the opposite, and the Skeptics would resolutely refuse to affirm either the original proposition or its negation. Epicurus, however, speaks for all three of the major schools when he says:

> Empty are the words of that philosopher who offers no therapy for human suffering. For just as there is no use in medical expertise if it does not provide therapy for bodily diseases, so too there is no use in philosophy if it does not expel the suffering of the soul. (Epicurus; quoted in Porphyry [1987], 155)

This generic conception of philosophy, as treating of sickness in the soul in a fashion usefully compared with the manner in which a physician treats of sickness in the body, was understood by the practitioners of all three of the major Hellenistic schools to have originally derived from the teaching of Socrates. Anthony Gottlieb sums up their relation to Socrates as follows:

> The new schools of thought owed more to Socrates than they did to Plato or Aristotle. It was Socrates who had stressed the practical relevance of philosophy. Its point, he urged, was to change your priorities and thereby your life. The Hellenistic philosophies tried to deliver on this Socratic promise. In particular, they claimed to be able to produce the sort of peace of mind and tranquil assurance that Socrates himself had conspicuously possessed. (Gottlieb 2000, 284)

During the Hellenistic and Roman eras, philosophy was a *way of life*. As Hadot tells us:

> This is not only to say that it was a specific type of moral conduct ... Rather it means that philosophy was a mode of existing-in-the world, which had to be practised at each instant, and the goal of which was to transform the whole of the individual's life. For the ancients, the mere word *philo-sophia* – the love of wisdom – was enough to express this conception of philosophy ... Philosophy was a method of spiritual progress which demanded a radical conversion and transformation of the individual's way of being ... Thus, philosophy was a way of life, both in its exercise and effort to achieve wisdom and in its goal, wisdom itself. For real wisdom does not merely cause us to know: it makes us "be" in a different way. (Hadot [1995], 265)

On this conception of philosophy, a philosopher's life just *is* the definitive expression of his philosophy. For such a philosopher, his writings (that is, that which we are tempted to identify as his "work") are a mere means to facilitate the achievement of that work on the self that is (properly identified as) a philosopher's work.

This has implications for the sorts of role that a form of writing aiming to depict the life of a philosopher is able to play in ground-level philosophical practice. The deployment in ancient Greek and Roman texts of

anecdotes and biographical details pertaining to the lives of the philosophers does not serve merely to spice up a text that should be primarily
about something else if it is to present a philosophy. On the contrary,
anecdotes about the philosopher's mode of life are adduced by the ancients
as an instrument not only for *exhibiting* but equally for *assessing* the
teaching in question.[7] As Arnoldo Momigliano, in *The Development of
Greek Biography*, puts it:

> Anecdotes [about philosophers] served to characterize modes of life, of
> thought, of style. If Phainias or Phanias of Eresus in his book on the
> Socratics said that Aristippus was the first of the Socratics to pay for tuition
> and to make money by teaching, the story must have been meant to
> characterize, or perhaps to discredit, the hedonistic inclinations of
> Aristippus. (Momigliano 1971, 71)

Momigliano distinguishes this ancient practice of liberally deploying *anecdotes* from the ancient practice of *biography* proper (that is, the practice of
constructing a narrative of an individual's whole life from birth to death).
Nevertheless, he argues that the two practices have at least this much in
common: both were "used by philosophers at large as a weapon against
hostile schools" (84). Arnold Davidson spells this point out as follows:

> The significance of philosophy as a way of life can be seen in the importance
> given to biographies in ancient philosophical work. ... A philosophical
> biography was not predominantly a narrative intended to allow one to
> understand an author and his doctrines; it was not just a report of what

---

[7] The question of exactly what role anecdotes about a philosopher's mode of life are meant to play in
ancient philosophical writings is a complex and delicate one. This much seems clear: if one thinks
that a consideration of the manner in which a philosopher lives can contribute in some way to an
assessment of the cogency of his philosophical doctrines, then this will have implications for what
one takes the role and standing of (what we would tend to consider merely) ad hominem forms of
argument to be. Nonetheless, it is difficult for a modern reader not to be struck by the abundance of
(what is apt to strike one as) apparently irrelevant biographical detail in ancient philosophers'
discussions of each other's views. As an amusing yet representative sample, consider the manner in
which Aristotle introduces his discussion of the political doctrines of Hippodamus:

> Hippodamus the son of Euryphon, a citizen of Miletus, was the first man without practical
> experience of politics who attempted to handle the theme of the best form of constitution. He
> was a man who invented the planning of towns in separate quarters, and laid out the Piraeus
> with regular roads. In his general life, too, [apart from these innovations] he was led into some
> eccentricity by a desire to attract attention; and this made a number of people feel that he lived
> in too studied and artificial a manner. He wore his hair long and expensively adorned: he had
> flowing robes, expensively decorated, made from a cheap but warm material, which he wore in
> summer time as well as in winter. ([1946] / *Politics* 2.5.1267b22–31)

Can the observation that a philosopher lives "in too studied and artificial a manner" shed light on
the character of his philosophy?

the author said and believed. Rather, "it was, in the first place, a tool of philosophical battle," since one could defend or condemn a philosophy by way of the characteristics of the mode of life of those who supported it. (Davidson 1995, 30; embedded quotation from Cambiano 1993, 81)

The role of biography proper (as opposed to a merely polemical deployment of anecdote) in the practice of ancient philosophy was by no means limited to the purely negative function of bringing out the limitations of a philosophy as something that could be embodied in a life. Ancient biography serves an important positive function as well: to furnish the most fundamental form of representation of the philosophical life as such. The tradition of philosophical biography, so conceived, is initiated by Plato's and Xenophon's respective accounts of the life of Socrates. The practice of this mode of representing a life is concerned with the embodiment of philosophy in life—something in which a human being through her manner of living cannot help but engage to some degree or other. This form of biography is therefore by no means confined to the representation of the lives of individuals whom we would today classify as philosophers. In ancient Greek and Roman times, all biography partakes of philosophical biography —of the philosophical dimension of the life of the exemplary individual. That life which the ancient art of biography seeks to depict, whatever else it may be, will be the embodiment of a conception of philosophy. Biography, so conceived, is an account of the life of the individual—whether it be the life of a poet, statesman, general, or saint—qua heroic, if albeit often heroically flawed, personality. That which such an account aims to highlight is that which is to be emulated and that which is not to be emulated in such a life— both what furnishes an exemplary model in its achievement and what functions as a cautionary tale in its limitations. The biography seeks to illuminate the exemplary individual's ascension to great heights, while equally drawing our attention to secondary biographical details of that life that may allow us to comprehend its overall arc—perhaps, for example, ending in tragic downfall—as a collection of not merely accidentally related moments. Momigliano argues, precisely because the point of the model of how to live furnished by such representations is to articulate a philosophical ideal—and not merely to record historical fact—that the practice of philosophical biography among the ancients must be carefully distinguished from that of history; hence he writes:

> The Socratics were infuriating in their own time. They are still infuriating in our time. They are never so infuriating as when approached from the point of view of biography. We like biography to be true or false, honest or

dishonest. Who can use such terminology for Plato's *Phaedo* or *Apology*, or even for Xenophon's *Memorabilia*? ... The fact we have to face is that biography acquired a new meaning when the Socratics moved to that zone between truth and fiction which is so bewildering to the professional historian. We shall not understand what biography was in the fourth century if we do not recognize that it came to occupy an ambiguous position between fact and imagination. Let us be in no doubt. With a man like Plato, and even with a smaller but by no means simpler man like Xenophon, this is a consciously chosen ambiguity. The Socratics experimented in biography, and the experiments were directed towards capturing the potentialities rather than the realities of individual lives. Socrates, the main subject of their considerations ..., was not so much the real Socrates as the potential Socrates. He was not a dead man whose life could be recounted. He was the guide to territories as yet unexplored. ... The Greeks and the Romans realized that writing about the life of a fellow man is not quite the same as writing history. ... By keeping biography separate from history the Greeks and the Romans were able to appreciate what constitutes a poet, a philosopher, a martyr, a saint. (Momigliano 1971, 46, 104)

What such an account of a life seeks to highlight, for the ancients, is not—and could not be—independent of what philosophy is. Plutarch's depiction of a life—say, that of an exemplary statesman or general—aims, in each case, to show how *philosophia* finds expression in a life.

To compare an ancient philosopher to Socrates and to notice various affinities between his life and that of Socrates is not to notice anything remarkable for the ancients. That there must be something along these lines to notice is, for the ancients, a grammatical truth. In this sense subsequent Hellenistic and Roman philosophers looked back to Socrates as someone who had introduced an irreversible kink into the history of thought. Cicero sums up his understanding of the historical situation as follows:

From the ancient days down to the time of Socrates ... philosophy dealt with numbers and movements, with the problem whence all things came, or whither they returned, and zealously inquired into the size of the stars, the spaces that divided them, their courses and all celestial phenomena; Socrates, on the other hand, was the first to call philosophy down from the heavens and set her in the cities of men ... and compel her to ask questions about life and morality and things good and evil. (Cicero [1927], 435 / *Tusculan Disputations* V, IV, 10)

A life utterly devoid of any Socratic aspect for an ancient Roman philosopher would have been a life in which *philosophia* itself finds no expression. The claim that an ancient philosopher's life in no way resembled that of Socrates would have been unintelligible. Conversely, the claim that some ancient philosopher, say, Diogenes or Epicurus, or Seneca or Cicero, sought to practice a conception of philosophy which bore certain resemblances to that of Socrates would have been a truism.

III   Socratic Aspects of Wittgenstein's Conception of Philosophy

One could reformulate this last point as follows: to say of an ancient philosopher that his conception of philosophy bears Socratic aspects is to utter a grammatical truth. To say something of this sort about your average contemporary professor of philosophy is to make a substantive and informative claim—one that could prove to be false.

Perhaps philosophy was *once* about living a certain sort of life—perhaps *back then* there was no such thing as separating an understanding of the life a particular philosophy enjoins its practitioners to lead from an understanding of the philosophy itself. But perhaps the relation between one's life and one's philosophy can no longer be *for us* what it was for the ancients. Nowadays, we will be told, philosophers no longer look to the *Sage* for an accurate standard or measure of anything. Nowadays, we are taught to look first and foremost to the well-reasoned philosophical *theory* for guidance in such matters, and one does not need to be a sage to put forward exemplary instances of such theory (all one needs to be is a good "philosopher").

This brings us to the following question: what does it show that even scholars who know both Socrates and Wittgenstein well can have difficulty answering the questions on our exam? No doubt, it shows a number of interesting things, but not least of them is that it can help to reveal that there is something altogether misleading about a certain widely disseminated caricature of Wittgenstein. For his conception of philosophy is often presented as if it were opposed to all previous understandings of philosophy—as if his aim were to bring anything and everything previously called "philosophy" to an end—that is, as if he represented a particularly pure incarnation of the anti-philosopher. Yet if one wishes to speak about Wittgenstein—that is, if one wishes to use the word "philosophy" to indicate, as he himself often does, the form of activity he seeks to exemplify in his writings—then arguably to say of *that* conception of philosophy that it bears Socratic aspects is, once again, to utter a grammatical truth.[8] This

---

[8] For a comparison of Socrates' and Wittgenstein's conceptions of philosophy offering detailed exegesis of both Plato's Socratic dialogues and Wittgenstein's writings, see Sebastian Sunday's "The Importance of Understanding Each Other in Philosophy" (2015).

suggests that Wittgenstein seeks to inherit considerably more of
a traditional conception of philosophy than the cliché of him as the pure
anti-philosopher can allow for. This is non-accidentally related to why the
questions on our exam can pose the sort of difficulty that they do.

In a manner strikingly reminiscent of ancient accounts of
a philosopher's thought, many accounts purporting to furnish an overview
of Wittgenstein's philosophy take the trouble to adduce a wealth of
anecdotes and biographical details regarding Wittgenstein's life.
Wittgenstein, like Socrates or Pythagoras, seems to many of his expositors
to require this sort of treatment. This is surely not merely because
Wittgenstein lived in a manner which caused anecdotes about him to
proliferate, but because the authors of such accounts take the anecdotes
and details in question to illuminate something about Wittgenstein qua
philosopher. Yes, he was an odd fellow who lived an unconventional life;
and, yes, of course, this provides colorful material for the occasional
entertaining digression. But the authors of the accounts of Wittgenstein's
philosophy at issue here do not take themselves to be *digressing* when
adducing the material in question; they tend to see an intimate if elusive
connection between the extraordinariness of Wittgenstein's life and the
difficulty of his thought.[9] And it is doubtful that most of them would
imagine that they are able to see such a connection if they did not take
themselves to be encouraged to look for one by something in
Wittgenstein's philosophical writings themselves. But by what?[10]
Consider these five passages from Wittgenstein:

1. Nothing is so difficult as not deceiving yourself. (CV 39e)
2. If anyone is unwilling to descend into himself ... he will remain
    superficial in his writing. (MS-120, 72v; translated in RW 174)
3. You cannot write more truly about yourself than you *are*. (CV 38e)
4. Work on philosophy ... is really more work on oneself. (CV 24e)
5. The revolutionary will be the one who can revolutionize himself.
    (CV 51e)

---

[9] The case of Saul Kripke can serve as a useful contrast here. There are many anecdotes about Kripke
circulating in contemporary philosophical circles. But no one is tempted to adduce any of them in
the context of explicating Kripke's philosophical writings. I discuss the question of the relation
between philosophy and biography—and why in the case of some philosophers the relation between
the two matters more to an understanding of their philosophy than in others—in my "Philosophy
and Biography" (2001).

[10] The third part of this text draws heavily on my "On Going the Bloody *Hard* Way in Philosophy"
(2002a).

I will call these "Socratic remarks." Remarks like these can be found scattered throughout Wittgenstein's writings.[11] Socratic remarks are apt to strike a certain kind of reader as a non sequitur, if she brings certain preconceptions to her reading of the text. When she happens upon such a remark, it may strike her as a departure from the business of the philosophical inquiry at hand and a sudden excursion into some unrelated and far more general methodological question. But the question is: what is the business at hand? If one of the five remarks were to occur, say, in the middle of an extended Wittgensteinian philosophical investigation (on, say, whether it is possible for me to give myself a private ostensive definition, or for another person to have my pains, or for there to be only one occasion on which someone obeys a rule), would that be a change of subject? Why do such Socratic remarks crop up in the midst of Wittgenstein's philosophical investigations?

When such a remark occurs in the midst of one of Wittgenstein's investigations, it does not introduce an abrupt change of topic; it interrupts the investigation in order to step back for a moment and comment on a difficulty in doing philosophy which one runs up against in such investigations. Thus, one will not understand what such remarks are about, unless one understands why they occur in the sorts of contexts in Wittgenstein's work in which they characteristically do.[12]

Consider the first of the remarks just quoted ("Nothing is so difficult as not deceiving yourself"). This is neither more nor less a remark about a difficulty of philosophy than it is a remark about a difficulty of life. One's ability to avoid self-deception *in* philosophy can be neither more nor less than one's ability to avoid it *outside* philosophy. Wittgenstein concludes a meditation on the effects which the all-but-inevitable tendency to "lie to oneself" has on one's writing with the remark: "If you are *unwilling* to

---

[11] "But these passages," someone might complain, "are mostly taken from a single work: *Culture and Value*—the work which Wittgenstein devotes exclusively to topics in ethics, aesthetics, and religion!" This is not true. Wittgenstein never wrote, nor ever planned to write, such a work. The passages in *Culture and Value* are drawn from all over Wittgenstein's *Nachlass*. (See the revised edition of *Culture and Value*, in particular the newly added appendix which includes a complete list of manuscript sources; see also Pichler 1991.) The passages from *Culture and Value* that are quoted here—like many such passages from *Culture and Value*—occur, in their original home in Wittgenstein's manuscripts, in the midst of investigations of questions such as "What is it to follow a rule?", or ". . . name an object?", or ". . . understand the meaning of a word?", etc.

[12] To put a somewhat more polemical edge on the point: one cannot understand many of the remarks that occur in an edition of Wittgenstein's writings such as *Culture and Value* by engaging in a close reading of it—that "work"—while neglecting Wittgenstein's investigations of the sorts of questions with which the bulk of his work is concerned—neglecting, that is, what he thought philosophy *is* as embodied in his philosophical practice.

know what you are, your writing is a form of deceit" (MS-120, 72v; translated in RW 174).[13] And he continues: "If anyone is unwilling to descend into himself . . . he will remain superficial in his writing." Thus, Wittgenstein's reasoning goes as follows: if you are unwilling to descend into yourself, then you will remain superficial in your thinking (and writing) generally, and a fortiori you will remain superficial in your efforts to write philosophy. Hence Wittgenstein writes Malcolm: "You can't think decently if you don't want to hurt yourself" (Letter to Norman Malcolm, November 16, 1944; also quoted in WAM 35). Is that a claim about how to live or how to philosophize?

Again (the second of the remarks quoted above): "If anyone is unwilling to descend into himself . . . he will remain superficial in his writing." Wittgenstein is equally committed to something close to the converse of this thought: if someone remains superficial in his thinking or writing, this can be a reflection of the character of the person whose thinking and writing it is. It is, for Wittgenstein, not only possible to discern aspects of a person's character in the character of their philosophizing, but essential to the formation of any true estimate of their philosophy that one be *able* to do so. The exercise of such discernment is never far below the surface in the judgments Wittgenstein himself offers of the philosophical work of others.[14] To put the point more positively and in a more Wittgensteinian idiom: the spirit of a person *shows itself* in the spirit of his philosophy, which in turn shows itself *in the way* he philosophizes. The other side of this point—its Plutarchian obverse, as it were—may be formulated as follows: the spirit of a person's philosophy shows itself in the way she lives.

The numerous remarks about other thinkers sprinkled throughout Wittgenstein's notebooks and recorded conversations furnish vivid documentation of the manifold sorts of ways in which Wittgenstein himself exercises such discernment of aspects of a person's character in the character of their philosophizing. Wittgenstein says about Frank Ramsey: "R.'s incapacity for genuine enthusiasm or for genuine reverence, which comes to the same thing, came finally to repulse me more & more" (MS-183, 7; also translated in PPO 15). Here Wittgenstein is commenting on

---

[13] See also the remark about the relation between cheating others and cheating oneself which Wittgenstein interjected, in code, in his "Notes for the 'Philosophical Lecture'": "If you cheat others, at least don't cheat yourself; and if you don't cheat yourself—why should you cheat the others?" (PO 450 / MS-166, 12r).

[14] The discernment of aspects of a person's character in the character of their philosophizing is essential to the capacity for distinguishing (genuine) *philosophy* from, what Wittgenstein was fond of calling, (mere) *cleverness*—a distinction which underlies a great many of Wittgenstein's judgments of the work of others.

something about Ramsey's sensibility that reflects itself in, but certainly not only in, the character of his response to philosophical problems. What is at issue here is a kind of limitation of sensibility that is neither merely personal nor merely philosophical, but rather equally (and, in Wittgenstein's eyes, equally fatefully) both. Maurice Drury once told Wittgenstein: "I always enjoy reading anything of William James. He is such a human person." Wittgenstein responded: "Yes, that is what makes him a good philosopher; he was a real human being" (RW 106). That James is "a real human being" is something Wittgenstein takes himself to be able to discern as a reader of James's philosophical writings. And the estimate he forms in this regard of James qua person is not utterly independent of his estimate of James qua philosopher. When Wittgenstein remarks about A. J. Ayer that he "has something to say, but he is incredibly shallow" (RW 159), it is, in the first instance, of course, a remark about the shallowness of Ayer's philosophizing. But it is not *merely* a remark about the quality of Ayer's efforts at philosophizing; it is not wholly without bearing on an estimate of the shallowness or depth of the sensibility of the person whose philosophizing it is.[15] Similarly, Wittgenstein says about the anthropologist James Frazer: "Frazer is much more savage than most of his savages" (PO 131). Again, this is a comment on both the man and his thought. It is a comment on something that shows itself in Frazer's writing about the forms of life he studies—where part of what shows itself is something about what sorts of possibilities of thought and life are (and are not) closed to Frazer himself.

Wittgenstein's remark "You cannot write more truly about yourself than you *are*" is simultaneously a remark about a personal and a philosophical difficulty; if you cannot write anything *about yourself* that is more truthful than you yourself are, then you cannot write anything *in philosophy* that is more truthful than you yourself are. For Wittgenstein, the two difficulties are inseparable—they are aspects of a single difficulty.[16] One can, if one

---

[15] See also Ray Monk's review of Ben Rogers's *A. J. Ayer: A Life* (Monk 1999, esp. 12).

[16] Another double-faced difficulty that surfaces repeatedly in Wittgenstein's notebooks as an urgent topic for him is the danger of *pride* (or *vanity*). Consider the following remark: "The *edifice of your pride* has to be dismantled. And that means frightful work" (CV 30e). And this "frightful work" is, by Wittgenstein's lights, of both a personal and a philosophical kind. In one of the possible prefaces he drafted for a possible book, Wittgenstein writes:

> I would like to say "This book is written to the glory of God," but nowadays that would be chicanery, that is, it would not be rightly understood. It means the book is written in good will, and in so far as it is not so written, but out of vanity, etc., the author would wish to see it condemned. *He cannot free it of these impurities further than he himself is free of them.*" (PR, foreword, my emphasis)

will, take the words "perspicuity" and "clarity" to stand for things Wittgenstein struggles to attain in philosophy. And one can, with equal justification, take the words "honesty" and *"Anständigkeit"* to stand for things one should struggle to attain in life.[17] If you evidently do practice philosophy, but most decidedly not in the spirit of Wittgenstein, then these two struggles may strike you as utterly independent of one another. But if you wish to think of yourself as practicing philosophy in anything like the spirit of Wittgenstein—or, for that matter, in anything like the spirit of Socrates—then these two struggles are twin aspects of a single struggle, each partially constitutive of the other.

When Wittgenstein writes his sister "Call me a truth-seeker and I will be satisfied," he specifies the character of his striving in terms of something that for him is equally a philosophical and an ethical ideal. All philosophical thinking and writing accordingly has, for Wittgenstein, its ethical aspect. Wittgenstein thought that what, and more importantly *how*, we think is revelatory of who we are and how we live; and that learning to think better (and, above all, to *change* the ways in which one thinks) is part of learning to be better, that is, part of becoming (what Wittgenstein calls) "a real human being."[18] So, even though Wittgenstein, in one sense, may appear to "'have' no ethics" (namely, if "ethics" names a branch of philosophy with its own proprietary subject matter[19]), in another sense, his thinking and writing, on every page of his work, takes place under the pressure of an ethical demand.[20] And if qua biographer one turns to examine his life, one will discover the pressure of such a demand equally

---

[17] I have not attempted here to translate the German word *"Anständigkeit"*—which can mean "decency" or "propriety," as well as "fairness" or "justice" or "fittingness," employed as a virtue term for someone who has a developed sense of what is fair, just, or fitting. There is no English word that has quite this semantic range. It was an important word for Wittgenstein and recurs in his correspondence and conversations.

[18] Thus, Wittgenstein does not only think that the limitations of a person qua person limit his possibilities of imagination and reflection qua philosopher; he also thinks that the activity of philosophy represents a possible means of overcoming limitations of a person qua person. Hence both the promise and the danger of philosophy: throughout Wittgenstein's life, an important ground of his motivation to philosophy (to, that is, what he hopes philosophy, at its best, can be) and of his fear of philosophy (of, that is, what he knows philosophy, at its worst, can do to a person) is the thought that in developing her philosophical sensibility a person is thereby (for better or worse) profoundly shaping herself as a person.

[19] I take it that the term "ethics" in Wittgenstein's vocabulary no more names an independent subject matter or separable area of philosophy than does the term "logic" (or "grammar"). For Wittgenstein, logic and ethics are each, and each differently, concerned with a pervasive dimension of human thought and action.

[20] For a discussion of the sense in which Wittgenstein does not "'have' an ethics," as well as of the sense in which his work is everywhere pervaded by an ethical concern, see my "What Ethics in the *Tractatus* Is Not" (2002c).

pervasively manifest in almost every aspect of his life and in his understanding of the relation between his philosophy and his life.

Such a philosopher will naturally attract biographers. If those biographers think of Wittgenstein's life as one thing and his philosophy as
another, their biographical narratives will necessarily give a distorted picture not only of the life but also of the thought. They will give a distorted
picture of the life of such a philosopher because there is no understanding
the life of such a man apart from an understanding of his thought.[21] They
will give a distorted picture of his thought because there is no understanding the thought of any contemporary philosopher—and certainly not
this one—as a straightforward function of his life, especially when the
requisite understanding of the life is taken to be unproblematically available independently of an understanding of the thought.[22]

Wittgenstein neither wanted to, nor thought he could, separate the task
of becoming the sort of human being he wanted to be from the task of
becoming the sort of philosopher he wanted to be. One sometimes hears
the following sort of thing said about Wittgenstein: there were two
different things Wittgenstein wanted to do—become a certain kind of
person and become a certain kind of philosopher—but he thought that
these two pursuits somehow presupposed one another or were in some way
entangled in one another. This is as wrong about Wittgenstein as it would
be about Socrates. These were not "two different things Wittgenstein
wanted to do." There is only one thing here. The dimension of living
that is here in question and the dimension of thinking that is here in
question were, for Wittgenstein, two different aspects of a single unitary
pursuit, which Wittgenstein called, as did Socrates long before him,
"philosophy."[23]

---

[21] In his review of W. W. Bartley's biography of Wittgenstein, Rush Rhees puts the point well: "Unless
you know what his [Wittgenstein's] work means to him and what he tries hardest to bring into his
work – and unless you know what other features of his living and his relations to other people he
counts important – you cannot say whether some ... desire or practice is significant or rather
insignificant in his character and his life" (Rhees 1974).

[22] Those who imagine, for example, that Wittgenstein's homoeroticism ("the love that dare not speak
its name") is the key to understanding everything else in his life, including his philosophical
preoccupations, invariably end up offering a shallow and skewed representation of his philosophical
thought. I discuss how this happens in the biographical representations of the relation between
Wittgenstein's philosophy and his sexuality offered by W. W. Bartley and Bruce Duffy in my
"Throwing Away the Top of the Ladder" (1991).

[23] Wittgenstein, both early and late, employs the words "philosopher," "philosophy," and "philosophical" in (among others) the following two distinct senses: to denote that which he seeks to combat
through his practice ("when philosophers use a word ...," PI §116; "how does the philosophical
problem ... arise? ... the decisive movement in the conjuring trick has been made, and it was the
very one that seemed to us quite innocent," PI §108; etc.) and to denote that practice itself

If this is correct, then it also suggests that we would do well not to be too quick to move from an observation about Wittgenstein's generally critical attitude, toward much of what contemporary academic philosophy stands for, to a claim about his attitude toward philosophy as such. The difficulty of our exam suggests that we go very wrong in our understanding of Wittgenstein, if we attribute to him a disdain toward everything that the very idea of philosophy—as it comes down to us through the tradition that begins with Socrates—has stood for. It is often and easily missed that Wittgenstein's quarrels with various contemporary dispensations of philosophy are conducted with an eye to the question: who does and who does not have the right to speak in the name of philosophy—to claim to be the true inheritor of the most fundamental aspirations of the tradition?

("philosophy is a struggle against the bewitchment of our understanding . . .," PI §109; "there is not a single philosophical method, though there are indeed methods, different therapies, as it were," §133; "what is your aim in philosophy? – To show the fly the way out of the fly-bottle," §309; etc.). And, for Wittgenstein, each of these two opposed senses of the word "philosophy" has equal claim to inherit the ancient sense of the word. I mean here to be referring only to his use of "philosophy" in the second of these two senses.

APPENDIX I

The Preliminary Exam

1. "Everyone has a simple test to tell whether a cobbler makes good shoes. There is no test of this sort to discover whether a philosopher does his job or not."
   Is this Socrates speaking or Wittgenstein?

2. "I give you permission to define each word the way you like just so long as you make clear the application of whatever word you use."
   Is this Socrates speaking or Wittgenstein?

3. "Call me a truth-seeker and I will be satisfied." Socrates or Wittgenstein?

4. Our philosopher notes, halfway through one of his dialectical excursions, that, at the point thus reached in the proceedings, ". . . we have helped [our interlocutor] to some extent toward finding the right answer; for now not only is he aware that he is ignorant of the answer, but he will be quite eager to look for it." Socrates or Wittgenstein?

5. Our philosopher remarks: "Anything [your interlocutor] can do for himself, leave it to [your interlocutor]." Socrates or Wittgenstein?

6. "He shows his interlocutors a projection of their own selves. . . . [He] splits himself into two, so that there are two [of him]: the [one] who knows in advance how the discussion is going to end, and the [one] who travels the entire dialectical path along with his interlocutor." Is this said here about Socrates or Wittgenstein?

7. "He was constantly fighting with the deepest philosophical problems. The solution of one problem led to another problem. [He] was uncompromising; he had to have *complete* understanding." Is this said about Socrates or Wittgenstein?

8. "It is a telling fact that everyone got carried away when they talked about [him], whether it was [someone] singing his praises or his enemies ranting against him." Said of Socrates or Wittgenstein?

9. "[He] had an extraordinary gift for divining the thoughts of the person with whom he was engaged in discussion. While the other struggled to put his thought into words [he] would perceive what it was and state it

for him. This power of his ... sometimes seemed uncanny." Said of Socrates or Wittgenstein?

10. "One of [his] beliefs was that philosophy ... cannot accurately be captured in a lecture or a treatise." Said of Socrates or Wittgenstein?

11. "When [he] invented an example ... in order to illustrate a point, he himself would grin at the absurdity of what he had imagined. But if any member of the [audience] were to chuckle, his expression would change to severity." Said of Socrates or Wittgenstein?

12. "Most of the paradoxical views that can be attributed to [him] are based on things which he said ... for a distinctive purpose and in a distinctive context." Said of Socrates or Wittgenstein?

13. "[He] was not an easy guru to follow, not least because a guru was the one thing that he resolutely refused to be. Still, it is hardly surprising that after his death several of his friends wanted to carry on the good work somehow. Since it was, and is, no simple matter to say exactly what the good work amounted to, it should be equally unsurprising that these would-be successors of [his] ended up championing very different causes." Said of Socrates or Wittgenstein?

APPENDIX II

The Exam Proper

I. *Which great philosopher lived an ascetic existence, spurning wealth and fame, but did not hold up his own way of life as a model to his friends and students, often encouraging them instead to take up ordinary professional trades and to immerse themselves in the world from which the philosopher himself had withdrawn?*

1a. Looking back upon his life, one of our philosophers finds he is able to claim the following about himself: "I did not care for the things that most people care about – making money, having a prosperous household, high military or civil rank." Socrates or Wittgenstein?

1b. Looking back upon the life of one of our philosophers, a comrade is able to remark the following: "A great simplicity, at times even an extreme frugality, became characteristic of his life." Socrates or Wittgenstein?

2. *Which great philosopher was especially renowned for the intensity of his intellectual concentration, liable to fall into a state of complete absorption in a philosophical problem – a state in which he became utterly oblivious to the world around him?*

2a. "When he was trying to draw a thought out of himself, he would prohibit, with a peremptory motion of the hand, any questions or remarks. There were frequent and prolonged periods of silence, with only an occasional mutter from [him], and the stillest attention from the others. During these silences, [he] was extremely tense and active. His gaze was concentrated; his face was alive; his hands made arresting movements; his expression was stern. One knew that one was in the presence of extreme seriousness, absorption, and force of intellect." Socrates or Wittgenstein?

2b. "He started wrestling with some problem or other about sunrise one morning, and stood there lost in thought, and when the answer wouldn't come he still stood there thinking and refused to give it up." Socrates or Wittgenstein?

3. *Which great philosopher's mode of discussion with others was no less intense than his aforementioned capacity for isolated absorption in thought?*

3a. "Each conversation with [him] was like living through the day of judgment. It was terrible. Everything had constantly to be dug up anew, questioned and subjected to the tests of truthfulness." Socrates or Wittgenstein?

3b. "Anyone who is close to [him] and enters into conversation with him is liable to be drawn into an argument, and whatever subject he may start, he will be continually carried round and round by him, until at last he finds that he has to give an account both of his present and his past life, and when [his interlocutor] is once entangled, [he] will not let him go until he has completely and thoroughly sifted him." Socrates or Wittgenstein?

4. *Which great philosopher received a military decoration for bravery in battle?*

4a. "You are mistaken ... if you think that a man who is worth anything ought to spend his time weighing up the prospects of life and death." Socrates or Wittgenstein?

4b. "Now I ... have an opportunity to be a decent human being, because I am face to face with death." Socrates or Wittgenstein?

4c. "I may die in an hour, I may die in two hours, I may die in a month, or not for a few years. I cannot know about it and I cannot do anything for or against it: *such is this life.* How then ought I to live in order to hold my own at that moment, to live amid the good and the beautiful until life stops of itself?" Socrates or Wittgenstein?

4d. "Those who pursue philosophy rightly, study to die." Socrates or Wittgenstein?

5. *Which great philosopher's decoration in battle was regarded by those who knew him as merely one conspicuous outward sign of a much broader capacity for self-mastery?*

5a. "He was by all accounts supremely disciplined and a master of rational self-control. Maybe that was the problem. Perhaps it explains why he had such impossibly high expectations for others ... It has been said of [him] that 'in the strength of his character lay the weakness of his philosophy.'" Socrates or Wittgenstein?

5b. "There was practically nothing he was not, or could not have been, able to do unusually well if it belonged at all to the sort of thing that can be brought under voluntary control, where training and practice are essential in the learning process." Socrates or Wittgenstein?

6. *Which great philosopher often seemed to cast a spell on others, either powerfully attracting or repelling those around him?*

6a. "It seems he cannot avoid casting a spell, and some are repelled by it as strongly as others are attracted. Those that are drawn to him, are bound by an affection which has in it something that can perhaps be called love. It happens to fishermen and farmers as well as to philosophers." Socrates or Wittgenstein?

6b. "I've been bitten in the heart, or the mind, or whatever you like to call it, by [his] philosophy, which clings like an adder to any young and gifted mind it can get a hold of." Socrates or Wittgenstein?

7. *Which great philosopher is often credited with the capacity of being able to see a philosophical problem as if for the first time?*

7a. "He would talk about almost anything and always with the same intensity. He impressed me, time and time again, by lifting familiar problems into the light as if he were the first to see the problem, unhampered by conventional and received views." Said of Socrates or Wittgenstein?

8. "Is it just *I* who cannot found a school, or can a philosopher never do so?" Is this Socrates or Wittgenstein?

9. "One *cannot* speak the truth if one has not yet conquered oneself. One *cannot* speak it—but not, because one is still not clever enough. The truth can be spoken only by someone who is already *at home* in it; not by someone who still lives in untruthfulness, and does no more than reach out towards it from within untruthfulness." Socrates or Wittgenstein?

10. "One must start out with error and convert it into truth. That is, one must reveal the source of error, otherwise hearing the truth won't do any good. The truth cannot force its way in when something else is occupying its place. To convince someone of the truth, it is not enough to state it, but rather one must find the *path* from error to truth." Socrates or Wittgenstein?

11. "If someone thinks, mustn't he think *something*? . . . And if he thinks something, mustn't it be something *real*?" Is this question asked by Wittgenstein or Socrates?

12. "And mustn't someone who is painting be painting something – and someone who is painting something be painting something real?" And this one: Socrates or Wittgenstein?

APPENDIX III

The Extra Credit Portion of the Exam

1. "[He] used a very simple language and [was] sure that [he] would be understood only by a few. [He] sought for friendship through philosophy and [was] certain that [he] would be rejected by many." Socrates or Wittgenstein?

2. "An encounter with [this philosopher] ... can be radically unsettling precisely insofar as it does not merely reveal that reality is not what it appeared to you to be, but that you no longer know how it appeared to you. It is not that your belief was mistaken or that nothing in the world answers to your desire; instead you lose your grasp, or rather realize that you never had a grasp, on *what* you 'desired' or 'believed' in the first place, on what should be most intimately your own." Does this describe an encounter with Socrates or Wittgenstein?

3. "It is no wonder that no new knowledge needs to be added to the philosophical work. The only thing needed is to work with what one already knows; for the problems are not problems external to ourselves but rather precisely a part of our selves." Said about Socrates or Wittgenstein?

4. "If there are no doctrines to be learnt, are there only things to be unlearnt? – And, importantly, here the answer should be: No. But . . . there is no one single determinate point to take home either." Is this said about Socrates or Wittgenstein?

APPENDIX IV

Answers to Exam Questions (with References)

The Preliminary Exam

1. Wittgenstein. Karl Britton, "Portrait of a Philosopher," in F. A. Flowers III, ed., *Portraits of Wittgenstein* (Thoemmes Press, 1999), volume 2, p. 209.
2. Socrates. *Charmides* 163d. Plato's dialogues are cited after *The Collected Dialogues of Plato*, edited by Edith Hamilton and Huntingdon Cairns (Princeton University Press, [1961]).
3. Wittgenstein. The remark occurs, in German, in a letter to his sister Helene Salzer (née Wittgenstein) dated "Saturday [1934]." See *Wittgenstein: Gesamtbriefwechsel / Complete Correspondence (Innsbrucker Electronic Edition)*, second release, edited by Anna Coda, Gabriel Citron, Barbara Halder, Allan Janik, Ulrich Lobis, Kerstin Mayr, Brian McGuinness, Michael Schorner, Monika Seekircher, Anton Unterkircher, and Joseph Wang (Intelex, 2004/11), www.nlx.com/collections/166.
4. Socrates. *Meno* 84b; translation amended.
5. Wittgenstein. *Culture and Value: A Selection from the Posthumous Remains*, edited by G. H. von Wright in collaboration with Heikki Nyman, revised edition of the text by Alois Pichler, translated by Peter Winch (Blackwell, 1977/98), p. 88e. The original quotation reads: "Anything the reader can do for himself, leave it to the reader."
6. Socrates. Pierre Hadot, "The Figure of Socrates," in *Philosophy as a Way of Life*, edited by Arnold I. Davidson, translated by Michael Chase (Blackwell, 1995), pp. 149 and 153.
7. Wittgenstein. Norman Malcolm, *Ludwig Wittgenstein: A Memoir*, second edition with Wittgenstein's letters to Malcolm (Clarendon Press, 1958/84), p. 26.
8. Socrates. Anthony Gottlieb, *The Dream of Reason: A History of Western Philosophy from the Greeks to the Renaissance* (Norton, 2000), p. 133.
9. Wittgenstein. Malcolm, *op. cit.*, p. 47.
10. Socrates. Gottlieb, *op. cit.*, p. 143.
11. Wittgenstein. Malcolm, *op. cit.*, p. 27.
12. Socrates. Gottlieb, *op. cit.*, p. 155.
13. Socrates. *Ibid.*, p. 160.

The Exam Proper

1a. Socrates. *Apology* 36b.
1b. Wittgenstein. Georg Henrik von Wright, *Wittgenstein* (Blackwell, 1982), p. 23.
2a. Wittgenstein. Malcolm, *op. cit.*, p. 25.

2b. Socrates. *Symposium* 220c.

3a. Wittgenstein. Georg Henrik von Wright, "Autobiography," in Paul Arthur Schilpp and Lewis Edwin Hahn, eds., *The Philosophy of Georg Henrik von Wright* (Open Court, 1989), p. 14.

3b. Socrates. *Laches* 187e.

4a. Socrates. *Apology* 28b.

4b. Wittgenstein. *Geheime Tagebücher, 1914–1916*, edited by Wilhelm Baum (Turia + Kant, [1991]), entry for 13.9.14 (translated from the original German).

4c. Wittgenstein. *Ibid.*, 7.10.14 (translated from the original German).

4d. Socrates. *Phaedo* 64a (translated from the original Greek).

5a. Socrates. Gottlieb, *op. cit.*, p. 154; the embedded quotation is a translation of Karl Joël, *Der echte und der Xenophontische Sokrates* (R. Gaertner, 1893), p. 256, quoted in W. K. C. Guthrie, *Socrates* (Cambridge University Press, 1971), p. 138.

5b. Wittgenstein. Knut Erik Tranøy, "Wittgenstein in Cambridge 1949–1951: Some Personal Recollections," in Flowers III (ed.), *op. cit.*, vol. 4, p. 126.

6a. Wittgenstein. *Ibid.*, pp. 128–9 (transposed into the present tense to better suit the purposes of the exam).

6b. Socrates. *Symposium* 218a.

7a. Wittgenstein. Tranøy, *op. cit.*, p. 125.

8. Wittgenstein. *Culture and Value*, op. cit., p. 69e.

9. Wittgenstein. *Ibid.*, p. 41e (punctuation altered).

10. Wittgenstein. *Philosophical Occasions: 1912–1951*, edited by James C. Klagge and Alfred Nordmann (Hackett, [1993]), p. 119.

11. Socrates. *Theaetetus* 189a (translation altered, and italics added, following Wittgenstein's rendition; see next answer).

12. Wittgenstein. *Philosophical Investigations*, edited by G. E. M. Anscombe and Rush Rhees, revised edition by P. M. S. Hacker and Joachim Schulte, translated by G. E. M. Anscombe, P. M. S. Hacker, and Joachim Schulte (Wiley-Blackwell, 1953/2009), §518 (after he quotes the above passage from the *Theaetetus*).

The Extra Credit Portion of the Exam

1. Both. Thomas Wallgren, "Radical Enlightenment Optimism: Socrates and Wittgenstein," in Luigi Perissinotto and Begoña Ramón Cámara, eds., *Wittgenstein and Plato* (Palgrave Macmillan, 2013), p. 298.

2. Both. Joel Backström, "On Wittgenstein, Socrates, and the Morals of Metaphysics," unpublished manuscript, p. 2.

3. Both. Niklas Toivakainen, "Socrates Examining, Wittgenstein Investigating," unpublished manuscript, p. 14.

4. Both. Sebastian Sunday Grève, "The Importance of Understanding Each Other in Philosophy," *Philosophy* 90 (2015), p. 292.

References

Works by or Originating from Wittgenstein with Abbreviations

[1930]   R. D. Townsend's Notes from Wittgenstein's Lectures, Michaelmas Term 1930, Cambridge (Wittgenstein 504, Trinity College Library, Cambridge).

[1934]   Notes Dictated to Francis Skinner (Add.Ms.a/407, Trinity College Library, Cambridge).

AWL   *Wittgenstein's Lectures, Cambridge 1932–1935: From the Notes of Alice Ambrose and Margaret MacDonald*, edited by Alice Ambrose (Blackwell, 1979).

BB   *The Blue and Brown Books*, second edition, edited by Rush Rhees (Blackwell, 1958/69).

BT   *The Big Typescript: TS 213*, edited and translated by C. G. Luckhardt and M. A. E. Aue (Wiley-Blackwell, 2005).

CV   *Culture and Value: A Selection from the Posthumous Remains*, edited by G. H. von Wright in collaboration with Heikki Nyman, revised edition of the text by Alois Pichler, translated by Peter Winch (Blackwell, 1977/98).

EPB   *Eine philosophische Betrachtung*, edited by Rush Rhees, translated by Petra von Morstein, in Ludwig Wittgenstein, *Schriften*, volume 5, edited by G. E. M. Anscombe, Rush Rhees, and G. H. von Wright (Suhrkamp, 1970).

GT   *Geheime Tagebücher, 1914–1916*, edited by Wilhelm Baum (Turia + Kant, 1991).

Letter   *Wittgenstein: Gesamtbriefwechsel / Complete Correspondence (Innsbrucker Electronic Edition)*, second release, edited by Anna Coda, Gabriel Citron, Barbara Halder, Allan Janik, Ulrich Lobis, Kerstin Mayr, Brian McGuinness, Michael Schorner, Monika Seekircher, Anton Unterkircher, and Joseph Wang (Intelex, 2004/11), www.nlx.com/collections/166.

LFM   *Wittgenstein's Lectures on the Foundations of Mathematics, Cambridge 1939: From the Notes of R. G. Bosanquet, Norman Malcolm, Rush*

Rhees, and Yorick Smythies, edited by Cora Diamond (Cornell University Press, 1976).

LPE Wittgenstein's Notes for Lectures on "Private Experience" and "Sense Data," edited by Rush Rhees, *The Philosophical Review* 77 (1968), 275–320; revised and expanded version, edited and with additional translations by David G. Stern, in PO. Cited after both editions.

LPP *Wittgenstein's Lectures on Philosophical Psychology 1946–47: Notes by P. T. Geach, K. J. Shah, and A. C. Jackson*, edited by P. T. Geach (Harvester, 1988).

LW I *Last Writings on the Philosophy of Psychology*, volume 1, edited by G. H. von Wright and Heikki Nyman, translated by C. G. Luckhardt and M. A. E. Aue (Blackwell, 1982).

M Wittgenstein's Lectures in 1930–33, edited by G. E. Moore from his own notes, *Mind* 63 (1954), 1–15, 289–316; *Mind* 64 (1955), 1–27, 264. Cited after the reprint in PO.

MS Manuscript, *Wittgenstein Source Bergen Nachlass Edition*, edited by the Wittgenstein Archives at the University of Bergen under the direction of Alois Pichler, in *Wittgenstein Source* (The Wittgenstein Archives at the University of Bergen, 2015–), www.wittgensteinsource.org. Cited by MS (or TS) number following G. H. von Wright's catalog (see von Wright, *Wittgenstein*, Blackwell, 1982, pp. 35ff; reprinted with an addendum in PO).

OC *On Certainty*, edited by G. E. M. Anscombe and G. H. von Wright, translated by Denis Paul and G. E. M. Anscombe (Blackwell, 1969/74).

PG *Philosophical Grammar*, edited by Rush Rhees, translated by Anthony Kenny (Blackwell, 1974).

PI *Philosophical Investigations*, second edition, edited by G. E. M. Anscombe and Rush Rhees, translated by G. E. M. Anscombe (Blackwell, 1953/8); fourth, revised edition, edited by P. M. S. Hacker and Joachim Schulte, translated by G. E. M. Anscombe, P. M. S. Hacker, and Joachim Schulte (Wiley-Blackwell, 2009). Cited after either edition. [In the fourth edition, what was previously known as "Part II" of *Philosophical Investigations* is edited as PPF.]

PLP *The Principles of Linguistic Philosophy*, by Friedrich Waismann, edited by Rom Harré (Macmillan, 1965).

PO *Philosophical Occasions: 1912–1951*, edited by James C. Klagge and Alfred Nordmann (Hackett, 1993).

PPF *Philosophy of Psychology – A Fragment*, in the fourth edition of PI. [In previous editions of PI, this was edited as "Part II" of *Philosophical Investigations*.]

PPO *Public and Private Occasions*, edited by James C. Klagge and Alfred Nordmann (Rowman & Littlefield, 2003).

PR *Philosophical Remarks*, edited by Rush Rhees, translated by Raymond Hargreaves and Roger White (Blackwell, 1975).

RAM	*Ludwig Wittgenstein: A Student's Memoir*, by Theodore Redpath (Duckworth, 1990).

RAM   *Ludwig Wittgenstein: A Student's Memoir*, by Theodore Redpath (Duckworth, 1990).

RFM   *Remarks on the Foundations of Mathematics*, third, revised and reset edition, edited by G. H. von Wright, Rush Rhees, and G. E. M. Anscombe, translated by G. E. M. Anscombe (Blackwell, 1956/78).

RPP I   *Remarks on the Philosophy of Psychology*, volume 1, edited by G. E. M. Anscombe and G. H. von Wright, translated by G. E. M. Anscombe (Blackwell, 1980).

RPP II   *Remarks on the Philosophy of Psychology*, volume 2, edited by G. H. von Wright and Heikki Nyman, translated by C. G. Luckhardt and M. A. E. Aue (Blackwell, 1980).

RW   *Recollections of Wittgenstein*, edited by Rush Rhees (Oxford University Press, 1984).

TLP   *Tractatus Logico-Philosophicus*, translated by C. K. Ogden (Kegan Paul, 1922); alternative translation by D. F. Pears and B. F. McGuinness (Routledge & Kegan Paul, 1961; revised edition, 1974). Cited after any edition.

TS   Typescript. [The source and method of citation are the same as for MS, above.]

VW   *The Voices of Wittgenstein: The Vienna Circle*, edited by Gordon Baker, translated by Gordon Baker, Michael Mackert, John Connolly, and Vasilis Politis (Routledge, 2003).

WAM   *Ludwig Wittgenstein: A Memoir*, second edition with Wittgenstein's letters to Malcolm, by Norman Malcolm, with a biographical sketch by G. H. von Wright (Clarendon Press, 1958/84).

WC   *Wittgenstein: Conversations 1949–1951*, by O. K. Bouwsma, edited by J. L. Craft and Ronald E. Hustwit (Hackett, 1986).

WVC   *Wittgenstein and the Vienna Circle: Conversations Recorded by Friedrich Waismann*, edited by Brian McGuinness, translated by Joachim Schulte and Brian McGuinness (Blackwell, 1979).

Z   *Zettel*, edited by G. E. M. Anscombe and G. H. von Wright, translated by G. E. M. Anscombe (Blackwell, 1967).

Other Works

Square brackets around a publication year are used to indicate posthumous publication of an author's work without their direct authorization.

Agam-Segal, Reshef. 2012. Reflecting on Language from "Sideways-on": Preparatory and Non-Preparatory Aspects-Seeing. *Journal for the History of Analytical Philosophy* 1: 1–17.

Alcoff, Linda Martín. 2010. Epistemic Identities. *Episteme* 7: 128–37.

Alston, William P. 1964. *Philosophy of Language*. Prentice-Hall.

    2000. *Illocutionary Acts and Sentence Meaning*. Cornell University Press.

Anderson, Elizabeth. 1995. Knowledge, Human Interests and Objectivity in Feminist Epistemology. *Philosophical Topics* 23: 27–58.

Aristotle. [1946]. *Politics*, translated by Ernest Barker. Oxford University Press.

[1955]. *Aristotelis Fragmenta Selecta*, edited by W. D. Ross. Oxford University Press.

[2000]. *Nicomachean Ethics*, translated and edited by Roger Crisp. Cambridge University Press.

Austin, J. L. 1946. Other Minds. *Proceedings of the Aristotelian Society, Supplementary Volume* 20: 148–87. Cited after the reprint in Austin [1961/79].

1957. A Plea for Excuses. *Proceedings of the Aristotelian Society* 57: 1–30. Cited after the reprint in Austin [1961/79].

[1961/79]. *Philosophical Papers*, third edition, edited by J. O. Urmson and G. J. Warnock. Clarendon Press.

[1962/75]. *How to Do Things with Words: The William James Lectures Delivered in Harvard University in 1955*, second edition, edited by J. O. Urmson and Marina Sbisà. Clarendon Press.

Baker, Gordon. [2004]. *Wittgenstein's Method: Neglected Aspects*, edited by Katherine J. Morris. Blackwell.

Baker, G. P. and P. M. S. Hacker. 1980/2009. *Wittgenstein: Understanding and Meaning*, second edition, extensively revised by P. M. S. Hacker. Wiley-Blackwell.

1984. *Language, Sense and Nonsense: A Critical Investigation into Modern Theories of Language*. Blackwell.

1985/2009. *Wittgenstein: Rules, Grammar, and Necessity*, second edition, extensively revised by P. M. S. Hacker. Wiley-Blackwell.

Baz, Avner. 2003. On When Words Are Called For: Cavell, McDowell, and the Wording of Our World. *Inquiry* 46: 473–500.

2010. On Learning from Wittgenstein, or What Does It Take to *See* the Grammar of Seeing Aspects? In William Day and Victor J. Krebs, eds., *Seeing Wittgenstein Anew*, Cambridge University Press.

2011. Seeing Aspects and Philosophical Difficulty. In Marie McGinn and Oskari Kuusela, eds., *The Oxford Handbook of Wittgenstein*, Oxford University Press.

2012. *When Words Are Called For: A Defense of Ordinary Language Philosophy*. Harvard University Press.

2016a. Aspects of Perception. In Gary Kemp and Gabriele M. Mras, eds., *Wollheim, Wittgenstein, and Pictorial Representation*, Routledge.

2016b. The Sound of Bedrock: Lines of Grammar between Kant, Wittgenstein, and Cavell. *European Journal of Philosophy* 24: 607–28.

2017. *The Crisis of Method in Contemporary Analytic Philosophy*. Oxford University Press.

Bealer, George. 1998. Intuition and the Autonomy of Philosophy. In Michael R. DePaul and William Ramsey, eds., *Rethinking Intuition*, Rowman & Littlefield.

1999. A Theory of the A Priori. *Philosophical Perspectives* 13: 29–55.

Beaney, Michael. 1996. *Frege: Making Sense*. Duckworth.

2005. *Imagination and Creativity*. The Open University.

2007. Frege's Use of Function-Argument Analysis and His Introduction of Truth-Values as Objects. *Grazer Philosophische Studien* 75: 93–123.

2017a. *Analytic Philosophy: A Very Short Introduction*. Oxford University Press.

2017b. Wittgenstein and Frege. In Hans-Johann Glock and John Hyman, eds., *A Companion to Wittgenstein*, Wiley-Blackwell.

2018. Conceptual Creativity in Philosophy and Logic. In Berys Gaut and Matthew Kieran, eds., *Creativity and Philosophy*, Routledge.

Beaney, Michael and Bob Clark. 2018. Seeing-As and Mathematical Creativity. In Brendan Harrington, Dominic Shaw, and Michael Beaney, eds., *Aspect Perception After Wittgenstein*, Routledge.

Black, Max. 1964. *A Companion to Wittgenstein's "Tractatus."* Cambridge University Press.

Boden, Margaret A. 1990/2004. *The Creative Mind: Myths and Mechanisms*, second edition. Routledge.

1994. What Is Creativity? In Margaret A. Boden, ed., *Dimensions of Creativity*, MIT Press.

2010. *Creativity and Art: Three Roads to Surprise*. Oxford University Press.

Boghossian, Paul. 1989. The Rule-Following Considerations. *Mind* 98: 507–49.

Brandom, Robert B. 1994. *Making It Explicit: Reasoning, Representing, and Discursive Commitment*. Harvard University Press.

2000. *Articulating Reasons: An Introduction to Inferentialism*. Harvard University Press.

Britton, Karl. 1999. Portrait of a Philosopher. In F. A. Flowers III, ed., *Portraits of Wittgenstein*, volume 2, Thoemmes Press.

Bronzo, Silver. 2017. Wittgenstein, Theories of Meaning, and Linguistic Disjunctivism. *European Journal of Philosophy* 25: 1340–63.

Burge, Tyler. 2005. Disjunctivism and Perceptual Psychology. *Philosophical Topics* 33: 1–78.

Cambiano, Giuseppe. 1993. La figura del filosofo e le altre forme del sapere. *Quaderni di Storia* 37: 75–87.

Cappelen, Herman. 2012. *Philosophy without Intuitions*. Oxford University Press.

Carnap, Rudolf. 1939. *Foundations of Logic and Mathematics*. University of Chicago Press.

1945. The Two Concepts of Probability. *Philosophy and Phenomenological Research* 5: 513–32.

1950. *Logical Foundations of Probability*. University of Chicago Press.

1963. P. F. Strawson on Linguistic Naturalism. In P. A. Schilpp, ed., *The Philosophy of Rudolf Carnap*, Open Court.

Carus, A. W. 2007. *Carnap and Twentieth-Century Thought: Explication as Enlightenment*. Cambridge University Press.

Cavell, Stanley. 1958. Must We Mean What We Say? *Inquiry* 1: 172–212.

1962. The Availability of Wittgenstein's Later Philosophy. *The Philosophical Review* 71: 67–93.

1969/2002. *Must We Mean What We Say? A Book of Essays*, updated edition. Cambridge University Press.

1979. *The Claim of Reason: Wittgenstein, Skepticism, Morality, and Tragedy*. Oxford University Press.

1996. Notes and Afterthoughts on the Opening of Wittgenstein's *Investigations*. In Hans Sluga and David G. Stern, eds., *The Cambridge Companion to Wittgenstein*, Cambridge University Press.

Child, William. 2010. Wittgenstein's Externalism. In Daniel Whiting, ed., *The Later Wittgenstein on Language*, Palgrave Macmillan.

2011. *Wittgenstein*. Routledge.

2017. Sensations, Natural Properties, and the Private Language Argument. In Kevin Cahill and Thomas Raleigh, eds., *Wittgenstein and Naturalism*, Routledge.

Churchland, Paul M. 2005. Cleansing Science. *Inquiry* 48: 464–77.

Cicero. [1927]. *Tusculan Disputations*, translated by J. E. King (Loeb Classical Library 141). Harvard University Press.

Code, Lorraine. 1991. *What Can She Know? Feminist Theory and the Construction of Knowledge*. Cornell University Press.

Conant, James. 1991. Throwing Away the Top of the Ladder. *The Yale Review* 79: 328–64.

2001. Philosophy and Biography. In James C. Klagge, ed., *Wittgenstein*, Cambridge University Press.

2002a. On Going the Bloody *Hard* Way in Philosophy. In John H. Whittaker, ed., *The Possibilities of Sense*, Palgrave Macmillan.

2002b. The Method of the *Tractatus*. In Erich H. Reck, ed., *From Frege to Wittgenstein*, Oxford University Press.

2002c. What Ethics in the *Tractatus* Is Not. In D. Z. Philipps, ed., *Wittgenstein on Ethics and Religion*, St. Martin's Press.

2005. The Dialectic of Perspectivism, I. *Sats – Nordic Journal of Philosophy* 6 (2): 5–50.

2006. The Dialectic of Perspectivism, II. *Sats – Nordic Journal of Philosophy* 7 (1): 6–57.

Crary, Alice. 2002a. What Do Feminists Want in an Epistemology? In Peg O'Connor and Naomi Scheman, eds., *Re-Reading the Canon*, Penn State Press.

2002b. Why Can't Moral Thought Be Everything It Seems? *Philosophical Forum* 33: 373–92.

2007. *Beyond Moral Judgment*. Harvard University Press.

2012. Dogs and Concepts. *Philosophy* 87: 215–37.

2016. *Inside Ethics: On the Demands of Moral Thought*. Harvard University Press.

2018. The Methodological Is Political: What's the Matter with "Analytic Feminism"? *Radical Philosophy* 202: 47–60.

Crystal, David. 1987. *The Cambridge Encyclopedia of Language*. Cambridge University Press.

Daston, Lorraine and Peter Galison. 2007. *Objectivity*. Zone Books.

Davidson, Arnold I. 1995. Introduction: Pierre Hadot and the Spiritual Phenomenon of Ancient Philosophy. In Pierre Hadot, *Philosophy as a Way of Life*, edited by Arnold I. Davidson, translated by Michael Chase, Blackwell.

Davidson, Donald. 1974. On the Very Idea of a Conceptual Scheme. *Proceedings and Addresses of the American Philosophical Association* 47: 5–20.

1984/2001. *Inquiries into Truth and Interpretation*, second edition. Clarendon Press.

1990. The Structure and Content of Truth. *The Journal of Philosophy* 87: 297–328.

2005. *Truth, Language, and History*. Clarendon Press.

De Mesel, Benjamin. 2017. Wittgenstein and Objectivity in Ethics: A Reply to Brandhorst. *Philosophical Investigations* 40: 40–63.

DePaul, Michael R. and William Ramsey (eds.). 1998. *Rethinking Intuition: The Psychology of Intuition and Its Role in Philosophical Inquiry*. Rowman & Littlefield.

Diamond, Cora. 1991. *The Realistic Spirit: Wittgenstein, Philosophy, and the Mind*. MIT Press.

Forthcoming. *Ethics: Shifting Perspectives*. Harvard University Press.

Dreyfus, Hubert L. 2005. Overcoming the Myth of the Mental: How Philosophers Can Profit from the Phenomenology of Everyday Expertise. *Proceedings and Addresses of the American Philosophical Association* 79: 47–65.

2007. Detachment, Involvement and Rationality: Are We Essentially Rational Animals? *Human Affairs* 17: 101–109.

2013. The Myth of the Pervasiveness of the Mental. In Joseph K. Schear, ed., *Mind, Reason, and Being-in-the-World*, Routledge.

Dummett, Michael. 1978. *Truth and Other Enigmas*. Duckworth.

1993a. *Origins of Analytical Philosophy*. Harvard University Press.

1993b. *The Seas of Language*. Clarendon Press.

Earlenbaugh, Joshua and Bernard Molyneux. 2009. Intuitions Are Inclinations to Believe. *Philosophical Studies* 145: 89–109.

Eddington, A. S. 1928. *The Nature of the Physical World*. Cambridge University Press.

Fodor, Jerry and Ernest Lepore. 1991. Why Meaning (Probably) Isn't Conceptual Role. *Mind & Language* 6: 328–43.

1992. *Holism: A Shopper's Guide*. Blackwell.

Frege, Gottlob. 1879. *Begriffsschrift: Eine der artihmetischen nachgebildeten Formelsprache des reinen Denkens*. L. Nebert.

1884. *Die Grundlagen der Arithmetik: Eine logisch-mathematische Untersuchung über den Begriff der Zahl*. W. Koebner. Cited after the translation in Frege [1997], 84–129.

1891. *Function und Begriff: Vortrag gehalten in der Sitzung vom 9. Januar 1891 der Jenaischen Gesellschaft für Medicin und Naturwissenschaft*. H. Pohle. Cited after the translation "Function and Concept," in Frege [1997].

1892. Über Begriff und Gegenstand. *Vierteljahrsschrift für wissenschaftliche Philosophie* 16: 192–205. Cited after the translation "On Concept and Object," in Frege [1997].

1918. Der Gedanke – Eine logische Untersuchung. *Beiträge zur Philosophie des deutschen Idealismus* 1: 58–77. Cited after the translation "Thought," in Frege [1997].

[1997]. *The Frege Reader*, edited by Michael Beaney. Blackwell.

Friedman, Michael. 2007. Introduction: Carnap's Revolution in Philosophy. In Michael Friedman and Richard Creath, eds., *The Cambridge Companion to Carnap*, Cambridge University Press.

Gaita, Raimond. 1998/2000. *A Common Humanity: Thinking About Love and Truth and Justice*, second edition. Routledge.

2002. *The Philosopher's Dog*. The Text Publishing Company.

Gellner, Ernest. 1959. *Words and Things: An Examination of, and an Attack on, Linguistic Philosophy*. V. Gollancz.

George, Alexander. 2000. On Washing the Fur without Wetting It: Quine, Carnap, and Analyticity. *Mind* 109: 1–24.

George, Alexander and Daniel J. Velleman. 2001. *Philosophies of Mathematics*. Blackwell.

Ginsborg, Hannah. 2011. Primitive Normativity and Skepticism about Rules. *The Journal of Philosophy* 108: 227–54.

Glock, Hans-Johann. 1996a. *A Wittgenstein Dictionary*. Blackwell.

1996b. Abusing Use. *Dialectica* 50: 205–23.

2003. *Quine and Davidson on Language, Thought and Reality*. Cambridge University Press.

2010. Concept: Between the Subjective and the Objective. In John Cottingham and P. M. S. Hacker, eds., *Mind, Method and Morality*, Oxford University Press.

2015. Meaning and Rule-Following. In James D. Wright, ed., *International Encyclopedia of Social and Behavioral Sciences*, second edition (volume 14), Elsevier.

2017. Philosophy and Philosophical Method. In Hans-Johann Glock and John Hyman, eds., *A Companion to Wittgenstein*, Wiley-Blackwell.

Glock, Hans-Johann and John Preston. 1995. Externalism and First-Person Authority. *The Monist* 78: 515–33.

Goldfarb, Warren. 1983. I Want You to Bring Me a Slab: Remarks on the Opening Sections of the *Philosophical Investigations*. *Synthese* 56: 269–72.

Goldman, Alvin and Joel Pust. 1998. Philosophical Theory and Intuitional Evidence. In Michael R. DePaul and William Ramsey, eds., *Rethinking Intuition*, Rowman & Littlefield.

Gottlieb, Anthony. 2000. *The Dream of Reason: A History of Western Philosophy from the Greeks to the Renaissance*. Norton.

Grice, Paul. 1989. *Studies in the Way of Words*. Harvard University Press.

Gustafsson, Martin. 2006. Quine on Explication and Elimination. *Canadian Journal of Philosophy* 36: 57–70.

2011. Eliminativism, Reference and Vocabulary Replacement: Sellarsian Roots of Rortian Pragmatism. In Jonathan Knowles and Henrik Rydenfelt, eds., *Pragmatism, Science and Naturalism*, Peter Lang.

2014a. Quine's Conception of Explication – and Why It Isn't Carnap's. In Gilbert Harman and Ernie Lepore, eds., *A Companion to W. V. O. Quine*, Wiley-Blackwell.

2014b. Review of *Wittgenstein's Metaphilosophy*, by Paul Horwich. *Mind* 123: 1195–201.

Guthrie, W. K. C. 1971. *Socrates*. Cambridge University Press.

Hacker, P. M. S. 1990. *Wittgenstein: Meaning and Mind*. Blackwell.

1996. *Wittgenstein: Mind and Will*. Blackwell.

Hadot, Pierre. 1995. The Figure of Socrates. In Pierre Hadot, *Philosophy as a Way of Life*, edited by Arnold I. Davidson, translated by Michael Chase, Blackwell.

Hallett, Garth. 1967. *Wittgenstein's Definition of Meaning as Use*. Fordham University Press.

1977. *A Companion to Wittgenstein's "Philosophical Investigations."* Cornell University Press.

Hanfling, Oswald. 2000. *Philosophy and Ordinary Language: The Bent and Genius of our Tongue*. Routledge.

Harding, Sandra. 1991. *Whose Science? Whose Knowledge: Thinking from Women's Lives*. Cornell University Press.

Hartsock, Nancy. 1983. The Feminist Standpoint: Developing Grounds for a Specifically Feminist Historical Materialism. In Sandra Harding and Merrill Hintikka, eds., *Discovering Reality*, D. Reidel.

Hattiangadi, Anandi. 2007. *Oughts and Thoughts: Rule-Following and the Normativity of Content*. Clarendon Press.

Hertz, Heinrich. 1894. *Die Prinzipien der Mechanik: In neuem Zusammenhange dargestellt*. J. A. Barth. Cited after the translation *The Principles of Mechanics*, translated by D. E. Jones and J. T. Walley (Macmillan, 1899).

Hintikka, Jaakko. 1999. The Emperor's New Intuitions. *The Journal of Philosophy* 96: 127–47.

Horwich, Paul. 1993. Meaning and Metaphilosophy. *Philosophical Issues* 4: 152–8.

1998. *Meaning*. Oxford University Press.

2005. *Reflections on Meaning*. Oxford University Press.

2008. Explaining Intentionality. *Manuscrito* 31: 467–82.

2010a. *Truth – Meaning – Reality*. Oxford University Press.

2010b. Wittgenstein's Definition of "Meaning" as "Use." In Daniel Whiting, ed., *The Later Wittgenstein on Language*, Palgrave Macmillan.

2012. *Wittgenstein's Metaphilosophy*. Clarendon Press.

2013. Naturalism, Deflationism and the Relative Priority of Language and Metaphysics. In Huw Price, ed., *Expressivism, Pragmatism, and Representationalism*, Cambridge University Press.

2014. Naturalism and the Linguistic Turn. In Bana Bashour and Hans D. Muller, eds., *Contemporary Philosophical Naturalism and Its Implications*, Routledge.

Hylton, Peter. 2007. *Quine*. Routledge.

Joël, Karl. 1893. *Der echte und der Xenophontische Sokrates*. R. Gaertner.

Johnson, Samuel. [2003]. *Samuel Johnson: Selected Essays*, edited by David Womersley. Penguin.

Johnston, Paul. 1993. *Wittgenstein: Rethinking the Inner*. Routledge.

Kant, Immanuel. 1781/7. *Kritk der reinen Vernunft*. J. F. Hartknoch. Cited after the translation *Critique of Pure Reason*, translated and edited by Paul Guyer and Allen W. Wood (Cambridge University Press, 1998).

    1790/3. *Kritik der Urteilskraft*. Lagarde und Friederich. Cited after the translation *Critique of the Power of Judgment*, edited by Paul Guyer, translated by Paul Guyer and Eric Matthews (Cambridge University Press, 2000).

Kearns, Stephen and Ofra Magidor. 2012. Semantic Sovereignty. *Philosophy and Phenomenological Research* 85: 322–50.

Klagge, James C. 2010. Das erlösende Wort. In Volker Munz, Klaus Puhl, and Joseph Wang, eds., *Language and World, Part Two*, Ontos.

Koffka, Kurt. 1921/8. *The Growth of the Mind: An Introduction to Child-Psychology* second edition (revised), translated by Robert Morris Ogden. Harcourt Brace and Company. Cited after the 2007 edition by Kessinger.

Köhler, Wolfgang. 1929/47. *Gestalt Psychology: An Introduction to New Concepts in Modern Psychology*. Liveright.

Kripke, Saul A. 1972/80. *Naming and Necessity* [slightly revised book edition of "Naming and Necessity," in Donald Davidson and Gilbert Harman, eds., *Semantics of Natural Language* (D. Reidel, 1972)]. Harvard University Press

    1982. *Wittgenstein on Rules and Private Language: An Elementary Exposition*. Harvard University Press.

Kusch, Martin. 2009. Objectivity and Historiography. *Isis* 100: 127–31.

Kuusela, Oskari. 2008. *The Struggle against Dogmatism: Wittgenstein and the Concept of Philosophy*. Harvard University Press.

    2014. The Method of Language-Games as a Method of Logic. *Philosophical Topics* 42: 129–60.

    2019. *Wittgenstein on Logic as the Method of Philosophy: Re-Examining the Roots and Development of Analytic Philosophy*. Oxford University Press.

Lewis, David. 1983. New Work for a Theory of Universals. *Australasian Journal of Philosophy* 6: 343–77.

    1984. Putnam's Paradox. *Australasian Journal of Philosophy* 62: 221–36.

Ludlow, Peter. 1997. Introduction [to Part I]. In Peter Ludlow, ed., *Readings in the Philosophy of Language*, MIT Press.

Ludwig, Kirk. 2010. Intuitions and Relativity. *Philosophical Psychology* 23: 427–45.

Lycan, William G. 1999. *Philosophy of Language: A Contemporary Introduction*. Routledge.

MacIntyre, Alasdair. 1999. *Dependent Rational Animals: Why Human Beings Need the Virtues*. Open Court.

Marcuse, Herbert. 1964. *One-Dimensional Man: Studies in the Ideology of Advanced Industrial Society*. Beacon Press.

McDowell, John. 1979. Virtue and Reason. *The Monist* 62: 331–50.

    1983. Aesthetic Value, Objectivity, and the Fabric of the World. In Eva Schaper, ed., *Pleasure, Preference and Value*, Cambridge University Press.

1981. Non-Cognitivism and Rule-Following. In Steven H. Holtzmann and Christopher M. Leich, eds., *Wittgenstein*, Routledge & Kegan Paul. Cited after the reprint in Alice Crary and Rupert Read, eds., *The New Wittgenstein* (Routledge, 2000).

1984. Wittgenstein on Following a Rule. *Synthese* 58: 325–63.

1986. Critical Notice [of *Ethics and the Limits of Philosophy*, by Bernard Williams]. *Mind* 95: 377–86.

1989. One Strand in the Private Language Argument. *Grazer Philosophische Studien* 33/4: 285–303.

1994/6. *Mind and World*, with a new introduction. Harvard University Press.

1998. *Mind, Value, and Reality*. Harvard University Press.

2007. What Myth? *Inquiry* 50: 338–51.

2008. Avoiding the Myth of the Given. In Jakob Lindgaard, ed., *John McDowell*, Blackwell. Cited after the reprint in McDowell 2009.

2009. *Having the World in View: Essays on Kant, Hegel, and Sellars*. Harvard University Press.

2013a. Concepts in Perceptual Experience: Putnam and Travis. In Maria Baghramian, ed., *Reading Putnam*, Routledge.

2013b. The Myth of the Mind as Detached. In Joseph K. Schear, ed., *Mind, Reason, and Being-in-the-World*, Routledge.

McFee, Graham. 1999. Wittgenstein on Art and Aspects. *Philosophical Investigations* 22: 262–84.

McGinn, Colin. 1984. *Wittgenstein on Meaning: An Interpretation and Evaluation*. Blackwell.

Merleau-Ponty, Maurice. 1945. *Phénoménologie de la perception*. Gallimard. Cited after both the 2002 edition of the translation *Phenomenology of Perception*, translated by Colin Smith (Routledge & Kegan Paul, 1962) and the translation *Phenomenology of Perception*, translated by Donald A. Landes (Routledge, 2012).

Mills, Charles W. 1988. Alternative Epistemologies. *Social Theory and Practice* 14: 237–63.

2005. "Ideal Theory" as Ideology. *Hypatia* 20: 165–83.

Momigliano, Arnoldo. 1971. *The Development of Greek Biography*. Harvard University Press.

Monk, Ray. 1999. Review of Ben Rogers's A. J. Ayer: A Life. *The Sunday Times*, June 13, book section.

Morris, Katherine J. 2007. Wittgenstein's Method: Ridding People of Philosophical Prejudices. In Guy Kahane, Edward Kanterian, and Oskari Kuusela, eds., *Wittgenstein and his Interpreters*, Blackwell.

2017. Wittgenstein and Merleau-Ponty on Gestalt Psychology. In Komarine Romdenh-Romluc, ed., *Wittgenstein and Merleau-Ponty*, Routledge.

Mulhall, Stephen. 1990. *On Being in the World: Wittgenstein and Heidegger on Seeing Aspects*. Routledge.

2001. Seeing Aspects. In Hans-Johann Glock, ed., *Wittgenstein*, Blackwell.

2009. *The Wounded Animal: J. M. Coetzee and the Difficulty of Reality in Literature and Philosophy*. Princeton University Press.

2010. The Work of Wittgenstein's Words: A Reply to Baz. In William Day and Victor J. Krebs, eds., *Seeing Wittgenstein Anew*, Cambridge University Press.

Nagel, Thomas. 1979. Subjective and Objective. In Thomas Nagel, *Mortal Questions*, Cambridge University Press.

1986. *The View from Nowhere*. Oxford University Press.

Novaes, Catarina Dutilh and Erich Reck. 2017. Carnapian Explication, Formalisms as Cognitive Tools, and the Paradox of Adequate Formalization. *Synthese* 194: 195–215.

Peacocke, Christopher. 2001. Phenomenology and Nonconceptual Content. *Philosophy and Phenomenological Research* 62: 609–15.

Pearson, James. 2017. Caring for Quine's Don't-Cares. *The Monist* 100: 266–87.

Peregrin, Jaroslav. 2014. *Inferentialism: Why Rules Matter*. Palgrave Macmillan.

Pichler, Alois. 1991. *Ludwig Wittgenstein,* Vermischte Bemerkungen*: Liste der Manuskriptquellen / Ludwig Wittgenstein,* Culture and Value*: A List of Source Manuscripts*. The Wittgenstein Archives at the University of Bergen.

Plato. [1961]. *The Collected Dialogues of Plato: Including the Letters*, edited by Edith Hamilton and Huntingdon Cairns. Princeton University Press.

Porphyry. [1987]. *To Marcella*, 31. In Anthony Long and David Sedley, eds., *The Hellenistic Philosophers*, Cambridge University Press.

Pust, Joel. 2004. On Explaining Knowledge of Necessity. *Dialectica* 58: 71–87.

Putnam, Hilary. 1975. The Meaning of "Meaning." *Minnesota Studies in the Philosophy of Science* 7: 131–93.

1977. Realism and Reason. *Proceedings and Addresses of the American Philosophical Association* 50: 483–98.

1981. *Reason, Truth and History*. Cambridge University Press.

1990. *Realism with a Human Face*, edited by James Conant. Harvard University Press.

2002. *The Collapse of the Fact/Value Distinction and Other Essays*. Harvard University Press.

Quine, W. V. O. 1950. *Methods of Logic*. Harvard University Press.

1951. Two Dogmas of Empiricism. *The Philosophical Review* 60: 20–43. Cited after the reprint in Quine 1953/61.

1953. Mr. Strawson on Logical Theory. *Mind* 62: 433–51.

1953/61. *From a Logical Point of View: Nine Logico-Philosophical Essays*, second edition, revised. Harvard University Press. Cited after the 1963 edition by Harper & Row.

1960. *Word and Object*. MIT Press.

1969. *Ontological Relativity and Other Essays*. Columbia University Press.

1981. *Theories and Things*. Harvard University Press.

Reck, Erich. 2012. Carnapian Explication: A Case Study and Critique. In Pierre Wagner, ed., *Carnap's Ideal of Explication and Naturalism*, Palgrave Macmillan.

Reddy, Vasudevi. 2008. *How Infants Know Minds*. Harvard University Press.

Rhees, Rush. 1974. Wittgenstein. *The Human World* 14 (February).

Richardson, Alan. 2004. Tolerating Semantics: Carnap's Philosophical Point of View. In Steve Awodey and Carsten Klein, eds., *Carnap Brought Home*, Open Court.

Ricketts, Thomas. 2003. Languages and Calculi. In Gary L. Hardcastle and Alan W. Richardson, eds., *Logical Empiricism in North America*, University of Minnesota Press.

Rorty, Richard. 1979. *Philosophy and the Mirror of Nature*. Princeton University Press.

   1982. *Consequences of Pragmatism*. University of Minnesota Press.

Rundle, Bede. 1979. *Grammar in Philosophy*. Clarendon Press.

   1990. *Wittgenstein and Contemporary Philosophy of Language*. Blackwell.

Ryle, Gilbert. 1945. *Philosophical Arguments: An Inaugural Lecture Delivered before the University of Oxford, 30 October 1945*. Clarendon Press. Cited after the reprint in Ryle 1971b.

   1951. Ludwig Wittgenstein. *Analysis* 12: 1–9.

   1953. Ordinary Language. *The Philosophical Review* 62: 167–86. Cited after the reprint in Ryle 1971b.

   1966. Jane Austen and the Moralists. *The Oxford Review* 1: 5–18.

   1971a. *Collected Papers Volume 1: Critical Essays*. Hutchinson. Cited after the 2009 edition by Routledge.

   1971b. *Collected Papers Volume 2: Collected Essays 1929–1968*. Hutchinson. Cited after the 2009 edition by Routledge.

von Savigny, Eike. 1983. *Zum Begriff der Sprache: Konvention, Bedeutung, Zeichen*. Reclam.

Schroeder, Severin. 2006. *Wittgenstein: The Way out of the Fly Bottle*. Polity.

   2010. A Tale of Two Problems: Wittgenstein's Discussion of Aspect Perception. In John Cottingham and P. M. S. Hacker, eds., *Mind, Method and Morality*, Oxford University Press.

Schulte, Joachim. 1987/93. *Experience and Expression: Wittgenstein's Philosophy of Psychology*. Clarendon Press.

Searle, John R. 1969. *Speech Acts: An Essay in the Philosophy of Language*. Cambridge University Press.

Sellars, Wilfrid. 1956. Empiricism and the Philosophy of Mind. *Minnesota Studies in the Philosophy of Science* 1: 253–329. Cited after the 1997 book edition by Harvard University Press.

   1974. Meaning as Functional Classification (A Perspective on the Relation of Syntax to Semantics). *Synthese* 27: 417–34.

Sosa, Ernest. 2006. Intuitions and Truth. In Partick Greenough and Michael P. Lynch, eds., *Truth and Realism*, Clarendon Press.

   2007. Experimental Philosophy and Philosophical Intuition. *Philosophical Studies* 132: 99–107.

   2009. A Defense of the Use of Intuitions in Philosophy. In Dominic Murphy and Michael Bishop, eds., *Stich and His Critics*, Wiley-Blackwell.

Stein, Howard. 1992. Was Carnap Entirely Wrong, after All? *Synthese* 93: 275–95.

Strawson, P. F. 1952. *Introduction to Logical Theory*. Methuen.

1959. *Individuals: An Essay in Descriptive Metaphysics*. Methuen.

1963. Carnap's Views on Constructed Systems vs. Natural Languages in Analytic Philosophy. In P. A. Schilpp, ed., *The Philosophy of Rudolf Carnap*, Open Court.

1966. *The Bounds of Sense: An Essay on Kant's* Critique of Pure Reason. Methuen.

1970. Imagination and Perception. In Lawrence Foster and J. W. Swanson, eds., *Experience and Theory*, University of Massachusetts Press. Cited after the reprint in P. F. Strawson, *Freedom and Resentment and Other Essays* (Methuen, 1974).

1992. *Analysis and Metaphysics: An Introduction to Philosophy*. Oxford University Press.

1995. My Philosophy. In Pranab Kumar Sen and Roop Rekha Verma, eds., *The Philosophy of P. F. Strawson*, Allied Publishers.

Stroud, Barry. 2000. *Meaning, Understanding, and Practice: Philosophical Essays*. Oxford University Press.

2012. Meaning and Understanding. In Jonathan Ellis and Daniel Guevara, eds., *Wittgenstein and the Philosophy of Mind*, Oxford University Press.

Sunday Grève, Sebastian. 2015. The Importance of Understanding Each Other in Philosophy. *Philosophy* 90: 213–39.

2018. Logic and Philosophy of Logic in Wittgenstein. *Australasian Journal of Philosophy* 96: 168–82.

Sunday Grève, Sebastian and Jakub Mácha (eds.). 2016. *Wittgenstein and the Creativity of Language*. Palgrave Macmillan.

Symons, John. 2008. Intuition and Philosophical Methodology. *Axiomathes* 18: 67–89.

Tanney, Julia. 2013. *Rules, Reasons, and Self-Knowledge*. Harvard University Press.

2014. Rule-Following, Intellectualism and Logical Reasoning: On the Importance of a Type-distinction Between Performances and "Propositional Knowledge" of the Norms That Govern Them. In Danièle Moyal-Sharrock, Volker Munz, and Annalisa Coliva, eds., *Mind, Language, and Action*, De Gruyter.

2019. What Knowledge Is Not: Reflections on Some Uses of the Verb "To Know." In Markos Valaris and Stephen Hetherington, eds., *Knowledge in Contemporary Philosophy*, Bloomsbury Academic.

Tranøy, Knut Erik. 1999. Wittgenstein in Cambridge 1949–1951: Some Personal Recollections. In F. A. Flowers III, ed., *Portraits of Wittgenstein*, volume 4. Thoemmes Press.

Travis, Charles. 2013. *Perception: Essays after Frege*. Oxford University Press.

2015. Suffering Intentionally? In Michael Campbell and Michael O'Sullivan, eds., *Wittgenstein and Perception*, Routledge.

2016. The Room in a View. In Gary Kemp and Gabriele M. Mras, eds., *Wollheim, Wittgenstein, and Pictorial Representation*, Routledge.

Vision, Gerald. 1998. Perceptual Content. *Philosophy* 73: 395–427.

Wagner, Pierre (ed.). 2012. *Carnap's Ideal of Explication and Naturalism*. Palgrave Macmillan.

Wallgren, Thomas. 2013. Radical Enlightenment Optimism: Socrates and Wittgenstein. In Luigi Perissinotto and Begoña Ramón Cámara, eds., *Wittgenstein and Plato*, Palgrave Macmillan.

Weinberg, Jonathan M., Shaun Nichols, and Stephen Stich. 2001. Normativity and Epistemic Intuitions. *Philosophical Topics* 29: 429–60.

Whiting, Daniel. 2018. Conceptual Role Semantics. In James Fieser and Bradley Dowden, eds., *The Internet Encyclopedia of Philosophy*, www.iep.utm.edu (last accessed on 15 August 2018).

Wiggins, David. 1987/2002. *Needs, Values, Truth: Essays in the Philosophy of Value*, third edition. Clarendon Press.

Williams, Bernard. 1978. *Descartes: The Project of Pure Enquiry*. Penguin.

1985. *Ethics and the Limits of Philosophy*. Fontana Press.

Williamson, Timothy. 2004. Philosophical "Intuitions" and Scepticism about Judgement. *Dialectica* 58: 109–53.

2007. *The Philosophy of Philosophy*. Blackwell.

Winch, Peter. 1981. "Eine Einstellung zur Seele." *Proceedings of the Aristotelian Society* 81: 1–16.

Wisdom, John. 1945. Gods. *Proceedings of the Aristotelian Society* 45: 185–206.

1991. *Proof and Explanation: The Virginia Lectures*, edited by Stephen F. Barker. University Press of America.

Wollheim, Richard. 1980. Seeing-as, Seeing-in, and Pictorial Representation. In Richard Wollheim, *Art and Its Objects*, second edition, Cambridge University Press.

2001. On Pictorial Representation. In Rob van Gerwen, ed., *Richard Wollheim on the Art of Painting*, Cambridge University Press.

Wright, Crispin. 1980. *Wittgenstein on the Foundations of Mathematics*. Duckworth.

von Wright, Georg Henrik. 1982. *Wittgenstein*. Blackwell.

1989. Autobiography. In P. A. Schilpp and Lewis Edwin Hahn, eds., *The Philosophy of Georg Henrik von Wright*, Open Court.

Zerilli, Linda M. G. 2016. *A Democratic Theory of Judgment*. University of Chicago Press.

Index

a posteriori, 65, 156, 162
a priori, 57, 65, 151–2, 154
  knowledge, 63
  synthetic, 160, 162
abstraction, 35–6, 40, 51–3, 58, 60–1, 105,
    113–14
  from subjective endowments, 51
  in mathematics, 52
  requirement, 51–3, 57, 60
abstractness, 52, 58
  ideal, 53–4
accuracy, 59
act
  creative, 129
  illocutionary, 41, 202–4
  linguistic, 201
  perlocutionary, 203
  speech, 202–4, 209
action, 26–8, 75, 174, 184, 190, 198, 213,
    226–7, 229
  human, 254
  intentional, 177, 228
  linguistic, 201
  non-linguistic, 201
activity
  linguistic, 151, 199
actuality, 43, 62
adjective, 29, 185, 201
adverb, 29, 185
aesthetics, 57, 61, 126, 251
Agam-Segal, Reshef, 111
Alcoff, Linda Martín, 61
alienation, 11, 15
Alston, William P., 202
ambiguity, 38–9, 92–3, 248
  in a picture vs. in the world, 92
  perceptual, 91–2
analogy, 9, 15, 18–19, 94, 120, 122, 128, 134, 137,
    142, 150, 156
  between language and a game, 194, 201
analysis, 7, 32

atomistic, 206
chemical, 207
conceptual, 41, 188, 190, 196, 206
connective, 187, 206–7, 209
function–argument, 119, 132–4, 138
mathematical, 135
philosophical, 207
reductive, 206–7
therapeutic, 138
analyticity, 4
Anderson, Elizabeth, 61
anecdote, 238, 242, 246–7, 250
anti-normativism, 195, 207–8
anti-philosopher, 249–50
appearance, 113
  vs. reality, 50–1
application
  condition, 202, 205, 208
  correct, 205
  future, 222
  of a term, 197
  of a word, 21, 166–7
  of an expression, 31, 33, 35, 41, 170–1,
    219, 222
Archimedes, 129
architecture, 110
argument, 26
  causal, 226
  form of, 226
  place, 132, 136
Aristippus, 246
Aristotle, 67, 81, 244–6
arithmetic, 132–3
  transfinite, 130, 136
article
  definite, 201
ascetic, 234, 259
asceticism, 235
aspect
  and concept, 111
  blindness, 97, 137

change, 86–7, 93, 125, 141, 190
  continuous seeing of an, 93, 95
  dawning, 111, 115
  in a picture vs. in the world, 91
  noticing of an, 109, 125–7
  perception, 107–8, 110–11, 113, 125, 141–2
  perceptual, 48
  seeing, 27, 84–8, 90–3, 95, 97–8, 108–9, 125
  switch, 93
  Wittgensteinian, 104, 107–11, 113–15, 118
assent, 165
assertion, 13, 28, 34, 113, 133–4, 155, 162, 198
assertability, 220
ataraxia, 244
Athens, 236, 243
attitude, 28, 88–9, 152, 216, 256
  Pyrrhonian, 113
  propositional, 64
Augustine of Hippo, ix–x, 15, 176–7
Austen, Jane, 43
Austin, J. L., 44, 186, 188, 190, 202, 205
Austria, 239
Ayer, A. J., 253

Bach, Johann Sebastian, 128
Backström, Joel, 264
Baker, Gordon, 141, 173, 189, 204
Bartley, W. W., III, 255
Baz, Avner, 86–7, 102–4, 107–8, 113
Bealer, George, 62–5, 70, 74, 76, 79,
    82–3
Beaney, Michael, 127, 130–1, 135, 137
beauty, 107
Bedeutung, 133–5, 191–2, 195
bedrock, 217–19, 222
behavior
  linguistic, 214, 217
behaviorism, 121–2, 165
being
  for the gaze, 92
  human, 239, 247, 253–5, 260
  in the world, 92, 117
  situated, 92
  rational, 64
belief, 28, 31, 63–4, 76, 113, 152, 198, 224,
    233, 258
Big Typescript, 121, 139, 150, 211
biography, 254–5
  ancient, 247
  ancient Greek, 246
  ancient practice of, 246
  art of, 247
  form of, 247
  nature of, 248
  of a philosopher, 245

philosophical, 246–7
  proper, 246–7
Black, Max, 6
blindness, 80, 98, 109
  aspect, 95, 97
  form, 97
  gestalt, 97
  meaning, 97
  thing, 95, 97
Blue Book, 2–3, 5, 8–13, 15, 17–18, 20–5, 189, 200
Boden, Margaret A., 127–8
body
  phenomenal, 118
  physical, 162
Boghossian, Paul, 211, 223
Bouwsma, O. K., 131
Bragg, Melvyn, 42
brain, 33, 85, 97
  state, 220–1
Brandom, Robert B., 57
Breitenbach, Angela, 83
Britton, Karl, 263
Bronzo, Silver, 183, 187
Brown Book, 20, 116–17, 219
builders, 175, 177–8, 199
Burge, Tyler, 105

Cairns, Huntingdon, 235
calculus, 153, 156
  conception of meaning, 34, 41
  logical, 158
calibration, 104
Cambiano, Giuseppe, 247
Cantor, Georg, 119, 129–30, 136
capacity
  classificatory, 217
  conceptual, 106
  sensory, 48
Cappelen, Herman, 65–6, 71
Carnap, Rudolf, 4, 144, 148–9, 152–8, 160,
    162, 192
Carroll, Gregory, 13, 27
Carus, A. W., 144
case, 43–4
  complex, 62, 66–7, 78–80, 190
  Gettier, 76
  intermediate, 2, 15, 91
  simple, 62, 66, 79, 190
cat, 29, 40, 226–9
category, 30–1, 87
  mistake, 185
  traditional psychological, 110
causality, 166, 184, 225, 227
  concept of, 221
  non-semantic, 226

Cavell, Stanley, 9, 11, 19, 61, 177
chair, 22, 76–7, 79, 176, 204
chemistry, 128
Child, William, 195, 211, 217
Chinese Room, 201
Chomsky, Noam, 200
Churchland, Paul M., 143
Cicero, 248–9
circularity, 166, 169, 179, 182, 184, 206–7
clarification, 5, 12, 14, 23, 34, 133, 138,
  141, 148, 157–8, 175, 183, 189, 192,
  204–5, 235
clarity, 95, 140, 146, 156, 162, 254
  complete, 157
  reflective, 80
Clark, Bob, 130
Code, Lorraine, 61
cognition, 64–5, 105–7, 165, 193
coherence, 60, 168
Collins, John, 83
color, 48, 87, 115
  physiognomy of, 96
commentator, 84–5, 87, 93, 95, 98, 177, 182, 232–3,
  242–3
communication, 34, 36, 106, 145–50,
  177–8, 197
  form of, 178
  linguistic, 192, 203
  ordinary, 148
  purpose of, 150
  system of, 178
community, 36, 215–17
  linguistic, 192–5, 199, 202
  religious, 29
comparison, 43, 141, 159
competence
  communicative, 203
  conceptual, 68–70, 73–4, 77
  intuitive, 65
  linguistic, 68–9, 73, 75, 198
  mathematical, 67
  modal, 68, 70–3
  moral, 67
complexity, 66, 78, 80
compositionality, 10, 37, 187, 200
Conant, James, 48–50, 145, 148
conceivability, 42–3, 49, 224–5
concept, 6, 21, 31–2, 42, 105–6
  and aspect, 111–12
  and function, 132–5, 138
  application, 63, 66, 69, 76–80
  as function, 119, 132, 134, 136, 139
  complex, 32, 81–2, 207
  comprehension of a, 69
  script, 37

empirical, 103, 111–12, 114–15, 118
  employment of a, 69
  extension of a, 132, 134
  formation of a, 130
  fundamental, 207
  concept of, 135
  perceptual, 130
  possession, 63, 74
  psychological, 212
  visual, 90
  vs. object, 132
  word, 133, 136
conceptual
  analysis, 41, 188, 190, 196, 206
  apparatus, 143, 160, 175
  capacity, 106
  change, 129–30
  claim, 206
  competence, 68–70, 73–4, 77
  confusion, 149
  connection, 204–5, 209
  content, 54, 133
  creativity, 119, 142
  engineering, 154
  inference, 198–9
  investigation, 41
  knowledge, 64
  machinery, 25
  modality, 62–3
  necessity, 62–3
  possibility, 62–3
  practice, 52
  priority, 180–1
  resources, 138
  role, 197–200
  scheme, 155
  space, 50, 126–30, 136–7, 141
  system, 128
conception
  alternative, 49
conceptualism, 101
  about perception, 54–5, 102, 111–12, 118
condition
  ideal, 65, 166–7
confusion, 4, 6, 9–10, 12, 14, 17, 19–20, 81, 121, 124
  131, 139, 146–51, 158–9, 162, 184
  philosophical, 12, 121, 123, 150
connective, 37, 185
connotation, 202
conservatism, 143
content
  intentional, 202, 212, 217
  linguistic, 165, 181
  modal, 73
  non-conceptual, 54

perceptual, 102
propositional, 40, 45, 63, 105, 199
representational, 105
truth-theoretic, 169
context, 10, 13, 16, 29, 36, 213, 228–9, 233
dependence, 116–17
everyday, 145
first-person, 25
independence, 41, 156
invariance, 37–8, 40–1
legal, 145
medical, 145
philosophical, 207
principle, 134, 201
scientific, 145
sensitivity, 41, 102, 104, 112, 117
suitable, 105, 110
third-person, 25
contextualism, 113
contextualization, 84, 98
contingency, 218
continuation, 119, 123–4, 219–21, 227
of a series, 181, 221
contradiction, 17
convention
linguistic, 202–3
conversation, 27, 41, 91, 131, 140, 238,
252, 260
cooperation, 33, 203
copula, 14, 18, 20–2, 201
correctness, 7, 26, 52, 69, 74–8, 105, 171, 213
semantic, 199, 205–9
cosmos, 244
Crary, Alice, 49, 51, 61
creativity, 136
combinational, 127, 137, 142
conceptual, 119, 142
connective, 137
exploratory, 127–8, 137, 142
transformational, 127–8, 137, 142
criterion, 41–2, 44, 69–70, 72, 74, 129–30, 145,
161–3, 206, 215
for understanding an expression, 210
of application, 69, 80
criticism
term of, 1–2, 11, 15–16
Crystal, David, 188
counterexample, 32, 76, 223–30
counterfactual, 229
Culture and Value, 15, 138, 140–2, 250–1, 253, 263–4
custom, 35, 40, 213

Daston, Lorraine, 47, 58–9
Davidson, Arnold I., 246
Davidson, Donald, 54, 79, 188, 195, 206

De Mesel, Benjamin, 61
death, 233, 236, 239, 244, 246, 258, 260
deception
self, 250–1
decontextualization, 96, 157
definition, 7, 32, 78, 207
analytic, 189
contextual, 189
ostensive, 55, 189, 198, 251
philosophical, 64
private, 55
recursive, 6–8, 189
Descartes, René, 100
description, ix, 12, 16, 18–19, 85–7, 125,
167, 217
definite, 186
mythological, 173–4
of a language-game, 177
of language, 177
of language use, 19
of use, 173, 211–12
pole of a, 190
proof of the excellence of a, 43
pure, 137
vs. explanation, ix, 136, 214
desire, 82, 164, 170, 220, 224, 242, 262
determination
causal, 172–5, 182–3, 195
dialectic, 232–3, 256–7
dialogue, ix–x
Socratic, 249
Diamond, Cora, 61, 110
dichotomy, 108
dictionary, 193, 195
difference
causal, 227
dispositional, 221–2, 227
non-physical, 223
non-semantic, 221–2, 227–9
physical, 221
teaching of, 23
Diogenes, 249
disagreement, 24, 27, 44
kind of, 24, 80
philosophical, 26
verbal, 78
discourse, 31, 37, 40, 113, 203
about creativity, 127
colloquial, 158
established, 144
everyday, 5, 36
mathematical, 53
mode of, 53
moral, 68
ordinary, 5

discovery, 9, 23, 27, 35, 45, 96, 129–30, 136–7, 140, 152, 231
　future, 122–3
　of meanings, 2
disposition, 165–7, 181, 211
　causal, 182
　linguistic, 216
　non-semantic, 220, 222
dispute, 22
　philosophical, 26
　verbal, 43
distortion, 166, 168–9
distraction, 235
diversity, 65, 68, 78, 191
drawing, 90, 110, 117
　ambiguous, 86
Dreyfus, Hubert L., 57
Drury, M. O'C., 23, 253
duck–rabbit, 86–7, 92–3, 95, 115, 125–6, 142
Duffy, Bruce, 255
Dummett, Michael, 188, 212

Eddington, A. S., 12–13
empiricism, 88–9, 107, 118, 162, 207
　classic, 54
entity
　mental, 70
　substantial, 225
environment
　external, 220
　physical, 216–17
Epicurean, 244
Epicurus, 245, 249
epistemology, 61
error, 53, 139
　source of, 241, 261
essentialism, 189
estrangement, 11
ethics, 50, 57, 61, 79, 251, 254
etymology, 204
Euclid, 128, 137
evidence, 23, 28, 44, 62–3, 65, 67, 75–9, 83, 87, 104
　basic source of, 65
　in philosophy, 76
　intuitive, 75
　philosophical, 64
example
　famous, ix, 128
exclamation, 123, 185, 195, 198
exegesis, 249
exemplification, 151, 189, 249
existence, 6
　possible, 224–5, 229
experience, 13, 22, 97

concept of, 126
　datum of, 64
　inner, 55–6
　intuitive, 71, 73
　nature of, 23
　perceptual, 54–5, 89, 100, 105, 109–11, 114, 116
　practical, 246
　sudden change in, 125
　visual, 110, 113, 125, 168–70
experiment, 26, 104, 248
　thought, 63, 76
expert, 206
expertise, 245
　logical, 67
　mathematical, 67
　moral, 67
　philosophical, 67
explanation, ix–x, 16, 68, 85, 126, 168, 211, 214
　causal, 189, 205–6, 220, 226–7, 230
　non-circular, 206
　of meaning, 28, 35, 44, 189, 198, 205, 207–9
　proof of the excellence of an, 43
　semantic, 205, 207
　type of, 205
　vs. description, ix, 136, 214
explication, 144, 154–6, 160–2, 192
expression
　algebraic, 124
　facial, 90
　form of, 2–3, 9, 11, 14, 16–17, 25, 171–3, 175
　functional, 132–3, 136
　linguistic, 13, 73, 82, 103, 144, 171, 195
　meaningful, 113, 185, 197
　mode of, 124, 149
　primitive, 181
　psychological, 25
　referring, 185
　super, 125
　type, 194, 202
　type of, 42
extension
　of a concept, 167
　of a predicate, 196
extensionality, 154, 192
externalism
　semantic, 216

fact
　non-semantic, 215–23, 227, 230
　bedrock, 217–19
　brute, 221, 228, 230
　grammatical, 108

historical, 247
  linguistic, 191
  physical, 220, 223–4
  sensory, 88
falsification, 196–7
falsity, 1, 11, 32, 37–8, 180, 224
fiction, 16, 199–200
fly-bottle, 120–1, 123, 127–8, 131, 136, 138–9,
    141, 256
Fodor, Jerry, 198, 200
force
  illocutionary, 203
  perlocutionary, 203
form
  linguistic, 198
  of life, 201–3, 236, 253
formalization, 12, 156, 202
Frazer, James G., 253
Frege, Gottlob, 6–8, 14, 37–8, 70, 108, 113, 119,
    131–9, 141, 195, 201
Friedman, Michael, 156
function, 6–7, 13, 36, 200
  and argument, 119, 131–4, 138
  mathematical, 135
  normative, 198
  plus, 216
  value of a, 135
functionalism
  in the philosophy of mind, 200

Gaita, Raimond, 61
Galison, Peter, 47, 58–9
Gellner, Ernest, 143
generality, 105–6, 108, 110–11, 115
genius, 58–9, 127
geographer, 16
geometry
  Euclidean, 128, 137
George, Alexander, 20, 25
gestalt
  blindness, 97
  psychology, 85, 89, 115
Gettier, Edmund L., 76
Ginsborg, Hannah, 214
given
  perceptually, 101, 106, 118
Glock, Hans-Johann, 175, 188–9, 191, 195, 198,
    204, 207, 216
God, 26, 82, 253
Goldfarb, Warren, 177
Goldman, Alvin, 70
Gottlieb, Anthony, 245, 263–4
grammar, 10, 14, 140, 173, 183, 200, 254
  logical, 146
  of "rule", 174

of "see", 108
  of a word, 181
  of aspects, 112
  surface, 18
grammatical
  dependence, 113–14
  fact, 108
  inquiry, 27
  investigation, 21, 27
  movement, 130
  parallelism, 14
  point, 174
  remark, 173–5
  truth, 248–9
  variant, 29
Greve, Anniken, 96
Grice, Paul, 25, 188, 194, 202–3
Ground, Ian, 88
guru, 233, 258
Gustafsson, Martin, 144, 149, 154, 183, 192
Guthrie, W. K. C., 264

habit, 151
  linguistic, 160–1
Hacker, P. M. S., 120, 123, 173,
    189, 204
Hadot, Pierre, 244–5, 263
Hallett, Garth, 188
Hamilton, Edith, 235
Hanfling, Oswald, 188
Harding, Sandra, 61
Hartsock, Nancy, 61
Hattiangadi, Anandi, 208
hearer, 194, 203, 209
hedonism, 246
Heidegger, Martin, 143
Hertz, Heinrich, 17
heuristic, 111
Hippodamus, 246
history, 192, 247
  of analytic philosophy, 25, 47
  of science, 54
  of thought, 248
holism, 117, 203
homoeroticism, 255
homosexuality, 202
Horwich, Paul, 164–70, 175–84, 188, 212
Hume, David, 2
Husserl, Edmund, 143
Hylton, Peter, 154

idea, 33
ideal, 157
  epistemic, 58
  metaphysical, 47

identity, 7, 14, 18, 20–1
ideology, 61, 144
idiolect, 197, 199–200
ignorance, 11, 23, 232, 257
illusion, 7–8, 12, 16, 66–7, 71, 127, 192
image
  mental, 33, 108, 126
imagination, 106–7, 177,
    248, 254
implication, 207
  logical, 34, 38–9
  normative, 167
implicature
  conventional, 203
  conversational, 39, 202–3
imprecision, 144
inclination
  to believe, 64–5
indeterminacy, 92, 102, 105, 112, 117
indexical, 185
individual, 65, 73, 79, 97, 199, 216–17, 247
inexactness, 144
inference, 31, 151–2, 198–200, 218
  conceptual, 198–9
  deductive, 198
  inductive, 198
  logical, 131, 199
  rule of, 198
inferentialism, 197–200, 209
infinity, 42, 171
  rails laid to, 52
inquiry
  empirical, 11, 18, 58
  scientific, 53, 191
insight, 23, 113, 136, 152, 201, 203, 216
  aesthetic, 61
  fundamental, 133
  moral, 61
  political, 61
intentionality, 165, 179, 183, 186, 192
  of perceptual experience, 105
intentional
  action, 177, 228
  activity, 200
  characterization, 165
  content, 202, 212, 217
  ghost, 157, 223–6
  notion, 166, 176–7, 181
  property, 224–5
  term, 168, 176, 178, 181, 212
interlocutor, x, 4, 44, 101, 122, 218–19, 222, 227,
    232–3, 235, 238, 257, 260
intersubjectivity, 107, 199
introspection, 63–4, 89–90
introspectionism, 88–9, 96

intuition, 31, 42, 56, 62–7, 71, 73–83, 119, 190
  about a philosophical case, 78
  about complex cases, 66, 78
  about simple cases, 66, 78
  account of, 70
  and perception, 65, 67, 74
  as a capacity/competence, 66–8
  as evidence, 65, 75, 78
  competence of, 65
  in philosophy, 42, 63, 75, 78
  Kantian, 106–7
  nature of, 64
  phenomenology of, 64
  philosophical, 78
  rational, 64
  reliability of, 65, 74–5
  vs. belief, 63–4
invention, 128, 141, 158, 233
  in philosophy, 136–7
Ireland, 235
isomorphism, 85

James, William, 253
Jesus, 44
Joël, Karl, 264
Johnson, Samuel, 1
Johnston, Paul, 111
judgment, 104–5, 113, 133
  act of, 108
  empirical, 102, 107, 112
  perceptual, 100, 102, 106, 108–9, 114
  trained, 59
jurisprudence, 192
justice, 21–2, 31, 58, 79, 81, 111, 125, 187, 189, 254
justification, 28, 71, 75, 77, 83, 133, 152–3, 254
  of an intuition, 67

Kant, Immanuel, 100–1, 103–7, 118, 225
Kearns, Stephen, 216, 223–30
Kekulé, August, 128–9
Kepler, Johannes, 168–9, 182
kind
  natural, 216
Klagge, James C., 140
knowledge, 58
  a priori, 63
  as justified true belief, 82
  logical, 63
  mathematical, 63, 160
  new, 242, 262
  modal, 64
  theory of, 42
  transmission of, 16
Koffka, Kurt, 115
Köhler, Wolfgang, 84–91, 96, 98

Kripke, Saul A., 78–9, 166–7, 169, 182, 211, 216–17, 220, 223, 250
Kripkenstein, 223
Kusch, Martin, 59
Kuusela, Oskari, 158

language
artificial, 4
colloquial, 145–55, 158–9
conception of, 103, 146
creativity of, 45, 127
English, 14, 18, 20, 24, 29, 31, 39–40, 127, 166, 169, 201, 216, 254
essence of, 176
everyday, 15, 18, 36, 81, 145–6, 150
formal, 4
German, 127, 191, 202, 238, 254
ideal, 39, 41
natural, 28, 31, 34, 38–40, 188, 198
ordinary, 4, 8, 10, 18, 21, 25, 39, 154, 161
philosophy of, 104, 188, 202
picture of, 120–1
primitive, 177–8
private, 55, 122, 124
simple, 138, 158, 175, 190, 242, 262
use of, 2, 19, 23, 25, 68–70, 80, 120, 136, 140, 142, 148–9, 151, 154–5, 158, 163, 176, 187, 212, 217
user, 16–18, 35, 66, 70, 78, 151, 223–4
whole, 200, 202
language-game, 15–16, 18–19, 124, 138, 158–9, 172, 175, 177–8, 190, 199, 201
concept of a, 137
Last Writings on the Philosophy of Psychology, 110, 200
law
causal, 181
natural, 169–70, 221
learning, 89, 180, 215
of a language, 37
of a language-game, 124
process of, 88, 214, 240, 260
situation of, 213
to be better, 254
to dance, 45
to die well, 239
to follow a rule, 214
to play chess, 193
to speak, 45
to think better, 254
to use an expression, 193
Lepore, Ernest, 198, 200
Lewis, David, 216
lexicography, 36

lexicon, 137, 197, 199, 205
liberation
moral, 61
life
academic, 236
and philosophy, 255
and work, 243
Athenian, 235
change of, 245
difficulty of, 251
embodiment of philosophy in, 247
good, 239
individual, 245, 248
kind of, 243–4
manner of, 247
mode of, 246–7
of the mind, 235
of the sage, 244
past, 238, 260
possible, 253
present, 238
prospects of, 239, 260
simple, 236
Socratic, 244
sort of, 235, 243, 249
unconventional, 250
way of, 35, 96, 234–6, 243–7, 252, 259
well-lived, 235–6
whole, 201, 246
limitation, 104, 138, 247, 254
linguistics, 168, 188, 192–3
logic, 13, 37, 132, 254
conception of, 146, 152–3
crystalline purity of, 152, 155, 157
formal, 7, 38, 192
mistake in, 145
modern, 38, 119
of language, 172
of natural language, 41
of our language, 131
of our words, 173
predicate, 154
quantificational, 39, 131, 133, 136, 141
symbolic, 72, 156–7
logical
calculus, 158
determination, 173–4, 182–3, 195
expertise, 67
form, 131
framework, 153, 162
grammar, 146
implication, 34, 38–9
inference, 131, 199
knowledge, 63
modality, 63

logical (cont.)
object, 132
operator, 198, 204
order, 18, 145–6, 149–50, 153, 155–9
perspicuity, 147
pluralism, 162
principle, 64
property, 153
relation, 135–6, 138
rigor, 154
situation, 148
structure, 7, 146–8, 150–3
symbolism, 154, 158–9
syntax, 145–6, 148, 151, 200–1
system, 131, 133, 153
theory, 134
unit, 146
logicism, 7, 132, 134
look, 110
objective, 109
looking
at the world vs. at paintings, 94
at the world vs. at pictures, 85
Ludlow, Peter, 37
Ludwig, Kirk, 70, 78
Lycan, William G., 188

Mácha, Jakub, 127
machine, 182
MacIntyre, Alasdair, 57
magic
effect, 227–9
Magidor, Ofra, 216, 223–30
Malcolm, Norman, 238, 252, 263
Marcuse, Herbert, 143
mathematician, 20, 41–2
mathematics, 52, 67–8, 81, 110, 124, 132, 134, 156
Matthew, 44
maxim
conversational, 203
McDowell, John, 50, 52–6, 61, 101, 104–5, 111, 113, 118, 166, 183, 211, 217–19, 222–3, 229
McFee, Graham, 84, 86, 95
McGinn, Colin, 211, 223
McGinn, Marie, 83
McGuinness, Brian (B. F.), 145
McTaggart, John M. E., 45
meaning
account of, 167–9, 184, 188, 191, 195, 222
analytic theory of, 188
and significance, 96
and understanding, 201
and use, 187, 191, 193, 209, 211
anti-reductionism about, 164, 183–4, 211–13, 217, 223

as use, ix, 188
behaviourist theory of, 188
blindness, 97
causal theory of, 188
change of, 39
concept of, 164, 169, 175, 188–9, 191–3, 206–7
conception of, 177, 183, 185, 188, 203
constitution of, 175, 177–81, 195, 197, 204, 212
constructive theory of, 188
conventional, 203
demystification of, 164, 170, 175
determination of, 217
difference of, 222–3
dispositional theory of, 166–7, 169, 181–2
eliminativism about, 191–2
epistemology of, 218, 222
explanation of, 187, 204, 206–7, 209
facts about, 212, 214–15, 217
idea of, 211
as use, 187–8, 193, 206, 211
knowledge of, 206, 218, 222, 232
lexical, 187, 197, 199, 201–4, 209
linguistic, 185, 187, 189, 192, 194–5, 206, 211, 217
metaphysics of, 222
nature of, 191
new, 202, 248
non-sentential, 179
notion of, 29, 164, 168, 184, 191–2, 204, 206–8
of a proposition, 6
of a sentence, 199
of a sign, 185
of a word, 10, 28, 45, 147, 166–7, 170, 176, 185, 187–8, 194, 196–7, 200–1, 204, 211
of an expression, 125, 170–2, 174, 181–3, 187, 193–5, 198–9, 205–6, 209
of things, 97
primitive form of, 178
reductionism, 164, 170, 177–8, 182–4, 187, 211, 214
reductionist theory of, 184
referential conception of, 185, 187, 191
referential theory of, 188
sameness of, 185, 192, 195, 202
seeing a, 96
speaker's, 187, 197
stimulus, 192
the question of, 185
theory of, 164–6, 184, 187–90
use conception of, ix
verificationist theory of, 188
meaninglessness, 194, 208–9
measurement, 15, 44, 104
meditation, 231, 251

mental, 16, 189
  accomplishment, 171
  access to the world, 60
  act, 171
  contact, 54–7, 60
  content, 165, 181
  cramp, 21, 189
  entity, 70
  episode, 70–1
  event, 161–2
  illness, 138
  image, 33, 108, 126
  life, 60, 126
  meaning, 191
  object, 187
  operation, 199
  phenomenon, 225
  predicate, 42
  process, 121–4, 140, 194, 201
  property, 226
  representation, 33
  seeming, 74
  state, 74, 122–3, 140, 161–2, 199,
    224
memoir, 242
Merleau-Ponty, Maurice, 85, 92–3, 96–8,
    117–18
metaphor, 16, 50, 120–1, 128, 137, 142
metaphysics, 39, 160, 183
  descriptive, 207
method
  evaluatively non-neutral, 61
  important, 15
  mathematical, 27
  philosophical, 16, 26–7, 43
  scientific, 27, 57
methodology, 58, 61–2, 79–80, 82, 156,
    191–3, 251
  philosophical, 65, 75
  revisionist, 144
Mills, Charles W., 61
mind
  Cartesian, 224
  dependence, 48
  independence, 47
  peace of, 245
  philosophy of, 61, 202
misconception, 175
misunderstanding, 2, 18–19, 27, 34, 40, 42, 159,
    172, 174–5
modality, 62–5, 67–75, 77, 79–80,
    83, 166
  conceptual, 63
  logical, 63
  mathematical, 63

metaphysical, 63
Momigliano, Arnoldo, 246–8
Monet, Claude, 93–5
Monk, Ray, 253
morality, 68, 248
Morris, Katherine J., 85, 91, 108
Mulhall, Stephen, 61, 86–7, 94–5,
    97, 111
music
  atonal, 128
  classical, 128
mystification, 175, 184
myth
  of the given, 5, 55, 101, 118
mythologization, 119, 127, 129

Nachlass, 251
Nagel, Thomas, 48, 51, 53
name, 3, 6–7, 122, 125, 201, 226
  proper, 185, 187, 195
narrative, 55, 58, 246
naturalism, 33, 165–6, 184, 199,
    207, 214
  contemporary, 165
naturalness, 216–17
nature
  description of, 59
necessity, 62–5, 80
Necker cube, 91, 109
negation, 245
Neo-Platonist, 244
neutrality, 61
Nichols, Shaun, 65, 78
non-conceptualism, 54–6, 101,
    106–7
  about perception, 54, 56, 102,
    118
  appeal of, 56
  argument against, 55
  critique of, 56
  defense of, 57
non-inferentialism, 199
non-intentionalness, 164–6, 168, 176, 178, 212,
    224–5
non-normativeness, 165–6, 168
non-objectivity, 49–50, 107
non-revisionism, 145–6, 148, 152, 155, 157,
    160, 162
nonsense, 2–3, 11, 14, 19, 103, 145,
    209, 232
notion
  normative, 165–6
  truth-theoretic, 168, 179
norm
  epistemic, 168

normativity, 34, 69, 165, 167, 194,
     209
  of meaning, 166–7, 169–70, 187, 197, 205,
     207, 209
  of use, 194
normativism, 204, 209
Norway, 235, 240
notation, 4–5, 7, 15, 17–21, 38, 144,
     146, 159
  logically perspicuous, 147–50
noun, 33
  abstract, 29
  accusative, 205
  mass, 185
  sortal, 185
Novaes, Catarina Dutilh,
     144
number, 6, 8, 166
  natural, 20, 52–3, 130
  rational, 130
  real, 130
  sameness of, 119, 130
  series, 53
  transfinite, 119, 129–30

object
  determinate, 103
  environmental, 109
  everyday, 87
  grasp of an, 97
  in the environment, 108, 110
  inner, 86
  itself, 94
  of comparison, ix, 2, 43–4, 158–9
  of perception, 108–9
  of sight, 87, 109, 114
  ordinary, 87
  perceived, 85, 116
  physical, 161
  spatio-temporal, 201
  three-dimensional, 89
objective
  authority, 61
  domain, 49
  judgment, 102, 113–14, 118
  look, 109
  naturalness, 217
  notion, 115
  perspective, 101
  point of view, 48
  property, 114, 116
  quality, 49
  similarity, 116
  thought, 118
  truth, 113

value, 50
world, 48, 102, 104, 109, 114–18
objectivity, 47–51, 53, 58–60, 81, 119
  concept of, 47–8, 50–1, 57–8, 60
  conception of, 47–51, 54, 57–61
  historical conception of, 58
  ideal of, 47, 53, 58
  in ethics, 50
  in science, 59
  narrower conception of, 50–1, 53, 57–8
  narrower vs. wider conception of, 49
  realm of, 48
  touchstone of, 47
  wholehearted, 49
  wider conception of, 60
objectivism, 103
observation, 9, 23, 57, 91, 96, 216
Ockham's razor, 73
Ogden, C. K., 148
On Certainty, 194, 200
ontology, 144, 148, 154, 156–7
operator, 12, 174
orthography, 146, 150
overdetermination, 226

pain, 7–9, 22–7
painting, 89, 93–5, 241, 261
paradox, 65, 86–7, 138, 192, 233
  of aspect-change, 86
  of the concept *horse*, 119, 132
  Russell's, 119, 132
particular, 105
Peacocke, Christopher, 57
Pears, D. F., 145
Pearson, James, 144
perceiver, 100–1, 105, 108, 117
perception, 50, 63, 105, 198
  account of, 107, 111, 117–18
  analytic, 97
  analytical vs. normal attitude in,
     88–9
  and intuition, 65, 67, 74
  fundamental question of, 100–2,
     104, 108
  human, 111, 117
  normal mode of, 95
  ordinary, 99
  philosophy of, 54
  vs. sensation, 88
perceptual
  ambiguity, 91–2
  apparatus, 105
  aspect, 48
  capacity, 56, 75
  concept, 130

content, 102
experience, 54–5, 89, 100, 105, 109–11, 114, 116
input, 56
judgment, 100, 102, 106, 108–9, 114
life, 55
notion, 115
physiognomy, 96
presentation, 2, 105, 108, 110–11
relation, 101
representation, 105
thought, 54, 57
Peregrin, Jaroslav, 197
perplexity, 10, 15, 23
person
  first, 22–5, 42, 196, 225
  third, 22–5, 42, 95, 101, 103, 115
perspective
  alternative, 50
  causal, 183
  literal, 50–1
  notion of, 50
  objectivist, 103
  spatial, 50
  theoretical, 103
  third-person, 101, 103, 115
perspicuity, 148, 254
  logical, 147
  notational, 149
Phanias of Eresus, 246
phenomenology, 64, 71, 92, 96, 118, 143
  difficulty of, 103
  of aspect dawning, 111
  of aspect perception, 112
  of intuition, 64
phenomenologist, 85, 92
phenomenon
  complex, 207
  mental, 225
  mysterious, 172, 174–5
  non-semantic, 226
  physical, 130, 194
  psychological, 80, 165, 221
philosopher, 9–12, 16, 27, 32, 121, 138–40, 231, 234–6, 241, 245–6, 248, 250, 255–7, 261
  analytic, x, 103, 117
  ancient, 248–9
  ancient Greek, 235
  ancient Roman, 248
  contemporary, 243, 249, 255
  good, 249, 253
  great, 234, 237–40, 259–61
  Hellenistic, 248
  life of a, 245, 255
  life of the, 243, 245–6

ordinary language, 25
post-Socratic, 236
simulacrum of a, 237
task of the, 162
traditional, 152–4
work of a, 245
philosophical
  aim, 145
  argument, 57, 59, 225
  competence, 67
  debate, 122
  definition, 64
  difficulty, 253
  dispute, 122, 126, 138
  doctrine, 246
  expertise, 67
  fantasy, 51, 155
  ideal, 247
  illness, 138
  inquiry, 61, 251
  interest, 16, 19, 242
  investigation, 1, 39, 251
  issue, 161
  life, 235–6, 247
  massage, 20
  method, 16, 138, 141, 185, 256
  methodology, 65, 75, 141
  point, 244
  practice, 255
  problem, ix–x, 19, 27, 81–3, 121, 132, 136–8, 140, 141, 156, 158–63, 190–1, 207, 233, 236–7, 240, 253, 255, 257–9, 261
  progress, 27
  purpose, 31, 201
  question, 160, 241
  reflection, 15, 89, 190
  repression, 101
  sensibility, 254
  statement, 78
  superlative, 125, 137
  theory, x, 63–4, 75–6, 80, 160, 189, 249
  thinking, 138, 254
  thought, 81–2, 255
  tradition, 82, 118, 256
  treatment, 81, 150, 159
  trouble, 148, 162–3
  view, x, 76, 78–9, 81, 83
  weight, 50
  work, x, 16, 56, 62, 64, 82, 235, 242, 252, 262
  worry, 155, 161
  writing, 140, 252–4
Philosophical Grammar, 123, 189–91, 193–4, 200

Philosophical Investigations, ix–x, 9, 12, 15–21, 23, 26–8, 36, 43, 52–3, 55–6, 59, 81, 84, 100, 106, 116, 119, 122–5, 127, 130, 136–8, 142–3, 152, 157–8, 170–2, 176–7, 180–1, 187, 201, 204, 206, 211, 219, 232, 255, 264
Philosophical Remarks, 131
philosophy
  academic, 236, 256
  activity of, 254
  aim of, 39
  analytic, x, 4, 47, 61, 113, 126, 143, 185
  ancient, 244–7, 256
  ancient Greek, 245
  ancient Roman, 245
  and life, 243–4, 255
  area of, 50, 60, 254
  as a way of life, 246, 252
  as such, 242, 256
  conception of, 18, 146, 231, 242, 244–5, 247, 249–50
  contemporary, x, 63, 100, 103, 113, 143, 216, 242–3, 249–50, 255–6
  difficulty of, 251
  experimental, 65
  expression of one's, 243–5
  Hellenistic, 244–5, 248
  history of, 2, 69, 137
  idea of, 256
  nature of, 17, 242, 244, 248, 251
  object of, 31, 40
  objectionable, x
  of food, 236
  ordinary language, 10, 19
  political, 61
  practice of, 11, 120, 140, 170–1, 175, 244–5, 251, 254
  purpose of, 32
  remarks on, 136
  traditional, 1–2, 152, 250
  transformative, 47, 245
  Western, 100
Philosophy of Psychology — A Fragment, 18, 55, 84, 86–7, 91, 93–5, 97, 109, 113–15, 125–6, 130, 140
phonetics, 146, 150
physical
  behavior, 161
  body, 162
  difference, 221, 223
  duplicate, 223
  environment, 216–17
  event, 184
  fact, 220, 223–4
  object, 161

phenomenon, 30, 165, 184, 194
property, 223–4, 226
process, 123
state, 123, 220, 222
subject, 223
term, 194
theory, 12
thing, 223
world, 184
physicalism, 161, 165
physicist, 12–13, 16, 123
physics, 165
physiognomy, 92, 96, 98, 112, 139–40
  of color, 96–7
  of shapes, 97
  perceived, 109, 116–17
physiology, 221
Pichler, Alois, 251
picture, 14, 26, 85, 87, 91–8, 120–1, 124, 128, 137, 142, 151
  accepted, 223
  face, 94
  inner, 86, 126
  inner vs. outer, 86
  philosophical, 37
  rabbit, 95
Plato, 235–6, 245, 247–9, 263
pleonasm, 211–13, 215
Plutarch, 248, 252
poem, 140
poet, 140, 247–8
politics, 246
Pope, 32
possibility, 63, 166
practice, 34, 176
  linguistic, 36, 40, 46, 74, 138, 144, 154, 191, 196 198–200
  of multiplication, 214–15
  rule-following, ix, 213
  rule-guided, 194
pragmatics
  vs. semantics, 39
pragmatism, 202, 204
precision, 144, 151, 155–7
  formal, 157
predicate, 14, 34, 196
  mental, 42
predication, 18, 20–1, 169
prediction, 214–15, 218
  genuine, 215
preposition, 185
presentation
  perceptual, 101–2, 105, 108, 110–11

Preston, John, 216
presupposition, 207
pride, 253
principle
　fundamental, 134
　cooperative, 203
privacy, 55
　metaphysical, 102, 108
　necessary, 122
problem
　philosophical, 10, 14, 17, 19, 27
process
　causal, 194
　mental, 124, 194
　psychological, 123
　scientific, 160
progress
　philosophical, 19
　scientific, 58
　spiritual, 245
pronoun, 186
proof, 44
　deductive, 43
property, 21, 33, 48, 50, 63, 70, 73–4, 104,
　164, 216
　dispositional, 220–1, 227–8
　fundamental, 221
　intentional, 224–5
　mental, 226
　modal, 69
　natural, 217
　non-physical, 223–4
　non-semantic, 221, 224–5,
　228–9
　objective, 116
　of an object, 115
　physical, 226
　semantic, 223, 225
　spatial, 50
proposition, 37, 150
　bipolar, 185
　elementary, 6, 151, 200
　general form of the, 180
　mathematical, 214–15
　notion of, 179–80
　philosophical, 2
　sense of a, 185, 211
　symbolical, 174–5
　vs. sentence, 40, 146
psychoanalysis, 14, 139
psychology, 85–6, 89, 122, 127
　empiricist, 88–9
psychologization, 64
Pust, Joel, 65, 70
Putnam, Hilary, 54, 216–17, 223

puzzlement, 20–1, 27, 84, 142,
　159, 183
Pythagoras, 250

quality
　affective, 48–9
　secondary, 48
　subject-dependent, 50–1
quantification
　theory, 6, 8
question
　philosophical, 19
　moral, 80
　rhetorical, 244
quietism, 211
Quine, W. V. O., 4–6, 38, 40, 144, 148–9, 152,
　154–8, 160–2, 188, 191–2, 207, 223

Ramsey, F. P., 252
rationality, 56
reader, ix, 16, 76, 139, 143, 212, 216–17, 251,
　253, 263
　modern, 246
realism, 22–4, 26–7, 41
reality, 39, 44, 158, 248
　conception of, 157
　feature of, 223
　layer of, 183
　structure of, 156–7
　vs. appearance, 50–1
realist, 22–7
realization, 16, 44
reason
　datum of, 64
reasoning
　case-by-case, 45
　deductive, 43
　form of, 26
　inferential, 63
　means–end, 25–6
　practical, 177
　techniques of, 26
Reck, Erich, 144, 157
Redpath, Theodore, 16
reference, 200
　condition, 179
　linguistic, 42, 45, 185
　notion of, 168
　of an expression, 216
　word, 176–7, 226–9
reflection
　mode of, 244
regimentation, 154–6, 158–9
regularity, 53–4, 60, 164–5,
　213–14

regularity (cont.)
law-like, 168
physiological, 221
psychological, 221
of use, 169
reification, 192, 207
relation
external, 53, 115–16
internal, 111, 115–18, 243
inferential, 146, 150–1, 198
logical, 135–6, 138
modal, 69
perceived, 115–6
perceptual, 101
reliability
of an intuition, 63
of intuition, 65, 74
religion, 29, 226, 251
Remarks on the Foundations of Mathematics,
212–15
Remarks on the Philosophy of Psychology, 84–6,
89–90, 95–7, 113, 190, 200
remedy, 27, 144, 149, 159
reminder, 1, 5, 27, 85, 112–13, 159–60,
173–4
representation, 102, 105
form of, 247
linguistic, 103
mental, 33
perspicuous, 18
species of, 94
representationalism
about language, 103
in the philosophy of mind,
202
resemblance, 18, 109
family, 36, 43, 59, 123, 189
retina, 88, 101, 103, 108–9
revisionism, 18, 143–4, 148–50, 152, 155, 157,
160, 196
Rhees, Rush, 255
Richardson, Alan, 156
Ricketts, Thomas, 154
rigor, 156
conception of, 157
Rogers, Ben, 253
Rorty, Richard, 144, 149
rule
governedness, 207
grasp of a, 53
guidedness, 194–6, 200
linguistic, 34, 198, 207
notion of a, 180
pragmatic, 187, 199, 202–3
semantic, 32

syntactic, 32, 156, 208
rule-following, ix, 52, 62, 69, 71, 106, 124, 213–15
217–18, 220
blind, 172–4
epistemology of, 222
implicit, 169
metaphysics of, 222
Rundle, Bede, 186, 193
Russell, Bertrand, 3, 6, 45, 131
Russell's paradox, 119, 132
Ryle, Gilbert, 28, 35, 39, 43, 45, 185,
190, 194

sage, 243–4, 249
saint, 247–8
Salzer, Helene, 263
Savigny, Eike von, 202
Schlick, Moritz, 140
Schoenberg, Arnold, 128
Schroeder, Severin, 84, 97, 111, 193
Schulte, Joachim, 84, 87
science, 39, 156
cognitive, 165, 192
conception of, 157
empirical, 168
natural, 49, 58, 189
nature of, 58
philosophy of, 49
scientism, 58
scientist, 12, 33, 54, 59, 156
Searle, John R., 25, 201, 204
seeing, 80, 84
a meaning, 85, 96
aspects vs. shapes and colors, 94
concept of, 91, 126
connections, 137
organisation vs. shapes and colors, 86
pictures, 97
shapes and colors vs. a meaning, 96
something as something, 97, 110, 117,
125–6, 130
the world, 95, 97
things, 45, 50, 90, 93–6
things vs. shapes and colors, 84, 88–90,
93–4
vs. thinking, 110–11
seeming, 71
intellectual, 64
sensory, 64
Sellars, Wilfrid, 5–6, 54–5, 58, 101, 198
semantic
anomaly, 200
competence, 204–6
compositionality, 37, 187
concept, 211–12

correctness, 199, 205–9
difference, 221–2, 227–9
dimension, 198, 200
disposition, 220–2
eliminativism, 192
explanation, 205–7
externalism, 216
fact, 216, 219–24, 227, 230
features, 25
mistake, 209
norm, 208
notion, 176–7, 181
phenomenon, 226, 230
principle, 208–9
property, 221–5, 228–9
question, 196
role, 200
rule, 4, 32, 157, 187, 196
sovereignty, 223
supervenience, 217–30
system, 153, 156
term, 176–81, 209, 212, 228,
    230
theory, 37
semantics, 4, 32, 176, 178, 185
conceptual role, 197, 199
formal, 188, 202, 208
vs. pragmatics, 39
Seneca, 249
sensation, 3, 55–6, 115, 122
vs. perception, 88
sense, 3, 45
and unity, 102, 107, 118
common, 64, 106, 218, 220
datum, 5, 64
linguistic, 117
of a sentence, 197, 200
ordinary, 5
perceived, 117
physiognomic, 114, 118
sensibility, 52, 58, 253–4
sentence, 165
Bedeutung of a, 134, 136
colloquial, 147–8, 150–1
complex, 200
component, 197, 199
declarative, 40, 196–8
indicative, 105
meaning, 179
non-declarative, 196–7
simple, 196
vs. proposition, 40, 146
series
continuation of a, 124
number, 53, 124, 219

set
finite, 130
infinite, 129
sex, 33
sexuality, 255
Shah, Nishi, 11, 25, 27
shopkeeper, ix, 175–8
sign
propositional, 151, 172
system, 70
significance, 96, 98
inflection of, 32, 45
natural, 187
perceived, 115, 117
teleological, 187
signification, 185
total, 203
silence, 237, 259
similarity
linguistic, 14
objective, 116
objectively establishable, 109
simplicity, 15, 63, 142, 168, 185, 234,
    259
absolute, 206
Sinn, 133–5, 192, 195
situatedness, 92, 100
situation
historical, 47, 248
Skeptic, 9, 244
skepticism, 60, 77
Skinner, Francis, 27
space, 31, 90
phenomenological, 33
Socrates, 189–90, 231–45, 247–51,
    254–61
Socratic, 246–8
solipsism, 22–4, 121
solution, 125–7, 198, 233
sophism, 237
Sosa, Ernest, 62–7, 70, 74, 76, 78–9,
    82–3
soul, 236, 245
spatiotemporality, 166, 201
speaker, 19, 105, 150–1, 153, 194–5, 202–3, 209,
    216–17, 222
competent, 41, 112, 147, 187, 193, 197,
    205–6
individual, 195, 200
speech
act, 184, 188
figure of, 113, 201
act theory, 188, 202, 204
spirit, 244
of one's philosophy, 252

standpoint, 50, 94
state
    physical, 123, 220, 222
Stein, Howard, 154
Stich, Stephen, 65, 78
Stoic, 244
Strawson, P. F., 34, 38, 43, 91–3, 111, 113, 190, 192, 206–7, 225
Stroud, Barry, 211, 223
structure
    normative, 56
study
    empirical, 78
stupidity, 89
subject, 107
    Cartesian, 225
    dependence, 49, 51, 60, 109
    individual, 225
    non-physical, 223
    normal, 98
    ordinary, 224
subjective
    constitution, 51
    contribution, 59
    element, 49
    endowment, 51
    experience, 64
    makeup, 51
    point of view, 48
    quality, 48–9, 60
    response, 52
    status, 47
    take, 53
    talk, 161
subjectivity, 47–9, 51, 53
    countering of, 47
    exclusion of, 47
    mere, 64
    of a researcher, 59
Sunday Grève, Sebastian, 127, 142, 158, 249, 264
supervenience
    base, 216–17, 220, 229
    non-semantic, 217, 220
    of meaning on use, 195
    of semantic facts on non-semantic facts, 215, 218, 220, 222, 228–9
    of the mental on the physical, 226
    semantic, 217–30
surprise, 27, 140
symbolism, 153–4, 157
    formal, 158
    logical, 158–9
synonymy, 192, 195
syntax, 13, 18, 200
system

formal, 153
generative, 127
linguistic, 200

table, 12, 120, 176, 235
Tanney, Julia, 40, 42, 204
Tarski, Alfred, 156
tautology, 231
teaching, 110, 245–6
telos, 244
temptation, 3, 80–1, 235
    empiricist, 89
tense
    present, 196
term
    general, 28, 32, 39, 100, 191, 196, 202, 208, 210
    singular, 196, 201
    non-intentional, 176, 178, 181
    non-semantic, 176–81, 212, 230
    normative, 168, 182, 195
testimony, 63
theory, 177, 244
    building, 190
    construction, 19, 187
    constructive, 188–9
    development of, 161
    empirical, 19, 190
    formation, 190
    organization of, 161
    philosophical, 63–4, 75
    scientific, 190, 198
    systematic, 188
therapy, 16, 27, 138, 245, 256
thing
    being as it is, 101, 105, 110
    blindness, 97
    non-physical, 223
    physical, 223
    sensible, 48
thinker, 4, 48, 53–4, 61, 100, 105, 137, 142, 224
thinking, 110–11
    conception of, 123
    tendency of, 26
    way of, 64, 151, 242
thought, 24, 31, 105–6, 125, 147
    act of, 108, 110
    experiment, 63, 76
    formation, 101
    Fregean, 37, 70
    human, 254
    mode of, 60
    objective, 118
    originality of, 45
    perceptual, 54

time, 15
Toivakainen, Niklas, 264
tolerance, 152, 154, 157, 162
tool, 24, 34, 36, 156, 200, 247
Tractatus Logico-Philosophicus, 5–8, 14, 17–18,
    120–1, 131, 140, 145–8, 151, 155, 159, 180, 185,
    192, 200
Tranøy, Knut Erik, 240, 264
transcendence, 50
transformation
    of one's life, 245
    political, 61
    self, 244
translation, 41, 84, 97, 123, 127, 145, 180,
    235, 254
transparency, 54, 90
Travis, Charles, 100–18
Tredennick, Hugh, 235
tribe, 201
trompe-l'œil, 94
truism, 45, 205, 249
truth, 37, 102, 106, 152, 162
    analysis of, 179
    analytic, 4, 40
    bearer, 32, 196
    common-sense, 218
    condition, 7, 78, 179, 208
    deflationary theory of, 179
    function, 6, 131
    in life, 241
    in philosophy, 241
    metaphysical, 16
    necessary, 63
    norm of, 208
    notion of, 168, 179–80
    objective, 113
    predicate, 208
    seeker, 232, 254, 257
    speaking the, 241, 261
    the question of, 185
    theory of, 131, 169
    tracking, 63
    value, 133–6, 197, 209, 224
truthfulness, 238, 253, 260
Twin Earth, 220

Übersicht, 137–8, 141
unclarity, 81, 87, 122
understanding, 21, 31, 53, 63
    a sentence, 209
    another, 45
    bewitchment of our, 256
    complete, 233, 257
    concept of, 175
    form of, 244

linguistic, 11, 13, 28, 170–1, 181, 208
mathematical, 52
mutual, 218
of a life, 249, 255
of someone's thought, 255
someone, 35, 218–19, 222
sudden, 119, 123–7, 129, 139–41
unicorn, 127, 227–9
United States of America, 238
universal, 42, 105, 166
universe, 50
untruthfulness, 241, 261
usage, 159, 194
    of an expression, 202
    ordinary, 5, 10–11, 160
use
    competent, 206, 210
    conception of, 194
    core, 32
    correct, 20, 194, 207
    different, 13, 17, 21, 23, 88–9, 91
    fact about, 27, 212, 215–16,
        222–4
    figurative, 29, 31
    grasping the, 125
    individuation of, 25
    linguistic, 18–19, 193–4, 196, 209
    literal, 29, 31
    meaningful, 146, 155, 201
    notion of, 194–5, 197, 211
    novel, 12–13
    of a concept, 57, 69, 77, 80, 217
    of a sentence, 40
    of a sign, 69–70
    of a term, 195
    of a word, ix, 18, 23, 27–8, 87, 91, 124, 141, 158,
        166, 168, 170, 172, 175, 178, 180, 195–6,
        203–4, 211, 217, 219, 224
    of an expression, 2, 8, 10, 13–15, 18–21, 23–4, 31,
        39, 125, 182, 194, 207, 211, 216, 219, 222
    of language, 15–16, 19, 69, 120, 161, 163,
        218
    of our language, 139
    of the word "see", 84, 86–8, 90–1, 95, 98, 108,
        114, 116
    ordinary, 3, 13, 19–20
    philosophical, 47
    theory, 164–6, 179, 187, 190–1, 193, 197,
        200–1
    whole, 124, 172, 175
uses
    contradiction between, 17
    totality of, 3, 10
using
    way of, 15, 162, 194–6, 200

validity, 40, 136
value, 166
  ethical, 50
  moral, 167
vanity, 253
Velleman, Daniel J., 20
verb, 29, 185
  deontic, 198
verification, 196–7
verificationism, 188, 196, 199
view
  intuitive, 54
  point of, 33, 50, 74, 76, 151, 247
  received, 240, 261
vision, 74, 85–6
  intellectual, 190
Vision, Gerald, 57
Voices of Wittgenstein, 9, 14
Vorstellung, 108–10

Wagner, Pierre, 144
Waismann, Friedrich, 140
Wallgren, Thomas, 264
Weinberg, Jonathan M., 65, 78
Whiting, Daniel, 197
Wiggins, David, 49, 61
will
  good, 253
  subject to the, 90, 95, 109
Williams, Bernard, 48, 51, 53, 225
Williamson, Timothy, 64, 66
Winch, Peter, 61, 238
wisdom, 243, 245
Wisdom, John, 26, 40, 43–4
Wittgenstein, Ludwig
  early, 120, 131, 140, 144–52, 155–6, 158–9, 255
  later, ix, 1, 47, 55, 120, 126, 131, 136, 138, 140–1,
    144, 152–3, 155, 157–60, 164, 185, 190, 194,
    201, 255
Wollheim, Richard, 94, 111, 113
word
  liberating, 139–40
  operation with a, ix, 176
  play, 201
  use of a, 165
work
  on oneself, 244, 250

world, 215
  actual, 48
  ancient, 243
  as it is in itself, 49, 58, 103
  as perceived and responded to, 100
  aspect of the, 47
  being in the, 92
  description of the, 152, 154, 162
  empirical, 104
  existing in the, 245
  external, 82, 113
  fabric of the, 51, 58
  in itself, 49
  independent of how we stand toward it,
    101, 103
  insertion in the, 94
  looking at the, 85, 91
  non-semantically duplicate, 223,
    226–8
  objective, 48, 102, 104, 109,
    114–15, 118
  of the aspect-blind, 97
  orientation towards the, 26
  perceived, 85, 100–2
  phenomenal, 101–4, 106–7, 111,
    115–18
  physical, 184
  physically duplicate, 223
  possible, 223–4, 226–9
  as presented vs. represented, 100
  real, 51
  repression of the, 101, 103–4, 107
  seeing the, 97
  situated in the, 92
  subject-dependent aspects of the, 60
  view of the, 51, 53
Wright, Crispin, 166
Wright, Georg Henrik von, 235, 238,
    263–4
writing, 252
  form of, 245

Xenophon, 247–8

Zerilli, Linda M. G., 61
Zettel, 84, 138, 140, 191,
    221

CPSIA information can be obtained
at www.ICGtesting.com
Printed in the USA
LVHW081338200521
688008LV00012B/247